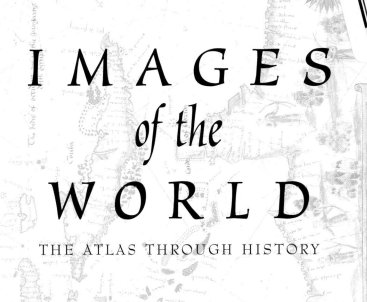

IMAGES
of the
WORLD

THE ATLAS THROUGH HISTORY

Edited by
John A. Wolter and Ronald E. Grim

LIBRARY OF CONGRESS
Washington, D.C.
1997

D0930894

Library of Congress Cataloging-in-Publication Data

    Images of the world : the atlas through history / Library of Congress
    John A. Wolter and Ronald E. Grim, editors.
        p.   cm.
    Includes bibliographical references and index.
    ISBN 0-07-071578-5
    1. Atlases—History.   I. Wolter, John Amadeus, 1925–
  II. Grim, Ronald E.   III. Library of Congress.
  GA300.I42   1997
  912'.09—dc20   97-15443
                                                CIP

McGraw-Hill

A Division of The McGraw·Hill Companies

Copyright © 1997 by the McGraw-Hill Companies, Inc. All rights reserved. Printed in the United States of America. Except as permitted under the United States Copyright Act of 1976, no part of this publication may be reproduced or distributed in any form or by any means, or stored in a data base or retrieval system, without the prior written permission of the publisher.

1 2 3 4 5 6 7 8 9 0 1IMP/1IMP 9 0 1 0 9 8 7 6

ISBN 0-07-071578-5

The editing supervisor for this book was Virginia Carroll, and the production supervisor was Suzanne W. B. Rapcavage. It was set in Janson by North Market Street Graphics.

Printed and bound in Hong Kong through Print Vision, Portland, Oregon.

McGraw-Hill books are available at special quantity discounts to use as premiums and sales promotions, or for use in corporate training programs. For more information, please write to the Director of Special Sales, McGraw-Hill, 11 West 19th Street, New York, NY 10011. Or contact your local bookstore.

Information contained in this work has been obtained by The McGraw-Hill Companies, Inc. ("McGraw-Hill") from sources believed to be reliable. However, neither McGraw-Hill nor its authors guarantees the accuracy or completeness of any information published herein and neither McGraw-Hill nor its authors shall be responsible for any errors, omissions, or damages arising out of use of this information. This work is published with the understanding that McGraw-Hill and its authors are supplying information but are not attempting to render engineering or other professional services. If such services are required, the assistance of an appropriate professional should be sought.

for

JOHN BRIAN HARLEY
1932–1991

BARBARA BARTZ PETCHENIK
1939–1992

HELEN WALLIS
1924–1995

esteemed
scholars, authors, friends, and colleagues

CAT Dec 9 96

ALLEGHENY COLLEGE LIBRARY

CONTENTS

Illustration Credits

While most of the illustrations in this book were selected from the collections of the Geography and Map Division of the Library of Congress, others are based on the research of the authors or furnished from the authors' collections. The remainder are reproduced here with the permission of the libraries, archives, museums, and private collections listed below and identified in the respective captions. The editors and publisher wish to thank these institutions and individuals for permitting the reproduction of these maps and images in this publication.

Archivio de Stato di Venezia 27, 28

Beijing Library 17, 18

Biblioteca Marciana, Venice 119

Biblioteca Nazionale Braidense, Milan 23

Bibliothèque Nationale de France, Paris, 1, 49, 53, 54, 55, 56, 73

The British Library, London 2, 3, 4, 5, 6, 7, 8, 9

Free Library of Philadelphia 147

Free University of Berlin 89, 90, 92, 94, 98

Frontenac County Schools Museum, Kingston, Ontario 189, 190

Henry E. Huntington Library and Art Gallery, San Marino, California 10, 11

Herzog August Bibliothek, Wolfenbüttel 59

Houghton Library, Harvard University 183

Koninklijke Bibliotheek, Brussels 37, 40

Maritiem Museum "Prins Hendrik," Rotterdam 69, 72

Nederlands Scheepvaartmuseum, Amsterdam 71, 74

The Newberry Library, Chicago 26

Pietro Crini Collection, Florence 124

Universiteitsbibliotheek, Amsterdam 35, 38, 41, 42, 45, 46, 47, 60, 68

Universiteitsbibliotheek, Utrecht 39

Foreword

JOHN Y. COLE

Director, Center for the Book
Library of Congress

The Library of Congress's cartographic collection, the largest and most comprehensive in the world, is one of the institution's chief glories. It includes more than 4.3 million maps and charts, 50,000 atlases, 300 historical globes, and 2,000 three-dimensional plastic relief models, and spans all dates, all geographic areas, and all subjects.

Maps, charts, and atlases have been part of its collections since the Library of Congress was established in 1800. When the Library moved from the U.S. Capitol to its own building in 1897, a separate Hall of Maps and Charts was established to house the collection of 47,000 maps and 1,200 atlases. This administrative unit, which has grown into today's Geography and Map Division, has a long tradition of scholarship and publication.

In 1984 the Geography and Map Division joined with one of the Library's newest offices, the Center for the Book (established in 1977) to sponsor the symposium and commission the papers published in this volume. The Center for the Book was created by Librarian of Congress Daniel J. Boorstin "to stimulate public interest and research in the role of the book in the diffusion of knowledge." Using private funds, it sponsors projects, symposia, and publications that, in Dr. Boorstin's words, "organize, focus, and dramatize our nation's interest and attention on the book."

The history of books has become an exciting field of study in the 1980s and the 1990s. Concerned broadly with the influence of printed materials on the development and transmission of culture, it combines bibliographic and textual studies with social and intellectual history. The atlas, as John A. Wolter points out in his introduction, is a unique, multipurpose book that has helped to shape civilization. The Library of Congress, through its Geography and Map Division and Center for the Book, is pleased to present this new look at the atlas and its role in history.

Introduction

JOHN A. WOLTER

Once subsidized and collected mostly by royalty, the nobility, and the wealthy merchant princes, atlases are so relatively inexpensive and commonly used today that their importance and the fascinating history of their development are often overlooked. Yet, in a manner at once scientific, philosophical, and artistic, atlases embody, in as compact a form as possible, the whole range of humankind's knowledge of the earth they occupy and of the heavens they observe—and now probe. Originally a compilation of maps uniform in concept and design, the atlas has evolved into a comprehensive summary of information of all kinds transformed into a cartographic format.

The atlas, as the term is understood today, originated in the late fifteenth century with the introduction into Italy from Constantinople of Claudius Ptolemy's *Geographia* of the second century A.D. Essentially a textbook on mapmaking, the *Geographia* had a profound effect on Renaissance man's understanding of the earth. Indeed, no more opportune time could have been chosen for its arrival than this, the age of the printing press and of the great voyages of discovery. This not only rapidly popularized the *Geographia*, but also demanded its modification almost immediately after its first printing with copperplate-engraved maps by Arnold Buckinck in Rome in 1478.

The first steps in the creation of the modern atlas were taken in the latter part of the fifteenth century by compilers who redrew and corrected Ptolemy's twenty-seven maps and added modern maps. With the increasing awareness of the inadequacy of Ptolemy's classical view, and the growing demand for maps reflecting the recent discoveries in the New World and elsewhere, Italian publishers began to bind these diversely printed modern maps into made-to-order collections. In Rome, publisher Antonio Lafreri added an engraved title page to the bound collections of maps he produced, giving the different-sized maps a sense of unity. Lafreri used the image of Atlas on this title page, marking the first time that the figure and the book of maps were associated.

The final steps in the early evolution of the atlas were taken in the late sixteenth century by Abraham Ortelius and Gerard Mercator. Ortelius was the first to produce an atlas with maps uniform in size and content, while Mercator was the first to use the name "atlas" as the title of such bound collections of maps. By the end of the century, the atlas had found a coherent format and evolved rapidly.

Since the beginning of the seventeenth century, the atlas has undergone additional and profound transformation. The renowned voyages of such explorers and space adventurers as Cook, Vancouver, Wilkes, Bering, Perry, Byrd, and Armstrong were supported by the powerful impulses over the intervening centuries of nationalism and the industrial revolution. Areas unknown to earlier explorers were gradually revealed, thus requiring the constant revision of contemporary maps. At the same time, new instruments such as the chronometer, sextant, barometer, and theodolite, as well as advances in science and mathematics, permitted greater accuracy in surveying and mapmaking, and more accurate measurements of the earth and its atmosphere.

In response to these developments, new conceptual frameworks about the nature of geography and its relation to cosmic and human experience were devised in the nineteenth century by such theorists as Alexander von Humboldt, Carl Ritter, George Perkins Marsh, and Paul Vidal de la Blache. Concurrently, great innovations in graphic technology such as wax engraving, lithography, and photography transformed the appearance of the atlas as well as the methods by which it was produced, making it almost universally understandable and, more importantly, less expensive and readily available. All these changes are visible in the landmark atlases which seem to summarize their age. Blaeu's works, for example, epitomize the seventeenth century or "golden age" of Dutch cartography; Sanson's more scientific approach, the reformation of cartography in France during the Age of Reason; Berghaus's and Johnston's, the significant broadening of the atlas framework—with the graphic display of economic and scientific data. Many of the works of contemporary atlas makers, which present complex spatial and statistical data in a pleasing and easily understood manner, printed for both the popular and education markets, are splendid examples of the cartographer's science and the printer's art.

The end of the twentieth century is also witness to an electronic revolution in atlas making. As several of the authors remind us in the essays that follow, the informed user can (and does) now create his or her own atlas on demand from data and formats provided by numerous software manufacturers.

Atlases are, indeed, remarkable cartographic objects which have become, since their origin in the fifteenth century, important and seldom-recognized social and economic forces. The several roles of the atlas throughout its history were discussed and debated at an international symposium held in the Library of Congress on October 25 and 26, 1984. The symposium was organized by John A. Wolter. It was cosponsored by the Center for the Book and the Geography and Map Division, and codirected by John Y. Cole and John A. Wolter.

Contributions to the atlas symposium, which are reproduced in this volume, were primarily concerned with the atlas as a book, since it was cosponsored by the Center for the Book. In other words, the atlas was considered not only as a cartographic object, but also as an important means of recording and disseminating spatial information of every kind. Atlases are made up of individual maps, each one having special areal or thematic characteristics (or perhaps both). However, the process of bringing maps together in a volume, or volumes, on similar scales and projections with standard symbolization, color codes, and so forth, brings them into the realm of the book. Thus, our interest was in the atlas as a book, as a cartographic object, and equally important, of course, as a social and economic force.

Along with the symposium, the Library mounted a major exhibition, *Images of the World: The Atlas Through History*, which traced some 500 years of atlas making from the earliest times to the present. It featured over 300 items from the Library's vast collection of more than 50,000 atlases, the largest collection of its kind in the world. The atlases and atlas plates displayed in the exhibition provided the viewer with a graphic record of the human occupancy of the earth. They vividly recorded the expansion of geographic and scientific knowledge that took place from the Age of Discovery during the Renaissance to the rise of the natural and social sciences during the nineteenth and twentieth centuries.

We hoped to increase public awareness of the atlas as an artistic and scientific work by means of our exhibition which included several of the most interesting, rare, and important volumes from the Library's magnificent collection. Atlases or groups of atlases which were discussed in the symposium were also prominently displayed.

With the above considerations in mind, symposium participants were asked to select from the geographical and topical areas of their individual cartographic interest and expertise, a subject which would fit into our general historical theme. The atlas, an intellectual as well as a physical object, could be discussed in several ways. We suggested that one way would be to describe a given edition or perhaps several editions as physical objects which show changes in format, design, printing, color, and other characteristics which reflect the period of production. Some of the nineteenth-century atlases, of course, show great advances in printing techniques and engraving (for example, lithography and photolithography); selected volumes exhibit these changes. Successive editions of Stieler's *Hand Atlas* were used in the exhibition as an example of this approach.

Additionally, the intellectual content of an atlas and its social and economic influence, if measurable, could also be described. The migration of atlas plates from one country to another or from one publisher to another within a country was an important factor which could also be discussed. The characteristic of distribution networks and the specific roles of the cartographer, printer, publisher, and vendor were also of interest. Recent literature on the history of cartography shows every indication of a new and vital look at this important aspect of the dissemination of the physical volume. One of most important questions asked was, How did the atlas influence the ruling classes and bourgeois? What role did the atlas play in education; for example, in establishing the Mercator projection as a world view and the standard for so many decades?

There are high points in the history of mapmaking that are well known and that have been described many times. However, we believed that a new look at the atlas as a volume of maps with special characteristics which have changed and increased in sophistication and geographical and intellectual content over the past five centuries was both necessary and desirable. Those important characteristics of the atlas (whether in the form of physical makeup; intellectual, scientific, social, or economic content; or cartographic depiction) all deserved attention. The rise of national atlases and the introduction of thematic content—indeed, the evolution of cartography to its present state in the late twentieth century—is exhibited in the pages of our Rand McNally, Bartholomew, Bos, or Westermann atlases as it was in the much earlier atlases of Saxton, Ortelius, Mercator, Blaeu, Coronelli, and Sanson. Most important, during the period of great geographical and social change in the nineteenth century, new techniques of representation were developed in the atlases of Berghaus, Stieler, Mitchell, Johnston, and Colton, to name but a few.

It is, as can be seen in the following pages, an enormously rich cartographic heritage. We are fortunate that so much of note has been preserved in original atlas format for study and contemplation in the libraries of the large public and private institutions in Europe and America.

The aim of the symposium was to pay homage to those who compiled and produced these magnificent publications and to evaluate, and in some cases reevaluate, their contributions. By including some of the lesser known atlas makers and their times, we hoped to make some important contributions to understanding the growth and evolving structure of this unique cartographic format.

The fifteen essays are divided into four distinct time periods following basically the same arrangement as the symposium. The first session was devoted to early manuscript and printed maps and was chaired by John A. Wolter (Chief, Geography and Map Division, Library of Congress). Session two was chaired by Norman J. W. Thrower (Director, William Andrews Clark Memorial Library, University of California, Los Angeles), and concerned atlases of the sixteenth to eighteenth centuries. The third session included atlases of the late eighteenth and nineteenth centuries and was chaired by Betty Kidd (then Director, National Map Collection, Public Archives of Canada). Jon Leverenz (Managing Editor, Atlas and Map Publication, Rand McNally & Co.) chaired the fourth and last session which dealt with atlases of the late nineteenth and twentieth centuries and the future of the atlas. The entire proceedings were recorded, including the lively and informative question-and-answer period following each presentation.

Authors were encouraged to consider any comments and criticisms when preparing the final version of their papers for submission. Due to the lengthy period between presentation and publication, they have had the opportunity to make changes in their papers as presented. Therefore, all of the essays have been revised to some extent to incorporate changes suggested by symposium participants, reviewers, and the editors. Although this lengthened the editorial process considerably and slowed the identification and photography of illustrations for the essays, I hope it will be agreed that it was well worth the extra time required.

Acknowledgments

JOHN A. WOLTER AND RONALD E. GRIM

Although this volume of essays was initially conceived and edited by John A. Wolter, Ronald E. Grim, the Geography and Map Division's Specialist in Cartographic History, assumed co-editorship of the volume in 1994. Previously, he had provided bibliographic assistance including the compilation of the references for Wolfgang Scharfe's essay, "German Atlas Development During the 19th Century."

Together, we wish to express our appreciation to Ralph E. Ehrenberg, friend and colleague for many years, who succeeded Dr. Wolter as Chief of the Geography and Map Division. Because of his interest and enthusiasm for this project, he has allowed us the necessary assistance of several Division staff members for its completion.

A special debt of gratitude is owed to these staff members for their valuable assistance. Former staff members Richard W. Stephenson and Andrew M. Modelski were particularly helpful during the early stages of the project as were atlas catalogers Barbara M. Christy and Barbara J. Story. Elizabeth U. Mangan provided her usual expert guidance in all word processing matters and Denise Gotay and Carla Busey typed the first drafts from authors' submissions. Marjorie Burgess, Dr. Wolter's secretary when he served for many months as acting director for Public Service and Collections Management I, was of inestimable help. She deserves credit for typing final drafts, which included many emendations and additions, a monumental task which was cheerfully, expeditiously, and above all skillfully completed.

Thanks are also due to Charlotte A. Houtz who provided much-needed assistance in acquiring several score illustrations, and to Edward J. Redmond, who has very ably assisted us in this and in several other projects undertaken during the past three years. Deanna Hammond of the Library's Congressional Research Service is commended for expertly translating Mireille Pastoureau's essay from the French. Additional editorial support and advice were provided by Eileen McConnell, Barbara O'Brien, and Charles Krewson, Geography and Map Division volunteers, as well as Cordell Yee, St. Johns College, Annapolis, Maryland, and Mary Sponberg Pedley, University of Michigan, Ann Arbor, Michigan.

The on-again, off-again nature of public funding and changing priorities contributed to the long delay in publication. Although the essays were all in hand by the fall of 1990, Dr. Wolter's additional administrative duties for two separate periods during that year and in 1991, as well as the curatorship of a major Library exhibition from 1992 to 1993, required him to temporarily set aside editorial duties. We are also grateful to Dana J. Pratt, former Director of the Library's Publishing Office, and Margaret Wagner, Editor, Publishing Office, for their continuing interest, advice, and expertise. Our special thanks go to Sybil Parker, Publisher, Technical Reference and New Media, McGraw-Hill Professional Book Group, who took an interest in this project and agreed to commit her company's resources to publishing it.

We wish to thank the authors of these essays. Without their continuing interest and enthusiasm for this project over the past decade, it would have been impossible to bring it to what we sincerely hope is a successful conclusion. Because of the timelessness of most of the essays and their chronological place in each author's overall work, they should be doubly interesting to the reader. It is our fond hope that each essay will help to fill in one or more of any noticeable gaps in our knowledge of the history of maps and atlas-making in many different countries during the past several centuries.

Finally, we thank our wives, Joan and Ottilie, who have been very patient, understanding, and supportive during the past years as we have worked on this extended project.

PART ONE

Early Manuscript and Printed Atlases

Sixteenth-Century Maritime Manuscript Atlases for Special Presentation

HELEN WALLIS

Maritime manuscript atlases are notable artifacts of the sixteenth-century geographical renaissance. Oceanic voyages were transforming the European view of the world. Explorers had broken out from the confines of the *orbis terrarum* of medieval geography to reveal the continents and oceans of the terraqueous globe. Their discoveries were recorded on charts made on the voyages or compiled in the chart makers' workshops. The charts were treated as secret documents, whose distribution was regulated by the schools of navigation of the leading exploring countries, the Casa de la Contratación at Seville in Spain and the Casa da India at Lisbon in Portugal. They not only documented the results of discovery and progress in colonial enterprise, but were also of geopolitical significance, showing how discoveries related to the division of the world between Spain and Portugal, according to the 1493 papal dispositions and the 1494 Treaty of Tordesillas.

Chart makers at the same time supplied a special need in making atlases for presentation to royal or noble persons and officers of state. These atlases might be commissioned, or freely offered as testimonials in expectation of favors. They were designed as masterpieces of the art and craft of maritime cartography. Less vulnerable than charts and working documents in general, special atlases tended sooner or later to find a home in private or public libraries, and were preserved for posterity.

Such atlases may be considered tools of statecraft. Portuguese chart makers, for example, served an absolute and monopolistic state. The empire, which by the 1530s was straddling half the globe, was the possession of the Crown. John II, the Great and the Perfect (1481–1495), had taken the title, Lord of Guinea. Manuel, the Fortunate (1495–1521), enlarging the title, had styled himself, Lord of the Navigation, Conquest, and Commerce of Ethiopia, Arabia, Persia, and India. By presentations to the sovereigns and royal princes of the House of Aviz, colonial governors and other officials could inform and flatter, promoting the imperial cause as well as advancing their own careers.

THE MILLER ATLAS, CIRCA 1519

One of the earliest Portuguese atlases made for presentation is something of a mystery. The Miller atlas (c. 1519), named after its last private owner, is now in the Bibliothèque Nationale de France.[1] This magnificent Portuguese portolan, as the Visconde de Santarém described it in 1855,[2] seems to have been made for a royal patron, probably Manuel. Its four vellum folios, displaying charts of the Atlantic and America, the Mediterranean, the Indian Ocean, and the Far East, are illuminated, probably by the painter Gregorio Lopes.[3]

A world map signed and dated by Lopo Homem (1519), and bought by Marcel Destombes in London, was identified by scholars in 1939 as having once belonged to the atlas. When the sheet is folded, an inscription on the right-hand side of the verso of the map forms a sort of frontispiece. The legend states that the chart was made by command of Manuel, glorious king of Portugal. The arms of Queen Catherine de Medici, displayed below the legend, were apparently added at a later date. Armando Cortesão and Avelino Teixeira da Mota have determined the original arrangement of the charts in the atlas, which is incomplete, showing where missing folios, covering Africa and elsewhere, were once inserted.[4]

Lopo Homem was "master of sea charts" in Lisbon from 1517, and had been granted, by letters patent of Manuel, the exclusive right "to make and correct all navigation compasses which may belong to our fleet."[5] The charts, preserved in the Miller atlas itself, appear to be the work of Pedro Reinel, Lopo's former master, and Pedro's son Jorge. The Reinels are the first known Portuguese cartographers. Their work, which is undated, has been placed between c. 1500 and c. 1540.[6] Cortesão and Teixeira da Mota suggest that Lopo Homem, as official cartographer, was commissioned by King Manuel to prepare an atlas of Portuguese discoveries, to be sent probably to Francis I of France, to show the young Valois king the extent of Portuguese dominions. Lopo Homem (it is inferred) sought the help of Pedro Reinel, who duly enlisted Jorge, then working in Seville.[7] The Miller atlas is, therefore, also known as the Lopo Homem–Reinels Atlas of 1519. It is significant that João de Castro, when Viceroy of India, recalled in a dispatch to King João III that "the King your father" (Manuel I, who died in 1521) had "commanded Jorge Reinel, master of nautical charts, to make for the King's information a chart (*padrão*) with the leagues from place to place as far as Suez, and from there all the land as far as Alexandria. . . ."[8]

The charts in the atlas show the world as revealed through recent discoveries prior to the voyage of Ferdinand Magellan's ship the *Victoria* round the world (1519–1522). Many features of the old world are derived from Ptolemy's

Geographia and from Marco Polo. Most notable of these are the Magnus Golfus Chinarum (fol. 3r) and the numerous islands of Far Eastern waters (fols. 2v and 3v). The chart of the Atlantic Ocean (see Figure 1) shows in midocean the northeast coasts of America, named Terra Corte Regalis, and comprising the discoveries of Gaspar and Miguel Corte Real for Portugal (1500–1504). Gaspar's discovery is described in a long legend. To the west, separated by a gulf, is Terra Frigida. This is the earliest cartographic record of the discoveries of another Portuguese, João Alvares Fagundes (c. 1519).[9] Some of the place-names marked on Terra Corte Regalis and Terra Frigida, such as "santa Ana," "sam Joam," and "honze mill virgeens," are the result of Fagundes's early voyage along the south coast of Newfoundland and into the Gulf of St. Lawrence. The letters patent granted to Fagundes for a 1521 voyage includes these places in its list of ten names which originated with Fagundes.[10]

Many leagues to the west of Terra Frigida, separated by open ocean, is the land Terra Bimene, lying roughly in the position of Florida. In one of the Fountain of Youth stories Bimini is described as an island north of Cuba. The Spanish explorer Juan Ponce de León sailed from Puerto Rico in search of it in 1513, discovering Florida, and then the Yucatan Peninsula, which he saw as an island. He named it "Beimini . . . another spelling of Bimini."[11]

The most detailed depiction of any part of "Mundus Novus," as the New World of America was named, is Brazil (fol. 4r). The arms of Portugal at 37° S

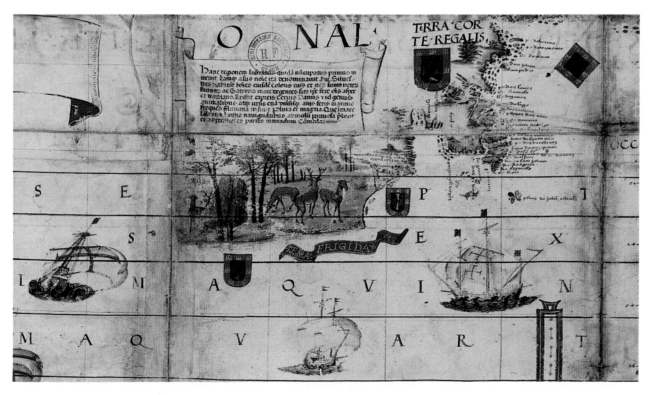

FIGURE 1   *Atlantic chart (detail) from Miller atlas, c. 1519.*
Bibliothèque Nationale de France.

suggest that the Portuguese (perhaps João de Lisboa and Estéban Froes, called Flores by the Spaniards, on their expedition of 1511 to 1512) had reached the mouth of the River Plate before Juan Diaz de Solis made his discovery for the king of Castile in 1516.[12] Lopo Homem's world map,[13] now regarded as part of the Miller atlas, is a curiosity. The coast of South America is connected to that of the southern continent, which sweeps eastward to join the eastern Ptolemaic coastline of Asia. The coast in the southwest Atlantic is somewhat similar in outline to that on the Atlantic chart, which was probably part of a world chart, by the Turkish admiral Piri Re'is (1513), who may have made a similar adaptation of Ptolemy, or was following a similar prototype.

The most outstanding feature of the Miller atlas is the sumptuous illumination of the Reinel charts. They display the usual coastlines and place-names plus a profusion of vignettes of towns and cities and scenes of local life. The Portuguese had established the practice of sending on exploring expeditions a "painter," whose task was to depict views and panoramas as well as to draw maps.[14] On the chart of Brazil, Indians are depicted hunting and collecting brazilwood in the forests. Pink, blue, and red parrots enhance the scene. On the Atlantic chart, several Africans are seen digging for golden nuggets on the northern mainland of South America. On all the charts, flags distinguish the possessions of Spain and Portugal, and many ships, beflagged and in full sail, are crossing the high seas.

ROTEIROS, PORTUGUESE COASTING PILOTS

Another type of mapmaking in which the Portuguese excelled was the production of *roteiros,* route books or coasting pilots. The Portuguese empire depended on long lines of communication. Only coastlines and islands were firmly held along the seaway round Africa, and across the Indian Ocean to India and the Far East. The *roteiro* was ideal for the depiction of this extensive empire and the *carreira da India,* the round-trip from Lisbon to Goa and back.

An early example of the technique of coastal depiction is found in the panoramic drawings illustrating the Book of Francisco Rodrigues, a manuscript describing his voyage in the Eastern Archipelago (1514). The finest practitioner of the technique was D. João de Castro, soldier, administrator, scientist, and cartographer. He was a pupil of Pedro Nuñes, mathematician and royal cosmographer. In 1538, he went to India, and during his service made hydrographic and magnetic observations from which he compiled three *roteiros* (Lisbon to Goa, Goa to Diu, and Goa to Suez). These *roteiros* are partly journals and partly sailing directions, and are illustrated by *távoas,* or harbor charts.

In the dedication of the *roteiro* from Goa to Diu, made to the Infant Luís, fourth son of King Manuel, friend and fellow pupil under the tutelage of Nuñes, De Castro recounted how he decided "to write about the situation of this Indian sea coast, with the cosmography of the lands comprised behind its long and formidable beaches." He mentioned how much these efforts had cost him: "how often I went beneath the rough waves . . . ," how "also to find the truth about the routes, the flowing of the sea, the twists and still waters of the rivers, anchorages of harbours, the shelter of bays, differences of needles, latitudes of cities, and to make *távoas* . . . of each place and river, which comprise the view of the land, shoals, reefs, routes, and how they must be entered; I lost much of my health and natural disposition."[15] A. E. Nordenskiöld in his *Periplus* (1897) described the harbor charts as "the first known of the kind and the earliest special maps of any part of the southern littoral of Asia."[16]

On the *távoas*, physical features and naval activities were depicted with equal care. The view of the port of Suk (Xeque) on the north side of the island of Socotra, for example, shows Portuguese ships (*ñaos*) lying off the port and rowing galleys on their way to Suez, where the Turkish forces prevented them from landing. (See Figure 2.)

De Castro made polite excuses for the technicalities of his work: "it is well known that I do not write this book to be read by ladies and lovers and to be used at courts and in royal places, but by those of Leça and Matosinhos," he wrote, adding a note in the margin, "places where mariners live."[17]

The most famous of the three *roteiros* is that of the Red Sea, written in 1541 and dedicated and presented to the Infant Luís. On December 31, 1540, De Castro had sailed from Goa in command of a galleon in the fleet sent to the Red Sea by Governor D. Estêvão da Gama. He returned to Goa on August 21, 1541. As he explained to Luís, the *roteiro* contained "the situation and picture of all the Arabian Sinus. I do not say that it had not been conquered to this point by some nations, but no one knew its length or the distances between its beaches, [or anything] of the natives who live and navigate in it. . . ." Such were the difficulties in navigation that he wondered whether the Portuguese had gained more glory and

FIGURE 2 *Suk, from De Castro's* roteiro *of the Red Sea, 1541. British Library.*

renown in their military triumph in the Red Sea or in discovering its coasts and rendering them navigable.[18]

The most beautiful exemplar of the *roteiro* of the Red Sea, and the source of all the printed editions, is that in the British Library (previously the British Museum). It is identified as the original fair copy presented by De Castro to Infant Luís and later donated by the Infant's younger brother, the Cardinal-King Henrique, to the College of the Society of Jesus at Évora.[19] The charts appear to have been redrawn in 1543 by Gaspar Aloisius, alias Gaspar Luís Viegas, an equerry at court who was also a cartographer.[20] The quality of his work is seen in the view of Suk. (See Figure 2.)

Later on, the manuscript was seized from a Portuguese ship by a privateer and was purchased by Sir Walter Raleigh for £60. The Elizabethan antiquary Sir Robert Cotton acquired it from Raleigh or from his collections after his death, and it came to the British Museum in the Cotton Collection in 1753.[21] Samuel Purchas, the chronicler, published an abridged version in *Hakluytus Posthumous, or Purchas his Pilgrimes* (London, 1625), stating that he made the translation at Raleigh's own request.[22]

De Castro was appointed Viceroy of India in 1547, but he died in 1548. One of the heroes in the founding of Portugal's eastern empire, he averred that military feats should be chronicled by someone of genius; he would keep silent for the sake of the honor of these great deeds, which did not belong in a *roteiro*.[23] However, the poet Luis de Camões (c. 1524–1580) undertook this task of commemorating heroes. In his epic poem, *The Lusiads*, published in 1572 to celebrate Portugal's advance to the distant Orient, he refers in the Tenth Book to the feats of Martím de Sousa and De Castro at Diu, the small island south of the Kathiawar Peninsula, in northern India, whose fortress De Castro had relieved in 1546 after its second great siege:

> *Such is that Martin, who from Mars his name*
> *Derives, together with his actions high.*
> *No less for arms shall he have lasting fame*
> *Than for wise thought and perspicacity,*
> *Castro will follow, who the oriflame*
> *Of Portugal shall make for ever fly,*
> *Of his forerunner the successor fit,*
> *For one built Diu, one defended it.*[24]

DIEGO HOMEM

If the work of official Portuguese cartographers was not in the same epic mold as that of De Castro, man of action as well as mathematical practitioner, their lives did not lack drama. Lopo Homem continued in office over a long period, from 1517 to 1565. He was knighted by the Governor of Azamor for his military feats in 1521, and was described as late as 1563 as "a noble knight of the household of the King our Lord, and master of the nautical charts of these Kingdoms of Portugal."[25] He had become the head of a family of chart makers, of whom his son Diego (or Diogo) was the most notable as an atlas maker.

Unlike his father, Diego worked in exile. The royal prohibition on the gift and sale of charts to foreigners did not prevent cosmographers and mapmakers from leaving their native country and offering their services to new masters. Diego Homem fled to London in 1547 on being accused of murder. Though offered a pardon by João III, he stayed abroad and was in London for some years, gaining his livelihood as a chart maker, and then about 1568, he moved to Venice. Diego was not a navigator or seaman but a *cartographe du cabinet*. Cortesão and Teixeira da Mota regard his work as showing little new, when compared with Lopo Homem's planisphere of 1554, and they suggest that Diego went on reproducing his father's prototypes.[26] If this is so, then the same might be said of his brother André Homem, also an exile, whose planisphere of 1559 bears many similarities to Lopo's and Diego's works.[27] Both Diego and André also incorporated features on their charts which derived from Dieppe hydrography.

Diego seems to have been the most prolific Portuguese cartographer in the sixteenth century, or, at least, more of his works survive, including twelve atlases. Of these, Queen Mary's Atlas, 1558, is one of the finest.[28] It appears to have been commissioned by Mary and her husband Philip II, since it contains no flowery dedication; or perhaps it was ordered by Mary as a gift for Philip, probably a New Year's gift. Homem decorated the chart of Western Europe with an escutcheon over Spain and an even larger one over England, impaling the arms of Philip and Mary. The left-hand half of the shield, with the arms of Philip, has been scratched out, leaving only traces. When Mary died on November 17, 1558, the world chart was probably not yet finished, and on this Homem put only the arms of England. It is surmised that when the atlas came into the hands of Elizabeth I, she had the arms of Philip scraped off the shield over England.[29]

The Homem atlas ranks as one of the most beautiful pictorial atlases of the sixteenth century. Some of the vignettes display traditional features, such as Prester John, the Christian King, enthroned in Ethiopia. The inscription "Mareleparamatiu" (Sea of Parmentier), inscribed in the northeast Pacific on the chart of the Atlantic and North America, commemorates the exploits of the celebrated Dieppe navigator Jean Parmentier, who led an expedition to Sumatra in 1529 to 1530.[30] (See Figure 3.)

FERNÃO VAZ DOURADO

In the second half of the sixteenth century, one of the greatest Portuguese cartographers was Fernão Vaz Dourado, who is considered unequaled as a cartographic illuminator.[31] He was born at Goa about 1520, was wounded at the siege of Diu in 1546, and served on the expedition of Vasco da Cunha to Bengal in

FIGURE 3   *Diego Homem, chart of North America and the Atlantic from Queen Mary's Atlas, 1558. British Library.*

1547 (or 1543–1544). His experiences in the East enabled him to compile much geographical and hydrographical information for the region, including tide tables for the coast of India.

Six of Vaz Dourado's atlases survive, a number of which he signed and dated at Goa, styling himself in his atlases of 1568 and 1571 as "*fronteiro* [frontier captain] in these parts of India."[32] He was in Portugal with the Viceroy from 1572, and there drew, in 1575, one of the most beautiful and complete of his atlases now in the British Library. It is dedicated to King Sebastião (1554–1578), who had ascended the throne at the age of three and assumed government of the country in 1568 at the age of fourteen.[33] The frontispiece has the image of St. Sebastião on the right and the royal coat of arms of Portugal on the left, with the author's legend below. The title of the atlas is written in capital letters round the frame: *Universalis. et integra totius orbis, hidrographia, ad verissimam Luzitoanorum, traditionem descripcio. Ferdinado Va.*

Comparing the more heavily illuminated charts of Vaz Dourado to those in some of the atlases of the Dieppe school, Cortesão and Teixeira da Mota consider the French works "however remarkable," as inferior to the beauty, delicacy, and good taste of most of Vaz Dourado's works.[34] While Vaz Dourado's style lacks the documentary vividness of the Dieppe school, it exercises an elegant and masterly restraint, as shown in the chart of the Indian Ocean. (See Figure 4.)

The atlas of 1575 was preserved in the royal palace of Lisbon until the earthquake of 1755, and was privately salvaged or stolen from the ruins. It was acquired by a certain Henry Chapman in 1772. The British Board of Admiralty purchased it from Chapman in 1792 and the Lords of the Admiralty presented it to the British Museum in 1872.[35]

Vaz Dourado's atlases depict the world shortly before the Spanish and Portuguese empires were united under the Crown of Spain. Sebastião's grandiose ambitions had ended in defeat and death at the Battle of the Three Kings in Morocco (1578). Henrique the Cardinal-King, who succeeded him, died in 1580. Philip II of Spain thereupon annexed the crown of Portugal, to become the most powerful Christian monarch in the world. Philip's personal motto and emblem, *Non sufficit orbis* (One world is not enough), proclaimed him in this role.

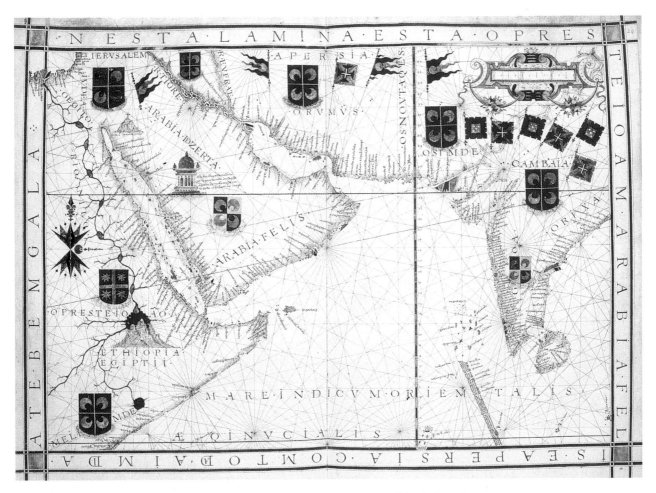

FIGURE 4   *Fernão Vaz Dourado, chart of the Indian Ocean*
in atlas of 1575. British Library.

SPANISH AND ITALIAN ATLASES

The Spanish dominions in the New World, resplendent with their kingdoms of Mexico and Peru, were the envy of Europe. To protect the rich lands and trade routes of the empire from intruders, the Spanish authorities enforced strict regulations limiting the circulation of the *padron real*, the official navigational chart. The works produced in Italy by chart-making workshops, which depicted the Spanish world, were therefore eagerly sought after. One center was at Messina in Sicily, Spain's outpost against the Turks. It seems that Jewish members of the Catalan school in Majorca, among others, had moved to another area of the Aragonese empire.[36]

A leading chart maker at Messina from 1550 to 1591 was Joan Martines, who was of Spanish descent. He made more than thirty atlases and charts in this period, and in his last years was working as royal cosmographer in Naples. Although many of his portolan charts covered the normal area of the Mediterranean and surrounding regions, some of his atlases included charts of the Americas. A fine example is an atlas now in the British Library (Harley MS 3450). The inscription reads "Joan Martines en Messina Año 1618," but the middle two fig-

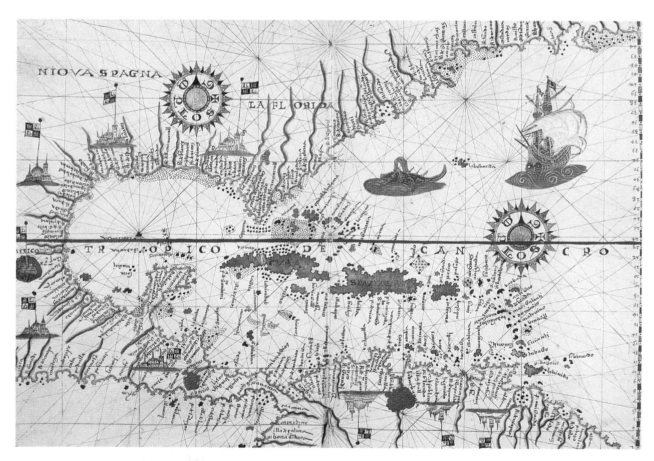

FIGURE 5 *Joan Martines, chart of the West Indies, in atlas of 1578. British Library.*

ures have been altered, and the original date appears to have been 1578. Six regional charts cover parts of America, beautifully illuminated and gilded to show Spain's hopes and achievements in her "Kingdoms of the Sun." The chart of the West Indies (Map 14, see Figure 5) depicts the heart of the Spanish empire, a favorite hunting ground for foreign privateers. Mexico City appears in a vignette in New Spain.[37]

Another workshop producing portolan-style decorative atlases for sale or presentation, based mainly on Spanish prototypes, was that of the Genoese Battista Agnese, who worked at Venice from about 1536 to 1564. He was one of the leading popularizers of the day, drawing on sources both Spanish and Portuguese.[38] For the first time, many Europeans would have seen on Agnese's maps the track of Magellan's ship, the *Victoria*, around the world. Some of the atlases bear personal dedications and the coat of arms of intended recipients, for example, those of Cosimo I in the Vatican Library atlas of 1542 (now missing). The so-called Charles V atlas (c. 1544) has a medallion portrait of Charles and the arms of Castile and Aragon.[39] The long-running successes of the workshops of Martines and Agnese at Messina and Venice, respectively, illustrate the great interest among Italians in overseas discovery and trading ventures. Their merchant houses in particular were avid for all recent news.

THE DIEPPE SCHOOL

In many ways the most remarkable group of manuscript atlases made for presentation was the work of the Dieppe hydrographers. These men did not serve a monopolistic state but were entrepreneurs pursuing a local policy of worldwide enterprise. As the historian Charles de la Roncière has remarked, "If you want to find the governing principle in the maritime politics of the day, you must seek it not at the Court of King Francis I, but at Dieppe."[40] Under the direction of Jean Ango the great *armateur* (a word with no exact English equivalent; literally, a fitter-out of ships), the seamen of Dieppe were sweeping the seas as interlopers in the Portuguese sphere of the world, seeking trade and dominion.

In support of these activities, a school of hydrography had developed at Dieppe which was second to none in Europe. The earliest reference to the school is that of Jean Parmentier, poet-cosmographer, the greatest of Ango's navigators in the 1520s:

> *Deux des plus clercs qui soient en leur école*
> *Pour composer . . .*
> *. . . astrolabes, sphères et mappemondes,*
> *Aussi cartes pour connaître le monde*
> *Tant qu'ont acquis un perpétuel nom*
> *Faisant fleurir de Dieppe le renom*[41]

A later reference indicating the school's international reputation was that of Lucas Jansz Waghenaer in 1601, "Diepe reputee comme l'escolle des bons Pilottes de ce Royaulme."[42] We know from a comment of Jean Rotz (1542), that there were many charts in Dieppe in the 1530s.[43] They were derived from Portuguese sources and from the records of the Dieppe voyages.

Against this background of local initiative undertaken in the face of government caution, and at times outright disapproval, the Dieppe hydrographers presented fine atlases and charts to royal and noble persons to advance the cause of French enterprise overseas. The first atlas made for presentation was the *Boke of Idrography* of Jean Rotz (1542). Rotz had intended the atlas for his sovereign Francis I of France. He had probably spent two years in Paris, 1540 to 1542, seeking a royal appointment, and then, disappointed, transferred to the service of Henry VIII in England. When the book was nearly finished, as Rotz piously remarked to Henry, God "chose to direct it elsewhere, to better fortune than I had hoped."[44] Rotz had brought with him, as testimonials, a manuscript-navigational treatise, the "Traicte des differences du compas aymante"; his *cadrant differential* (a differential quadrant), which was a navigating instrument of his own invention described in the treatise; and the *Boke of Idrography*. When the first two gifts had been well received, he went on to present the Boke. He was rewarded about September 1542 with an appointment as royal hydrographer, which he held until Henry's death in January 1547.

The Boke was part of Rotz's special stock-in-trade as a hydrographer. In his dedication of the Boke to Henry, written in French, Rotz explained how he had come to make it for Francis I; and he described it as the first of its kind:

. . . believing the world was already well supplied with the common sort of marine charts, I formed the opinion it would be best to make a book for him containing all hydrography or marine science; both because I had never seen such a thing, and also because it would be more useful and profitable, more significant, and easier and more convenient to handle and to look at, than a single chart four or five yards in length.[45]

The dedication to Henry is followed by an introduction in the form of a navigational manual, written in English, and then by eleven regional charts described as "the lands and sea coasts of the World in so far as by mariners and other sailors it is known; the which description of lands is set by order so that every leaf does begin there where the precedent of it did leave [off]." Rotz's charts are drawn on a uniform scale, which at the Equator works out at 1:9,000,000. Photocopies of the charts have been built into a mosaic which reveals the model as a world chart thirteen feet broad and seven feet high. By transforming the world chart into a series of atlas maps, Rotz was able to omit unknown regions, such as northeast

Asia. He made a neat fit, keeping to a minimum the duplication of regions on adjoining charts.[46]

Rotz completed the atlas with a world map in two hemispheres, described as "the whole description of the sea chart made in roundness after the manner of cosmography." (See Figure 6.) Whereas the regional charts have south at the top, the world map follows the more commonly accepted convention for maps, with north at the top. The map appears to be the only example of the equatorial form of the stereographic projection dating from the first half of the sixteenth century. The decorative borders are inscribed to Henry: "H.R. VIII. God save the Regis Maieste." This dates the map's completion in 1542, whereas the regional charts appear to have been drawn before 1540 and represent an earlier state of knowledge.

The Boke is notable as the earliest surviving major work of Dieppe hydrography. As Rotz claimed, it was a new form of atlas, comprising a large chart converted into book form. It was also much more than a compendium of hydrography or marine science. Rotz had elaborated its charts with panoramas of the lives of peoples encountered overseas by the Dieppe voyagers. These scenes were

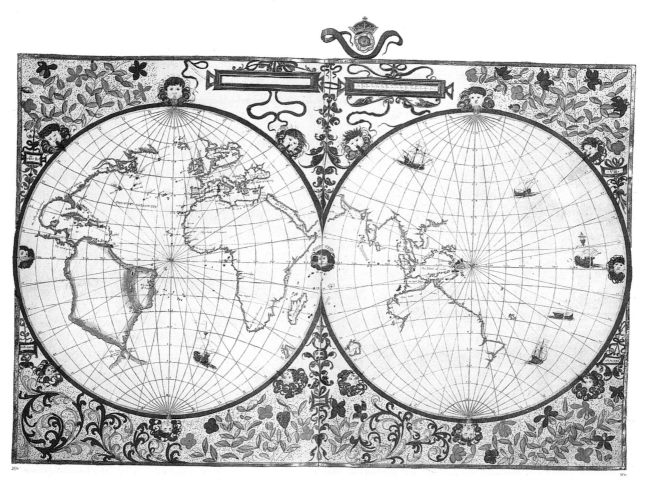

FIGURE 6   *World map in Jean Rotz,* Boke of Idrography, *1542. British Library.*

15

ALLEGHENY COLLEGE LIBRARY

intended originally for the eyes of Francis I, from whom Rotz was seeking not only a position at court, but also (we may surmise) support for the armateurs of Dieppe, of whom he was one. Francis pursued throughout his reign a policy of "good friendship, alliance, and confederacy" with the Portuguese king, "my good brother, cousin, and ally."[47] He sponsored only one voyage, that of Giovanni da Verrazzano to North America in 1524.[48] He prohibited, in 1539 to 1540, the Norman voyages overseas, and Ango's fortunes were threatened.[49] As a merchant adventurer himself, Rotz had every reason to impress on Francis the advantages of an active overseas policy.

When Rotz, disappointed in these hopes, took himself off with his family to England and turned to Henry VIII as patron in 1542, he adapted the Boke to his new situation. He now intended it for the instruction of Henry's sailors and for Henry's personal enlightenment:

For in this work, Sire, after labouring for the affairs and public good of your most excellent Kingdom and people, you may for the recreation of your noble mind observe and learn which coastal lands adjoin or face one another, how many leagues apart they are and in what latitude, together with the style and manner of houses, clothes and skin-colour, as well as arms and other features of the inhabitants of all those coasts which are least known to us.[50]

Rotz added that he had chosen to write the whole book "in the common language of this country, as well as I can." He hoped that the work, being in English, might be printed "to the great profit and use of all the navigators and seamen of this flourishing kingdom, if such be your pleasure."[51] The text of the Boke (other than the dedicatory letter) and the main legends on the charts are written in a somewhat anglicized late Middle Scots, as Rotz's father, David Ross, was a Scot who had emigrated to Dieppe.

The Boke was thus documentary and didactic in conception. Rotz showed only discovered coasts, as he explained to Henry: "All this I have set down as exactly and truly as possible, drawing as much from my own experience as from the certain experience of my friends and fellow navigators."[52] He did not venture into hypothetical geography. Even the decorative features in the continental interiors are mainly coastal scenes drawn *ad vivum*, evidently made on Rotz's own voyages with some additional material derived from other Dieppe expeditions. The voyage of Parmentier from Dieppe to Sumatra (1529–1530) is the source for a series of vignettes drawn in Africa, Madagascar, and Asia. The chart of southeast Africa shows an incident at Madagascar in July 1529 when three of Parmentier's crew were killed by the local inhabitants. Scenes in Sumatra recorded during the expedition's visit to the island (and depicted for convenience to the north of the Malay peninsula) include a military procession of the rajah of Ticou

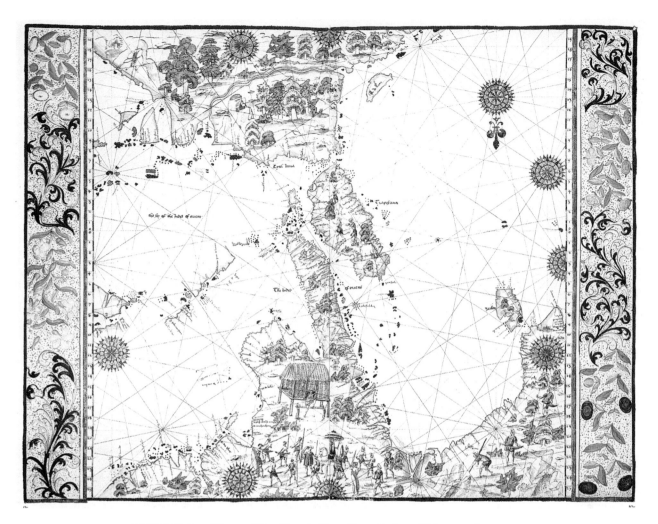

FIGURE 7   *Chart of Far East in Jean Rotz*, Boke of Idrography, *1542.*
South is at the top. British Library.

and a Sumatran house. (See Figure 7.) On the way home the ships anchored without landing at the Cape of Good Hope. This explains why Rotz was able to include some of the earliest pictures of Hottentots in their animal skins. That Rotz was on the voyage himself is suggested by the accuracy of the depictions and a statement in his treatise that he was in the Far East in January 1530.[53]

Other references show that Rotz visited Guinea and Brazil in 1539. His portrayal of the homes and peoples of the Guinea coast is thus from first hand. The usual picture of the Portuguese fortress El Mina dominating the scene is missing. Instead, Rotz shows the huts of African villages that the French would see on their expeditions to the Cap des Trois Pontes, lying ten leagues away from the Portuguese fortress. Most remarkable of all the pictures is Rotz's record of a Tupinambá village in Brazil, including a visiting party of French traders in brazilwood, all drawn *ad vivum*. (See Figure 8.) In contrast, the Indian huts in the northeastern parts of North America, important as the earliest to be found on a

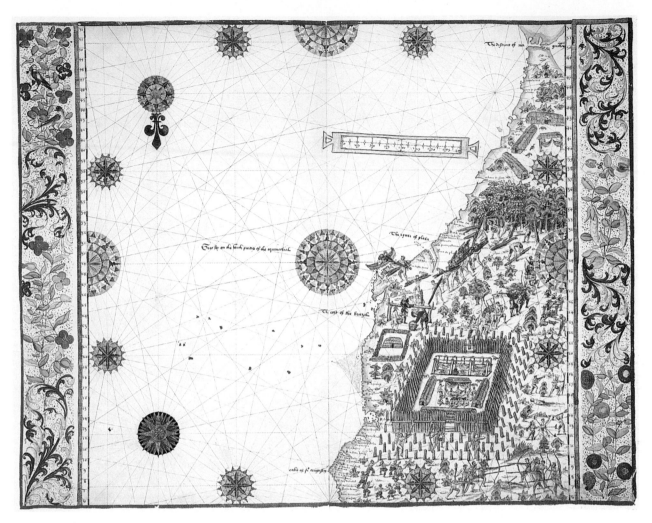

FIGURE 8   *Chart of Brazil in Jean Rotz,* Boke of Idrography, *1542.*
South is at the top. British Library.

map, are presumably derived from the drawings of other Norman voyagers. (See Figure 9.) As with Portuguese voyages, it was customary for French expeditions to carry a "painter" who would draw the sights and scenes as well as make maps. Rotz's atlas combined the chart work of a hydrographer with an artist's work of illumination. It is this feature which has made Rotz's Boke and the other atlases of the Dieppe school outstanding examples of Renaissance maritime cartography.

The Boke was not printed in Rotz's own day nor for many years to come.[54] Instead, it found a safe home on the shelves of the Royal Library in Westminster. Rotz returned to Dieppe in 1547 and soon received from the new King Henri II royal commissions to build ships. In 1553, now the leading merchant captain in Dieppe, he was ennobled. There is no evidence to suggest that he made further hydrographic works for royal presentation.

Two special atlases of Dieppe origin dating from the 1540s reveal curious similarities to Rotz's Boke: "The Hague" atlas, which dates from about 1545, and the atlas of Nicolas Vallard of Dieppe (1547). Like Rotz's Boke, they show evidence of Portuguese influence and so have been characterized (with the Boke) as Luso-French.[55]

Little is known about the circumstances in which The Hague atlas was made. It was in the Duke de la Vallière's collection until 1783 and then passed to the Bolognaro-Crevenna collection. It was finally purchased by auction for the Koninklijke Bibliotheek, The Hague, in 1790.[56] Its fourteen beautifully decorated charts cover the Americas, the Atlantic Ocean, Europe, and the Aegean and Adriatic seas. These are followed by tables of solar declination and nautical regiments and diagrams of tides and winds, written in another hand. The atlas is neither signed nor dated, but bears the arms of Henri as Dauphin of France (1536–1547). Each chart is decorated with a fleur-de-lis, the symbol of Henri, pointing north and, in a corresponding position to the south, a crescent moon, the symbol of Diane de Poitiers, who in 1540 became officially *la dame du Dauphin*. This dates the atlas as not earlier than 1540.[57]

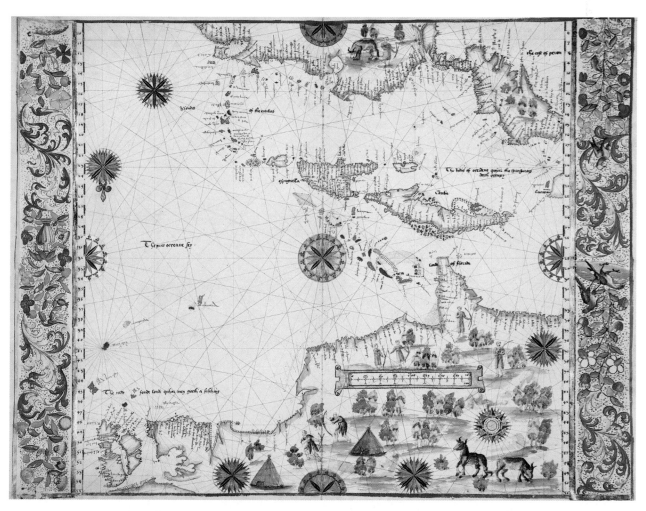

FIGURE 9   *Chart of North America in Jean Rotz*, Boke of Idrography, *1542.*
South is at the top. British Library.

The geographical features of South America suggest a date c. 1545, as do the tide tables which Guillaume Brouscon of Le Conquet in Brittany was issuing in the mid-1540s. The atlas seems to be the work of a Portuguese, probably a resident of Dieppe. The fact that there is no sign of Cartier's voyages explains an earlier dating of c. 1538, given (mistakenly) by Cortesão, Teixeira da Mota, and others who have overlooked the heraldic evidence. Altogether, the atlas provides a fine record of discoveries covering the Atlantic region and would have given the Dauphin an excellent idea of prospects for French enterprise.

The Vallard atlas is inscribed "Nicolas Vallard de Dieppe, 1547." Formerly in the possession of Talleyrand, it was purchased in 1816 by Sir Thomas Phillipps, the great bibliophile and manuscript collector. It is now in the Huntington Library, San Marino, California.[58] The author appears to have been Portuguese, although regional names (in a larger hand) are mainly in French. The work is remarkable for its elaborate iconography.

Of special interest is the map of the land mass Java-la-Grande, shown south of the Eastern Archipelago. (See Figure 10.) In Rotz's Boke there was room only for the northern part of Java-la-Grande on the chart of southeast Asia (see Figure 7), although the world map (see Figure 6) shows in outline its full extent, revealing it as a land of continental proportions. The Vallard atlas depicts the land in detail, with numerous place-names along the coasts and an array of ethnographical scenes. A comparison with Rotz's Boke shows these scenes to be Sumatran and derived from the same source as Rotz's vignettes.[59] Vallard's Java-la-Grande appeared thus to be a substantial and authentic discovery and inspired Sir

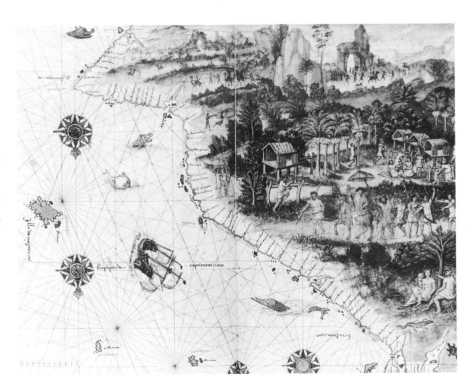

FIGURE 10 *Java-la-Grande in the atlas of Nicolas Vallard, 1547. South is at the top. Henry E. Huntington Library and Art Gallery, San Marino, CA.*

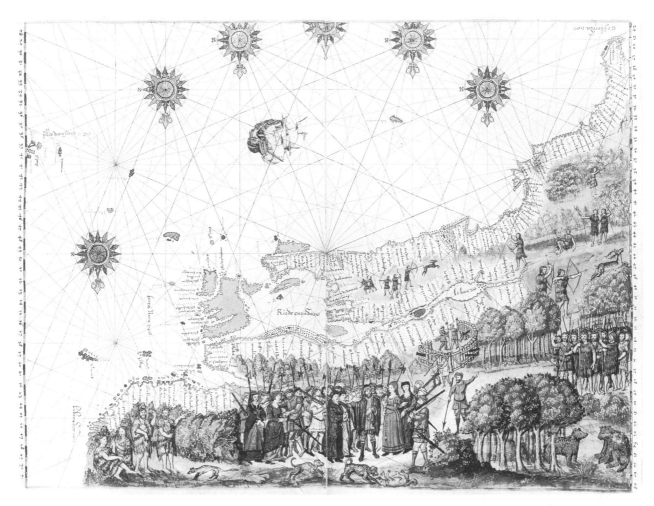

FIGURE 11 *North America in the atlas of Nicolas Vallard, 1547. South is at the top.*
Henry E. Huntington Library and Art Gallery, San Marino, CA.

Thomas Phillipps to publish in 1856 a facsimile of the map by chromolithography and to style it "The first map of Australia."

The Vallard atlas is outstanding also in showing the French colony of New France established on the St. Lawrence River in the years 1542 to 1543 in the course of Jacques Cartier's third voyage. Le Sieur de Roberval, commander of the expedition, and his party of colonists, men and women, stand in a large group facing a body of Indians, with the fort at Montreal in the background. (See Figure 11.) The regional chart of North America in Rotz's Boke (see Figure 9), in contrast, shows only the mouth of the St. Lawrence River, based on the discoveries of the Dieppe voyages and possibly also of Cartier's first voyage (1534), while the world map has the course of the river as known from Cartier's second voyage (1535). (See Figure 6.)

With the exception of these differences in the Canadian area, the striking similarities between Rotz's Boke and the Vallard atlas, and the general resemblance of both to The Hague atlas, raise questions as to their relationship. Since Rotz left Dieppe in 1542, or perhaps earlier, in 1540, his Boke could not have influenced the work of later Dieppe chart makers. With the more accurate dating of the works which has now proved possible, the answer is clear. It appears that the authors of The Hague atlas and the Vallard atlas in the 1540s were drawing on the same sources which Rotz had used or had himself created in the later 1530s. The two later atlases with their beautiful miniatures reveal an artistry compared to which Rotz's illustrations may seem amateurish. In fact, Rotz's Boke provides the more authentic record because the scenes have a documentary realism.

JAVA-LA-GRANDE

The three atlases are among the show pieces of Dieppe hydrography. With the companion works of Pierre Desceliers, priest-cosmographer of Arques, and others, they contribute a remarkable corpus of material dating from about 1540 to 1570. Nearly all the surviving pieces were made for presentation. It would appear that the many ordinary charts which were in Dieppe in the 1530s and 1540s perished when the English fleet bombarded the town in 1694. The special atlases and charts had already left Dieppe and so escaped destruction. They were dispersed among various libraries and collections of Europe, and their provenance was not recognized until the early or later years of the nineteenth century. They were not at first identified as being associated with the Dieppe school. Yet, as they came to light, one by one, learned authorities noticed the common feature of Java-la-Grande, and the question of whether it represented the early discovery of Australia became the subject of public discussion in London and Paris.

The British hydrographer Alexander Dalrymple opened the debate in the 1780s, dealing with the Harleian map. John Pinkerton the geographer and James (later Admiral) Burney offered Rotz's Boke (with high commendation) for comparison with the map. In 1803, Charles Étienne Coquebert de Montbret brought to the attention of the Société Philomatique of Paris the two atlases preserved in France, the Vallard and the atlas in the sale of the Duke de la Vallière's library. As he had not seen it, he was unaware that The Hague atlas (as it was later called) did not extend to the Far East, and so did not show Java-la-Grande, but he identified the similarities of style.[60]

The Dieppe atlases, together with the charts which complemented them, thus became famous particularly in the context of the debate concerning Java-la-Grande. Whereas scholars had noted the combined French and Portuguese sources revealed, no one could explain how the Portuguese discovery of Java-la-Grande (as they identified it) came to appear on French maps, whereas it was not displayed on Portuguese charts of the same date. That the discoverers were Portuguese was evident from the form of the place-names and the Portuguese flags attached to the territory on the charts of one of the later Dieppe hydrographers,

Nicolas Desliens, dating from 1561, 1566, and 1567. The atlases of Diego Homem and Vaz Dourado, in contrast, show no sign of Java-la-Grande.

Rotz's Boke, the earliest and most authoritative extant work of Dieppe hydrography, now provides the key to the answer. It documents unambiguously Parmentier's voyage to Sumatra (1529–1530). The journal of the voyage by the expedition's pilot-astronomer Pierre Crignon, together with other contemporary or later sources, reveals that the French, while in Sumatra, obtained intelligence about a recent Portuguese voyage (1528) to Java-la-Grande, ending up in Sumatra.[61] Records of this otherwise unknown voyage were brought home and incorporated in the charts maintained in Dieppe. Crignon, poet-cosmographer, was the most influential figure in hydrographic circles in Dieppe in the 1530s, and was also well known in Paris. It was presumably through Crignon that Diego and Andre Homem came to record the Sea of Parmentier in the north Pacific, for this fulfilled Crignon's pious hope that if another Frenchman should venture beyond the frontiers of the East into the Pacific, he would name the sea after Parmentier.

Il nommera ceste mer parmentiere
Et en fera memoire a tout iamais.[62]

Most of Crignon's manuscript works have been lost, including presumably the charts which recorded the Sea of Parmentier and the land of Java-la-Grande. Only Rotz's Boke preserves the visual record of Parmentier's historic voyage. The sequel to Rotz, the Vallard atlas, shows how the new continent delineated south of Sumatra, obtained a Sumatran ethnography, flora, and fauna. Whether the land was, indeed, Australia, is still in question. The balance of evidence would seem to be in favor, although recently challenged by some Australian scholars.[63] If the evidence is accepted, the Dieppe atlases can be claimed to preserve for posterity the record of a great discovery on the edge of the Portuguese empire that never entered the mainstream of Portuguese history.

THE INFLUENCE OF MANUSCRIPT PRESENTATION ATLASES

The production of manuscript maritime atlases for presentation was one form of celebration of the European renaissance and the achievements of overseas discovery. Pageantry, the writing of cosmographical poetry by such practitioners as Jean Parmentier and Pierre Crignon, and atlas making were associated activities. The great fête held at Rouen in 1550, in which a complete Tupinambá village was constructed, provided a dramatic ephemeral version of the scene depicted in Rotz's Boke. The pictures in the stained-glass windows of the church of Saint-Jacques de Dieppe have preserved in another form the exotic sights observed on the expeditions sent out by Ango across the seas.[64]

How far the atlases prepared for presentation spurred monarchs and ministers to greater enterprise overseas is an interesting question. The policy of secrecy, which was imposed in Spain and Portugal to protect their empires, must have limited the access to this material. The official chart or *padrón* (*padrão*), which was the standard chart for ships, was closely guarded. On the other hand, some of the atlas makers were also responsible for compiling the official charts. The *padrón real* of the Spanish Casa de la Contratación was based on the planisphere of Jorge Reinel, corrected by his father Pedro Reinel, both of whom are regarded as authors or part authors of the Miller atlas, the Lopo Homem–Reinels Atlas of 1519.[65] Jaime Cortesão comments that the map of the New World in the Miller atlas (which he attributed to Lopo Homem) remained for two centuries a model for the official *padrón* of Portugal.[66]

When the atlases of Spain and Portugal found their way overseas, they sometimes gained a new reputation. Cortesão and Teixeira da Mota comment on João de Castro's *Roteiro* of the Red Sea (the BM Codex, now in the British Library): "If, on the one hand, we cannot but regret that this, like many other early Portuguese codices and charts, was taken out of Portugal, on the other hand it was fortunate that it went to England; otherwise it is most unlikely that it would have been translated, even if only as an abstract, into English, and then into Latin and French, which made it widely known."[67] Sir Walter Raleigh's initiative and Purchas's industry as chroniclers gave the codex world fame.

The influence of the Dieppe school of hydrographers was limited by the distraction of the kings of England and France with affairs of war. In his last years, Henry VIII drifted into war with France and became involved in Scottish affairs and the danger of a French invasion of Scotland. Henri II of France was mainly interested in the struggle for command of the Narrow Seas and for control of territory in Northern France and Scotland. When peace with England followed (1560–1562), France was soon to be engulfed in religious wars. Rotz himself, on his return to France in 1547, became a merchant-captain, and no charts or atlases by him survive from this period.[68]

The later history of Rotz's Boke is also relevant. The inventory of Henry's belongings in his palaces made after his death in 1547 show that he possessed many maps and astronomical instruments, but individual books are not listed.[69] Rotz's Boke and Traicté disappeared into the collections of the royal library. In the reign of Elizabeth I, they escaped the searching eyes of Sir Humphrey Gilbert and Richard Hakluyt, promoters of overseas discovery, who consulted and described the maps and globes to be seen in the Queen's private gallery in Whitehall.

The old Royal Library, still in Henry's Palace at Westminster (known as Whitehall from 1542), had no keeper until about 1605 when Patrick Young (Patricus Junius) was appointed Librarian on the advice of his father Sir Peter Young. After the death of Prince Henry, the heir to the throne, in 1612, the Library was moved from Whitehall to St. James, and Patrick Young began eliminating duplicates. We know he had Rotz's treatise in his possession since a label in the volume reads "From Mr Patrick Young, 1616."[70]

With the accession of Charles II in 1660, there was a revival of interest in the Royal Library and also the royal map collection, which was now kept in the King's private library at Whitehall. The first reference to Rotz's Boke since Rotz's lifetime appears in c. 1681 when Samuel Pepys wrote in his Naval Minutes, "Examine very well the King's Library at St. James's, and particularly the hydrographical draughts presented to Henry 8th by John Rotz, a servant of his." He added the comment "Q. whether an Englishmen or no."[71] Since Rotz's volumes were housed at St. James, they escaped the fire which swept through the Palace of Whitehall in 1698 and destroyed the royal map collections.

After Rotz's Boke and treatise had been passed to the British Museum with the Old Royal Library collection in 1757, the Boke became well known through the comments of Pinkerton and Burney in 1802 and 1803. In Paris in 1807, Barbié du Bocage cited the Boke as evidence of the Portuguese discovery of Australia.[72] Although "Jean Rotz or Roty" (so called) the author remained obscure, his Boke had now entered the mainstream of history.

Queen Mary's atlas by Diego Homem (1538) may have become known in Elizabeth's reign, if Elizabeth vengefully scratched out Philip II's arms on the map of England, as appears probable.[73] The major works in the Palace of Whitehall at that time were the world map of Sebastian Cabot (1549) and the world chart of Sir Francis Drake recording his circumnavigation of 1577–1580 (still secret, but later on display). These were testimonials to England's claim to North America. They were exhibited side by side at the Palace when Purchas consulted them in 1618.

The most important map of North America, made to promote Elizabeth's interests, was John Dee's manuscript map (1580).[74] This marks the "G. de S. m^a" (Gulf of Sta. Maria), which was the objective of the Roanoke voyagers for the colony of 1585. It was the only large bay marked on the coast in the right latitude for preying on Spanish ships. Significantly, the map shows the bay in a form similar to its appearance on the map of America in Diego Homem's atlas (1558). This may be further evidence of the use of Homem's atlas in England.[75]

Some of the special atlases achieved fame in their own day and others became known many years later. They reflect both hopes and achievements: the hopes of the bold armateurs of Dieppe and the achievements of the great imperial powers of Portugal and Spain. They record not only the hydrography of the seas but also the marvels of new lands and unknown peoples. For posterity they have yielded a rich heritage.

NOTES

1 Bibliothèque Nationale de France, Cartes et Plans, Rés. Ge. DD. 683 and Rés. Ge. AA. 640. See Armando Cortesão and Avelino Teixeira da Mota, *Portugaliae Monumenta Cartographica* (hereafter *PMC*), vol. 1 (Lisbon, 1960), pp. 55–61, pl. 16-24. A second edition of *PMC*, comprising a facsimile of the 1960 edition, with a new Introduction (in volume 1) and Supplement (in volume 6), written by Alfredo Pinheiro

Marques, was published at Lisbon by the Imprensa Nacional-Casa da Moeda, in 1987. This updated the 1960 edition and includes all known examples of Portuguese cartography up to the beginning of the eighteenth century.

2 Visconde de Santarém, *Estudos de Cartographia Antiga* (Lisbon, 1919), 1:225 (published posthumously).

3 Michel Mollat de Jourdain and Monique de la Roncière, et al., *Sea Charts of the Early Explorers, 13th to 17th Century*, trans. L. le R. Dethan (New York, 1984), p. 219. Monique Pelletier, et al., *Á la Découverte de la Terre. Dix siècles de Cartographie. Trésors du Département des Cartes et Plans* (Paris: Bibliothèque Nationale, 1979), pp. 18–20.

4 *PMC*, 1:55–61.

5 *PMC*, 1:49.

6 *PMC*, 1:xiv.

7 *PMC*, 1:60–61.

8 *PMC*, 1:130. Also Armando Cortesão and Luís de Albuquerque (ed.), *Obras completas de D. João de Castro* (Coimbra, 1968), 3:44.

9 Samuel Eliot Morison, *The European Discovery of America: The Northern Voyages*, A.D. *500–1600* (New York, 1971), pp. 230–231.

10 Bernard G. Hoffman, *Cabot to Cartier: Sources for a Historical Ethnography of Northeastern North America, 1497–1550* (Toronto, 1961), pp. 56–57.

11 Morison, *The European Discovery of America: The Southern Voyages*, A.D. *1492–1616* (New York, 1974), pp. 502–504, 510–512.

12 Morison, ibid., pp. 300–301.

13 Bibliothèque Nationale de France, Rés. Ge D 26179.

14 D. B. Quinn, "Artists and Illustrators in the Early Mapping of North America," *The Mariner's Mirror* 72 (1986):249. Helen Wallis, "The Role of the Painter in Renaissance Marine Cartography," in Carla Clivio Marzoli (ed.), *Imago et Mensura Mundi* (Rome, 1985), 2:515.

15 *PMC*, 1:135.

16 A. E. Nordenskiöld, *Periplus* (Stockholm, 1897), p. 157a. See also Helen Wallis, *Material on Nautical Cartography in the British Library, 1550–1650*, Centro de Estudos de História e Cartografia Antiga, Série Separatas, no. 162 (Lisbon, 1984), pp. 190–191.

17 Cortesão and Albuquerque (1968), 4:406.

18 *PMC*, 1:139.

19 *PMC*, 1:139–141.

20 The manuscript ends with the inscription, "Gaspar Aloisius scribebat M.D. XLIII."

21 British Library, Cotton MS. Tiberius D. IX. See *Prince Henry the Navigator and Portuguese Maritime Enterprise: Catalogue of an Exhibition at the British Museum, September–October 1960* (London, 1960), pp. 24–25.

22 Samuel Purchas, *Purchas his Pilgrimes* (Glasgow: MacLehose, 1905), 7:236.

23 Cortesão and Albuquerque (1968), 4:407.

24 Leonard Bacon (trans.), *The Lusiads of Luis de Camões* (New York, 1950), Book X, 67, pp. 365, 395. The original title is *Os Lusiadas*, "the epic of the nation of Lusus," i.e., the Portuguese, a classical allusion.

25 *PMC*, 1:50–53.

26 *PMC*, 1:49; 2:5–7.

27 *PMC*, 1:67–68; 2:10.

28 British Library. Add. MS 5415A. The atlas must have been in the Royal Library, but is not recorded in the Old Royal Library catalogs. On arriving in the British Museum it was given the above classmark.

29 *PMC*, 2:13.

30 *PMC*, 2:15. Helen Wallis (ed.) *The Maps and Text of the Boke of Idrography Presented by Jean Rotz to Henry VIII* (Oxford, 1981), pp. 66–67.

31 *PMC*, 3:xiii.

32 *PMC*, 3:6.

33 *PMC*, 3:23.

34 *PMC*, 3:xiii.

35 British Library, Add. MS 31317.

36 Mollat and De la Roncière (1984), p. 241.

37 *Catalogue of the Manuscript Maps, Charts, and Plans . . . in the British Museum* (1844, reprinted 1962), 1:29–30.

38 Mollat and De la Roncière (1984), p. 227.

39 Henry R. Wagner, *The Manuscript Atlases of Battista Agnese*, Papers of the Bibliographical Society of America, vol. 25 (Chicago, 1931), pp. 69, 74.

40 Charles de la Roncière, *Histoire de la marine françoise* (Paris, 1906), 3:244. Wallis, *Rotz* (1981), pp. 4, 24.

41 Pierre Crignon, *Poésies* (1541), quoted by Marcel Chicoteau, *Australie terre légendaire* (Brisbane, 1965), p. 22. See also Wallis, *Rotz* (1981), p. 74, n. 6.

42 Lucas Jansz. Waghenaer, *Thresorerie ou Cabinet de la Routte marinesque* (Calais, 1601), sig. *2v.

43 In Rotz's dedication to Henry, Wallis, *Rotz* (1981), pp. 79–80.

44 Wallis, *Rotz* (1981), p. 80.

45 Ibid.

46 Wallis, *Rotz* (1981), pp. 36–37.

47 Letter of Francis I to Vice Admiral de Chillon, May 6, 1523, in Norman J. W. Thrower, "New Light on the 1524 Voyage of Verrazzano," *Terrae Incognitae* 11 (1979), p. 63.

48 Thrower (1979), pp. 60–61, 65.

49 Wallis, *Rotz* (1981), p. 8.

50 Wallis, *Rotz* (1981), p. 80.

51 Ibid.

52 Wallis, *Rotz* (1981), pp. 6, 80.

53 Wallis, *Rotz* (1981), p. 6.

54 The first facsimile is that of 1981, published for the Roxburghe Club by Viscount Eccles, ed. Helen Wallis. See note 30.

55 *PMC*, 5:132.

56 Koninklijke Bibliotheek, The Hague, MS 129 A. 24.

57 Wallis, *Rotz* (1981), p. 41.

58 The Huntington Library, San Marino, California, MS HM. 29.

59 Wallis, *Rotz* (1981), pp. 59–60.

60 Wallis, "Java-la-Grande: The Enigma of the Dieppe Maps," Chapter 2 in Glyndwr Williams and Alan Frost (eds.), *Terra Australis to Australia* (Melbourne, 1988), p. 73.

61 Wallis, *Rotz* (1981), pp. 60–61, 65–66.

62 Wallis, *Rotz* (1981), p. 66. Jean Parmentier, *Description novvelle des merveiles de ce mõde et de la dignite de lhomme*, ed. Pierre Crignon (1531; reprint, Boston, 1920), fol. hiiii^v.

63 For illustrations of all the Dieppe maps showing Java-la-Grande and a full discussion of the evidence, see Wallis, "Java-la-Grande," in Williams and Frost, *Terra Australis* (1988), pp. 38–81. Wallis, *Rotz* (1981) also includes a detailed exposition. K. G. McIntyre's book, *The Secret Discovery of Australia* (Medindie and London, 1977), claiming a Portuguese discovery in the early sixteenth century, became very popular in Australia. More recently W. A. R. Richardson has set out a theory that Java-la-Grande is a composite of the coast of southwest Java and Vietnam (known as Champa in the early sixteenth century). See Wallis, "Java-la-Grande and Australia," and W. A. R. Richardson, "Java-la-Grande is not Australia," in "Unfolding Australia: Proceedings of the Joint Meeting of the International Map Collectors' Society (IMCOS) and the Australia Map Circle, Sydney, Australia 17–21 November 1991," *The Globe*, special issue no. 37 (1992), pp. 12–13 and 13–16. See also Richardson, "Is Java-la-Grande Australia? The Linguistic Evidence Concerning the West Coast," *The Globe*, no. 19 (1983), pp. 9–46. A review of the evidence, with the conclusion that Java-la-Grande comprised the incompletely mapped islands of Java and Sumbawa, is set out by Stuart Duncan, "Shaving with Ockham's Razor: A Reappraisal of the Portuguese Priority Hypothesis," *The Globe*, no. 39 (1993), pp. 1–9. The Australian commentators have not taken cognizance of Wallis's evidence of how the Dieppe hydrographers obtained their intelligence on the Portuguese discoveries. See Wallis, in Williams and Frost, *Terra Australis* (1988), pp. 40–48, 77.

64 Mollat du Jourdin and Jacques Habert, *Giovanni et Girolamo Verrazano, navigateurs de Francois Ier* (Paris, 1982), pp. 148–149.

65 *PMC*, 1:61, 89.

66 Jaime Cortesão, *História do Brasil nos Velhos Mapas* (Rio de Janeiro, 1965), 1:322.

67 *PMC*, 1:141.

68 Wallis, *Rotz* (1981), p. 23.

69 Ibid., p. 73. British Library, Harleian MS 1414 A and B.

70 Ibid., pp. 73–74.

71 J. R. Tanner (ed.), *Samuel Pepys's Naval Minutes* (London, 1926), p. 96; Wallis, *Rotz* (1981), p. 74.

72 Wallis, *Rotz* (1981), p. 74.

73 Helen Wallis, *Raleigh and Roanoke: The First English Colony in America, 1584–1590* (Raleigh, NC, 1985), item 3, p. 23.

74 British Library, Cotton MS, Augustus I.I.I.

75 William P. Cumming, *Mapping the North Carolina Coast: Sixteenth-Century Cartography and the Roanoke Voyages* (Raleigh, NC, 1988), plates 14, 18.

An Inquiry into Early Chinese Atlases through the Ming Dynasty

MEI-LING HSU

The beginning of mapmaking in historic China can be traced to at least the Zhou Dynasty in the eleventh century B.C. The making of a map or drawing (*tu*) is first mentioned in a chapter entitled "Luo Gao" in the *Shu Jing* (Book of History) which records the construction of the eastern capital of the Zhou Dynasty around 1100 B.C.[1] The term "map" (*di tu*; literally, a picture of the land) appeared as a chapter heading in a book *Guan Zi*, written in the Warring States period (475–221 B.C.).[2] By this time in ancient China, there were abundant literary records of mapmaking, map use, and officials in charge of cartographic activities.[3]

We need concrete, graphic evidence, however, to substantiate the written accounts and to provide visual images of the early Chinese cartographic works. Fortunately, four invaluable ancient examples were unearthed in China during the 1970s. Prior to this time, the earliest cartographic works extant in China were the two maps *Hua Yi Tu* and *Yu Ji Tu*, carved on stone in A.D. 1136. (See Figure 12.) The four maps, however, predate the stone maps by a millennium and a half. The oldest map of the four, the *Zhao Yu Tu*, a planning map of a burial ground, was made on a bronze plate sometime before 310 B.C. and was found during the 1974 to 1978 excavation in Pingshan Xian, Hebei Province.[4] The other three maps were made before 168 B.C. during the Western Han period (206 B.C.–A.D. 8) and are more important. They were found in 1973 at the excavation site in Mawangduei, Hunan Province.[5]

Two of the Han maps, one topographic and another military, have been carefully restored and studied; the third one, a city map, is, unfortunately, severely deteriorated. The two restored maps are extraordinary in the accuracy of the scale of the maps, sophistication of symbol use, and large amount of information. They reveal that a high level of cartographic achievement existed in China before the birth of Christ.[6] (See Figures 13 and 14.)

31

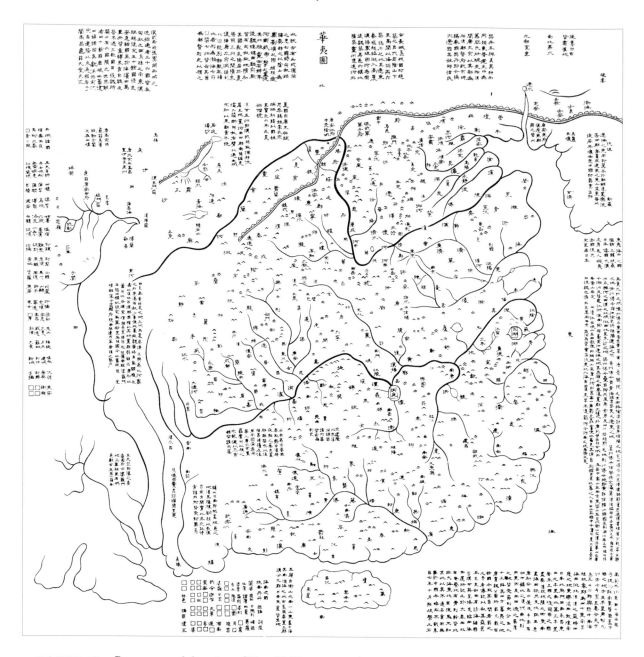

FIGURE 12 *Reconstructed drawing of* Hua Yi Tu, *engraved on stone in A.D. 1136. Original is housed in the Provincial Museum in Xian City. From* An Atlas of Ancient Maps in China, *eds., Wanru Cao and others (Beijing: Cultural Relics Publishing House, 1990).*

More recently, in 1986, seven maps were unearthed from a tomb of the Qin Kingdom which were dated around 300 B.C., the Warring States period (475–221 B.C.). Today these are the earliest extant Chinese maps which cover an area about 107 × 68 square kilometers south of Tianshui City in Gansu Province.[7] These are simple maps which show locations, rivers, and so forth, but on three of the maps there are notes indicating the kinds and locations of timber to be found in the

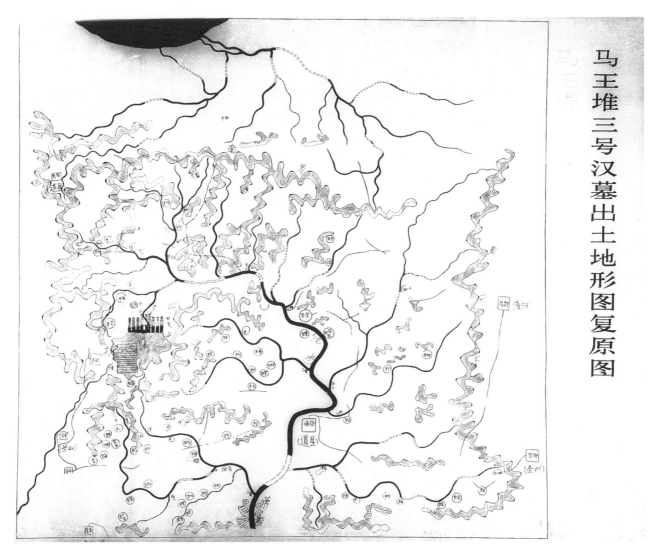

马王堆三号汉墓出土地形图复原图

FIGURE 13 *The reconstructed Han topographic map, which covers an area between 110° and 112° 30′ East and 24° 30′ and 26° North. South is at the top. The original map is kept in the Provincial Museum in Changsha, Hunan. From* Wen Wu, *1975, no. 2.*

forests. These must be some of the earliest, if not the earliest, economic maps in the world.

All these recently discovered ancient maps were unearthed from the tombs of high-ranking civilian and military officials. This is a result of at least two factors: (1) Maps were valuable military and political tools, which were usually secured in safe places or destroyed with defeat in war; (2) there was the early custom of leaving articles dear to the deceased in his tomb; thus, Han maps are found in the tombs of high-ranking officers in charge of the mapped area.

According to the literary records, the first Chinese attempt to produce an atlas occurred some six centuries after the Qin maps. Pei Xiu (A.D. 223–271), who is known as the father of scientific cartography in China and who conceptualized

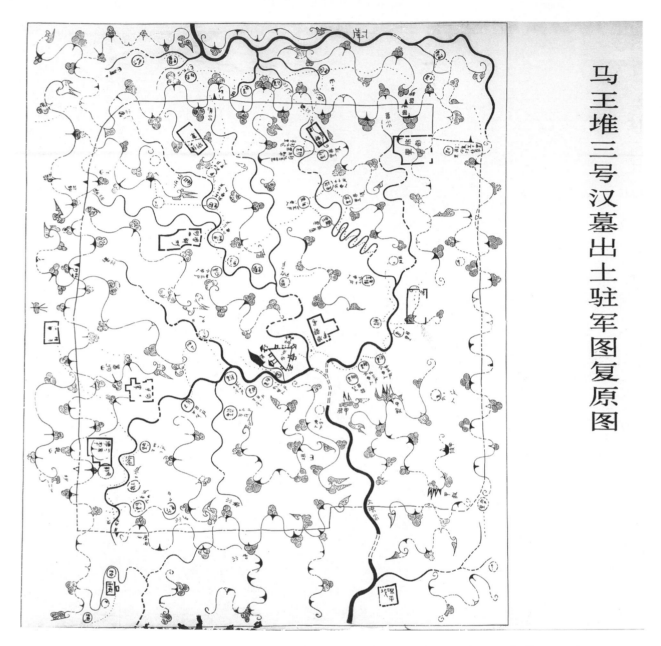

马王堆三号汉墓出土驻军图复原图

FIGURE 14 *The reconstructed Han military map. The original map is kept in the Provincial Museum in Changsha, Hunan. From* Wen Wu, *1976, no. 1.*

the well-known six principles of mapmaking, evidently spent the last three years of his life compiling an eighteen-section atlas, entitled *Yu Gong Di Yu Tu* (Maps of Regions in the "Tribute to Yu"). Yu was the first king of the Xia Dynasty (twenty-first to sixteenth centuries B.C.).[8] The atlas itself was lost over the centuries, but its preface has survived. Our knowledge of the content of this atlas derives from its preface and a few other historical documents.[9]

Activities of mapmaking and map use multiplied after Pei Xiu's time, yet the production of atlases was fairly small. Considerable time elapsed between Pei's pioneering contribution and the subsequent compilation of other major atlases. According to literary accounts, atlas making became a significant component of cartographic production only after the tenth century. The earliest of these atlases extant is thought to be the *Li Dai Di Li Zhi Zhang Tu* (Geographical Maps of Successive Dynasties), probably compiled in the twelfth century (authorship uncertain).[10] Four centuries later, Luo Hongxian compiled the *Guang Yu Tu* (Enlarged Terrestrial Atlas), which was first published in A.D. 1555.[11] This atlas was reproduced in five more editions over the next two and a half centuries and became a major source for the compilation of many later cartographic works.

This essay examines early Chinese atlas making through the Ming Dynasty (A.D. 1368–1644). Because atlas production did not have sustained growth during this period, source materials are scarce, and it is difficult to systematically discern the process through which this particular type of cartographic work developed. Consequently, only the three important atlases that are briefly mentioned above, will be examined here. These include the earliest atlas known to have been made in China, the earliest extant atlas, and the atlas that was the most influential through the eighteenth century.

Toward the end of the Ming Dynasty, in 1582, the Jesuit priest Matteo Ricci arrived in China and established the first Roman Catholic mission. He was followed by many others. Later in the early Qing Dynasty, the Jesuit priests became quite influential in Chinese cartographic work, but their activities form a separate topic and are outside the scope of this study.

YU GONG DI YU TU (MAPS OF REGIONS IN THE "TRIBUTE TO YU")

The earliest atlas known to have been made in China was *Yu Gong Di Yu Tu* (Maps of Regions in the "Tribute to Yu"). It was compiled by Pei Xiu, who was born into a powerful family and was in government service all his adult life. While engaged in the compilation of the atlas from A.D. 268 to 271, he held the position of Minister of Works (*Si-kong*), which gave him easy access to government documents and court collections. Presumably, he was the chief editor, while most of the work of producing the atlas was performed by his assistants.[12]

The atlas was an eighteen-section historical study of the territorial changes and internal administrative boundary alterations from the earliest known records to the Jin Dynasty (A.D. 265–316). It portrayed the ancient administrative regions (*jiu zhou*, nine provinces) as well as those established during the Jin period (*shiliu zhou*, sixteen provinces), and it recorded the names and capitals of various levels of administrative units, independent and dynastic kingdoms, and allied countries.[13] It also showed mountains, water bodies, hydrological works, and transportation routes. The atlas recorded changes in the names of geographical features and noted important ancient names that were no longer in use by the time of the Jin Dynasty. Pei's intention in making such an atlas could have been to promote political awareness and the unification of China, because he lived in a time of disunity and under a newly established regime.[14]

According to the scholar Chen, the scale of the maps in the atlas was approximately 1:9,000,000. An excellent base map, called *Fang Zhang Tu* (Ten-Foot Square Map), at a scale of 1:1,800,000, was prepared especially for the compilation of this atlas.[15] The focus of the atlas strongly suggests that most maps in the volume were administrative or political in nature. It is likely, therefore, that only simple point and line symbols were used to portray the various types of boundaries, settlements, and physical features. More abstract notions, like distances, may have been noted in writing on the maps.[16] Given that the many types of information included in the atlas could hardly have all been depicted on small-scale maps, it is quite likely that textual material accompanied the maps.[17] It is not known, however, if the texts were a part of the atlas or presented in a separate volume.

In the extant preface to his atlas, Pei elaborated on how maps should be made and described the six principles of mapmaking which he had formulated. The first three relate to scale, direction, and road distance. Direction was to be obtained by using horizontal sightings similar to those employed later in plane-table surveys. The other three principles dealt with the conversion of actual ground distances, which are curved on both the horizontal and vertical planes, to straight-line distances projected onto a flat map.[18] Pei's statement on mapping principles was a brilliant synthesis of early knowledge and practice. It provided the cartographic methodology for centuries to come and constituted a significant contribution to the practice of cartography. Based on these principles, we can be confident that the compilation of Pei's atlas was carried out with rigid standards. Because China was already a large country during Pei's time, the survey work probably could not have reached the high accuracy of scale and direction which Pei had conceptualized in his methodological statement.

The compilation of the *Yu Gong Di Yu Tu* had another methodological influence in cartography. To understand it, we must consider the dynastic history of the Western Han. The publication of dynastic histories constituted a valuable literary treasure of Chinese civilization and an important source of materials for the study of cartographic history. In the first century A.D., the term *di li* (geography) was used for the first time in a chapter heading in the *Han Shu* (Book of Han History). This chapter, the "Di-li Zhi" (Treatise of Geography), used the political boundaries and administrative divisions of a given time to organize geographical space and information. The geography of these divisions was discussed, but the major focus of the chapter was the history and boundary changes of administrative divisions and settlements. Because this was the first treatise of this kind, it had the effect of setting a precedent. Thus, the particular and somewhat narrow methodological approach and scope of the chapter became firmly established as the *model*, and was followed in treatises on geography in later dynastic histories and in many other geographical writings for the next two millennia.[19] Eventually, it led to the development of an important branch of geography termed *yan-ge di li*, which may be loosely translated as "historical geography of successive territorial/boundary changes." Pei's atlas was the first significant cartographic work to use this particular approach by emphasizing the territorial changes and boundary alterations within and between dynasties; thus, he reinforced the methodology that originated in the *Han Shu*. Perhaps Pei's reputation as a scholar and the merits of the atlas caused this particular theme to be used as an example by many later cartographers in China.

LI DAI DI LI ZHI ZHANG TU (GEOGRAPHICAL MAPS OF SUCCESSIVE DYNASTIES)

The authorship and date of publication of the earliest extant Chinese atlas, *Li Dai Di Li Zhi Zhang Tu* (Geographical Maps of Successive Dynasties), are uncertain. Early scholars attributed the atlas to either Shui Anli (died between 1098 and 1101) or Su Shih (a literary giant, 1036–1101), or made no attribution. Both Shui and Su lived in the Northern Song period (A.D. 960–1127). The atlas mainly contains information on the Northern Song and earlier dynasties, except for the last map which records changes in some administrative units that occurred in A.D. 1162. It is possible, therefore, that the atlas was compiled during the Northern Song period and the last map was added at a later time.[20] The several copies of this atlas that still exist in China are publications of the Ming Dynasty. A copy of the Song edition is preserved in Japan,[21] and one copy of a Ming edition is in the Library of Congress.[22]

As the title indicates, the atlas focuses on the administrative and political changes that occurred in successive dynasties. It is made up of several volumes and consists of a total of forty-four maps: (a) Two general maps; (b) thirty-eight administrative maps of successive dynasties from the eras of two legendary kings (Ti Ku and Yu Shun) to the Xia Dynasty (twenty-first to sixteenth centuries B.C.) and to the Northern Song period (A.D. 960–1127). They include, primarily, one map for each political period, along with more maps for the three important dynasties; four each for the Han Dynasty (206 B.C.–A.D. 220) and the Tang Dynasty (A.D. 618–907) and five for the Song Dynasty (i.e., the thirty-eight maps cover a total of twenty-eight different political periods); (c) four other maps, which for convenience are called the miscellaneous group, will be explained later. In addition, there are texts accompanying each map. A little more than one-third of the pages are devoted to maps; the remainder to texts.

Map symbols used in the atlas are quite straightforward and basically are point and line symbols (see Figure 15); however, some small variations in symbol design are found among the different editions of the atlas. These probably occurred when craftsmen produced the wood blocks for printing the atlas. On the whole, the design of the symbols in this atlas is very much within the tradition of Chinese maps prior to modern times. For example, a wave-like pattern depicts the sea and an outline is used to enclose the name of a place or feature. On

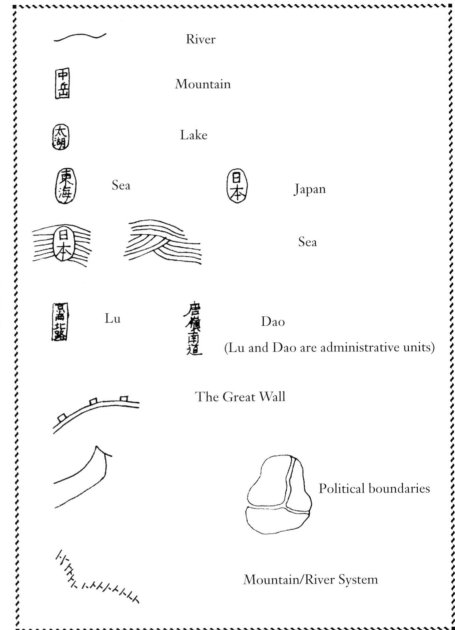

FIGURE 15 *Some symbols employed in the* Li Dai Di Li Zhi Zhang Tu *(Geographical Maps of Successive Dynasties).*

a number of maps, however, each administrative unit is surrounded by a border, thus creating the appearance of "double boundaries" on the map.[23]

The first map in the atlas is "Gu Jin Hua Yi Qu Yu Zong Yao Tu" (General Map of Territories from the Ancient to Present, of China and Foreign Countries). (See Figure 16.) Within China, the map shows the provinces (*lu*) established during the Song Dynasty and some *zhou* and *jun* (two different levels of administrative units) of the past and present. It also depicts the Great Wall, mountains, lakes, rivers, and the seas off the coast. The locations of rivers and coastlines are not very accurate. Korea (at the northeast corner of the map) and the foreign areas and countries west of China are placed fairly accurately, but other foreign territories (e.g., Japan, Vietnam, India, and other realms) are only approximately identified. It should be noted that the rivers, coastlines, and Great Wall portrayed on this map and the content of the accompanying text are similar to the portrayals and text carved on the well-known stone map, *Hua Yi Tu* (Map of China and Foreign Territories), dated A.D. 1136. (See Figure 12.) Therefore, it is highly likely that both maps were compiled from an identical source, perhaps a work of the well-known scholar Jia Dan of the Tang Dynasty.[24] The importance of this general map lies in its representation of administrative units of the Song period and earlier, but the map is inferior to the *Hua Yi Tu* in depicting other geographic features, such as coastlines, rivers, and so forth.

The second general map in the atlas is entitled the "Li Dai Yi Shan Chuan Ming Tu" (Map of Names of Mountains and Rivers of China and Foreign Coun-

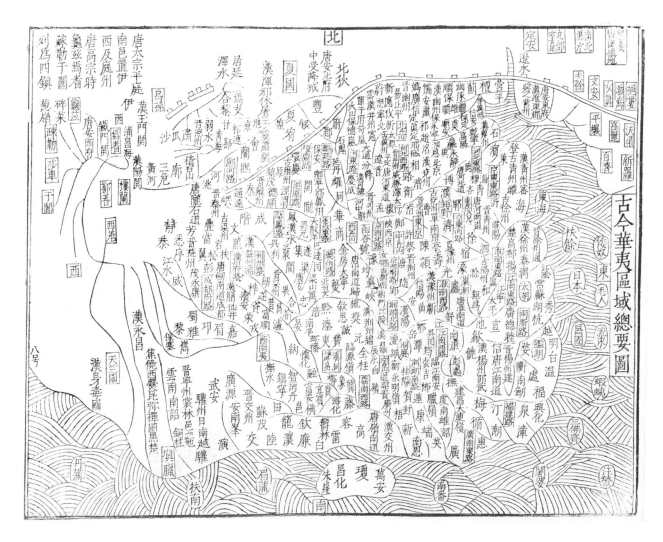

FIGURE 16 *"Gu Jin Hua Yi Qu Yu Zong Yao Tu" (General Map of Territories from the Ancient to Present, of China and Foreign Countries)* in Li Dai Di Li Zhi Zhang Tu, *vol 1. Published during the Ming Wan Li period (1573–1620). Library of Congress.*

tries through the Ages). It is more detailed than the first general map in regard to the names of mountains and rivers, but otherwise it is inferior. A unique contribution of this atlas is the inclusion of the name of a lake, Xing-shu-hai, shown in the central-western portion of the map "Tang Shi Dao Tu" (Map of Ten Provinces of the Tang Dynasty); the lake is in the source area of the Huang River. This may well be the first time that this name was printed on a map and it reflects the author's up-to-date knowledge of the source of the Huang.

One map in the miscellaneous group shows historical place names; however, the other three maps are more interesting. They reflect certain spatial concepts or points of view as well as providing information. Two of the maps depict the concept of astronomical sectionalization (*fen ye*, or *tian wen fen ye*). It is an old concept that first appeared in the literature in the Chunqiu period (770–476 B.C.) and became associated with mapping in the Tang Dynasty.[25] In brief, scholars, many of them Taoists, who held the view of *fen ye*, tried to relate political terrestrial units to celestial divisions and bodies, for example, the fixed stars. This relation was considered desirable because "the celestial bodies are suspended up in the heavens; they never change. But the names and boundaries of earthly districts and kingdoms change repeatedly."[26] To relate the two, then, was thought to provide some stability to terrestrial affairs. This effort was futile, of course.

One of the maps associated with the *fen ye* concept is the "Tian Xiang Fen Ye Tu" (Astronomical Sectionalized Map). It looks like an ordinary map in that it shows political units, lakes, rivers, and so forth, but it also includes the names of celestial divisions. Each of these names is printed within a symbol of a rectangular outline, and, in turn, each such symbol is placed below the name of the state, which is thought to be related to the particular celestial division. These states existed during the Warring States period. Another map in this subgroup is actually a diagram that is called "Er-shi-ba She Chen Ci Fen Ye Zhi Tu" (Diagram of the Twenty-Eight Constellations and Astronomical Sectionalization). In the diagram, the twelve Earthly Branches (*Di Zhi*) are shown within an inner circle, the twenty-eight constellations (*xiu*) are marked inside an outer circle, and the earthly places related to *fen ye* are named outside the outer circle.

The fourth map in the miscellaneous group is the "Tang Yi Xing Shan He Liang Jie Tu" (Map of the Two Great Mountain-River Systems Conceived by Yi Xing of the Tang Dynasty), which depicts the geopolitical strategic view of the monk, Yi Xing (A.D. 683–727). He was an astronomer, known for his pilgrimage to India, who also probably believed in the concept of *fen ye*. According to Yi Xing, there were two systems of mountains that began in western China. Initially joined at the mountain Taihua (east of today's Xian City), the systems separated, one to the northeast and the other to the southeast. These mountain systems, reinforced by the two major rivers, the Huang and Chang Jiang (Yangtze), formed two natural barriers which helped to keep out the non-Chinese (non-Han) peoples to the north and south.

This atlas includes three types of maps, and by examining their contents, it is clear that the main focus of the atlas is the territorial and boundary changes of administrative units within and between successive dynasties in China, from the earliest time to the Song Dynasty. Thus, this atlas supports the statement made earlier that many later works followed the theme and methodology initiated by Pei Xiu in his atlas. The four maps in the miscellaneous group were placed after the two general maps and the thirty-three administrative maps, which cover the periods prior to the Northern Song, and before the last five administrative maps devoted to the Song Dynasty. Why should an ordinary administrative atlas, such as this one, include a group of very different maps? And why were they placed between maps of pre- and post-Song periods? These are intriguing questions that need further investigation. The answers may provide some clues to the date and the author's intention in publishing this atlas. It is possible that the first section and the miscellaneous group were pre-Song compilations, and the remainder were post-Song. There were perhaps two different authors (or groups of authors) for the composite publication.

GUANG YU TU (ENLARGED TERRESTRIAL ATLAS)

The most substantial and influential atlas made in China up through the Ming Dynasty was the *Guang Yu Tu* (Enlarged Terrestrial Atlas) by Luo Hongxian (A.D. 1504–1564).[27] In its preface, Luo indicated that he had been searching for accurate maps and had found an excellent one, the *Yu Di Tu* (Terrestrial Map), compiled by Zhu Siben (A.D. 1273–1333). He went on to say that Zhu's map was too large (approximately 173 × 173 cm) and difficult to handle; thus, Luo divided Zhu's large map into smaller maps, by provinces, and put them into book form. Moreover, Luo greatly broadened the scope of the volume and named it the *Guang Yu Tu* (Enlarged Terrestrial Atlas), which clearly implied that the atlas was an expansion of Zhu's map.

The manuscript for Luo's atlas was probably completed around 1541 and first printed in 1555. Subsequently, five more editions were produced, the last one in 1799.[28] The original manuscript was lost in the 1550s, but Luo's preface in the printed editions describes its content very well: thirty-eight titles and forty-five sheets of maps. The titles include one general map (see Figure 17); fifteen provincial maps; ten maps of the (nine) northern border regions; five of the (four) southwestern border regions; one map of each of the following: Huang River, Grand Canal, and sea routes; and one map of each of the foreign territories: Korea, the northern deserts (i.e., Mongolia), Annam (today's Vietnam), and the western territories.

Most historians agree that the compilation of the general map and provincial maps was based on Zhu Siben's *Yu Di Tu*, which, in the main, covered the domain of China. Zhu's original map is lost, but fortunately, the preface to his

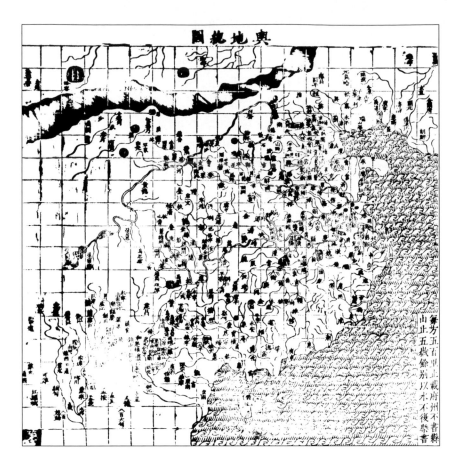

FIGURE 17 *"Yu Di Cong Tu" in* Guang Yu Tu *(Enlarged Terrestrial Atlas), 1561 edition. Beijing Library.*

map is included in Luo's atlas. Thus we know that Zhu Siben spent ten years compiling his map and that he traveled extensively to collect new data and subjected existing cartographic information to careful examination before incorporating it. Consequently, Zhu's map was highly accurate for its time. Luo Hongxian has been praised by historians for having incorporated, and thus preserved, Zhu's valuable work. We can be sure, therefore, that the first sixteen maps in the atlas are of good quality. Luo also exercised great care in compiling the remaining maps because he indicated that he had consulted fourteen major references.[29]

One example of Luo's ability to choose good sources and preserve map accuracy is his addition of two maps portraying Southeast Asia and Southwest Asia for the first printing of the manuscript in 1555. (See Figure 18.)[30] Apparently, Luo adopted these maps from Li Zemin's *Shen Jiao Guang Bei Tu* (Map for Extension of Instructions), a world map dated around 1330. Li's map is lost, but it had been incorporated into a Korean map, copies of which are kept in Japan and China.[31] When the two atlas maps are placed side by side, one finds an image that probably is a fair replica of the Asia portion of Li's original map. Li's map covered a vast area including all of Asia as well as Europe and Africa; it extended from Japan to the Azores and from central Russia to southern Africa. Luo also included south-

FIGURE 18 *"Xi Nan Hai Yi Tu" (The Map of Southwest-Sea Foreign Areas) in* Guang Yu Tu *(Enlarged Terrestrial Atlas), 1561 edition. Beijing Library.*

ern Africa (at the northwest corner of Figure 18), an addition praised by Walter Fuchs, who has observed that around A.D. 1300, Chinese mapmakers had already recognized the triangular shape of Africa with its tip pointing southward, whereas European-Arabic maps of this period depicted the tip of Africa as pointing eastward.[32] Fuchs indicated that because Luo used the early Chinese maps for reference, he was able to show the correct shape and orientation of Africa.

In addition to the two new maps of Southeast Asia and Southwest Asia that were included in the first printed edition of the atlas in 1555, the one-sheet map of the northern deserts was expanded into two. In the third edition, published in 1561, three more maps, one of Japan, another of Liuqiu (Okinawa), and one "Hua Yi Cong Tu" (General Map of China and Foreign Countries) were added by the author/publisher, Hu Song.[33] By then the atlas included forty-three different titles and fifty-one sheets of maps. No expansion in the number of maps was subsequently made. In addition to the maps, there were accompanying texts; thus, the 1541 manuscript had a total of 114 pages of maps and text. The number was increased to 117 in the first few editions of the atlas.

Much information is given in the text. For example, following each provincial map, there is a complete tabulation of all levels of administrative units within the jurisdiction of the province, statistics and discussions on population and households, government officials and military personnel, taxation, selected goods shipments, and so on. In short, the scope of the atlas is broad. It summarizes China's geographical knowledge of the mid-sixteenth century and reflects the country's geopolitical concerns at the time. It covers China's own territories, its inland and coastal waterways, border regions to the north and southwest, and adjacent foreign areas.

The significance of the *Guang Yu Tu* (Enlarged Terrestrial Atlas), of course, goes beyond its spatial and topical coverage. Two other elements of this work—its scale and symbolism—must also be evaluated. We read in Luo's preface that he valued highly the square grid system used on Zhu Siben's *Yu Di Tu*. (See Figure 17.) This system, called "*ji li hua fang*" (literally, a square grid drawn to the scale for distance measurement), provides a reference for scale and distance calculations. By employing this system, Luo commented, "the actual [geographical] shape can be referenced." Furthermore, "if one divides the map into east and west portions and later puts them back together, they will not be placed wrongly."[34] Thus, Luo was able to divide Zhu's large map into smaller provincial maps for inclusion in an atlas.

Several past scholars have credited Pei Xiu with being the originator of the square grid system on the basis that the essential idea for deriving such a system was embedded in Pei's first two principles of mapmaking that are concerned with scale and direction.[35] It was said that Pei had used the grid system in his atlas, *Yu Gong Di Yu Tu*. However, Pei Xiu himself never made any direct reference to such a system, nor did he link it to the six mapping principles. Today, therefore, many scholars do not think that Pei actually used the grid in his atlas.

On each map in the *Guang Yu Tu* (Enlarged Terrestrial Atlas), a statement indicates the number of *li* (the Chinese mile) represented by one grid length; the number varies from 40 to 500 *li*. On most maps, however, one grid length represents 100 *li*, which converts to a scale of approximately 1:3,200,000.[36] The smallest scale is 1:15,500,000, at 500 *li* per grid length. When comparing some of Luo's maps with today's provincial maps, one finds that the former look impressively accurate.

Accuracy of scale and map content are maintained much better in maps of central China than in those of border regions and foreign areas. It is also evident that in earlier editions the square grids were carefully reproduced. In later editions, however, care was not taken and the grid system was severely distorted. Consequently, the scale and hence the accuracy of the map were also distorted. (See Figure 19.) Fuchs pointed out that later publishers tried to fill up the page by stretching the squares of the grid into rectangles.[37] Nevertheless, sometimes improvements and corrections were made in later editions. For instance, on the first map of the *Ji Zhou Bian Tu Yi* (Ji Zhou Border Region), a tributary of a river in the central portion of the map was shortened considerably from its incorrect representation in an earlier edition.

Another important feature of the enlarged atlas is the symbol design and use. In the preface, Luo stated, "because of the complexity and crisscross of rivers,

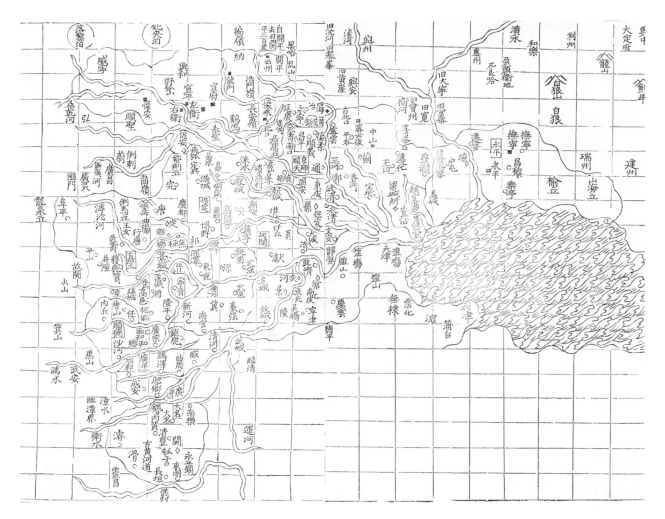

FIGURE 19   *Map of the Northern Zhi Li Province in* Guang Yu Tu *(Enlarged Terrestrial Atlas), published during Ming Wan Li period (1573–1620). Library of Congress.*

mountains, cities, and their names it was difficult to describe them all; thus twenty-four [signs] were used in order to save words and to make it clear. . . ." He then went on to list twenty-four point and line symbols used in the atlas. This list constitutes an early example of a map legend in China and other countries. (See Figure 20.) Actually, the list is incomplete, for many other symbols are found in the atlas; for example, the symbols used for the Great Wall, deserts, lakes, and so on. (See Figure 21.) Since there are more maps in the atlas portraying the border and foreign areas and coastal and inland waterways than those showing the provinces of China, it is not surprising that a large number of signs are used to depict guard stations, defense sites, and related military features. The early editions of the atlas show much better execution of the symbol designs than do the later ones.

Previously, Chinese historians considered the symbolism of this atlas to be advanced for its time and, as such, to be a significant achievement. Now that

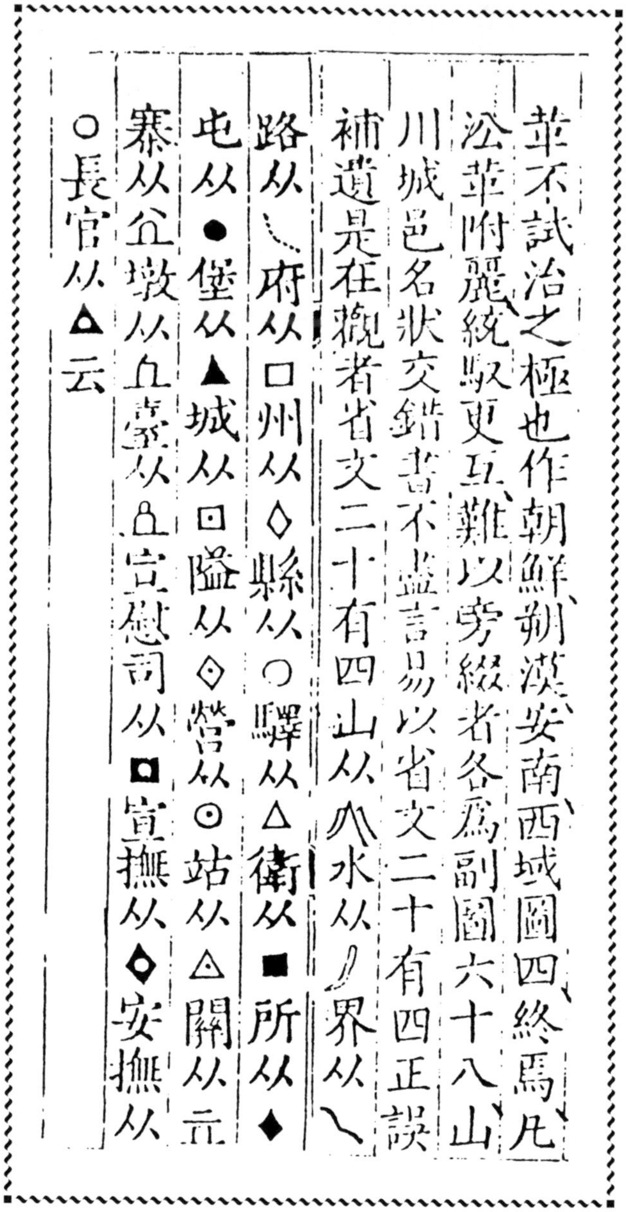
華不試治之極也作朝鮮、朔漠、安南、西域圖四、終焉凡
沿華附麗統馭更互、難以旁綴者各為副圖六十八山
川城邑名狀交錯書不盡言易以省文二十有四正誤
補遺是在觀者省文二十有四山从∧水从/界从㇏
路从、府从口州从◇縣从○驛从△衛从■所从◆
屯从●堡从▲城从回隘从◇營从⊙站从△關从亓
寨从亓墩从亼臺从亼宣慰司从◘宣撫从◆安撫从
○長官从△云

FIGURE 20 *Legend included in the preface of the* Guang Yu Tu *(Enlarged Terrestrial Atlas).*

much new information has been acquired from archaeological finds and the rediscovery of some earlier maps which had been misplaced or miscataloged in museums, we know that China has had a long tradition of symbolizing map features.[38] Today, the general view is that Luo Hongxian probably adopted some of the symbols from Zhu Siben's excellent map and that the design of this atlas reflects the cartographic practice in China at that time.

CONCLUSION

Three Chinese atlases that were compiled before the seventeenth century are discussed in this paper. Of them, the *Guang Yu Tu* (Enlarged Terrestrial Atlas) is the

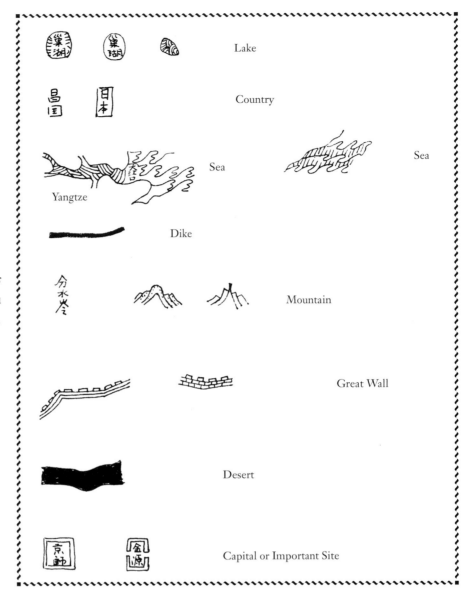

FIGURE 21 *Some symbols employed in the* Guang Yu Tu *(Enlarged Terrestrial Atlas).*

most important. It is in book form and summarizes the geographical information known in China up to the time of its publication. In the two and one-half centuries from the 1550s to the end of the eighteenth century, this atlas, including both maps and texts, was the major source of reference for a large number of cartographic works produced in China.[39]

Although there is no explicit citation to link this work to Matteo Ricci's mapping activities, there is ample evidence to indicate that Ricci and other priests used Luo Hongxian's atlas in their efforts to map China and Asia. For example, two desert areas in northern and western China are shown on Ricci's world map *Kun Yu Wan Guo Quan Tu*, dated 1602; one is labeled "desert" and another, the "great shifting sand." Both the locations and the terms on Ricci's map are identical to those in Luo's atlas.[40] On the other hand, no desert is shown in Africa on Ricci's map. Furthermore, no desert is shown in Mercator's world map of 1569. Thus, we may conclude that deserts had not been explicitly represented on European maps up to this time.[41] Lastly, we know definitely that Luo's atlas provided the foundation for the 1655 atlas of China (*Novus Atlas Sinensis*) produced by Martin Martini.[42] Thus the *Guang Yu Tu* (Enlarged Terrestrial Atlas) marks the climax of Chinese atlas making through the Ming Dynasty.

NOTES

1 *Shu Jing* is one of the five classics of ancient China. It is also known as the *Classic of Documents*, dated second century B.C.

2 In the chapter, the author provided an insightful discussion on the usefulness of a terrain map to military affairs.

3 Yong Wang, *Zhong Guo Di Tu Shi Gang* (Beijing: Shan-Lian Book Company, 1958), chapter 1. Joseph Needham and Ling Wang (collaborator), *Science and Civilization in China* (Cambridge: Cambridge University Press, 1959), 3:533–543.

4 The four maps were discovered in ancient tombs and are dated according to the time of tomb construction; these maps, of course, were made earlier. Mei-Ling Hsu, "A Chinese Planning Map of the Fourth Century B.C.," paper presented at the Tenth International Conference on the History of Cartography, August 1983, Dublin. Hongxun Yang, "A Study of the King's Mausoleum and Zhao Yu Tu of the Zhongshan Kingdom in the Warring States Period," *Kaogu Xuebao*, 1980, no. 1:119–138.

5 Qixiang Tan, "A Map of More Than Two Thousand and One Hundred Years Ago," *Wen Wu*, 1975, no. 2:43–48.

6 Mei-Ling Hsu, "The Han Maps and Early Chinese Cartography," *Annals of the Association of American Geographers* 68 (1978): 45–60.

7 Mei-Ling Hsu, "The Qin Maps: A Clue to Later Chinese Cartographic Development," *Imago Mundi* 45 (1993): 90–100.

8 Wang, *Zhong Guo Di Tu Shi Gang*, chapter 3.

9 Liankai Chen, "The First Historical Atlas of Ancient China: A Preliminary Study of Pei Xiu's *Yu Gong Di Yu Tu*," *Min Zu Xuebao*, 1978, no. 3:76–84.

10 Wanru Cao, "The Earliest Extant Historical Atlas—*Li Dai Di Li Zhi Zhang Tu*," *Ke Xue Shi Ji Kan*, 1982, no. 10:65–73.

11 Needham, pp. 551–556.

12 Chen, "The First Historical . . ."

13 Ibid.

14 Ibid.

15 We assume that the atlas contains more than one map. The map scale is derived by Chen, "The First Historical . . . ," p. 82.

16 Yong Wang, "From Pei Xiu's Map Making to A Discussion of the Origin of Chinese Maps," *Di Li Zhi Shih* 5, no. 7 (1954): 193–195.

17 Chen, "The First Historical . . ."; and Liankai Chen, "Characteristics and Contributions of *Yu Gong Di Yu Tu* and *Chunjiu Meng Huei Tu*" *Wen Shi* 16 (1982): 35–43.

18 Hsu, "The Han Maps . . ."

19 Ibid.

20 Cao, "The Earliest Extant . . . ," pp. 66–67.

21 A copy of the atlas dated 1140 (in Southern Song period) is kept in the Toyo Bunko Library in Japan. See Kazutaka Unno, "The Geographical Thought of the Chinese People: With Special Reference to Ideas of Terrestrial Features," *Memoirs of the Research Department of the Toyo Bunko* 41 (1983): 83–97.

22 The atlas housed in the Library of Congress is a copy of the fifth edition (1579). One map, "Tang Jun Ming Tu," is missing, so the atlas has only forty-three maps.

23 In the copy kept in the library of the Chinese Academy of Sciences in Beijing, there are ten maps using this kind of boundary symbol.

24 Cao, "The Earliest Extant . . . ," p. 67.

25 Needham, p. 545.

26 The quotation is from *Jiu Tang Shu* (Old History of the Tang Dynasty), vol. 36, Astronomy Section.

27 Hongxian Luo, *Guang Yu Tu* (1562). See also Cordell D. K. Yee, "Reinterpreting Traditional Chinese Geographical Maps," chapter 3, pp. 35–70, in *Cartography in Traditional East and Southeast Asian Societies*, vol. 2, book 2 of *The History of Cartography*, eds. J. B. Harley and David Woodward (Chicago: University of Chicago Press, 1994).

28 Gao Jun, "Compilation and Production of National and Provincial Atlases in the Ming and Qing Dynasties," *Ce Hui Xue Bao* 4 (1962): 289–306.

29 Kazutaka Unno, "The Original Sources of the Kuang-Yu-tu," *The Studies in the Humanities and Social Sciences* 15 (Osaka University, 1967): 19–46.

30 We assume that these two maps were added by Luo before the first printing. See also Unno, "The Original Sources . . ."

31 Kazutaka Unno, "On the Anonymous Map of China Owned by the Tenri Central Library," *Osaka Gakugei Daigaku Kiyo* 6 (1958): 60–67.

32 Walter Fuchs, "The Mongol Atlas of China by Chu Ssu-pen and the Kuang-Yu Tu, with forty-eight facsimile maps dating from about 1555," *Monumenta Serica*, Monograph VIII (Beijing: Fu Jen University, 1946).

33 Gao, "Compilation and Production . . ."

34 Quotation taken from Luo's preface in the atlas.

35 Hsu, "The Han Maps . . ."

36 Gao, "Compilation and Production . . . ," p. 295.

37 Fuchs, "The Mongol Atlas . . . ," p. 21.

38 An example of the rediscovered maps is discussed in: Xihuang Zheng, "My Humble Opinion on the Map Postscripted by Yang Ziqi," *Studies in the History of Natural Sciences* 3, no. 1 (1984): 52–58. Yang's map is dated 1526.

39 Kazutaka Unno, "Kuang-yu-tu-type Maps Illustrating Books Published in Ming and Ching Dynasties," *The Studies in the Humanities and Social Sciences* 23 (Osaka University, 1975): 10–34; and "The Kuang-yu-tu in Europe—Early Chinese Influence upon the Western Cartography," *The Studies in the Humanities and Social Sciences* 26, part 1 (1978): 2–28; and 27, part 2 (1979): 40–86. Wang, *Zhong Guo Di Tu Shi Gang*, pp. 63–72.

40 Wanru Cao and others, "World Maps by Matteo Ricci Extant in China," *Wen Wu,* 1982, no. 12:57–70.

41 G. R. Crone, *Maps and Their Makers* (5th ed., Folkestone, England: William Dawson, 1973), p. 77.

42 Fuchs, "The Mongol Atlas . . . ," p. 11; Unno, "The Kuang-yu-tu in . . ."

Italian Composite Atlases of the Sixteenth Century

DAVID WOODWARD

INTRODUCTION

From the decade of the 1560s until the end of the sixteenth century, largely in the centers of Venice and Rome, Italian publishers issued atlases consisting of separately published maps and views assembled to the order of individual clients. The significance of these sixteenth-century Italian atlases to the wider history of cartography can be discussed around three main themes. They represent an example of the Renaissance independence of cartographers from classical authority and engravers from noble patronage. Second, they illustrate the important but not yet fully explored relationship between the map trade and the print trade of sixteenth-century Italy. Finally, the atlases demonstrate the role as a preserving agent, not only for the collector in the sixteenth century, but also as the primary means by which the map prints of Renaissance Italy have come down to us. The scientific, artistic, economic, and cultural achievements of the Italian Renaissance are clearly evident in its maps and atlases. While the Italian contribution to atlas making stopped short of a critical anthology of maps in the Ortelian sense, there were more maps printed in Italy between 1550 and 1570 than in any other country in Europe.

The importance of the Italian map trade in this period has frequently been expressed. Bagrow stated that "it was in Italy, and particularly in Venice, that the map trade, which was to influence profoundly the course of cartographic history, was most highly developed during the first half of the sixteenth century."[1]

The common designation "Lafreri Atlas" to include any Italian composite atlas or atlas factice of the sixteenth century is highly misleading. Of the surviving Italian sixteenth-century composite atlases, only about a quarter bear the well-known title page issued by Antonio Lafreri.[2] Antonio Lafreri (Antoine Lafréry) came to Rome from France in 1544 as a publisher and engraver. He worked for over thirty years in his shop in the via del Parione, some of them in partnership with Antonio Salamanca, and is perhaps best known for his *Speculum*

Romanae Magnificentiae, a massive collection of prints relating to the antiquities and topography of ancient and Renaissance Rome. However, most collections of maps were published in Venice, and Lafreri had no direct hand in the issuance of these. It is, therefore, suggested (without much hope of success) that the term "Lafreri atlas" no longer be used in a generic sense, but that the term "Venetian composite atlas" be adopted for Lafreri's Venetian counterpart.[3]

Of the two prominent map publishing centers of the time (see Figure 22), the activity in maps destined for the composite atlases peaked earlier and lingered longer in Rome where Lafreri was active. However, map engraving and printing was far more intense in Venice. At the height of the Venetian trade during the 1560s, map publishers might have viewed themselves as being on top of the world, as Venice's symbol, the Lion of St. Mark, suggests. (See Figure 23.) There were probably 500 to 600 copperplates for maps in active use in Venice, and perhaps half that number in Rome. The peak in Venice for map publishing occurred around 1566, followed by a dramatic decline after 1570. It had dwindled to

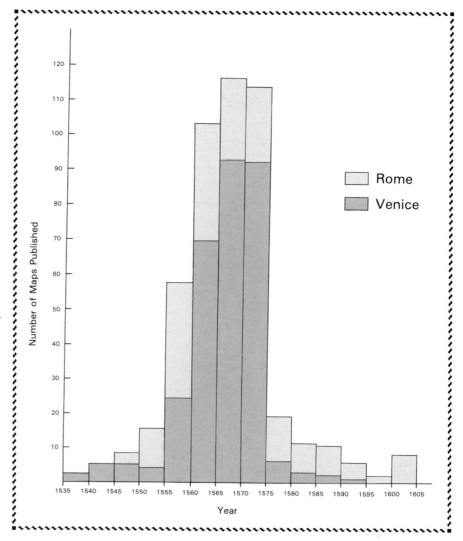

FIGURE 22 *Number of maps bearing Roman and Venetian imprints by five-year categories from 1535 to 1605. Based on the list by R. V. Tooley, "Maps in Italian Atlases of the Sixteenth Century," Imago Mundi 3 (1939): 12–47. University of Wisconsin Cartographic Laboratory.*

FIGURE 23 *Cartouche from* Nova descrittione del Friuli *(Venice: Donato Bertelli). Biblioteca Nazionale Braidense, Milan.*

almost nothing after the plague of 1575 to 1577, in which more than 46,000 people died, and thereafter the Venetian engravers and cartographers could hardly compete with the atlases of Ortelius, De Jode, and Mercator of the late sixteenth century. During this period, however, the life of the Roman trade was extended and even slightly revived by the reissues from the Lafreri plates by Claudio Duchetti, Giovanni Orlandi, and Petrus de' Nobilibus.

INDEPENDENCE

The overtness with which Italian cartography expressed its independence during the late Renaissance is particularly striking. It was revealed in several ways. By the time of the appearance of the Italian composite atlases in the 1560s, the authority of the traditions of Claudius Ptolemy was decidedly ambiguous. Editions of the *Geographia* were still being published in which both Ptolemaic and modern maps existed in the same volume. In the second century A.D., Ptolemy had set out clear instructions for the order of maps in an atlas; this was acknowledged by Antonio Lafreri in the title page to collections of maps emanating from Rome in the early 1570s. (See Figure 24.) It reads: "Geography. Modern maps of most of the world by various authors collected and put in Ptolemy's order with views of many cities and forts from various regions. Published from copperplates with care and diligence in Rome." Beyond this nominal acknowledgment of classical

FIGURE 24 *Title page accompanying some of the composite atlases of Antonio Lafreri in Rome. Library of Congress.*

GEOGRAFIA

TAVOLE MODERNE DI GEOGRAFIA
DE LA MAGGIOR PARTE DEL MONDO
DI DIVERSI AVTORI
RACCOLTE ET MESSE SECONDO L'ORDINE
DI TOLOMEO
CON IDISEGNI DI MOLTE CITTA ET
FORTEZZE DI DIVERSE PROVINTIE
STAMPATE IN RAME CON STVDIO
ET DILIGENZA
IN ROMA

learning, there are only passing allusions in the maps to Ptolemaic content or structure.

There was also a growing independence from the direct financing of publishing from noble patrons. Since the days of the successful map and print shop of Francesco Rosselli in late fifteenth- and early sixteenth-century Florence, the feasibility of making a living by selling maps and prints had been demonstrated.[4] This had perhaps allowed the cartographer and engraver to engage in a broader range of activities than the constraints of a patron would have allowed, but the need to please the market provided its own limitations. This had several implications. The marketing strategy was now clearly to provide the reader with *new* and purportedly *accurate* maps. Thus, the use of the word "modern" in Lafreri's title page, and the frequent use of adjectives such as "new," "recent," "true," "exact," "copious," and "latest" in many of the maps is no accident.[5]

Another clue to the market forces behind the sixteenth-century Italian atlases is the common use of vernacular Italian rather than Latin in the map titles and legends. The use of the vernacular could serve both to limit and enlarge a market for books and maps in the sixteenth century. On the one hand, it made works available to the merchant classes and thus may have increased demand for them. On the other hand, Latin was still the most commonly read language of Europe among the scholarly classes, and the use of a little-known vernacular language would clearly limit the market (this was certainly true of the use of Dutch in the sixteenth century).[6] The maps in the *Cosmographia* of Sebastian Münster, of course, made the best of both worlds by being published not only in Latin but in several vernacular editions. For the Italian composite atlases, however, Italian was the rule, and while there are individual exceptions to it, only two categories of maps form general exceptions: world maps and maps of islands. The former were probably in Latin in order to capitalize on a market wider than the domestic. The routine use of Latin for maps of islands is perhaps in deference to the concept of papal sovereignty over islands.

The demands of the printed-map market also seem to have influenced the choice of subject matter in the maps of the Italian atlases. Figure 25 summarizes the approximate percentages of coverage in various map categories: world, continental, large subcontinental regions (including countries), small subnational regions, town views, battle views, and miscellaneous prints. On account of their scale, we would expect there to be more regional maps than continental or world maps. Atlases commonly included only one world map (sometimes two) and general maps of Europe, Asia, Africa, and sometimes the Americas. The proportions are similar for both the Roman and the Venetian trades (with some three-quarters of the output for regional and town maps). The Venetian atlases tend to have more world and continental maps than the Roman, and the latter had significantly more town views to make up for it. This points to a difference in the two markets that has been explained by the more cosmopolitan taste of the clients of the Venetian trade, but clearly more documentation of this supposition would be desirable.[7]

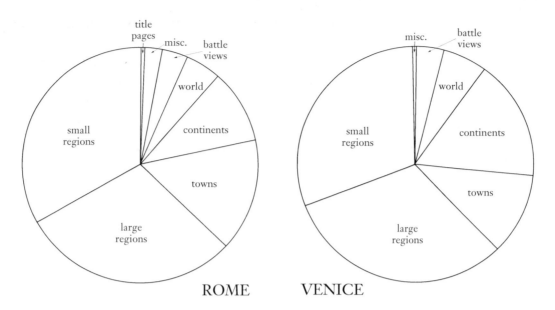

ROME   VENICE

FIGURE 25   *The average proportion of maps in various scale and subject categories in atlases of Roman and Venetian origin. Compiled by the author from data in R. V. Tooley, "Maps in Italian Atlases of the Sixteenth Century," Imago Mundi 3 (1939): 12–47, supplemented with data from atlases not listed by Tooley. University of Wisconsin Cartographic Laboratory.*

LINKS WITH THE BOOK AND PRINT TRADE

It is impossible to understand the nature of the Italian atlas trade in the sixteenth century without realizing that it was part of the larger engraving, printing, and publishing trades.[8] The major figures in the Venetian map trade, for example, Matteo Pagano, Giovanni Andrea Vavassore, Michele Tramezzini, Bolognino Zaltieri, Giovanni Francesco Camocio, Ferrando Bertelli, Domenico Zenoi, and Paolo Forlani, were all associated closely with the book trade. Donato Bertelli was listed as one of the founding members of the guild of booksellers, printers, and binders in 1578.[9] Of the fourteen pages of Lafreri's list of prints of antiquities, myths and legends, religious images, and portraits available at his shop in Rome in 1572, only three are devoted to maps.[10] It is thus difficult to escape the conclusion that these printed maps and the atlases they composed were primarily intended for the informed collector. Cartographic and topographical prints were already being collected for their own sake in the sixteenth century. Their manuscript counterparts—for example, the manuscript atlases of Battista Agnese or Francesco Ghisolfo—were finely executed and (no doubt) expensive commissions. Can we surmise that the small printed collections of town and fortress views by Forlani (1567) and Ballino (1568), based on an early model from Lyons by Guillaume Gueroult (1552), were the poor collector's equivalent of the manuscript atlases?[11] The manuscript and printed genres of the atlas appear to have been separate and parallel developments appealing to clients of different social classes.

In view of the strong links between the sixteenth-century Italian atlas trade and Italian engraving in general, it is unfortunate that research has progressed in two separate camps: the cartographic and the art historical. For example, the detailed description of the "Lafreri" collections in the Biblioteca nazionale, Florence, by Fabia Borroni Salvadori is the fullest account of the literature of the Roman and Venetian engraving trades yet published and forms an excellent basis for a more analytical study of the comparison of the printed map and atlas trade of the two centers.[12] Similar detailed work has been done relating to Lafreri's *Speculum Romanae Magnificentiae*.[13]

The cross-relationships of the prints and maps that came from Lafreri's shop still have to be systematically analyzed using physical evidence such as the examination of offsets is able to provide. To understand the significance of this evidence, it is necessary to explain a step in the printing process. After printing, if maps were stacked in a pile before the ink was dry, an impression of the lower map might be set off on the verso of the map above. This accidental image is called an offset. The occurrence of offsets is strong evidence that two copperplates were in the same place at the same time.[14] In the example shown in Figure 26, the offset is from the engraving by Cornelis Cort of *St. Francis Receiving the Stigmata*, in its second state.[15]

FIGURE 26 *Offset of Cornelis Cort's print* The Stigmatization of St. Francis, *1568; state 2 with imprint of Antonio Lafreri, two cocks bottom left, and "Heironymo Muciano Brixiano Invent." The offset appears on the back of a map entitled Marca di Ancona 1564 (Tooley 102). The Newberry Library, Chicago, Novacco Collection Map 2F165.*

The physical evidence afforded by these maps and prints is made all the more important by the fact that other forms of evidence—such as primary manuscript evidence—are in extremely short supply. Scholars in cartography and print history have sought in vain for inventories, cost books, and correspondence relating to the map-engraving trade of sixteenth-century Italy. The most promising source so far has been in the applications for privileges of copyright, and these have not only yielded information about the precise dating of maps (for example, the privilege for Antonio Floriano's world map is dated January 18, 1555 (mv) = A.D. 1556.[16] (See Figure 27.) They have also provided us with samples of the handwriting of cartographers, for example, Giacomo Gastaldi, as shown in Figure 28. Since the records of such depositories as the State Archives of Venice are, by their very nature, official, detailed clues to the activities of a modest class of individuals such as engravers or print sellers are elusive. For the most part, map and atlas engraving seems to have been an innocuous activity as far as the church or state was concerned.[17] One of the few encounters of the sixteenth-century Venetian engravers with the Inquisition was with the *Esecutori contro la Bestemmia* (Executors against Blasphemy) in connection with other activities. The *esecutori* fined Giovanni Francesco Camocio, an active map engraver and seller, for having stocked "highly indecent sonnets" printed by Domenico Zenoi, another map engraver and publisher, and for having "inserted among them several highly indecent drawings."[18]

The close association of the Italian atlases with the print-engraving trade also resulted in a generally high quality of artistic skill and taste which is reflected in clear layout, fine copperplate engraving, exemplary calligraphy, crisp impressions on fine paper, and a general restraint of color. A typical example of this is in the

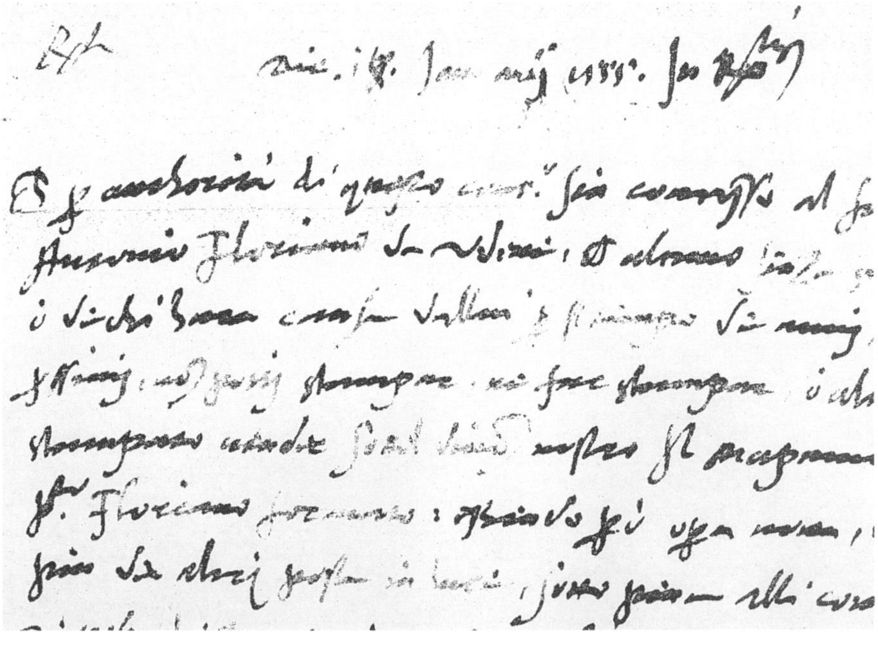

FIGURE 27 *Application by Antonio Floriano for a twenty-year privilege to print a world map. It was granted by the Senato Terra on January 18, 1555, (modo veneziano) = January 15, 1556. Archivio di Stato di Venezia, Senato Terra, Filza 22. Supplica e privilegio.*

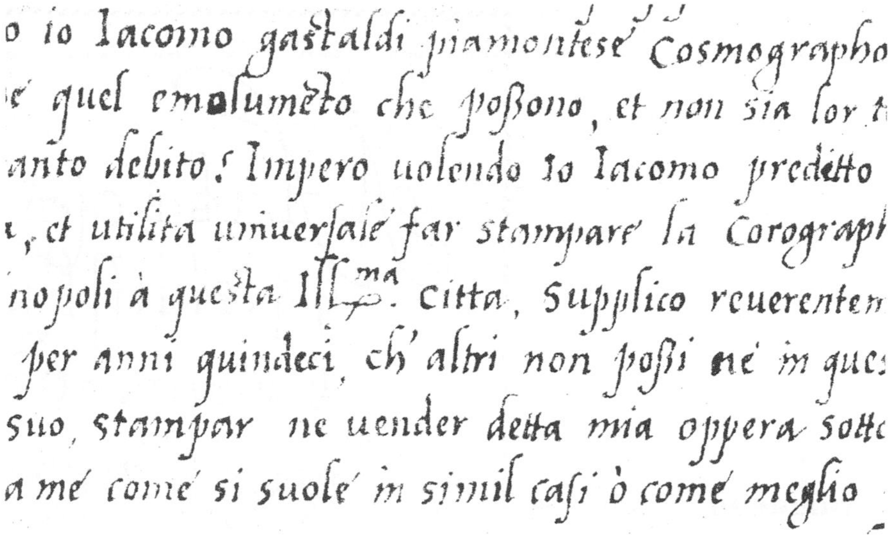

o io Iacomo gastaldi piamontese Cosmographo
e quel emolumeto che poßono, et non sia lor t
anto debito: Impero uolendo Io Iacomo predetto
i, et utilita uniuerfale far stampare la Corograph
nopoli à questa Ill.ma citta, Supplico reuerenten
per anni quindeci, ch'altri non poßi ne in ques
suo, stampar ne uender detta mia oppera sotto
a me come si suole in simil casi ò come meglio

FIGURE 28 *A specimen of the handwriting of Giacomo Gastaldi in an application for a fifteen-year privilege to print a map of Natolia and of the route between Constantinople and Venice. Archivio di Stato di Venezia, Senato Terra, Filza 29. Supplica 29 April 1559.*

Italian engraving of Mercator's world map of 1538 (see Figure 29) inserted in many atlases of the period. As an example, a closer description of the calligraphy on this and other Italian maps may illustrate the links between the calligraphic and cartographic trades of sixteenth-century Italy.[19] The main adopted lettering style was the chancery cursive, a compact, semiformal hand adopted in the Vatican Chancery, whence it derives its name. It formed the basis for the first italic type cut in 1500 for Aldus Manutius and the printed copybooks of Ludovico degli Arrighi Vicentino (c. 1522) and Giovanniantonio Tagliente (1524). (See Figure 30.) The style became popular throughout Europe in the sixteenth century, and the sixteenth-century map engravers excelled in it. Following the printed copybooks of Arrighi and Tagliente, the form became popular in engraved work.

FIGURE 29 *Detail of calligraphy from Antonio Lafreri's state of the reengraving of Gerardus Mercator's double cordiform world map by Antonio Salamanca (Rome, ca. 1560?). Library of Congress.*

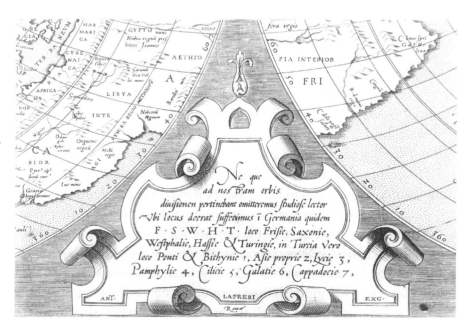

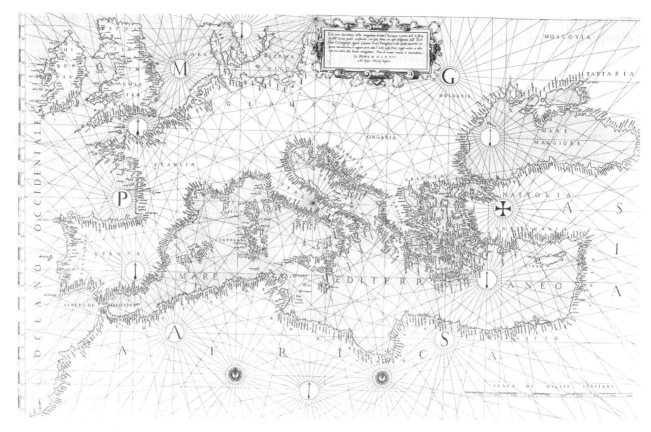

FIGURE 32   *Antonio Lafreri's state (1572) of the portolan chart of the Mediterranean Sea engraved after Diogo Homem by Paolo Forlani (1569). Library of Congress.*

monly worked for Duchetti. One of them, of Ancona, carries the date 1585, the date of Duchetti's death. At this time, a portion of the stock of plates certainly went to Giovanni Orlandi, who had a print shop in the Pasquino, usually adding the imprint "Ioannes Orlandi formis romae 1602." This imprint is also found on plates originating from Vincenzo Luchini and other Roman publishers. Another portion of the Lafreri-Duchetti plates, on the other hand, went to Petrus de' Nobilibus, including the rare second state of the Lafreri title page, which bears his imprint.[25]

Another example of the interrelationship between the Roman and Venetian centers of map publishing in sixteenth-century Italy is afforded by the publishing firm of Tramezzino.[26] Toward the middle of the century, Michele Tramezzino, a Venetian publisher and printer, with his brother Francesco, began to publish maps in Rome that were later to be incorporated into the composite atlases. While not of the stature of Antonio Salamanca or Antonio Lafreri, who were the most conspicuous of Rome's *librai*, Tramezzino was the first to introduce the large maps of Cornelisz. Anthonisz. and Jacob van Deventer, publishing them in more manageable dimensions than the originals published in the Low Countries. (See Figure 33.) Tramezzino's maps were published between 1552 and 1563 in Rome and offered for sale both in his shop in the via del Pellegrino as well as in the one he possessed in Venice at the sign of the Sibyl. His shop in Rome, along with that of Salamanca in the Parione, was, according to an eyewitness of the early 1550s, a haunt of archeologists and antiquarians interested in ancient Rome.[27]

Four *librai* in Venice were particularly active in the 1560s and early 1570s: Domenico Zenoi, Giovanni Francesco Camocio, Paolo Forlani, and Ferrando Bertelli. All either engraved or published maps that were included in the Venetian composite atlases that seem to have been assembled from 1565 onward. While these atlases do not have title pages or other marks of authorship, tenta-

FIGURE 33 *Michele Tramezzino's version of the map of Gelderland by Jacob van Deventer (Rome, 1566). Library of Congress.*

tive attribution has been attempted on the basis of the maps included, the name of Ferrando Bertelli being associated most frequently, as in the Quaritch atlas. The earliest collection may be the atlas preserved in the Biblioteca Marciana, which has no map dated after 1565. The atlases in the Biblioteca Marucelliana, the Biblioteca Casanatense, and the Newberry Library have no maps dated after 1567, and the Doria atlas has no maps dated after 1570. The dating of these atlases is also aided by the identification of the watermarks of the marginal strips pasted to the edges of the maps to bring them up to a standard size for binding.[28]

THE ROLE AS A PRESERVING AGENT

One of the purposes of the Italian atlases of the 1560s was apparently to preserve the geographical content and events of the age. In this, their purpose was quite different from that of the *Speculum Romanae Magnificentiae*, which depicted the classical antiquities of the city of Rome. The large composite atlases of the Roman and Venetian map sellers, while miscellaneous in authorship and format, were a kind of contemporary cartographic anthology—a garland of choice pieces, tastefully arranged—which is perhaps analogous to other kinds of printed anthologies which were developing in the sixteenth century. Richard Tottel's *Songes and Sonnetes,* for example, thought by some to be among the first anthologies of English literary criticism, made their appearance in 1557. The idea of a critical anthology of maps, of course, would shortly take form in Abraham Ortelius's *Theatrum Orbis Terrarum,* but the beginnings may be seen not only in the modest town atlas of Guerroult, already mentioned, but in its successors of Forlani, Ballino, and Bertelli in the 1560s.

The Italian composite atlases have also preserved maps in quite another way. Almost the entire corpus of sixteenth-century Italian cartography that now survives—perhaps ninety-five percent—has at some time been in bound form. Many collections were dispersed before Tooley's 1939 checklist. Some were destroyed or lost during the Second World War.[29] Since that time, as the market value of the maps has increased dramatically, more of the atlases have been broken up, destroying valuable bibliographical evidence.[30] It would be a worthwhile task to reconstruct the volumes of which the parts are thought to exist from physical evidence. A critical catalog of sixteenth-century Italian printed maps is still lacking.[31] Compared to the study of the atlases of other countries in Europe of the sixteenth century, the Italian composite atlas has only begun to attract attention, and it is important that the efforts of historians of cartography and historians of printmaking be combined to achieve it. The attraction of this map genre—in both a historical and in an aesthetic sense—is as great to the modern viewer as it was to the most famous of Italian cartographers, Giacomo Gastaldi, who, on his first printed map (that of Spain published in 1544), exhorted his readers to "look at it, read it, and live happy!" (See Figure 34.)

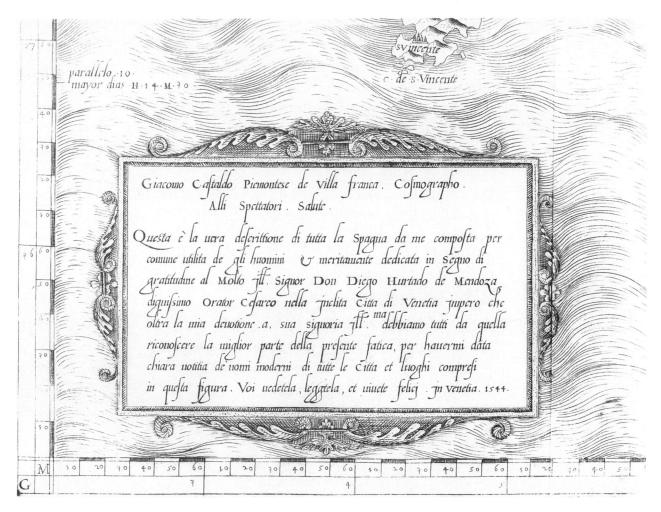

FIGURE 34 *Detail of legend from Giacomo Gastaldi's* La Spaña *(Venice, 1544). Library of Congress.*

NOTES

1 Leo Bagrow, *History of Cartography*, revised and enlarged by R. A. Skelton (London: C. A. Watts, 1964), p. 133.

2 These atlases include those in the Birmingham Public Library; the atlas known as the Beans-Henry Stevens atlas; the Library of Congress; Biblioteca nacional, Madrid; both the Wyld and Peckover copies at the Royal Geographical Society, London; Biblioteca nazionale centrale, Rome; the Bertarelli Collection, Biblioteca Trivulziana, Milan; Biblioteca nazionale, Florence; and a separate sheet in The Newberry Library originally from an atlas in the Ayer Collection (Ayer *135 L5 1575).

3 George H. Beans suggested the term "IATO atlas," meaning "Italian Assembled to Order," but this assumes only one scenario of how the atlases were produced. It is possible that some atlases were also printed to order. For an early use of the term, see George H. Beans, "Some Sixteenth-Century Watermarks Found in Maps Prevalent

in the 'IATO' Atlases," *George H. Beans Library Publications*, no. 13 (Jenkintown, Pa.: George H. Beans Library, 1938).

4 The inventory of the contents of the shop of Alessandro di Francesco Rosselli (Francesco's son), together with earlier references to this inventory, has been published by Arthur Mayger Hind, *Early Italian Engraving: A Critical Catalogue with Complete Reproduction of all the Prints Described* (New York: M. Knoedler, 1938), pp. 304–309.

5 Frequent words used in the titles are "universalis," "exactissima," "vera," "verissima," "exacta," "moderna," "novo," "novissima," "recens," "copiosa," and "ultima."

6 For a discussion of this issue, see Elizabeth L. Eisenstein, *The Printing Press as an Agent of Change* (Cambridge: Cambridge University Press, 1979), 1:543–566, esp. 545–546.

7 The allusion to this difference between the Venetian and Roman market in R. V. Tooley, "Maps in Italian Atlases of the Sixteenth Century," *Imago Mundi* 3 (1939): 12 clearly needs further elaboration.

8 See the excellent work by David Landau and Peter Parshall, *The Renaissance Print, 1470–1550* (New Haven: Yale University Press, 1994).

9 Arte dei Libreri, Stampatori e Ligadori, *Atti* no. 1, 3 March 1571, Archivio di Stato di Venezia.

10 Antonio Lafreri, *A' Lettori* [Rome, 1572?]. A unique copy of this pamphlet is in the Biblioteca Marucelliana, Florence.

11 These were derived from Guillaume Gueroult, *Premier livre des figures et pourtraitz des villes plus illustres et renommees d'Europe* (Lyon: B. Arnoullet, 1552). No copy is known. See Juergen Schulz, *The Printed Plans and Panoramic Views of Venice (1486–1797)*, Saggi e memorie di storia dell'arte 7 (Florence: Leo S. Olschki, 1970), no. 8. The full references are: Paolo Forlani, *Il primo libro delle citta, et fortezze principali del mondo* (Venice, 1567), see Schulz, *Printed Plans of Venice*, no. 18; Giulio Ballino, *Civitatum Aliquot Insigniorum, et locorum, magis munitorum exacta delineatio: Cum omnium quae ad eorum pertinent, breui enarratione. Disegni di alcune piu illustri citta, et fortezze del mondo, con un breue historia delle cose, a loro pertinenti* (Venice: B. Zalterij, 1568), see Schulz, *Printed Plans of Venice*, no. 18. See also Albert Ganado, "The Forlani-Zenoi Town Books of 1567," in P. H. Köhl and P. H. Meurer (eds.), *Florilegium Cartographicum. Beiträge zur Kartographiegeschichte und Vedutenkunde des 16. bis 18. Jahrhunderts. Freundesgabe für Fritz Hellwig* (Leipzig: Dietrich Pfaehler, 1993), pp. 21–34, which was also reprinted in *Speculum Orbis, Zeitschrift für Alte Kartographie und Vedutenkunde* 4 (1988–1993): 21–34.

12 Fabia Borroni Salvadori, *Carte, piante e stampe storiche delle raccolte lafreriane della Biblioteca Nazionale di Firenze*, Indici e Cataloghi, Nuova serie XI (Rome: Istituto Poligrafico e Zecca dello Stato, 1980).

13 See, for example, Lawrence R. McGinniss, *Catalogue of the Earl of Crawford's "Speculum Romanae Magnificentiae" now in the Avery Architectural Library* (New York: Avery Architectural Library, Columbia University, 1976) for a list of references.

14 A full reconstruction by author of the possible scenarios in which offsets could have taken place is found in "The Evidence of Offsets in Renaissance Italian Prints and Maps," *Print Quarterly* 8 (1991): 235–251.

15 J. C. J. Bierens de Haan, *L'oeuvre grave de Cornelis Cort, Graveur Hollandais, 1533–1578* (La Haye: Martinus Nijhoff, 1948).

16 Archivio di Stato di Venezia, Senato Terra, Filza 22. Supplica e privilegio. "mv" means "modo veneziano" the Venetian method of dating from March 1 each year.

17 This assertion cannot be pushed very far. For example, the so-called "Hadji Admad" cordiform map of the world in Arabic, for which the blocks were made in 1560, was suppressed and not published until the eighteenth century on the grounds that its information would be of use to the Turkish enemy. See George Kish, *The Suppressed Turkish Map of 1560* (Ann Arbor: William L. Clements Library, 1957).

18 For the archival references to this case, see Rodolfo Gallo, "Gioan Francesco Camocio and his Large Map of Europe," *Imago Mundi* 7 (1950): 94.

19 See David Woodward, "Calligraphy, Typography, and Cartography," in David Woodward, ed., *Art and Cartography: Six Historical Essays* (Chicago: University of Chicago Press, 1987).

20 [Carlo Pasero], "Giacomo Franco, editore, incisore e calcografo nei secoli XVI e XVII," *La Bibliofilia* 37 (1936): 332–356.

21 The atlas (Call number Ayer *f135 L2 1575 AI) is catalogued "Rome: Antonio Lafreri, ca. 1575" but contains evidence that it was published in Venice c. 1567 without the help of Lafreri. There is also an atlas in the Biblioteca Marciana, Venice, containing no map dated after 1565. See Rodolfo Gallo, *Carte geografiche cinquecentesche a stampa della Biblioteca Marciana e della Biblioteca del Museo Correr di Venezia* (Venice: Istituto Veneto di Scienze, Lettere ed Arti, 1954).

22 The technical evidence summarized here is presented in David Woodward, "The Study of the Italian Map Trade in the Sixteenth Century: Needs and Opportunities," *Wolfenbütteler Forschungen* 7 (1980): 137–146; "New Bibliographical Approaches to the History of Sixteenth-Century Italian Map Publishing," unpublished paper delivered to the 8th International Conference on the History of Cartography, Berlin, 1979; "New Tools for the Study of Watermarks on Sixteenth-Century Italian Printed Maps: Beta Radiography and Scanning Densitometry," in Carla Clivio Marzoli, ed., *Imago et Mensura Mundi. Atti del IX Congresso Internazionale di Storia della Cartografia* (Rome: Istituto della Enciclopedia Italiana, 1985) 2:541–552; and "The Analysis of Paper and Ink in Early Maps: Opportunities and Realities," in Stephen Spector, ed., *Essays in Paper Analysis* (Washington: Folger Books, 1987), pp. 200–221. See also *Maps and Prints in the Italian Renaissance: Makers, Distributors, Consumers*, 1995 Panizzi Lectures (London: British Library, forthcoming).

23 According to Mr. Tooley (correspondence of April 25, 1984), this revision was to have been published by Holland Press, but the manuscript cannot now be traced.

PART TWO

Atlas Cartography in the Low Countries in the Sixteenth, Seventeenth, and Eighteenth Centuries

CORNELIS KOEMAN

THE ORTELIUS-MERCATOR PERIOD

During the years following the publication of Abraham Ortelius's *Theatrum Orbis Terrarum* in 1570 (see Figure 35), booksellers and printers in Antwerp in the southern part of the Low Countries discovered that the atlas was a good selling item. From 1570 to 1580, booksellers could offer a variety of map books: four versions of the *Theatrum*, in Latin, Dutch, French, and German (see Figure 36); three versions of the pocket edition of the *Theatrum*, in Latin, Dutch, and French; the first two parts of the townbooks by Georg Braun and Franz Hogenberg; a competitive world atlas, *Speculum Orbis Terrarum*, by Gerard de Jode; an *Itinerarium Orbis Christiani* by Michael von Eitzing; and an edition of Ptolemy's *Geographia* by Gerardus Mercator.

The various theories explaining the origin of the atlas identify several significant circumstances which contributed to the appearance of this new phenomenon.[1] Ptolemy's classic handbook of cartography, with its twenty-eight maps of uniform size and its "tabulae novae," was essentially nonfunctional but, nevertheless, was intended to serve as a source of geographical information. In Italy, one solution was provided by Antonio Lafreri, who assembled collections of maps into bound volumes between 1550 and 1577. However, these volumes had no text and included maps of various formats. Sebastian Münster's *Cosmographia*, first printed in 1544 in Basel and published in Latin, German, French, and Italian editions, provided another solution with descriptions of the countries of the world and over fifty maps and seventy town plans. The friendly correspondence between Gerardus Mercator and Abraham Ortelius provided the inspiration, while the need for up-to-date, adequate maps, was expressed by the merchants of Antwerp. Accord-

FIGURE 35 *Frontispiece of the first edition of Abraham Ortelius's* Theatrum *(Antwerp, 1570). The copperplate has been reengraved at least three times. (See Figure 36.) This print has been censored. Universiteitsbibliotheek, Amsterdam.*

ing to a letter written by Jan Raedemaker,[2] one of these merchants, called Hooftman, persuaded him (Raedemaker) to assemble modern Italian, French, and German maps, obtained through Ortelius, into a prototype for a world atlas. Ortelius's significance in this sequence was that he organized the publication of the atlas, including the writing of the text and enlarging it with supplements.

Almost instantaneously, the book trade had enlarged its assortment with an attractive but expensive product—the atlas. It was attractive because of the graphical presentation of the kingdoms, cities, and peoples, in Europe and elsewhere. It was expensive because of the cost of engraving the copperplates, the size and weight of the paper, and the binding. Peter Heyn's pocket atlas, published in

FIGURE 36 *Frontispiece of the German edition of Abraham Ortelius's* Theatrum *(Antwerp, 1580). Library of Congress.*

1577, clearly demonstrated that only folio-size sheets would satisfy the customers. This small map book was not well received by the customers, who were already spoiled by the splendor of the *Theatrum*.

A letter to Ortelius, dated October 15, 1579, from Jacobus Monaw of Breslau stated: "I have seen an epitome as it were of your 'Theatrum,' . . . but it contains fewer maps, and is not so well engraved."[3] Since then, this feeling about a too small rendering of a too complex picture has been a trial to the buyer of a pocket atlas. The history of atlas publishing since Ortelius's *Theatrum* has been associated with the problem of how much an atlas is worth. Since the first sale of a bound or unbound copy of the *Theatrum* with fifty-three map sheets, the buyer of a folio-size world atlas had to be willing to pay a high price. And yet atlases sold readily. Ever since then publishers have been eager to bring atlases on the market because they do not give offense, which was a very good selling point during the years of persecution for heresy in the Europe of that period.

The origins of commercial atlas production in the Low Countries took place during those emotional years when there were major changes in political and religious life, including the separation of the Northern Netherlands from Spain, the Reformation, and the establishment of an intellectual middle class. The last factor produced favorable conditions for the flourishing of the Antwerp publishing houses, with Antwerp becoming the major European distribution center for scientific cartography.

The printing house of Plantin, established in 1555, played a prominent role in map distribution, as can be seen from the account books of Plantin's shop, which, surprisingly, have been preserved and published.[4] Several entries from 1564 onward are from London booksellers, which is understandable, following the publication of Mercator's large wall map of the British Isles in Duisburg (1564). Were it not for religious oppression, Mercator's greatest cartographic works would no doubt have also been published in Antwerp.

The success of commercial cartography in this area also stemmed from the development of scientific cartography in Leuven, the seat of the oldest university in the Low Countries (founded in 1425). Without scholars like Gemma Frisius, Caspard van der Heyden (also known as Amyrica or Amyricus), Franciscus Monachus, Jacob van Deventer, and Gerardus Mercator, Antwerp could not have become the trading center for cartography.

While mathematics, astronomy, and land surveying are basic contributions, they were not enough to compile an atlas. Antwerp's original contributions to the creation of the traditional world atlas included:

1. Drawing and engraving of atlas maps. Abraham Ortelius himself reduced large wall maps to the handsome size of one folio sheet, while Joris Hoefnagel did most of the engraving.

2. Acquisition of new maps from various sources. Ortelius's correspondence includes letters exchanged with cartographers from all over Europe. One of the major merits of his atlas is the "Catalogus auctorum tabularum geographicarum," which lists the names of cartographers whose maps Ortelius used in the atlas.[5]

3. Printing of the text on the verso of an atlas sheet. (1570 Latin text; 1571 Dutch; 1572 German; 1578 French; 1588 Spanish; 1608 Italian by Jan Baptist Vrients).

4. Editing of new editions. For the first time, the system of *Additamenta* was introduced. (See Figure 37.) Between 1570 and 1598, five supplements were issued, each containing about twenty-five new maps.

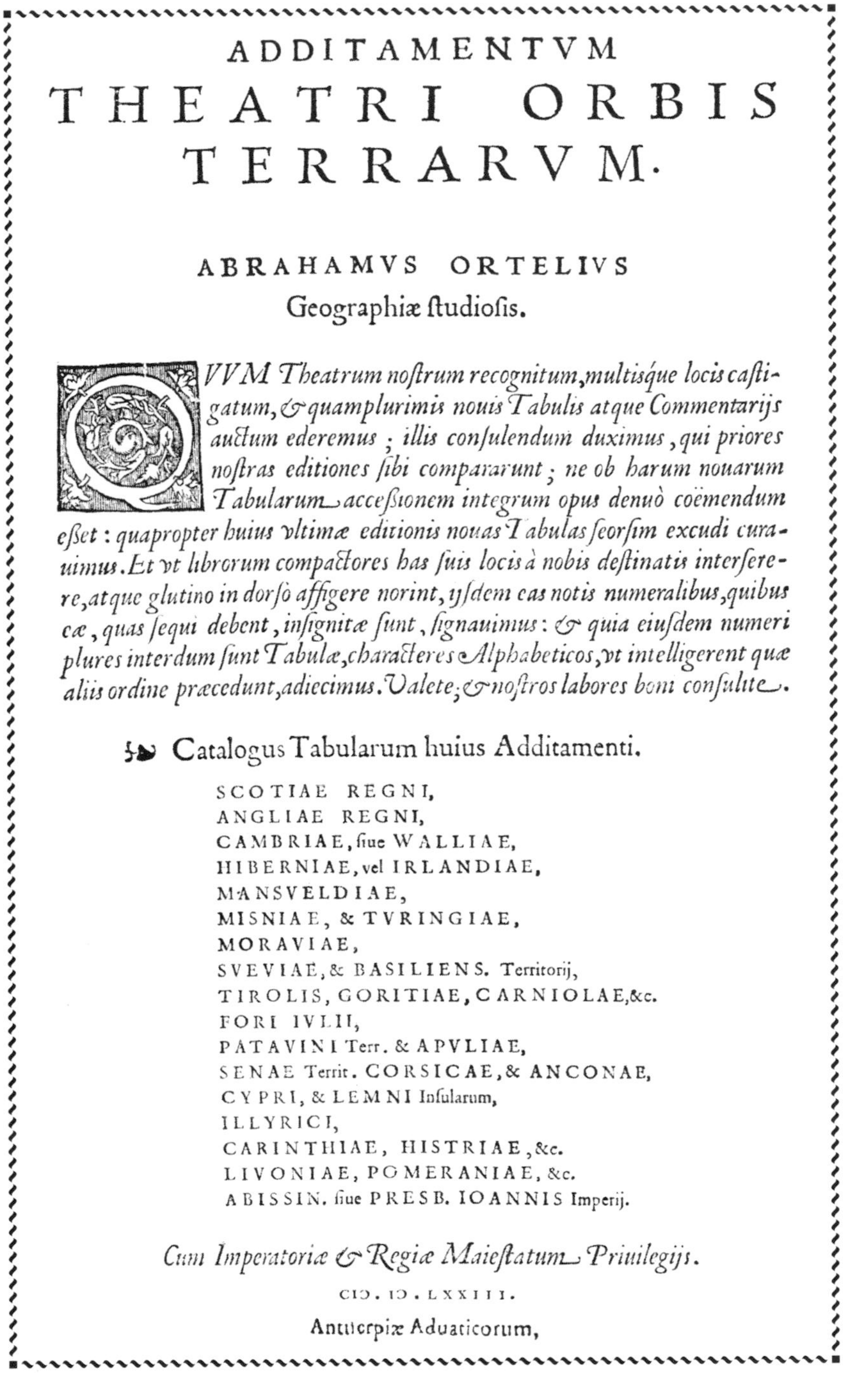

ADDITAMENTVM
THEATRI ORBIS TERRARVM.

ABRAHAMVS ORTELIVS
Geographiæ ſtudioſis.

VVM Theatrum noſtrum recognitum, multisque locis caſti-gatum, & quamplurimis nouis Tabulis atque Commentarijs auctum ederemus ; illis conſulendum duximus, qui priores noſtras editiones ſibi comparavunt ; ne ob harum nouarum Tabularum acceſsionem integrum opus denuò coëmendum eſſet : quapropter huius vltimæ editionis nouas Tabulas ſeorſim excudi cura-uimus. Et vt librorum compactores has ſuis locis à nobis deſtinatis interſere-re, atque glutino in dorſo affigere norint, yſdem eas notis numeralibus, quibus cæ, quas ſequi debent, inſignitæ ſunt, ſignauimus : & quia eiuſdem numeri plures interdum ſunt Tabulæ, characteres Alphabeticos, vt intelligerent quæ aliis ordine præcedunt, adiecimus. Valete; & noſtros labores boni conſulite.

ॐ Catalogus Tabularum huius Additamenti.

SCOTIAE REGNI,
ANGLIAE REGNI,
CAMBRIAE, ſiue WALLIAE,
HIBERNIAE, vel IRLANDIAE,
MANSVELDIAE,
MISNIAE, & TVRINGIAE,
MORAVIAE,
SVEVIAE, & BASILIENS. Territorij,
TIROLIS, GORITIAE, CARNIOLAE, &c.
FORI IVLII,
PATAVINI Terr. & APVLIAE,
SENAE Territ. CORSICAE, & ANCONAE,
CYPRI, & LEMNI Inſularum,
ILLYRICI,
CARINTHIAE, HISTRIAE, &c.
LIVONIAE, POMERANIAE, &c.
ABISSIN. ſiue PRESB. IOANNIS Imperij.

Cum Imperatoriæ & Regiæ Maieſtatum Priuilegijs.

CIƆ.IƆ.LXXIII.

Antuerpiæ Aduaticorum,

FIGURE 37 *Title page of the* Additamentum *for Abraham Ortelius's* Theatrum, *Latin text (Antwerp, 1573). Koninklijke Bibliotheek, Brussels.*

Since these were not substitutes for obsolete maps, the *Theatrum* grew into a thick body of 167 map sheets, including the *Parergon*. The system of *Additamenta* was obviously appreciated by the public, because Jodocus Hondius, later on between 1630 and 1640, applied the same system to the Mercator-Hondius atlas, naming the supplement an *Appendix*. Willem Janszoon Blaeu also followed this example.

from 1598 onward until 1724. However, notable as Italian craftsmen were for their imitations, they did not venture to copy a folio edition of any of the great Dutch atlases.

For German readers, Matthias Quad (1557–1613) wrote a text, accompanying eighty-two maps engraved by himself, called the *Geographisch Handtbuch*, which was printed by Johann Busemacher at Cologne in 1600.[10] Earlier, Busemacher had printed a collection of forty-eight maps with the title, *Europea totius orbis terrarum praestantissimae . . .* (Cologne, 1592). In his maps, Quad followed the models by Ortelius and Mercator. The title page was an almost faithful copy of the frontispiece of the *Theatrum*. Cologne became famous for its topographical works, not because of the *Geographisch Handtbuch*, which was reprinted only once in 1608, but because of the famous townbook, *Civitates Orbis Terrarum* by Georg Braun and Franz Hogenberg.

The other German city noted for its printing of maps was Duisburg, where Mercator's *Atlas* and wall maps were published. Mercator's work in classical cartography (Ptolemy's *Geographia*) paralleled his highly original work in modern cartography, especially his major *Atlas sive cosmographicae meditationes de fabrica mundi et fabricati figura*, published between 1585 and 1595. (See Figure 38.) Unlike the maps in Abraham Ortelius's *Theatrum Orbis Terrarum*, Mercator's maps were all originally designed by him, based on an integration of available geographical information and drawn in a uniform style. He also engraved the 107 plates, with the assistance of his talented son, Arnold, after about 1555.[11] His youngest son Rumoldus took part in the completion of his father's gigantic undertaking when he finally settled in Duisburg some time after 1588. Following his father's death in 1594, Rumoldus also completed the publication of the last part of the *Atlas* in 1595. The most important aspect of Mercator's atlas project was the way in which it contributed to the development of commercial atlas production in Amsterdam after 1606.

Although the works by Braun and Hogenberg and Mercator were written, engraved, and printed in Cologne and Duisburg, respectively, they are considered to belong to the Dutch school of cartography. Both Antwerp and later Amsterdam, with their world atlases, leaned heavily on the German market. Two years after its first edition, Ortelius's atlas was printed with Dutch text, and Willem Janszoon Blaeu had his new atlas of 1634 first printed in German. A study of Willem Janszoon Blaeu's publishing policy proves that he also favored the German market over the French or Italian markets.

TRANSITION FROM THE SOUTHERN TO THE NORTHERN NETHERLANDS

During the period which saw the successful appearance of the *Theatrum* and *Civitates*, the typographical scene changed completely. The best engravers, including the Van Deutecom brothers, Jodocus Hondius, and Pieter van den Keere, left Antwerp and settled in London in order to escape from the exigencies of the

FIGURE 38 *Frontispiece of the first edition of Gerardus Mercator's* Atlas *(Duisburg, 1595). Universiteitsbibliotheek, Amsterdam.*

Spanish military occupation of the Southern Netherlands. Even Plantin established a branch in Leiden in 1583, just to play it safe in case things went wrong in Antwerp. In 1584, the first sea atlas, Lucas Janszoon Waghenaer's *Spieghel der Zeevaerdt*, was printed in Leiden. Things had indeed gone wrong in Antwerp and, as a result, capital and trade moved to the north.

Among the many printers in Amsterdam, Cornelis Claesz specialized in maps, pilot guides, and books on the art of navigation. Before 1606, when Jodocus Hondius published his first edition of the Mercator *Atlas*, Cornelis Claesz had printed several editions of Waghenaer's chart book, *Spieghel der Zeevaerdt,* as well as a very charming and successful pocket atlas with 169 maps, the *Caert-thresoor,* first edition 1598 (*Atlantes Neerlandici,* entry Lan 1, hereafter cited as A.N. Lan 1; see note 12), with Barent Langenes of Middelburg as a co-publisher. This was the first world atlas printed in the Northern Netherlands. It was also published in Latin (text by Petrus Bertius) and in French, and went into several editions continuing well into the first half of the seventeenth century.

In 1604, Jodocus Hondius bought the copperplates of Mercator's atlases (Ptolemy's *Geographia* and the *Atlas*). In 1605, he published the *Geographia* with both Latin and Greek texts, the first book with a Greek text printed in Amsterdam. The next year, the *Atlas* appeared with a partially new Latin text written by Petrus Montanus and the number of maps increased from 107 to 144. (See Figure 39.) The new maps were drawn and engraved by Jodocus Hondius who had borrowed them from various authors. The printer of both atlases was, of course, Cornelis Claesz. At the same time, Jodocus Hondius had the maps reduced in order to publish them as the *Atlas Minor* in 1607. (See Figure 40.) These were crucial steps in the history of atlas production in the Netherlands, and until the end of the century, atlases from Amsterdam dominated the international book trade.

By 1612, Ortelius's *Theatrum* had appeared in its final edition with the majority of its plates some forty years old. The plates were not used again, a peculiar fact in view of the long life of the plates of Mercator's *Atlas* and those of the Blaeu atlases. Consequently, the Mercator-Hondius atlas dominated the market until 1630 when Willem Jansz. Blaeu entered the competition. When Jodocus Hondius, the great reformer of Dutch cartography, died suddenly in 1612, his widow and her seven children obtained assistance from a new son-in-law, Jan Janssen (or Johannes Janssonius), a printer from Arnhem, who had married Elizabeth Hondius. Atlas production was carried on until about 1660 under the imprint of Johannes Janssonius. Together with his brothers-in-law, Jodocus Hondius, Jr., and Henricus Hondius, Janssonius further enlarged the Mercator atlas and replaced old Mercator maps with new maps until the character of the contents had changed to such an extent that he had to alter the title to *Novus Atlas* in 1636. (See Figure 41.) By that time its 320 maps had to be divided among three volumes.

Another member of the Hondius clan, Pieter van den Keere (Petrus Kaerius, 1571–1646), one of the most versatile engravers of the period, collaborated in the engraving of the *Atlas Minor* but also published his own maps and map books. In 1617, van den Keere issued a very fine atlas of the Netherlands, *Germania Inferior,* with twenty-five maps and an elaborate text. A much smaller national atlas, the *Nieuw Nederlandtsch Caertboeck,* had been published in 1616 by his cousin Abra-

FIGURE 39 *Frontispiece of the second edition of the* Mercator-Hondius *Atlas (Amsterdam, 1607). Universiteitsbibliotheek, Utrecht.*

ham Goos. Apparently, Henricus Hondius too had his own business, aside from his partnership. His market was France, as can be seen from the appearance of his name on the many editions of the *Atlas* with French text, published between 1609 and 1630, and on the maps of French provinces (qui) "se vendent à Paris chez Melchior Tavernier à la sphere."

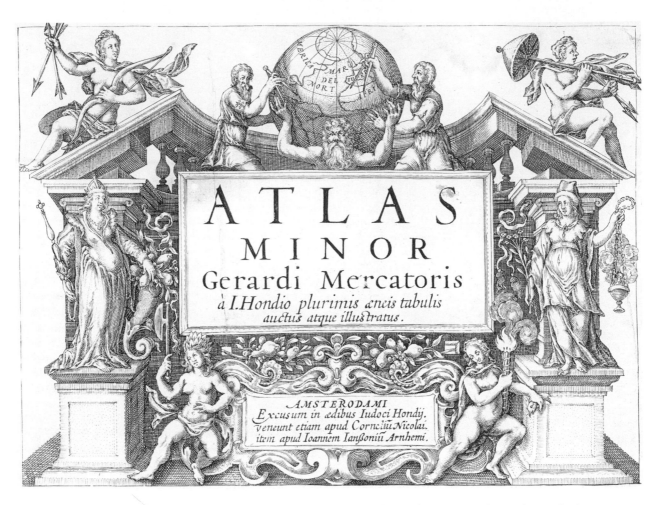

FIGURE 40   *Frontispiece of Jodocus Hondius's edition of the* Atlas Minor *(Amsterdam, 1607).*
Koninklijke Bibliotheek, Brussels.

Short Title List of the Mercator-Hondius Atlas Editions Published between 1585 and 1628

Date	Short title	Publisher	Entry[12]
1585	Galliae Tabulae Geographicae		A.N. Me 9
1589	Italiae Sclavoniae et Graeciae		A.N. Me 11
1595	Atlantis Pars Altera		A.N. Me 12
1595	Atlas sive cosm. médit.		A.N. Me 13
1602	Id.		A.N. Me 14
1606	Id.	Jodocus Hondius	A.N. Me 15
1607	Id.	J. H. and Cornelis Claesz	A.N. Me 16
1609	L'atlas ou méditations cosm.	Jod. Hondius (French)	A.N. Me 19
1611	Atlas sive cosm. médit.	Jod. Hondius (French)	A.N. Me 20
1613	Atlas sive cosm. médit.	Jod. Hondius (French)	A.N. Me 22
1613	L'atlas ou méditations cosm.	Jod. Hondius (French)	A.N. Me 23
1619	L'atlas ou méditations cosm.	Jod. Hondius (French)	A.N. Me 26
1623	Atlas sive cosm. médit.	Henr. Hondius	A.N. Me 27
1628	Atlas sive cosm. médit.	Henr. Hondius (French)	A.N. Me 28

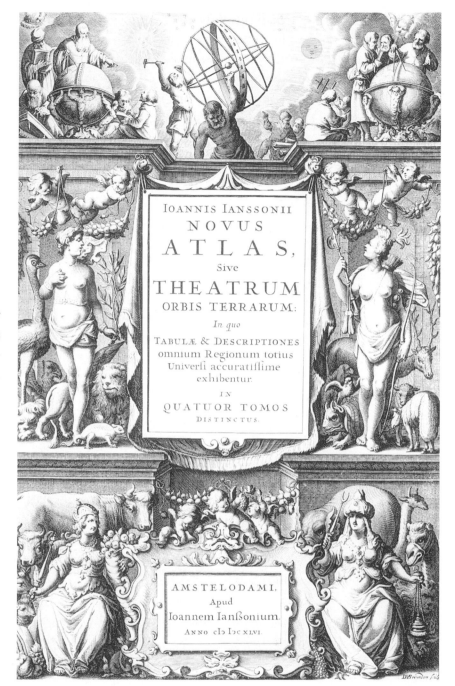

FIGURE 41 *Frontispiece of the first volume of Janssonius's* Novus Atlas *(Amsterdam, 1646). Universiteitsbibliotheek, Amsterdam.*

WILLEM JANSZOON BLAEU

When Willem Janszoon Blaeu (1571–1638) entered into competition with the Mercator-Hondius atlas, he was nearly sixty years old. Consequently, the famous Blaeu atlas was developed mainly by his sons Cornelis and Joan.[13] About 1599 Willem Janszoon established a ship-chandler's shop on the Amsterdam waterfront where he sold instruments, globes, and maps. In 1605 he moved to the Damrak to a house called "In de Vergulde Sonnewijser" (the gilt sundial), where he began business as a bookseller and printer. From 1618 on, Johannes Jansso-nius lived next door, which may have caused Janszoon to add "Blaeu" to his name in order to make the distinction between himself and his neighbor and competi-tor clearer.

His most important books were the two pilot guides, *Het Licht der Zeevaert* (1608) and the *Zeespiegel* (1623), along with subsequent editions of both. Without rivals, apart from some editions of the *Licht der Zeevaert* pirated by his neighbor, Willem Janszoon Blaeu dominated the market in pilot books until 1623 when Jacob Aertsz. Colom entered into competition with his folio size *Vyrighe Colom* (Fyrie Columne).

Apart from his business in instruments, globes, and charts, Willem Janszoon Blaeu published about thirty separate maps between 1604 and 1630, thirteen of which were incorporated in *Atlantis Appendix, sive pars altera . . .* , his first world atlas, published in 1630. The majority of its sixty maps were printed from plates acquired from Jodocus Hondius, Jr. When Jodocus Hondius died on August 18, 1629, his brother Henricus and his brother-in-law Johannes Janssonius greatly deplored this sale of plates to their rival, Willem Jansz. Blaeu, who had replaced Hondius's name with his own and published them in a hurry in his *Atlantis Appendix*, which was essentially a "supplement" to the Mercator-Hondius atlas.[14]

In order to supply their urgent need for plates, Janssonius and Henricus Hondius commissioned the engravers Evert Sijmontsz. Hamersvelt and Salomon Rogiers in 1630 to cut thirty-six new plates within eighteen months. The maps should "be accurate and fine . . . not less in quality than the maps given to the engraver" (i.e., the Hondius maps sold to Blaeu).[15] As a result, almost identical maps are found in Blaeu's and Janssonius's atlases. In order to compete success-fully with Blaeu, Hondius and Janssonius decided to do several things. First, they brought out immediately an Appendix of their own, *Atlantis Maioris Appendix* (1630, with eighty maps).[16] Second, they developed an entirely new atlas project without making use of the Mercator maps. Some very rare separate volumes are known: *Theatrum Universae Galliae* (1631), *Theatrum Imperii Germanici* (1632), and *Theatrum Italiae* (1636). Finally, they continued to produce and enlarge the Mercator-Hondius atlas. The idea of supplements proved to be very sensible and was continued until 1641.

By these means, Hondius and Janssonius were able to keep pace with Blaeu's development of a gigantic world atlas.[17] In 1634, Blaeu dropped the name *Appendix* and never used it again. At first, he tried *Atlas Novus* but in 1638 he finally settled on *Theatrum Orbis Terrarum* (*Le Théatre du Monde*), a traditional title which he could freely use because Ortelius's atlas had disappeared from the scene. (See Figure 42.) The title *Atlas Novus*, discarded by Blaeu, was taken up by Hondius-Janssonius, but altered as *Novus Atlas* (*Nouvel Atlas*) and used until 1670.

Hundreds of pages of text would be required to describe the unique story of the contest between the Blaeus and Janssonius. However, it has all been described in great detail in my *Atlantes Neerlandici* (see note 12). Blaeu was first to publish a

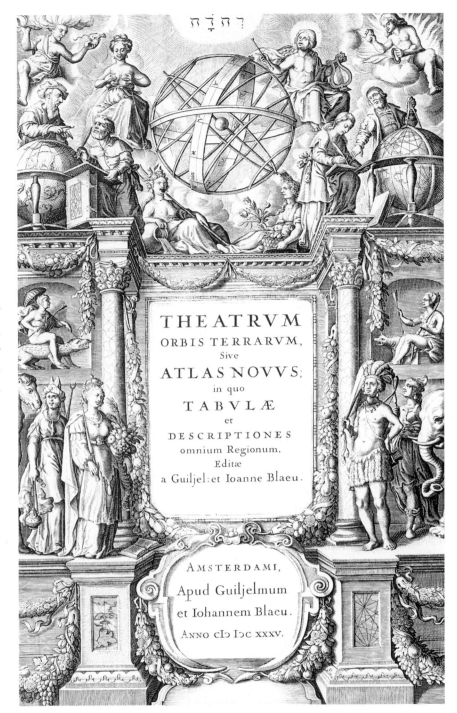

FIGURE 42 *Frontispiece of the first volume of the* Theatrum Orbis Terrarum, *published by Willem and Joan Blaeu (Amsterdam, 1635). Universiteitsbibliotheek, Amsterdam.*

two-volume world atlas (in German text) with 204 maps in 1634, but Janssonius was first to publish a three-volume world atlas (in Latin text) with 318 maps in 1638. And so on and so on. This contest culminated in a six-volume *Theatrum* by Joan Blaeu in 1655 and a six-volume *Novus Atlas* by Johannes Janssonius in 1658. Joan Blaeu was largely responsible for completing the *Theatrum* (Willem Blaeu had died in 1638). Following the death of Henricus Hondius in 1657, Johannes Janssonius took charge of developing the *Novus Atlas*. He died in 1664.

POCKET ATLASES

Overshadowed by the monumental folio atlases are the small pocket atlases. The Blaeus never went in for this "trifling stuff." However, Jodocus Hondius the elder, produced a series of charming, small world atlases which should not really be called pocket atlases. Pocket atlases, in the real sense of the word, were the *Epitomes* of Ortelius's *Theatrum*, measuring about 12 × 18 cm; the *Caert-thresoor*, measuring 11 × 17 cm; and some other, rather rare atlases such as Zacharias Heyns's *Miroir du Monde* (1599).

The *Atlas Minor*, based on Mercator's *Atlas*, appeared in 1607 with 152 maps, presumably all engraved by Jodocus Hondius, Sr. This atlas measures about 17 × 22 cm. In 1628 an entirely new edition with maps engraved and signed by Pieter van den Keere appeared. The old plates had been sold in England where they were used for *Purchas His Pilgrims* (1625) and subsequently for the translation of the Mercator atlas, *Historia Mundi*, by Thomas Cotes for Michael Sparke and Samuel Cartwright in 1635. In 1628 a rival work was published by Johannes Cloppenburgh. It was larger (21 × 28 cm), and contained some 180 maps, most of them engraved by Pieter van den Keere. Instead of being called *Atlas Minor*, it received a full-blown title, *Gerardi Mercatoris Atlas sive Cosmographicae Meditationes*. Editions of the *Atlas Minor* with French or German text were sold in large quantities, as can be deduced from their presence in libraries all over the world. Editions with Dutch or Latin text were even more popular.

BLAEU'S COMPETITORS

It is difficult to say which of the folio editions of the Blaeu and Hondius atlases enjoyed the largest edition. Probably the Hondius Latin edition was the most popular and the English and Spanish editions, the rarest. Blaeu never contemplated an English version, not even of his atlas of Scotland (1654). The rather complete documentation on the birth of this volume V from the *Theatrum* is very interesting.[18] Research by Skelton and his Scottish colleagues has demonstrated that Blaeu's intention to publish a separate atlas of Scotland, with maps surveyed by Timothy Pont and revised and drawn by Robert Gordon, dates back to some years before 1638. For his atlas of England (first edition, 1645), Blaeu copied plates already published in Speed's *Theatre of the Empire of Great Britaine* (1627), and borrowed (or pirated?) the text from Camden's *Britannia*.

Apparently Blaeu did not see a market for an English version of his world atlas because Hondius had published one in 1636. This consisted of a two-volume edition of Mercator's *Atlas*, with text translated into English by Henry Hexham, "Quartermaister to the Regiment of Colonell Goring."[19] Janssonius was first to publish an atlas with Spanish text, in four volumes in 1653 and in 1666.[20] Joan Blaeu started printing a Spanish text in 1658 and had nearly finished when his entire stock was burned in 1672.

Besides the two giants, several smaller map and atlas producers flourished in Amsterdam in the seventeenth century: Claes Janszoon Visscher, Abraham Goos, Cornelis and Justus Danckertsz, and Frederik de Wit. Apart from these, a dozen ship's chandlers along the quays also traded in atlases, maps, and globes. The most important name is that of Claes Jansz. Visscher (1587–1652), founder of the famous print and map shop "In de Visscher." He was an artist, an engraver, and one of the very few craftsmen about whom there is fairly complete biographical information available.[21] He was the most productive engraver of his period and is admired by both art and map collectors.

Visscher bought copperplates from Pieter van den Keere for his first atlas. These formed the nucleus of his 1634 atlas of the Low Countries, *Belgium sive Germania Inferior*, with forty-three maps. This had grown to sixty-one maps by 1645 and nearly all of them were Visscher's own work. After his death, his son Nicolaes (1618–1679) carried on the business and made a number of improvements, which made him the most serious competitor of the Blaeus and Janssonius. Between 1657 and 1677 he published some 100 atlas maps, assembled into an *Atlas Contractus* of varying size. He was the first to introduce modern French maps to the Netherlands: "authore N. Sansonio Abbevillensi, Geographus Regis Galliae," as his title proclaimed. In many ways Visscher's maps were superior to the (often out-of-date) maps in the atlases of the Blaeus or Janssonius.

After Visscher's death, his son Nicolaes (1649–1702) took over the shop. Thanks to a 1682 shop catalog, we have accurate information about the maps, prints, and views he sold. He was no less energetic than his father and enlarged his stock of atlas maps, which were assembled to order, with a printed index, into what he called his *Atlas Minor*. In spite of the modesty expressed in the title, an Atlas Minor often consisted of two hundred maps, bound in two large folio volumes and was much sought after by foreigners who visited Amsterdam's print and map shops. Visscher's atlases and collections of maps were widely distributed and can be found all over the world today. They were given a further lease on life when in 1726, after the death of Nicolaes Visscher II's widow, the copperplates were transferred to the firm of Schenk.

BLAEU'S *ATLAS MAIOR*

In Nicolaes Visscher's own eyes, he had created an Atlas Maior, but he had to name it *Atlas Minor*, because Joan Blaeu's *magnum opus* was already called *Atlas Maior*. In 1662, the eleven-volume edition of Blaeu's major work, with Latin text, came from the presses. The renown of *Atlas Maior* was not primarily based on the high standard of scholarship in the maps and text. It was rather the superb typography, the beauty of the six hundred hand-colored maps, and notably the unrivaled size that made the atlas desirable. (See Figures 43 and 44.)

Patricians of the period had a propensity for pompous display, not the least in their libraries. In this respect, Blaeu's *Atlas Maior* suited their often rather snob-

an ambitious project which did not succeed. The enterprise collapsed after the fourth volume due to financial difficulties.

WALL MAPS AND TOWNBOOKS

Two other very important categories of Dutch maps will be described briefly: wall maps and town plans and views. They were often bound together in a book or atlas format.

Multisheet wall maps of the world, continents, and various countries were printed by numerous map sellers in the Southern and Northern Netherlands in the sixteenth and seventeenth centuries. Very few of these maps have survived, due to exposure to light and humidity and because of their size. When kept as loose leaves in books, they may last for centuries. One specific type of Dutch multisheet map, frequently bound in atlases, is the polder map. These large-scale topographic maps, published between about 1610 and 1750, often comprised sixteen sheets, plus marginal decorations in the shape of town views or coats of arms.[23] When bound in atlases, they often had contemporary coloring.

A number of seventeenth-century Dutch multisheet wall maps of countries and continents have been assembled and are preserved in the only three giant atlases known in the world: the *Klencke Atlas* in the British Museum (170 × 120 cm) with thirty-four sheets; the *Rostock Atlas* in the University Library at Rostock (about 170 × 120 cm) with thirty-two sheets; and the *Kurfürsten Atlas* in the Staatsbibliothek in Berlin (170 × 110 cm) with thirty-eight sheets.[24] The *Klencke Atlas* was presented to the English King Charles II in 1660 by a delegation of Amsterdam merchants under Mr. Joan Klencke.

The second category, seventeenth-century town plans, deserves special mention because they have also been assembled into atlases, following the tradition of the sixteenth-century townbook, *Civitates Orbis Terrarum*.[25] In 1653, Johannes Janssonius acquired the plates for the *Civitates* from Abraham Hogenberg. The majority were incorporated into eight townbooks, the *Theatrum Urbium Celebriorum* (1657) containing no less than 500 plans and views of European cities. Janssonius ordered copperplates, newly engraved after the originals by Blaeu, for many plates of the cities of the Netherlands. In 1694 these copperplates were acquired by Frederik de Wit who used them again, under his own imprint, for his undated townbooks. Of all the Blaeu atlases, the townbooks of the Northern and Southern Netherlands, two volumes with 223 plates and descriptions published in 1649 and 1650, are held in the highest esteem in the Netherlands. This is partly due to the fact that their composition is linked with the Dutch Republic's struggle for independence from Spain in the seventeenth century. Reflecting the most dramatic and heroic period in the shaping of the Dutch state, they show the proud and industrious cities of the North in their full splendor.

Blaeu's townbooks of Italy, Piedmont, and Savoy are rather baroque in conception, unlike the plain and consistent presentation of the Dutch cities. Architectural drawings, statues, and landscapes give these large folio books an appearance quite different from a town atlas. However, by virtue of the variety of subjects, the splendor of the engravings and, above all, because of their number, they rank among the finest topographical works ever published. In 1663, the Latin text was published in three parts: Vatican City (74 plates), Rome (41 plates), and Naples and Sicily (33 plates). In 1682, under the imprint of Joan Blaeu heirs, two additional parts appeared: Savoy (71 plates) and Piedmont (69 plates).

PRINTING HISTORY OF THE *THEATRUM SABAUDIAE*

Unlike the printing history of Ortelius's *Theatrum* and Mercator's *Atlas*, the documentation on atlas publishing by the Hondius and Blaeu firms is slight. Thanks to the Plantin Archives in Antwerp and the Ortelius letters, there is sufficient information about printing and the printer at work in the second half of the sixteenth century. Unfortunately, no account books or office records of the Hondius, Janssonius, or Blaeu firms have been preserved. No one knows what happened to these business archives, of which hardly a scrap of paper is left. Presumably, part of the Blaeu archives were destroyed by the fire of February 28, 1672, which ruined the printing house in the Gravenstraat, where the atlases were printed. Research in the Blaeu papers maintained outside the Netherlands partially compensates for their loss. Recently a quantity of correspondence conducted by Joan Blaeu and his son Pieter was discovered in Italian archives. In the Archivio di Stato, Florence, thirteen letters exchanged between Pieter Blaeu (1637–1706) and Cosimo de Medici, Prince of Tuscany, from June 1666 through September 1667, are preserved. Dr. Joan Blaeu's son, Pieter, conducted most of the firm's foreign relations. Pieter, who was fluent in Italian, French, and German, was called the "roving agent of business, travelling tirelessly through Europe to sell and buy books and to seek assistance in completing the plans launched by his father."[26] He was also Prince Cosimo's private escort and guide during the prince's travels in the Netherlands in 1667 and 1669, serving as an intermediator in encounters with high officials.

Of equal importance is a collection of forty letters exchanged between Pieter Blaeu and Cardinal Prince Leopoldo de Medici, dated between December 1667 and September 1675. These and a set of twelve letters exchanged in 1690 and 1691 with the Grand Duke of Tuscany are also kept by the Archivio di Stato at Florence. The largest collection of Blaeu letters preserved in Italy consists of 108 letters written between 1660 and 1675 by Pieter Blaeu to Antonio Magliabechi, the librarian of the Biblioteca Laurenziana, kept by the Biblioteca Nazionale Centrale at Florence together with the letters written by Dr. Joan Blaeu to the Grand Duke Carlo Emanuele II of Savoy and Piedmont.[27]

Several new facts about the production of Joan Blaeu's *Atlas Maior* and the townbooks of Italy have emerged from this vast corpus of letters. It is generally known that Joan Blaeu not only produced a two-volume town atlas containing

were unfamiliar with Joan Blaeu's financial backing by the Grand Duke of Savoy and we also did not know about the well-advanced project of an atlas of cities in Tuscany, which was never realized. As Pieter Blaeu wrote in 1660 to Magliabechi:

When I was in Florence I had the good fortune to be able to call on Their Most Serene Highnesses the Grand Duke and the Granprincipe, as well as on His Most Serene Highness Prince Leopoldo, to whom I imparted my father's plan to print books on all the towns of Italy. I told them that since he had almost finished the book on the Papal State he was eager to begin on the Grand Duchy of Tuscany, but that he lacks drawings of that most flourishing of states and that I had come to Florence to beg their Most Serene Highnesses to assist my father, etc. As your Worship will remember the reply was that I should dispatch some completed drawing so that Their Most Serene Highnesses could see how they should be executed in order to tally with the others. I am now sending to Mr. Carlo Dati one of Florence and one of Siena. These are the only two drawings of Tuscany which my father possesses, and I therefore beg you with all my heart to intercede for us before Their Most Serene Highnesses, so that my father can have drawings of the other towns in Tuscany . . . I would also be most grateful if we could have drawings and descriptions of the Galleria, the Statues and the Capella de Gran Duchi, as well as of the other objects of interest . . .[28]

The Blaeus not only wanted drawings, but they also lacked capital to finance a project of that size as a *Theatrum Civitatum et Admirandorum Italiae*. In guarded terms, Joan Blaeu solicited a grant from the Grand Duke of Tuscany, as indicated in a letter of October 27, 1661, from his son Pieter to Magliabechi:

Finally I wish to ask two favours . . . The other is to procure the drawings of the towns, buildings and other objects of interest in Tuscany. The Duke of Savoye sends my father all the towns and other objects of interest in his state, and has also agreed to pay for everything which my father will spend on the drawings. I am not telling Your Worship this because I want His Most Serene Highness the Grand Duke to do the same, but only to show that other great princes are doing their utmost to honour the work of my father.[29]

The outcome was favorable; at the expense of the Grand Duke of Tuscany, drawings were made but, as far as we know, were never published by the Blaeus. However, these may have been obtained by Pieter Mortier after 1705, from the Blaeus' estate. For the other volume under preparation, the Grand Duke of

Savoy paid for the drawings as well as for the engraving and printing. The Grand Duke's devotion to Pieter Blaeu is demonstrated by the letters exchanged. We can only speculate about the reason for this intimacy. In fact, Duke Carlo Emanuele II paid a great sum of money to compensate for the losses suffered by the fire of February 23, 1672. It was in the middle of the production of the town-books of Savoy and Piedmont that Blaeu's printing office at the Gravenstraat was destroyed by fire. Pieter Blaeu immediately reported the disaster in letters to his princely correspondents. The fire destroyed fourteen presses, all the copper-plates of the atlas maps (with a few exceptions), all the type punches, a great number of printed books, and paper. The gift of the Duke of Savoy is reported in a letter of May 9, 1675, three years afterward, to Magliabechi:

> *I must tell Your Worship, as our most benevolent and affectionate patron, about how we have set up a new press on the same site where my father had his first printing-shop. It is a particularly convenient site, and we will have all that is necessary towards the end of this month. At the beginning of next month we shall start printing the rest of Grotius' theological works, half of which have already been printed. We shall also start printing a Roman breviary in 24-mo. and in four parts in red and black. We intend now to specialize in books in red and black. We are having the copperplates engraved as quickly as possible for the book on the states of the Duke of Savoye. We are obliged to do this since the Duke performed an act of extraordinary generosity towards our firm after the fire, an act worthy of so great a prince. I tell you this in confidence for the first time being, but we shall soon publish it in the preface to this particular book.[30]*

"Soon" in this case translated into seven years; the year of publication of the *Theatrum Sabaudiae* was 1682!

Most curious are the contents of letters exchanged with Cardinal Leopold. Often, the cardinal ordered books, atlases, and globes, but he also ordered objects of art including paintings by Dutch artists. Pieter Blaeu acted as a go-between for these transactions. The cardinal-prince showed himself most eager to obtain seascapes by Willem van de Velde, of which he managed to acquire a large piece in 1670.

When one reflects about the truth behind the politeness expressed in the letters, one presumes a professional relationship between merchants and their clients. But what was the origin of the relationship between the wealthiest clientele of Europe and the Blaeus, the most famous of all printers? There was a circle of Amsterdam bankers and investors which also included Italian bankers and private investors. For example, Laurence van der Hem (known to historians of cartography from the Van der Hem atlas in the Österreichische National Bibliothek) belonged to that circle. His name occurs in the correspondence of Cardinal Leopoldo, who was interested in buying books from the estate of Van der Hem.

One may also ask why there was such a close business relation between the printer Blaeu, living in the environment of the reformed church society of the Republic of the United Provinces of the Netherlands, and the Roman Catholic princes of the Italian states. Presumably, the religious conviction of Joan Blaeu and his sons was not of the extreme severity of the Calvinistic faith but rather a benign disposition toward the Roman Catholic church. As a printer of books for the church, the Blaeus were well known throughout Europe, as is demonstrated by Leti in his *Theatro Belgico* (Amsterdam, 1690).[31] Catechisms and breviaries were published under the imprint of a printer at Cologne in order not to give offense to the municipal or state officials in the Netherlands. Financial backing by the Duke of Savoy was in the interest of propagating the Roman Catholic religion as well, because Blaeu published and distributed many, many breviaries and catechisms, as previously noted. Finally, when we make an assessment of business relations in 1675, would not the higher clergy, who could pave the way or ease the connections, have collected provision money from the Blaeus? However, as is usual in matters of this kind, evidence of this is not disclosed by letters.

According to recently published letters from the Archivio di Stato at Torino, it appears that the making of the *Theatrum Sabaudiae* was a tedious operation. These letters have been used in the text, accompanying the facsimile edition of that book, published by the city of Torino in 1984.[32] On August 3, 1660, the municipality of Torino decided to cover the expenses involved with the incorporation of the plans and drawings of the city in Blaeu's townbooks of Italy. (See Figure 47.) This decision, forced by Grand Duke Carlo Emanuele II, marks the beginning of an operation which lasted over twenty years. It was not the delay caused by the fire in Blaeu's printing shop, but financial disputes and conflicts that were responsible for the slow progress. The financial settlement was not concluded between the State of Savoy and the Blaeu brothers before 1692. Further, one has to consider the troubled political situation in Europe at that time. ". . . Due to the wars at sea, paper is scarce and expensive . . . ," wrote Pieter Blaeu to Prince Cosimo de Medici in 1667. The reason that a delay in the financial settlement occurred was not a political one, but rather the presentation of an unreasonably high bill by the Blaeus.

The cost was almost too much for the small state of Savoy. However, the Grand Duke, based on a promise made to Joan Blaeu in 1660, had committed himself to pay for the drawings and the engraving of the plates. After the Grand Duke's death in 1675, every bill presented by the Blaeus had to be approved by the State's treasurer, which often gave rise to conflicts. Fortunately, Joan Blaeu II's confidant, the city of Torino's upper Justice Carcagni, decided these conflicts mostly in favor of the printer. Internal conflicts between the Grand Duke and the towns of Tuscany arose when the Duke ordered a town to have its topography surveyed and depicted, because the town itself had to bear the expenses of the

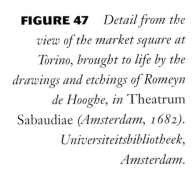

FIGURE 47 *Detail from the view of the market square at Torino, brought to life by the drawings and etchings of Romeyn de Hooghe, in* Theatrum Sabaudiae *(Amsterdam, 1682). Universiteitsbibliotheek, Amsterdam.*

survey and the drawing. Thanks to the documents in the Archivio di Stato, the names of the draftsmen who did the drawings are known. Some of them were military engineers, some were artists, for example: J. Th. Borgonius, Juvenalis Boetius, and so forth. However, we do not possess the names of all the engravers who worked for Blaeu at Amsterdam. A number of the seventy-one plates required etching and were signed by Johannes de Ram, Romeyn de Hooghe, Cornelis Decker, and Joannes de Broen. The documents in the Archivio di Stato also provide information on the date of the surveys and their costs, all very clear, unlike the record of the costs of the operations in Amsterdam, of which not a scrap has been preserved.

Finally, in a letter dated November 12, 1681, the Blaeu brothers wrote to Duke Vittorio Amadeo II that forty-five copies of "des Estats de Son Altesse Royale de Savoye" had been shipped. However, the date on the frontispiece reads 1682. This shipment was of particular interest. Some years before, the State of Savoy had placed another order in Amsterdam: the building of two warships. The Blaeus considered it most appropriate to ship the townbooks on the two new men of war, the "Saint Victor" and the "Saint Jean Baptiste." Apart from these forty-five uncolored copies, four illuminated copies and one black and white were expedited overland, via the Alps, to Torino. The bill presented by the Blaeus for the fifty copies amounted to 28,900 guilders!

In order to obtain an evaluation of this figure, one should consult the Blaeus's catalog of c. 1671, wherein the *Theatrum Italiae*, three volumes published in 1663, was priced at thirty-five guilders per volume; illuminated, seventy-five guilders per volume. It appears from the excessive amount of nearly thirty thousand guilders that the Blaeus billed the State of Savoy for the entire production of the book. For additional comparison, the warships built at Amsterdam cost seventy-five thousand guilders each.

Of course, the treasury made heavy objections about this large figure for a product produced over about twenty years time. Ambassadors, bankers, and lawyers intervened and at long last, in 1692, the final proposal for an agreement arrived in Torino. The Blaeus demanded payment for only fifty copies, shipment and taxes included, as well as the payment for extra work, commissioned long before by Grand Duke Carlo Emanuele II, altogether some 6,365 guilders, which seems to have settled the conflict.

What became of the Blaeus's townbooks of Italy and of the townbooks of Savoy and Piedmont after 1682? (See Figure 48.) In 1693, the Blaeu heirs printed an edition of the townbooks of Savoy and Piedmont with Dutch text, which was reissued by Adriaen Moetjens at The Hague in 1697.[33] Obviously, all the 287 copperplates used for the 1663 edition of the townbooks of Italy escaped destruction by the 1672 fire. The great and prosperous publisher Pieter Mortier printed a new edition from Blaeu's plates in 1704/1705 (A.N. Bl 84–Bl 94). On several plates Mortier made small corrections. He also added no less than 107 new plates; seventy-nine of them were assembled in a volume called "Lombardia," which also covered some of the towns of Tuscany. In the title Mortier states that the plates have been made "naar de tekeninge van Zaliger den Heer Joan Blaeu" (after the drawings of the late Mr. Joan Blaeu). Further investigation is necessary to determine if the originals from which the 107 new town-view plates were engraved were the extra ones Joan Blaeu II obtained from Italy but never published. Between 1724 and 1726, Rutger Christoffel Alberts at The Hague published a new edition with 281 plates (both the Blaeu and Mortier plates) as well as the townbooks of Savoy and Piedmont.[34]

FIGURE 48 *Scheme of the townbooks of Italy, published by the Blaeus.*

	Dutch text	French text	Latin text
		SCHEME OF THE TOWNBOOKS OF ITALY	
1663 J. Blaeu			1. Citta del Vaticano 2. Roma 3. Napoli & Sicilia
1682 J. Blaeu heirs			1. Piemonte 2. Savoye
1693 P. & J. Blaeu	1. Piemonte 2. Savoye		
1697 A. Moetjens	1. Piemonte 2. Savoye		
1700 A. Moetjens		1. Piemonte & Savoye I 2. Piemonte & Savoye II	
1704/05 P. Mortier	1. Lombardia 2. Citta del Vaticano 3. Napoli & Sicilia 4. Roma	1. Savoye & Piemonte 2. Citta del Vaticano 3. Napoli & Sicilia 4. Roma	1. Savoye & Piemonte 2. Citta del Vaticano 3. Napoli & Sicilia 4. Roma
1724 R. Chr. Alberts	1. Lombardia 2. Citta del Vaticano 3. Napoli & Sicilia 4. Roma	1. Lombardia 2. Citta del Vaticano 3. Napoli & Sicilia 4. Roma	1. Lombardia 2. Citta del Vaticano 3. Napoli & Sicilia 4. Roma
1725 R. Chr. Alberts	1. Piemonte & Savoye I 2. Piemonte & Savoye II	1. Piemonte & Savoye I 2. Piemonte & Savoye II	
1726 R. Chr. Alberts			1. Piemonte & Savoye I 2. Piemonte & Savoye II

Unlike Blaeu's geographical atlases, and also unlike the townbooks of the Netherlands, the townbooks of Italy were printed in small numbers only. In the Netherlands there are only ten copies known. The Library of Congress possesses some eight copies. Very seldom is a copy offered for sale and, when one is auctioned, it has fetched only a small price for a work with such a wealth of fine etchings and engravings.[35] Loose plates are very seldom seen, which indicates that the volumes that were sold were hardly ever touched.

COLLECTORS' ATLASES

The widespread mania for collecting coincided with the enormous output and diversity of map printing in the Netherlands. Private libraries of well-to-do citizens frequently contained collections of maps, views, and prints, assembled into volumes. These were different from the sixteenth- or early seventeenth-century *atlas factice* which was comparatively modest in composition. When map and print production increased greatly in the late seventeenth and the first half of the eighteenth century, collectors' atlases grew in proportion and frequently reached over a hundred volumes. Of the forty or so largest collections recorded in literature and in auction catalogs, only three or four have remained intact until today.

The development of map collecting in the Netherlands through the ages forms the subject of a thesis and cannot be recounted here.[36] However, the non plus ultra among collectors' atlases, the *Atlas van der Hem* or *Eugenius atlas*, originally assembled by the Amsterdam lawyer and millionaire Laurens van der Hem between 1640 and 1678, acquired by Prince Eugene of Savoy in 1730, and now one of the jewels of the Österreichische National Bibliothek in Vienna, must be mentioned. This atlas was based on Joan Blaeu's *Atlas Maior*, illuminated and heightened with gold by the greatest "enluminator" of the period, Dirck Jansz. van Santen. The collection, including additional printed maps, manuscript maps, and a great many ink and watercolor drawings, was bound in forty-six folio volumes. The most interesting and valuable volumes are those incorporating the manuscripts, charts, and drawings from the so-called "Secret Atlas" of the Dutch East India Company. Among the notable artists who supplied works for Van der Hem were Lambert Doorner, Jan Hackaert, Adriaan Matham, Roelandt Savery, Willem Schellinks, and Reinier Zeeman.[37] Two more private collectors' atlases which have been preserved are Goswinus Uilenbroeck *Grand Théâtre de l'Univers*, in forty-two volumes, sold in 1735 and now in the Biblioteca Nacional, Rio de Janeiro and C. Beudeker's *Atlas der 17 Nederlandsche Provincies*, consisting of twenty-seven volumes, sold in 1778, and now in the British Library.

Throughout the eighteenth century the atlases produced in the Netherlands, mainly in Amsterdam, were notable for their size and splendor. During the same period that the Visschers were diligently increasing the city's stock of new maps, another reformer, Frederik de Wit (1630–1706) entered the market. His original maps, though there were not more than about a hundred of them, were very

Generally speaking, the Dutch school, famous for the carefully planned atlas editions published between 1570 and about 1700, ended with an uncontrolled production of an enormous mass of maps, rather haphazardly distributed over large folio volumes some of which have luckily escaped the destruction of the wars of the twentieth century.

NOTES

1 C. Koeman, "The History of Abraham Ortelius and his *Theatrum Orbis Terrarum*," written to accompany the facsimile edition of the *Theatrum* (Amsterdam-Lausanne: Elsevier-Sequoia S. A., 1964).

2 J. H. Hessels, *Abrahami Ortelii et virorum eruditorum epistolae* (Cambridge, 1887), pp. 772–779, letter no. 330, dated July 25, 1603.

3 Ibid., pp. 210–213, letter no. 89.

4 J. Denucé, *Oud-Nederlandsche Kaartmakers in betrekking met Plantijn*, 2 vols. ('s Gravenhage-Antwerp, 1912–1913). A facsimile was also reprinted by Meridian Publishing Company, Amsterdam, 1964.

5 Leo Bagrow, *A. Ortellii Catalogus Cartographorum*, Petermann's Geographische Mitteilungen, Ergänzungsheft 199 and 210 (Gotha: Justus Perthes, 1928, 1930). This excellent work contains the biographies of all the cartographers mentioned by Ortelius in the first and subsequent editions of his *Theatrum*. In the first edition about ninety and in the 1603 edition some 183 names are given. For more recent publications that update these biographies, see Peter H. Meurer, *Fontes Cartographici Orteliani: Das "Theatrum Orbis Terrarum" von Abraham Ortelius und seine Kartenquellen* (Weinheim: VCH, Acta Humaniora, 1991), and Robert W. Karrow, Jr., *Mapmakers of the Sixteenth Century and their Maps: Bio-bibliographies of the Cartographers of Abraham Ortelius, 1570* (Chicago: Speculum Orbis Press for The Newberry Library, 1993).

6 Mireille Pastoureau, "Les atlas imprimés en France avant 1700," *Imago Mundi* 32 (1980): 45–72.

7 Mary Sponberg Pedley, "The Map Trade in Paris, 1650–1825," *Imago Mundi* 33 (1981): 33–45.

8 R. A. Skelton, "Bibliographical Note," to the facsimile edition of the English edition of the *Theatrum* (Amsterdam: Theatrum Orbis Terrarum, 1968).

9 Ibid. No surviving copies are known on the European continent. Locations: British Library (2 copies), National Maritime Museum Greenwich, Bodleian Library, John Carter Brown Library, Newberry Library, and the W. L. Clements Library.

10 W. Bonacker, "Introduction," to the facsimile edition of Matthias Quad's *Geographische Handtbuch* (Cologne, 1600; reprinted, Amsterdam: Theatrum Orbis Terrarum, 1969).

11 In 1962, 450 years after Mercator's birth, many excellent publications appeared on the occasion of various celebrations. Outstanding among many other good articles is the compilation of expert treatises published in volume 6 (1992) of the *Duisburger Forschungen*, edited by Günter von Roden. Primary sources for Mercator's private life are Walther Ghim's *Vita Mercatoris*, which was translated by Hans-Heinrich Geske into German and published in *Duisburger Forschungen* 6 (1962): 244–276. See also A. S. Osley, *Mercator*, which is a monograph on the lettering of maps, and so on, in sixteenth-century Netherlands with a facsimile and translation of his treatise on the italic hand and a translation of Ghim's *Vita Mercatoris* (London: Faber and Faber, 1969).

12 C. Koeman, *Atlantes Neerlandici. Bibliography of Terrestrial, Maritime and Celestial Atlases and Pilot Books, Published in the Netherlands up to 1880*, 5 vols. (Amsterdam: Theatrum Orbis Terrarum, 1967–1971). Volume VI (Alphen aan den Rijn: Canaletto, 1985).

13 J. Keuning and Marijke Donkersloot-De Vrij, *Willem Jansz. Blaeu: A Biography and History of his Work as a Cartographer and Publisher* (Amsterdam: Theatrum Orbis Terrarum, 1973), and C. Koeman, *Joan Blaeu and his Grand Atlas*, which is a monograph written to accompany the facsimile edition of the *Grand Atlas* (1673) (Amsterdam: Theatrum Orbis Terrarum, 1970).

14 Only five copies are known: Universiteitsbibliotheek, Amsterdam; Library of the Groot Seminarie Liesbosch-Princenhage, Breda; Museum Plantin-Moretus, Antwerp; The British Library; Fürstliche Wallenstein Oetingen Bibliothek, Harburg. The maps are without text on the back, unlike the subsequent edition of 1613, *Appendix Theatri A. Ortellii et Atlantis G. Mercatoris* with ninety-eight maps.

15 M. M. Kleerkooper and W. P. van Stockum, Jr., *De boekhandel te Amsterdam, voornamelijk in de 17e eeuw* (Den Haag, 1914–1916). A source book of original documents (notary contracts, etc.) pertaining to the book trade. For the Hondius-Janssonius contract, see pp. 1490–1491.

16 Only four copies are known: Bibliothèque St. Géneviève, Paris; Municipal Library, Geneva; University Library, Erlangen; and one in private possession, England.

17 J. Keuning, "The History of an Atlas," *Imago Mundi* 4 (1947): 37–62, and J. Keuning, "Jodocus Hondius Jr.," *Imago Mundi* 5 (1948): 63–71.

18 R. A. Skelton, *Country Atlases of the British Isles, 1579–1703* (London: Carta Press, 1970).

19 R. A. Skelton, "Bibliographical Note," to the facsimile of the English edition of the *Mercator-Hondius Atlas of 1636* (Amsterdam: Theatrum Orbis Terrarum, 1968). Copies of the 1636 English edition can be found *inter alia* in the British Library, the Bodleian Library, the Library of Congress, and the Maritime Museum, Amsterdam. A second edition was published in 1641; the only copy known is in the John Carter Brown Library.

20 Copies of the 1653 edition are found in the Servicio Geografico de Ejercito, Madrid; Biblioteca Nacional, Madrid; and the Library of Congress. A copy of the 1666 edition is in the Maritime Museum, Rotterdam.

21 Maria Simon, *Claes Jansz. Visscher*, Inaugural-Dissertation. (Freiburg im. Breisgau: Albert-Ludwig Universität, 1958).

22 C. Koeman, *Joan Blaeu* . . . , p. 41.

23 Walter W. Ristow, "Dutch Polder Maps," *The Quarterly Journal of the Library of Congress* 31 (1974): 136–149.

24 Egon Klemp, *Dokumentation zur Atlas des grossen Kurfürsten* (Leipzig: Edition Leipzig, 1971).

25 R. A. Skelton, "Introduction," to the *Civitates Orbis Terrarum*, vol. 3 (Amsterdam: Theatrum Orbis Terrarum, 1966).

26 Henk Th. van Veen, "Pieter Blaeu and Antonio Magliabechi," *Quaerendo* 12 (1982): 130–158. Quote: p. 133.

27 Ibid.

28 Ibid., p. 142.

29 Ibid.

30 Ibid., p. 157.

31 C. Koeman, *Joan Blaeu and his Grand Atlas* (Amsterdam, 1970), p. 107.

32 Citta di Torino, *Theatrum Sabaudiae* (*Theatro degli stati del Duca di Savoia*), a cura di Luigi Firpo con la collaborazione di Giuseppe Bocchino, Ada Peyrot, Isabella Ricci e Rossanna Roccia, vol. 1 (Torino, 1984), with seventy-one facsimiles in color.

33 E. F. Kossman, *De boekhandel te 's Gravenhage tot het eind van de 18e eeuw* ('s Gravenhage: M. Nijhoff, 1937), p. 273.

34 Ibid., p. 5.

35 Auction at Sotheby, vol. 8 (London, 1968), 1724–1725, £3000. id. 1975, 4 volumes, 1724, £4800. The most beautiful copy in the Netherlands is in the Museum Meermanno-Westreenianum at The Hague, affiliated with the Royal Library. This copy, which Albertus Magnus bought from the Blaeus, was illuminated by the greatest of all Dutch illuminators, Dirck Jansz. van Santen. In the eighteenth century, Professor Hadrianus Relandus of Utrecht acquired the set, and at an auction in 1761 the work was bought by Mr. Gerard Meerman, the founder of the Museum Meermanno-Westreenianum. It is one of six illuminated copies known in the world.

36 C. Koeman, *Collections of Maps and Atlases in the Netherlands. Their History and Present State* (Leiden, 1961).

37 Karl Ausserer, "Der 'Atlas Blaeu der Wiener National-Bibliothek'," *Beiträge zur historischen Geographie, Kulturgeographie, Ethnographie und Kartographie* . . . , ed. Hans Mzik (Leipzig and Wien: Franz Deuticke, 1929), pp. 1–40.

38 C. Koeman, "Krijgsgeschiedkundige Kaarten," *Armamentaria* 8 (1973).

39 Examples can be examined in the Universiteitsbibliotheek Amsterdam and in the Teylers Museum, Haarlem.

40 Philip Lee Phillips, *A List of Geographical Atlases in the Library of Congress*, vol. 2 (Washington: Government Printing Office, 1914), p. 288 (entry 3485). Other copies outside The Netherlands are preserved at the Bibliothèque Nationale, Paris; The British Library, London; Koninklijke Bibliotheek, Brussels; Österreichische Nationalbibliothek, Vienna; Newberry Library, Chicago; Yale University, New Haven; Lilly Library, Bloomington; and Biblioteca Nacional, Mexico City.

French School Atlases: Sixteenth to Eighteenth Centuries*

MIREILLE PASTOUREAU

While geography was considered the science of princes for several centuries,[1] the discipline has experienced continuous popularization, putting it within the reach not only of many amateurs, but also of more young students. Today the role of atlases in geographic instruction is no longer contested, and from the age of seven, twentieth-century children learn to recognize cartographic images.

In France, this was the result of a long evolution. By focusing on school atlas production during the sixteenth to eighteenth centuries, the first three centuries of this evolution are addressed in this study. The present remarks are based on a recent catalog devoted to French atlases of the sixteenth and seventeenth centuries,[2] which will be followed by a second volume (for the eighteenth century), currently in preparation. This catalog inventories and describes in detail all the atlases printed in France; it presents information on geographers and their publishers, printing techniques, and commercial relations practiced in French geographic circles.

Moreover, the intellectual climate in which these atlases were prepared, the different pedagogical methods utilized, and the place given children's education in the France of the Ancien Régime have been studied. (See Figure 49.) Since the history of education is currently the subject of active research by French historians, several recent works were useful in this study.[3] Above all, this article is dedicated to the much missed Father François de Dainville, who was fascinated by the

---

* This essay was translated from the French by Deanna Hammond, Congressional Research Services Language Service, Library of Congress. Although direct quotations have also been translated into English, they are still set off with quotation marks to signify the author's intentions of using a direct quotation.

FIGURE 49 *A. Bosse, "Le Maistre d'escole," c. 1635. Bibliothèque Nationale de France.*

history of both cartography and education, and who left us an in-depth study of the role of the Jesuits in the advancement of geography.[4]

In the history of school atlases, two periods can be distinguished. The first extends to the end of the reign of Louis XIV (1715), when one sees the birth of atlases designed especially for instruction. At the end of this first phase (i.e., the beginning of the eighteenth century), one sees traditional methods being questioned; they were judged ineffective and new educational approaches were set forth, multiplying in the eighteenth century, and culminating with the Revolution (1789–1799). The second period focuses on the rivalry between the old atlases and those of a new type, as well as on the diversification of atlas contents which acquired the composition still in use today.

SIXTEENTH AND SEVENTEENTH CENTURIES: THE BIRTH OF SCHOOL ATLASES

1570–1640: The Absence of French School Atlases

Definition of School Atlas Any atlas could be termed "school," to the extent that it makes information visible and presents maps too large to be consulted easily in miniaturized form, utilizing a format that is easy to handle. However, here the term "school atlases" will be used only for inexpensive works, of moderate dimensions, conceived to inculcate the cartographic knowledge considered essential. The preparation of these atlases thus involves a value judgment on the content of education (what does one need to know as a matter of priority?) and on its form (what is the most favorable presentation for memorization?).

Taking into account these criteria, it is evident that the first French atlases were not pedagogical instruments and that they were developed outside of educational environments. Maurice Bouguereau's *Le Théâtre Françoys* (1594) imitated Ortelius and Mercator, but the focus was primarily political and commercial. (See Figure 50.) In fact, Bouguereau was a printer and not a professor or scholar. For him it was a matter of showing the king and the court, taking refuge in his

FIGURE 50 *Frontispiece from Maurice Bouguereau,* Le Théâtre Françoys *(Tours, 1594). Library of Congress.*

city of Tours, the image of provinces joined together at the end of a civil war that had torn the country apart. The new maps that he incorporated into his atlases were not the work of scholars, rather that of an archeologist, a jurist, and a road planner.

French Editions of Flemish and Dutch School Atlases   If Bouguereau's enterprise was unknown in academic circles, it was perhaps because the first Flemish and Dutch school atlases were already available in France in both Latin and French editions. The *Epitome*, which Philippe Galle produced from Ortelius's *Theatrum Orbis Terrarum*, was translated into French in 1579 under the title, *Miroir du Monde*. It enjoyed considerable commercial success.[5] Its subtitle indicated that it was "appropriate for the education of all clever students." Without a doubt, this was the first cartographic manual for French students.

Shortly afterward, a second work, the *Atlas Minor* of Mercator-Hondius (first French edition, 1609) became available.[6] Its introduction was even more explicit about its intended use:

> *. . . since large books cannot be moved easily from place to place, and parents often being poor, not having their purses well-lined, we have reduced the aforesaid Atlas of Mercator into a small volume, so that in this way we can obviate such drawbacks and together benefit studious young people and avoid any cause for complaint.*[7]

Origins of French Engraved Cartography Outside the University   The delay in map publishing in France has been stressed many times. It was due to technical, economic, and political reasons, but also to the separation of learned circles from those of printing. At the end of the sixteenth century, there was no longer in existence the equivalent of an Oronce Finé, the learned mathematics professor whose maps with elaborate projections had been printed on many occasions.

Finé was in fact an exception. French engraved cartography was originally developed outside the circle of intellectuals and in particular outside of the University. The University teachers in Paris distrusted images and did not want to speak and read except in Latin. Their power over Parisian publishing prevented innovation and experimentation.

It was, therefore, not by chance that the first copperplate engraving prints made in France were produced in 1488 in Lyon and not in Paris. These were seven views of Mediterranean ports illustrating the Bernhard von Breidenbach's journey to the Holy Land; the rest, moreover, were contributed by engravers from Germany. Lyon, a rich commercial town, was located at the crossroads of Germanic and Italian influences. The merchants living there were a choice clientele for illustrated books in the vernacular language. They particularly loved travel accounts and geographic literature, especially if they were substantial accounts. Consequently, "atlases" were published in Lyon before literature; they were rich in views of cities, such as those found in the *Epitome . . . d'Europe* by Guillaume Guéroult (1552–1553) and the *Plantz, pourtraitz . . . de plusieurs villes* by Antoine Du Pinet (1564). (See Figure 51.)

FIGURE 51 *Title page from Antoine Du Pinet,* Plantz, pourtraitz et descriptions . . . *(Lyon, 1564). Library of Congress.*

Sebastian Munster's *Cosmographia*, a European best-seller, was the inspiration for these works. It also underwent a French adaptation in 1575, considerably enriched with maps of French cities. This edition appeared in Paris, taking over from Lyon, which was in decline at the end of the century. However, the spirit of geographic publications did not change; they were more documentary than learned, contributing more information than knowledge.

Bougereau followed the same line; he wanted his *Théâtre Françoys* (1594) to serve tax agents, the military, and merchants. His successors, Jean Leclerc, Jean Boisseau, the Bereys, and Melchior Tavernier, who published the series *Théâtres de France*, did not foster ties with educational circles. The only one to publish some maps of historical geography was Tavernier. In particular, he became the French publisher of Petrus Bertius's *Geographia Vetus* in 1628 to 1630. This small atlas was assembled from imported Flemish maps.

An example of Tavernier's lack of interest in historical cartography can be found in his association with Nicolas Sanson. In fact, the latter began to show an interest in historical cartography when he published a map of ancient Gaul in 1627. Tavernier proposed that Sanson join him, but he resolutely directed him toward current cartography (roads of France in 1632, rivers in 1634, etc.). Sanson was, therefore, compelled to repress his interest in the study of antiquity. In order to reprint educational works, he became his own printer.

First French Atlases Used by Students It is actually in another direction that one must search for the maps used by French students at the beginning of the seventeenth century. What do we find, for example, in a printed geography course for college students?[8] Regional maps of France were taken from the small atlases of Christophe Tassin. However, Tassin had nothing to do with education. He was a military engineer, who for three years between 1633 and 1635 published maps and atlases. He printed atlases in a small format, which were very popular: *Cartes générales . . . de France et d'Espagne* (1633), *Cartes générales . . . d'Allemagne* (1633), *Plans et profils des villes de France* (1634), and *Description du pays des Suisses* (1635). (See Figure 52.) However, Tassin's work, based on compilation, did not satisfy the partisans of geography as well as of science. Consequently, true school atlases were produced shortly thereafter within the educational establishment itself.

1640–1680: The First School Atlases

French Education in the Mid-Seventeenth Century The primary characteristic of education in France in the middle of the seventeenth century was the diversification of its structures. Establishments of religious orders, particularly those of the Jesuits and Oratorians, competed with the University. The emphasis on mass education should not allow one to overlook the private lessons given by tutors, or especially for geography, the numerous courses offered by engineers

FIGURE 52 *Divisional title leaf for map section of Christophe Tassin's* Cartes generales des provinces de France et d'Espagne *(Paris, 1633). Library of Congress.*

and geographers. It is known, for example, that in 1655 Nicolas Sanson gave public lectures in Paris on Wednesdays from four to five o'clock.[9]

Although the "college" was the predominant establishment of "higher" learning, several types existed. Some were within the University (in Paris, for example, the School of Arts had ten),[10] and others were run by religious orders. In this area, the Jesuits attracted a large number of students, and in 1710, their Parisian college Louis-le-Grand had 3,000 students, or about as many as the thirty-six colleges of the Latin Quarter.[11]

To this structural diversity was added the diversity of the students' ages. College studies in general took place between the ages of ten and seventeen years, but sometimes students would enter at the age of seven, while others were still there at the age of twenty-four. The precocity of some students was particularly remarkable since the child, in the seventeenth century, was pushed into the adult world with a minimum of transition. Father de Dainville determined that a difference of ten to fifteen years could exist between the youngest and oldest students in the class.[12] Under these conditions, it became extremely difficult to put a planned pedagogy into operation. It was even more difficult since the numbers of students in the classes were excessive, somewhere between 60 and 100 students per class.

The heterogeneity of the college population was masked by the organization of daily life and the prevailing, rather strict discipline most often applied to the live-in students. If one adds the fact that the majority of the class hours were dedicated to the study of the Latin language and Latin writers, that all courses were given in Latin, and that the students were forced to speak Latin continually, even among themselves, then it is evident that the schoolboy's youth was spent totally apart from the rest of society.

115

The teaching of geography, as it was carried out by the Jesuits, has been studied in depth by Father de Dainville.[13] Without a doubt, because he was a member of the Society, he probably did not emphasize enough the strong, negative reactions that these methods provoked. This reaction continued to grow, culminating in 1764 with the expulsion of the Jesuits from France and the confiscation of their schools.

The Jesuits and Geography   Father de Dainville has shown that until about 1660, geographic science experienced rapid development; he called it "the blossoming of humanism in geography." The Jesuits were convinced of the need for world knowledge in order to fulfill their mission of evangelization. In addition, they knew that the government, with which they wanted to be allied, had need of both good maps and citizens who knew the geography of the country.

Consequently, the Jesuit fathers achieved a leading place in this science, which was otherwise in its infancy. From the first third of the seventeenth century, they taught it through courses dictated to the students. With the lack of an adequate atlas, students stuck small maps of diverse origins in their copybooks. Father de Dainville also observed that the colleges obtained spheres, globes, and maps, but this material, of course, was not sufficient.

A Jesuit father himself, Philippe Briet, composed an atlas more adapted to this kind of instruction. The *Parallela geographiae veteris et novae* appeared in 1648 to 1649, in the form of a long treatise in Latin, illustrated with 144 maps. (See Figure 53.) The maps then appeared again in 1653, in the form of two atlases, one of modern geography, the *Théâtre géographique de l'Europe*, and the other of ancient geography, the *Theatrum geographicum Europae veteris*. The volumes planned for Asia and Africa were never published.

The *Parallela* reflected well mid-seventeenth century geography instruction: the modern maps were barely more numerous than the maps of ancient geography (seventy-nine compared to fifty-seven). Also, the coexistence of the most archaic information (taken from Ptolemy, for example) and the most modern methods (such as blank grids graduated in latitudes and longitudes so that the students could practice drawing the map of France) is evident. In addition, the *Parallela* is the atlas for which the largest number of copies were found in the course of this study.

The Atlases of Sanson and Duval   The other mid-seventeenth century school atlases were based on principles identical to those of Briet: the importance of maps depicting ancient history, and maps supporting nomenclature. Since this nomenclature was proposed in abundance, the need to order it through tables or "methods" was recognized.

Nicolas Sanson (1600–1677) was the creator in France of these "geographic tables" that categorized the types of names appearing on the maps, classifying them from the largest to the smallest. These tables were either mixed in with the

FIGURE 53 *Frontispiece from Philippe Briet,* Parallela geographiae *(Paris, 1648). Bibliothèque Nationale de France.*

maps in the atlases or they constituted separate collections.[14] Since their success was considerable, they were often copied and imitated.

It must be recognized that Sanson was a teacher and that his work was extremely didactic. However, he always addressed an adult audience, often of a high level, especially when he gave geography courses to King Louis XIII and to the princes of royal blood. His cartography was intended to be very erudite and because of that, it often led to confusion.

Nevertheless, his influence was considerable in France, since he was the first French cartographer to offer a complete series of maps of France and the world. The apparent coherence of his work was kept by maintaining consistent construction, format, and scale. His vision of the world was reassuring, since all the territories were carefully divided by diagrammatic borders, giving the impression of spaces perfectly controlled intellectually. His successor and disciple, Didier

Robert de Vaugondy, wrote in 1755: "With this method, one needs no more than eyes and maps."[15] (See Figure 54.)

With Pierre Duval (1619–1683), French cartography again left academic circles and became less expensive. He was the first in France to publish geography books and pocket atlases that were within the reach of students with little money. Didier Robert de Vaugondy wrote, "The popularity of geography, which was introduced in the colleges, led him to make maps *in douze* and *in quarto* for the intelligence of the classical authors, and he reached so far that no school boy was well received by his teacher if he was not supplied with his Duval."[16]

FIGURE 54 *Title page from Didier Robert de Vaugondy,* Nouvel atlas portatif *(6th ed., Paris, 1795). Bibliothèque Nationale de France.*

FIGURE 55 *Title page from Pierre Duval,* La Géographie universelle *(Paris, 1682). Bibliothèque Nationale de France.*

The Duval atlases were much less oriented toward antiquity than those of Briet and Sanson. They offered resumes of modern maps of France (*La Géographie française en plusieurs cartes*, 1659); Europe (*L'Europe et ses descriptions*, 1686), and of the world (*La Géographie universelle en plusieurs cartes*, 1661). (See Figure 55.) While Duval included ancient geography, he no longer expressed himself entirely in Latin. On the contrary, he incorporated his historic atlas into a more general work dedicated to contemporary travels and chronology.[17]

Like Duval, other authors tried to get out of the elitist circle of the traditional teaching of geography. Their works illustrated a new type of education, more practical and aimed at a professional or working life, described as follows.

1680–1710: More Concrete Instruction

College instruction did not answer the needs of all school clientele. The predominance of classical studies prepared students only for the legal or ecclesiastical professions. Consequently, the need for different training was felt. A specific method of teaching geography was created for them, which gave birth to new types of atlases.

The "Academies" The "academies," which appeared in the first third of the seventeenth century, offered a half-academic, half-military education. Young nobles would attend and prepare themselves for the profession of arms. Sometimes after a stay at a college, this training was called, "doing one's drills."[18] Weaponry, dancing, mathematics, fortifications, and notions of geography were taught. Future officers also needed to know fencing, horseback riding, and the art of drawing plans. Therefore, this mixture of theory and practice required new types of school manuals.

Among the "academies," those of the king were very much in demand, in particular the two schools for pages, the Grande and the Petite Ecurie. A mathematics teacher at the Petite Ecurie, Allain Manneson-Mallet, compiled three atlases for this type of instruction. The first, *Les Travaux de Mars* (1671), was also a complete course in fortification. The second, the *Description de l'Univers* (1683), was a general geography manual, enriched with close to 700 plates. The third, the *Géométrie pratique* (1702), was more technical and oriented toward map preparation, land measuring, and surveying. (See Figure 56.)

Nicolas de Fer's atlas, the *Forces de l'Europe*, composed of maps of the main fortified cities of Europe, was also originally designed to be a pedagogical work.

FIGURE 56 *Surveying diagram showing use of "demi-cercle" in Allain Manesson-Mallet,* La Géométrie pratique *(Paris, 1702). Bibliothèque Nationale de France.*

Its first installment appeared in 1690 under the title of *Introduction à la Fortification*, and was announced as follows in the *Journal des Sçavans*: "Nothing could be more useful than this small work, to give young people engaged in the arms profession a first acquaintance with the knowledge necessary to defend and attack places."[19] This characteristic, however, disappeared with the subsequent installments. De Fer also prepared a school atlas of general geography, the *Petit et Nouveau Atlas* (1697). (See Figure 57.) In nineteen maps, he offered students a convenient summary.[20]

Schools of Hydrography[21]   The teaching of hydrography in France underwent an important expansion from 1670 to 1680. After the beginning of the century, the Jesuits had taken the initiative in teaching it in their colleges, but an additional momentum was given when, in 1669, some of these schools acquired royal chairs, which in turn attracted students outside of the establishment. Hydrography was also taught in the public schools, where the structure and programs were officially organized in 1681 and 1689. They dealt with mathematics, navigation, and the use of nautical instruments. Three naval-guard schools were also created in 1682, with instruction at the same time general, military, and scientific.

The publication of hydrographic atlases was very modest in France, and for a long time pilots were trained with the assistance of Dutch rutters.[22] The nautical atlases published in France before the great *Le Neptune François* (1693) were only

FIGURE 57 *Title page from Nicolas de Fer, Petit et nouveau atlas (Paris, 1697). Library of Congress.*

was considered easy. P. Bernard Lamy noted, "Geography is an easy science and one of which children are capable, because one only needs eyes and a little memory."[25] This expression is found again and again in Nicolas Lenglet Dufresnoy, Didier Robert de Vaugondy, and numerous other authors.

The importance of the memory was often emphasized. Lenglet Dufresnoy wrote, "Young people ordinarily have more memory than judgement; it is thus necessary to use the one to train the other."[26] He bragged to the rest about inculcating the principles of geography in less than two months to anyone and even to the young girls in the convents! Every lesson was conceived by Lenglet Dufresnoy to be learned "by the least certain memory" in about half an hour.

For the teachers, maps and atlases were above all to be memory aids. They were presented as often as possible in the child's presence.

All the art of a schoolmaster should consist of imitating and following nature. He will present to his students a world map until they know the different parts and their respective location perfectly; from time to time he will put it under their eyes, and he will use it for all the other maps. . . . This is not a study here that demands an understanding of foreign terms, or that is founded on abstract ideas. One talks to the senses and therefore the most limited child can make as much progress in it as another who has more intelligence and an open mind.[27]

In the same respect, Abbé Grenet wrote: "Geography is mainly the science of the eyes; it is thus only by looking at a map often that they will be able to learn it."[28]

Poor Results The learning of geography, as it was presented, was full of contradictions; elitist and ambitious in its program, it was, however, proposed for very young and not even very bright children. It is not surprising, therefore, that the results were presented as catastrophic. Didier Robert de Vaugondy wrote, "The students are discouraged and do not know anything, the teachers regret the efforts they have made, and the parents are upset because of what it has cost them."[29] Abbé Boutillier pointed out "so many poor subjects that lag behind languidly in their study program and who leave our hands with such little knowledge and knowledge so imperfect."[30] Lenglet Dufresnoy also pointed out the crude errors made in society: "What can one think of a man or woman, educated moreover, when one hears them ask if Brittany is not in fact the straightest route to get to Poland?"[31]

Several authors attributed this pedagogical failure to the small number of maps and atlases in the hands of students during the courses. In fact, it seemed that the circulation of these documents was a cause of agitation in the classes. Brion wrote, "The utility of geography is in general recognized; everyone agrees that it should be a part of public education; for that it would be necessary to have maps that a large number of school children could see and follow comfortably. Experience has shown that this study caused a lot of unruliness among young people and that they gained nothing from it."[32]

New Methods

So that students would assimilate knowledge better by consulting more maps, new methods were devised. These innovations included introducing wall maps instead of atlas maps, creating atlases especially for children, and developing new memorization techniques.

Atlas or Wall Maps   All teachers seemed convinced of the need to show maps to their students. But how and in what form? A debate took place between advocates of atlases and advocates of wall maps. It occurred at an already late date (1775), but it amply illustrates the difficulties encountered by eighteenth-century teachers in the area of cartography.

The "promoter" of school wall maps was Abbé Boutillier, who wrote,

Small maps, of which geography treatises are full, those even of one page, which are used together, will never be able to make a great impression on the minds of children. The names with which they are filled, the rivers by which they are cut, the forests and mountains with which they are covered, often tire the eyesight of a young viewer and he does not remember absolutely anything.

But give him maps six feet in size, with well-spaced out objects, easily distinguished, and printed in large characters that stand out at first glance, and this sight will attract his attention, expand his imagination, brighten up his spirit, and impress on his memory a map in brief of our globe that will never be erased.

I do not blame ordinary maps . . . but I say that large maps, such as I just represented them, would help beginners considerably, they would give new charms to this study already so entertaining, and they are absolutely necessary for the instruction of young people, to whom one wishes to teach this science in the colleges and in all educational establishments.

In fact, in order to reach this goal, without detriment to the study of Literature, which is our principal goal, we need maps where the objects are presented in such a way that 100 school boys can see them without moving, or upsetting in the least the discipline and good order which should reign in a class.[33]

This plan was approved by the University tribunal, which in this respect emphasized the faults of atlases:

Ordinary maps are too small to be able to be distinguished from all parts of the class. They are too large, too awkward, and too costly, to require that every school boy carry a small atlas for his personal use.

Those who feared that this novelty (wall maps) would cause distractions for the school boys in their other studies will agree that this danger applies only to the first days.

With respect to the difficulty of placing maps of this size in classes that are sometimes very small, it is true that it will be necessary to stack them one on another; but with a little industry, one can imagine different means of showing the one needed on each occasion without obstacles.

It would be unfortunate if the price of maps announced at twelve pounds each, without canvas and mounting, stopped those who should acquire them.[34]

This wall map plan seemed unrealistic to many. It was probably premature and not adaptable. Classes were too large, and the poor eyesight of schoolboys, which was not corrected by glasses, caused further problems. Abbé Grenet became the defender of the atlas method; large maps, he said,

are almost entirely useless. In fact, however large they may be, it is impossible for one to distinguish the objects from one end of the class to the other; therefore, it is necessary for school boys to leave their places and gather around the map which cannot be done without disorder and trouble. Even supposing that good order would not suffer from this movement, how could one want, in a class of 60, 80, 100 school boys, everyone to be able to see the locations of cities that the teacher pointed out? It is only the first rows that see anything, and then in a rather confusing manner; as for the rest, they do not see anything.

In addition, in all classes there are some young people who have poor eyesight: so, I ask, of what use are large maps to them? It is evident that if they do not have other assistance, they will never learn geography.[35]

Abbé Grenet emphasized that wall maps were visible only in the classroom and that schoolboys should have maps they could consult at home and in their study rooms. "It is necessary to put maps into their hands: that is the only way to succeed."

With this same concern of putting the student into contact with the map, Lenglet Dufresnoy in 1740 became enthused over the "mechanism" of M. du Mondran, which also would have been able to replace atlases if it had been successful: "It is a type of small cabinet, or like a screen to put before the fire, about five feet tall and three feet wide. In the inside, which is nine to ten inches, one puts rolls of maps; and even in the number one wants, by the means of these rolls, which can be placed there and removed at will." The inventor received a royal privilege for the construction of his apparatus which "would make it unnecessary to open a large number of volumes successively, the mere movement of the crank being enough to make the necessary map appear."[36]

Progressive Atlases Adapted to Children   The defenders of atlases were thus the majority. Some also favored a great innovation, which consisted of creating atlases especially for children and even better, adapting them to each age of childhood.

In the _Enfant géographe_ (1769), publisher Jacques Nicolas Bellin proposed six extremely simplified maps aimed at beginners. He wrote, "only the main divisions, large rivers, and capital cities of each province have been marked. The names are written there without confusion." He expressed the concern that "knowledge increase and develop by degrees."

This concern is also found with Abbé Grenet, who conceived an atlas in volumes:

In the Sixth form, it would contain only the world map, the general maps of Europe and Asia, and the map of France, which it is appropriate to get to know early on. Africa and America will be for another class. Guards will be fixed there on the maps that will be needed every year. In the Fifth form, the children being a little more educated, one will go further, in proportion to the knowledge that they will already have. It will be pointed out to them that such and such a country, which at another time had such and such a name, today bears another; that the Peloponnese, for example, is now called Morea, and so for the rest.

The teacher, by indicating at the beginning of the year the books that he will explain, will at the same time indicate the maps that he judges appropriate to have them see: those of Greece, Italy, Africa, or some other area relative to the author that he will have explained.

The same thing shall be observed in Fourth, Third, Second, and Rhetoric forms, where the atlas shall be complete.

It will be good if each teacher not require more than four maps, or less than three, so that the expense will be modest, and more or less equal in each class: it will not exceed the price of ordinary classical books.[37]

The presentation of atlas maps was also adapted to the school public. Difficult terms and foreign words were explained in inset maps. In the margins, text and tables helped in understanding the map.[38]

Consequently, atlases that could be used without the aid of a teacher, that is, by the student alone, or with his parents, began to be created. Edme Mentelle encouraged fathers "and even mothers" to apply his method to their children. He noted, however, that "the presence of a stranger is sometimes more favorable for the young person." Louis Charles Desnos went further, writing on the *Atlas général:* "Experience has shown that with this atlas, fathers and mothers, and the least educated teachers could teach the different sciences that are the object of it; that even the assistance of a teacher was not necessary."

For Active Memorization Several methods were suggested to assist children in remembering the content of maps, some classical, others more original. A particular effort was made to involve the student physically in studies too austere and intellectual for such young minds.

Children were encouraged to play an active role in their learning by filling in blank maps themselves. Bellin, in the *Enfant géographe*, matched all his maps with a blank one. Brion, in turn, stated: "It is well understood that children will not produce a final copy of a map. Geography teachers are not design teachers. But nothing prevents them from proposing some locations and from ensuring that they are classified as necessary in the head of their students. It is a new object of emulation, which it seems should not be neglected."[39]

Edme Mentelle, the great geography teacher of the eighteenth century, was also in favor of blank maps: "I consider it an important exercise to drill children who are beginning to recognize the large divisions and positions of cities on small blank maps, without names and without coloring. When they are familiar with them, they can even be granted, as an award, the pleasure of writing these names on their small map themselves, and then coloring it in."[40]

The imagination of teachers often took them quite far. So that students would become more interested in maps, some proposed introducing them to a place with dimensions that could physically be entered.

The first to express this proposal was Baron de Bouis in 1737.[41] His idea was to make the child's house or the garden that he frequented into an immense geographic map. The cardinal points would be marked there and each room would become a part of the earth, of a continent, or of a country. Strips on the ground would note the river, and stumps of wood would symbolize the cities.

In the same way, Abbé Teisserenc, in 1754, imagined changing all the nomenclature of the map of Paris, and giving the streets of the capital the names of towns and regions of France, keeping their respective locations. So, thought the Abbé, "the inhabitant of Paris, without leaving it and without the assistance of any schoolmaster, will learn the location and name of the provinces, different countries, and cities of the kingdom, as if he were actually traveling whenever he attends to his affairs in the city." The city of Paris would itself become a "public school, perpetual, and free."[42]

A similar scheme arose again during the Revolution with a more political orientation, when they imagined creating patriotic gardens in 1789.[43] The gardens would be divided into sections, each representing one of the newly created departments of the young Republic. In each square, the products of the respective department would be grown. They would also bear signs describing memorable events and particularities of the department.

Numerous geographic games were also produced in the seventeenth and eighteenth centuries. Card games, snakes and ladders, puzzles, and so forth, had the goal of "making study pleasurable." They certainly seemed less forbidding than the traditional atlases, but this is not the purpose of this essay.

Toward a Common School Atlas

The end of the eighteenth century was particularly important for school questions for two major reasons. First, the expulsion of the Jesuits from France between 1762 and 1764 required a replacement, both in terms of personnel and methods. Second, from 1789 onward, the Revolution undertook to place teaching in the service of new ideas. These reform movements had a point in common: the concern over standardizing instruction and offering the same schools and books to everyone.

Educational Plans after the Expulsion of the Jesuits Between 1762 and 1764, the Jesuits were forced to abandon the 106 colleges that they managed—from a quarter to a third of the "secondary" establishments of the kingdom. In reaction against the teaching of the fathers, accused of preparing students only for ecclesiastical careers, a plan to reform education was drawn up by several parliamentarians.[44] In reading these plans, it can be seen that the authors were, unfortunately, not familiar with geographical atlases. Neither Caradeuc de la Chalotais nor Guyton de Morveau, whose plans would, however, become classic, suggested any more than that atlases could improve the teaching of geography.

La Chalotais recommended beginning geography studies at the age of five. Rejecting previous methods, he criticized Lenglet Dufresnoy, whom he found "dry and boring" and he advised instead educating children with the assistance of travel stories. It was evident to him that a geographical map was consulted, but was no longer learned by heart. Maps were thus used to create a favorable environment for studies and were not an object of study by themselves. He wrote, "It would be desirable for children to become familiar early with globes, maps, spheres, thermometers, barometers. . . ."[45]

Guyton de Morveau, in advocating the need to teach the sciences, continued to subordinate geography to history. The history course, according to him, should begin with a synopsis of geography, but only at the rate of one and a half hours a day for two months. A land map of the world would be placed on the wall, and all the additional cartographic material to be used would also be placed there.[46]

These schemes presented two important characteristics. On the one hand, all reformers emphasized the lack of school manuals and advised standardizing the programs and class books. La Chalotais proposed that once the object of the study had been set, the king should be the one to have "elementary classic books" composed. Guyton de Morveau felt that "it is a considerable abuse to leave to teachers the absolute choice of books that they give to the students."

In addition, the appeal for memorization was rejected on behalf of reasoning, which was a considerable and important development in the teaching of geography. "The study of geography does not consist of putting in one's memory some hundreds of names of towns more or less, but rather of grasping the spirit of the matter and envisioning the elementary principles that lift it to the category of sciences," wrote Abbé Morin.[47]

The Work of the Revolution   The men of the Revolution adopted and systematized the plans worked out in preceding years. The book in general seemed important to them, since it contributed to making education public and open to everyone. They knew, in addition, that the approval of youth was the condition for their success.

From the point of view of atlases, there appeared a new genre, the departmental atlas. It was designed above all to be useful and support the political action of the Revolution. It offered a cartography that school children would experience and infuse into their daily life.

In 1791, the *Atlas National Portatif de la France destiné à l'instruction publique* was published, followed by several imitations. It was produced by the committee that prepared the large *Atlas National*, which took much longer to appear. The *Atlas National Portatif* was considered the first official French school atlas, since it emanated from the same source that had conceived the administrative division. Although official, this atlas was not neutral. Its authors' goal was to put "the student who wishes to instruct himself in order to learn of the old and abusive France, as well as the new regenerated France, into the position of judging for himself what he feels is the best."

Another aspect of the *Atlas National Portatif* was the deliberate and major emphasis on France. The authors dedicated two general maps to the French colonies, but refused to describe them at length: "Removed from these climates, separated from ours by seas, not having almost any hope of getting to know them on the spot, or this hope not being that of more than a few people, it is a knowledge of detail barely useful."

The Revolution went further in the creation of official instruction. In 1794, the Public Education Commission ordered the drafting of several school manuals. Edme Mentelle and Jean Nicholas Buache de la Neuville were chosen to write those for geography. They were also named to occupy the chair of this discipline in the new Ecole Normale, created in 1795 and dedicated to training fair and competent teachers.

Mentelle and Buache were experienced and respected geographers, but they were too old to introduce additional changes. Comments on their lectures, raised again the eternal criticisms made of geographers. They were judged to be boring and it was said that they were "frozen by routine."[48] Nevertheless, their work remains and the work of Mentelle, who was the principal geography teacher of the eighteenth century, will be examined.

Mentelle and School Atlases of the End of the Century   Mentelle's career continued until his death in 1815 at the age of eighty-five. Through his effort, the composition of general school atlases was established, a composition that has remained practically unchanged until the present time. One of Mentelle's major innovations was the introduction of physical maps in school atlases. His *Atlas Nouveau* (1784) offered several of them. Concern over representation in relief had already surfaced when Mentelle constructed a large raised-relief globe for the education of the son and heir apparent of Louis XVI in 1781.

During the same period, thematic maps began to be included in a number of school atlases. In 1781, Abbé Grenet's *Atlas portatif* included maps of winds and monsoons. In Philippe de Prétot's *Atlas universel d'étude*, one finds maps of tides, magnetic declination, and voyages of discovery. As previously observed, Mentelle advised the use of outline maps. He also advocated the introduction of some city maps, and in the end, he added an index of places, which he called a "nomenclature."[49]

Although an innovator in some respects, Mentelle was, nevertheless, faithful to traditional geography. In particular, he accorded great importance to ancient history, and he introduced in his *Atlas Nouveau* a "comparative map" of the modern and ancient divisions of the inhabited world. However, it was primarily the order in which he described the countries that clarified his point of view. He felt that an atlas should begin with maps of Turkey in Asia and Europe, since the sites of Ancient Greece were there. Then Italy, seat of the Roman Empire, should be studied, followed by Spain and Portugal.

Under the pressure of new ideas, these traditional concepts naturally had to change a little. Joining Mentelle was a geographer from the Revolution: Pierre Grégoire Chanlaire, who was one of the authors of the *Atlas National*, which has already been discussed. Mentelle and Chanlaire completed an *Atlas des Commençans*, which appeared under the Empire, in 1805. It was the official school atlas of the *lycées* and secondary schools and was approved by the Public Instruction Commission. This seventeen-map atlas was the manual recommended for decades by educational reformers. Historical geography was eliminated and a new aspect appeared, entitled "Introduction to the knowledge and usage of maps." By presenting details of four types of large-scale maps, it prepared the child to understand cartographic materials of more precision than those offered by a general atlas.

Thus it can be seen that, by 1800, France had satisfactory school atlases, which responded to the desires of teachers and students. These atlases were available in sufficient numbers for everyone, and in principle, all students had access to the same knowledge. Teachers now wanted to further expand student learning by pursuing another goal: to train them in the direct reading of topographical maps. This new pedagogical endeavor would be undertaken in the nineteenth century.

NOTES

1 "Geography is in a peculiar manner the science of princes," wrote George Adam to George III. Quoted by Helen Wallis in "A Banquet of Maps," *The Map Collector*, no. 28 (September 1984), p. 3.

2 Mireille Pastoureau, *Les Atlas Français, XVIe–XVIIe siècles. Répertoire bibliographique et étude* (Paris: Bibliothèque Nationale, 1984), 700pp., 166 illustrations. See also "Les Atlas imprimés en France aux XVIe et XVIIe siècles," *Imago Mundi* 32 (1980): 45–72.

3 Philippe Ariès, *L'Enfant et la vie familiale sous l'Ancien Régime* (1st ed., 1960; Paris: Plon, 1973); Roger Chartier, Dominique Julia, and Marie-Madeleine Compère, *L'éducation en France du XVIe au XVIIIe siècle* (Paris: SEDES, 1976); Georges Snyders, *La pédagogie en France aux XVIIe et XVIIIe siècles* (Paris: Presses universitaires de France, 1976); and *Enseignement et diffusion des sciences en France au XVIIIe siècle*, under the direction of R. Taton (Paris: Hermann, 1964).

4 François de Dainville, *La Géographie des Humanistes* (Paris: Beauchesne, 1940).

5 Cornelis Koeman, *Atlantes Neerlandici* (Amsterdam: Theatrum Orbis Terrarum, 1969), 3:71.

6 Ibid., 2:508–509.

7 Gerardus Mercator, *Atlas minor de Guerard Mercator traduict de latin en françois par le sieur de la Popelinière gentilhomme françois anno 1613* (Amsterdam, 1613), p. ii.

8 Bibliothèque Nationale de France, Cartes et Plans, Ge. FF. 14441.

9 Dainville, p. 365.

10 These ten "full exercise" colleges were: Harcourt, Cardinal Lemoine, Navarre, Lisieux, Plessis-Sorbonne, de la Marche, des Grassins, Montaigu, Mazarin, and after the expulsion of the Jesuits in 1764, Louis-le-Grand.

11 Snyders, p. 35.

12 François de Dainville, "Effectif des collèges et scolarité aux XVIIe et XVIIIe siècles," *Population*, 1955, no. 3, quoted by Snyders, p. 35.

13 See note 4.

14 Mireille Pastoureau, *Les Sanson (1630–1730): un siècle de cartographie française* (Paris, 1981), 623pp.

15 Didier Robert de Vaugondy, *Essai sur l'histoire de la géographie* (Paris: A. Boudet, 1755).

16 Ibid., p. 225, quoted by Dainville, p. 408.

17 Duval's historical atlas *Cartes géographiques dressées pour bien entendre les historiens* (1665), is the third volume of his *Diverses cartes et tables pour la géographie ancienne, pour la chronologie et pour les itinéraires et voyages modernes* (Paris, 1665).

18 Ariès, pp. 222–223.

19 *Journal des Sçavans*, July 31, 1690.

20 The maps are: Celestial sphere, world map, Europe, Asia, Africa, North and South America, France, environs of Paris, the Netherlands, the British Isles, Germany, Scandinavia, Poland, Moscow, Hungary, Spain, Italy, and Greece.

21 See F. Russo, "L'Hydrographie en France aux XVIIe et XVIIIe siècles. Ecoles et ouvrages d'enseignement," *Enseignement et diffusion des sciences*, pp. 419–440.

22 See Isabelle Raynaud-Nguyen, "Lucas Jansz. Waghenaer et l'hydrographie française," in *Lucas Jansz. Waghenaer van Enckhuysen* (Enkhuysen: Zuiderseemuseum, 1984), pp. 96–103, and A. Anthiaume, *Evolution et enseignement de la science nautique en France* (Paris: E. Dumont, 1920).

23 Didier Robert de Vaugondy, "Discours sur l'étude de la géographie," in *Nouvel Atlas Portatif* (Paris: Robert de Vaugondy, 1762), pp. 3–6.

24 Louis Brion de la Tour, *Atlas et tables élémantaires de géographie ancienne et moderne* (Paris, 1777).

25 P. Bernard Lamy, *Entretiens sur les sciences*, 3d book (1684). Quoted by Snyders, p. 98.

26 Nicolas Lenglet Dufresnoy, *Géographie abrégée* (6th ed., Paris, 1752).

27 Brion, *Atlas et tables*, op. cit.

28 Grenet, *Atlas portatif*, op. cit.

29 Robert de Vaugondy, "Discours," op. cit.

30 Abbé Boutillier, *Abrégé méthodique de la géographie ancienne et moderne avec des cartes de six pieds de hauteur pour l'Instruction publique de la Jeunesse* (Paris, 1779).

31 Nicolas Lenglet Dufresnoy, *Géographie des enfans* (1736).

32 Brion, *Atlas et tables*, op. cit.

33 Boutillier, *Abrégé méthodique*, op. cit.

34 Délibération du Tribunal de l'Université, May 27, 1775.

35 Prospectus in Grenet, *Atlas portatif*, op. cit.

36 Lenglet Dufresnoy, *Géographie des enfans* (4th ed., 1740), pp. viii–ix.

37 Grenet, *Atlas portatif*, op. cit.

38 See, in particular, Didier Robert de Vaugondy, *Atlas d'étude pour l'instruction de la jeunesse* (Paris: Delamarche, 1797).

39 Brion, *Atlas et tables*, op. cit.

40 Edme Mentelle, *Géographie ou annonce de quelques ouvrages relatifs à cette science avec quelques vues sur la manière de l'enseigner* (Paris, 1784).

41 Baron de Bouis, *Le Parterre géographique et historique, ou nouvelle méthode d'enseigner la géographie et l'histoire* . . . (Paris, 1737). Reprinted in 1753.

42 Abbé Teisserenc, *Plan de Paris mis en carte géographique du royaume de France,* and *Géographie parisienne en forme de dictionnaire contenant l'explication de Paris ou de son plan mis en carte* . . . (Paris, 1754).

43 Quoted by Dominique Julia, *Les trois couleurs du tableau noir. La Révolution* (Paris: Belin, 1981), p. 232.

44 Jean Morange and Jean-François Chassaing, *Le mouvement de réforme de l'enseignement en France, 1760–1798* (Paris: Presses universitaires de France, 1974).

45 Caradeuc de la Chalotais, *Essai d'éducation nationale ou Plan d'étude pour la jeunesse* (1763).

46 Guyton de Morveau, *Mémoire sur l'éducation publique, avec le prospectus d'un collège* (1764).

47 Abbé Morin, *Leçons de géographie ancienne et moderne abrégées d'une forme nouvelle propres à l'éducation des jeunes gens de l'un et l'autre sexe* (2d ed., Paris, 1785).

48 Numa Broc, *La géographie des philosophes. Géographes et voyageurs français au XVIIIe siècle* (Paris: Editions Ophrys, 1975), p. 468.

49 See note 40.

Lucas Janszoon Waghenaer's Nautical Atlases and Pilot Books

GÜNTER SCHILDER

INTRODUCTION

In 1984 map historians celebrated the four hundredth anniversary of Lucas Jansz. Waghenaer's now famous *Spieghel der Zeevaerdt*, the oldest printed folio-size pilot book, with charts, which was printed on the Leiden presses of Christopher Plantin early in 1584.[1] With this publication, as well as *Thresoor der Zeevaert* (1592) and *Enchuyser Zee-caert-boeck* (1598), Waghenaer provided an indispensable resource to seamen navigating European shores from Norway to the Columns of Hercules. Not only Dutch pilots, but also seafarers of other nations profited from Waghenaer's guides when they were issued in translation.

WAGHENAER'S PREDECESSORS

Before the appearance of the epoch-making *Spieghel der Zeevaerdt*, seamen navigating the English Channel, northern waters and the Baltic, used nautical instruments and accessories such as the compass, sounding-lead, log and Jacob staff, and manuscript and printed sailing instructions, called *leeskaarten* (rutters). These rutters were compiled by "old salts," who had gained the necessary and reliable knowledge of European waters, by long seafaring experience. By the first quarter of the sixteenth century these rutters began to appear on the market and were readily bought by masters and ship owners.[2] They were printed and issued as octavo booklets.

The oldest printed rutter still in existence, entitled *De Kaert vaderzee*, appeared in 1532. It was issued by Jan Severszoon, who was born on the Isle of Terschelling but at that time was living in Amsterdam. The only existing copy is in the Royal Library in Brussels. The rutters published by various printers in the subsequent years were all issued in the same format with roughly the same contents.[3] There are also two manuscript rutters kept in the Municipal Library in Antwerp and in the Royal Library in Brussels. All of these manuscripts were composed of three elements: rough sketches of charts, coastal views, and sailing instructions.[4]

Although very little is known about the authors of early manuscript and printed rutters, some names from the second half of the sixteenth century have survived. These authors were responsible for the compilation of sailing instructions. Several examples include Govert Willemsz. van Hollesloot with his *Caerte vande Oost ende Westzee* (Harlingen, 1578)[5] and Adriaen Gerritsz. with his work *Zeevaert ende onderwijsinge der gantscher Oostersche ende Westersche Zeevaertwater* (Amsterdam, 1588).[6]

The oldest known example of Dutch chart making is a woodcut chart by Jan van Hoirne, published in Antwerp in 1526.[7] Unfortunately, this chart is preserved in fragments, but when assembled it provides a reasonable picture of the Dutch, German, and Danish coasts. It also suggests that a brisk trade existed between the United Netherlands and Baltic ports during the first decades of the sixteenth century.

An important milestone in the further development of Dutch marine cartography is the famous *Caerte van Oostlant* by Cornelis Anthonisz. (See Figure 59.) There is no extant copy of the original which was published in 1543 in Amsterdam. However, a later copy of his chart is preserved in the Herzog August Bibliothek at Wolfenbüttel.[8] It consists of nine sheets printed from nine woodblocks, and was produced and marketed by the Antwerp publisher Arnoldus Nicolai. This chart was especially designed for navigation in the Baltic. In a Latin legend the author promised to issue, within a short time, a rutter for eastern Baltic navigation, since it was not possible for him to incorporate into his 1543 chart all the relevant information he had gathered. The combination of chart and rutter was supposed to guarantee seamen safe navigation. The third edition, the only extant copy of this rutter (published in Amsterdam in 1558), is preserved at Harvard University.[9] Comprised of forty-two pages, this treatise is the oldest known Dutch instruction book of its kind. The first part is a general introduction to the art of navigation. The second part, however, titled *Hier beghint die Caerte van die Oosterse See* (Here Begins the Chart of the Baltic), provides extensive nautical information concerning the sea route to the Baltic. Although the older rutters treat western as well as eastern navigation, Cornelis Anthonisz. limited his booklet to the sea route from Amsterdam to the Baltic.

THE ECONOMIC AND HISTORICAL PREREQUISITES FOR WAGHENAER'S PILOT BOOKS

Because the Dutch were still dependent on Spanish and Portuguese charts and sailing instructions for their navigation outside European waters, the appearance of Waghenaer's *Spieghel* in 1584 and 1585 brought about quite a revolution in West European marine cartography. Based on the very large distribution of

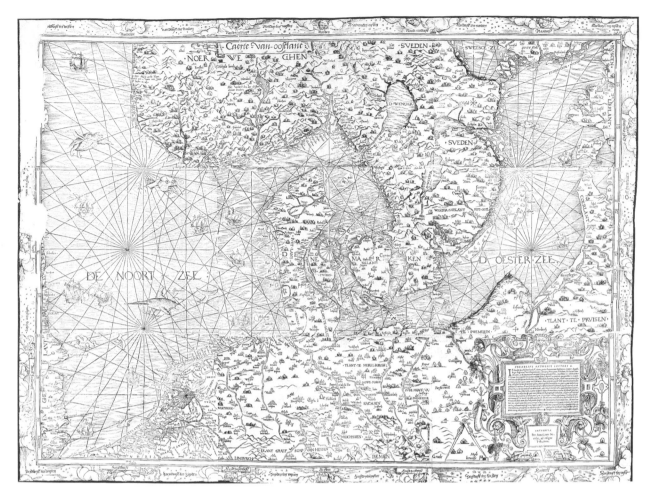

FIGURE 59 *Cornelis Anthonisz.,* Caerte van Oostlant *(3d. ed., Antwerp, c. 1560). Copper engraving in 9 sheets, 79 × 104 cm. Herzog August Bibliothek, Wolfenbüttel.*

Waghenaer's *Spieghel*, there is every reason to assume that it indeed supplied a long-felt need. At the same time it provided an indication of the advanced theoretical knowledge that was expected of a Dutch master mariner. Its publication represented the beginning of a very important period in marine cartography in the Netherlands, one which ultimately led to its preeminence in the science and art of chart and mapmaking during the next century.

The international distribution of Waghenaer's pilot books should be examined in the context of the general economic development of international trade and shipping. This trade consisted, for the most part, of an exchange of merchandise within European waters in which the Dutch shipowner played the important role of buyer, seller, middleman, and shipper. Moreover, the policy of multiple ownership, a favorable insurance system, and last but not least, the all-purpose *fluitschip* designed and built in Hoorn in the 1590s, made the Dutch merchant/owner the freight carrier of Europe. It was also quite clear that maintaining this position required the best navigational aids and charts.

Lucas Jansz. Waghenaer, born and raised in Enkhuizen (1533/34–1606), became a pioneer in the development of better and safer navigation on the European trade routes.[10] The coastal cities of the Zuyderzee became important ports and as such underwent rapid development. Enkhuizen, for example, grew from a city of 3,500 inhabitants to almost 16,000 during Waghenaer's lifetime. At the same time the city itself experienced significant physical growth. A bigger harbor, new wharfs, and enlarged quay walls including warehouses were built. This planned development was reflected in Waghenaer's first cartographic work, a city plan of Enkhuizen. (See Figure 60.) This map, which is now very rare, was printed from a copperplate engraved by Harmen Jansz. Muller in 1577.[11]

Waghenaer wrote in his 1592 *Thresoor* that he issued this pilot book "*tot verclaringhe van de zeevaart, daerinneick van jongs aan opgetoghen ende oudt gheworden ben* (in explication of seafaring in which I have been born and bred and grown old)." However, Waghenaer's career at sea did not last as long as he claimed; from 1579 onward, he was already at work in Enkhuizen. Before the appearance of his *Spieghel der Zeevaerdt* in 1584, Waghenaer had shown great ability as a designer

FIGURE 60 *Lucas Jansz. Waghenaer, Map of Enkhuizen (1577). Universiteitsbibliotheek, Amsterdam.*

of charts. These early charts, however, have not been preserved and their existence can only be determined from notary acts found in the city archives.[12]

THE *SPIEGHEL DER ZEEVAERDT* (LEYDEN, 1584–1585)

As previously stated, the publication of the first printed folio-size pilot book marked a turning point in the development of chart production. The *Spieghel* was a new concept in form, content, and execution, and started a trend toward the marketing of a completely new type of pilot book.[13] The small, insufficient, and obsolete rutters were no longer favored by seamen and remained unsold in the nautical establishments of the times.

In the introductions and dedications of his texts, Waghenaer gave a hint of how the material for his pilot books was compiled and worked out. It is evident that during his active employment as a pilot, while sailing the expansive and dangerous waters between Cadiz and the west coast of Norway, he was already actively preparing charts and textual material which gave rise to his future work. Waghenaer repeatedly refers to the papers in which he noted soundings and bearings, when sailing as a mate on Enkhuizen ships. Two factors were responsible for the high quality of his first and later editions of the *Spieghel*. In the first place, Waghenaer selected Christopher Plantin, the most famous printer/publisher of the time, who was also quite willing to publish his manuscript. Due to religious troubles in Antwerp, Plantin fled that city leaving his printing firm in the hands of his two sons-in-law. In 1583, he succeeded Willem Silvius as official printer at Leiden University. This was not, however, the first atlas printed by Plantin since he had printed Ortelius's *Theatrum Orbis Terrarum* in 1579. It is interesting to note that he chose the same format and a similar layout for the *Spieghel*.

A second important factor was his selection of a map engraver/decorator of the same high, artistic level, Johan van Deutecum, who was not only a very accurate map and chart engraver but also a gifted artist. The atlas as a whole, embellished with glorious Renaissance-style cartouches, scrolls, and garlands, and presented in its new and unusual format and layout, was a revelation to the seventeenth-century seaman. Although it may have been viewed initially with some skepticism, it far surpassed the existing crude and simple rutters in style and content. The imprint notes that Plantin printed the *Spieghel* at the expense of Lucas Jansz. Waghenaer. How then did he finance this venture? We must assume that his wealthy friend Francois Maelson, Burgomaster of Enkhuizen, helped him. In the preface to the second part, Waghenaer identifies Maelson as the person who actually came to his aid "*met raet ende daet goede hulpe ghedaen heeft* (who gave advice and actual help)."

The first part of the *Spieghel* was published in 1584. In the dedication copy to Prince Willem of Orange, the Spanish privilege was deliberately left out. This copy, with the dedication in gold, is preserved in the University Library at

Utrecht. In its richly decorated leather binding, it is one of the library's sixteenth-century treasures.

The *Spieghel der Zeevaerdt* begins with the title page, a specimen of the exquisite craftsmanship of the engraver Johan van Deutecum. (See Figure 61.) The center of the page is taken up by a cabinet, something often found in the paintings of Dutch and Flemish masters. The bookshelves are screened by the title which is flanked by the figures of a shipmaster in winter dress to the left, and summer clothes to the right, both sounding with a lead line. The lower part of the cabinet is standing on a base that is washed by the sea. In the sea in the fore-

FIGURE 61 *Frontispiece of the first part of Lucas Jansz. Waghenaer's* Spieghel der Zee-vaerdt *(Leiden: Christoffel Plantijn, 1585). Library of Congress.*

ground, we observe a forerunner of the *fluitschip* displaying the flags of the province of Holland and the city of Enkhuizen. Five sailors on top of the cabinet are looking (for advice?) into a mirror; a trainee, admonished by Waghenaer in his text, stands aside on the left. On the verso of the title page is a sonnet by Joannes Douza (Trustee of the Leiden University). The next several pages include the dedication to Willem of Orange (dated October 31, 1583) and two additional laudatory poems by Jan van Hout and Jan Walraven. Waghenaer's friend Maelson probably introduced him to these members of Leiden's literary circle. The main part of the text that follows is taken up by an introduction to the art of navigation. Waghenaer admonishes all young seamen who really want to learn something, to keep a sharp lookout for buildings, castles, towers, churches, recognizable mountains, dunes, mills, and other landmarks, when leaving or approaching land, river, or port. He further advises them "to make a sketch with the pen or else draw it." A total of some thirty-three pages are devoted to a summary of cosmography and navigation which includes the following: tables of the lunar declination, the declination of the sun, lists of the fixed stars with their declination, instruction on how to use these tables, and for observation, how to construct a cross-staff and its division into degrees. (See Figure 62.) Instructions on how to draw a *pascaerte* (portolan chart) are also included. There are three pages with the distance and coastal bearings from Holland as far south as Spain and north to the Baltic. There are also tide tables, direction of currents along the Dutch and Flemish coasts, and various depths and shallows in the North Sea and the English Channel. The text is illustrated by many explanatory woodcuts and copper engravings, some of them full page. The standardization of various symbols for buoys, seamarks and landmarks, anchorages, reefs, rocks and shoals, and so on, described in a legend and drawn on the charts appears for the first time in the history of chart making.

Following this introductory material, unique in design and elaboration, the atlas proper begins. Part I begins with a small-scale outline chart of Western Europe covering the area covered by the individual charts in Parts I and II. (See Figure 63.) Following this chart, Part I contains twenty-three charts on larger scales, numbered two through twenty-two (in Arabic numerals on the text side) and one unnumbered chart. Part II, dated 1585, begins with a dedication to the Lords of the States of Holland and West Friesland. This part contains twenty-two charts, numbered I through XXI (in Roman numerals). Based on the Western European outline chart in Part I, the location and extent of forty-four large-scale charts have been plotted on an index sheet by the Geographical Institute in Utrecht.[14] It is interesting to observe how systematically Waghenaer arranged the charts in the *Spieghel*. (See Figure 64.) While the economic development of the Dutch shipping trade has been previously noted, a closer look at the charts in the *Spieghel* makes it quite clear that Waghenaer's work is a true reflection of the beginning of this late sixteenth-century phenomenon, that is, the Dutch trade routes and the commodities sold and bought enroute.

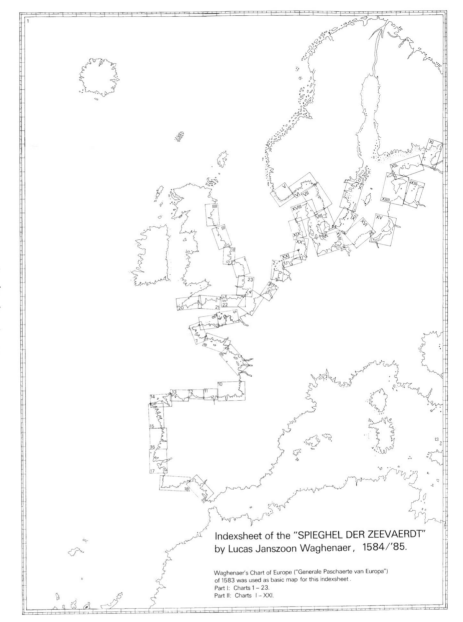

Indexsheet of the "SPIEGHEL DER ZEEVAERDT"
by Lucas Janszoon Waghenaer, 1584/'85.

Waghenaer's Chart of Europe ("Generale Paschaerte van Europa")
of 1583 was used as basic map for this indexsheet.
Part I: Charts 1 – 23.
Part II: Charts I – XXI.

FIGURE 64 *Index sheet show-ing the charts preserved in Lucas Jansz. Waghenaer's* Spieghel der Zeevaerdt *(1584–1585). Universiteit, Utrecht.*

The explanation for the exceptions on the blank verso pages is that they clearly divide the atlas into three separate sets of charts. The first set ends with chart 19 (Gibraltar). On the verso of the right side of chart 19, text appears for the first time. The second set begins with chart 20 (Part I) and ends with chart IV (Part II). Here for the second and last time Waghenaer uses the verso. Chart V (Norway) begins the third and last set of charts. How the crossing from Aberdeen to the Norwegian coast is made is not explained.

The initial impression of the charts is the artistry of the noncartographic elements. The genius and artistic versatility of Johan van Deutecum as an engraver is unmistakable. (See Figure 65.) The hand of the master is recognized in the richly decorated cartouches. No two are the same, although there is some uni-

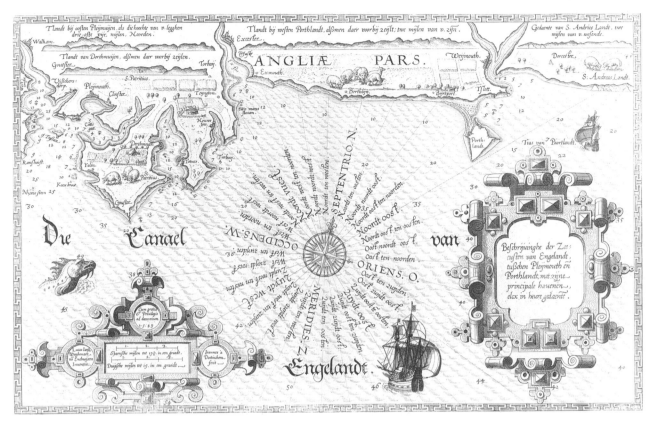

FIGURE 65   *"Beschrijvinghe der Zee custen van Engelandt . . . ,"* Spieghel der Zeevaerdt
(1584–1585). Library of Congress.

formity in the design for the scale cartouches and the text cartouches. He
enlivens the expanses of water with illustrations of various types of ships, beautifully decorated wind roses, a variety of fishes and sea monsters. This explosion of
artistic fantasy is contrasted with Waghenaer's more realistic sketches of the
coastline in the original manuscript submitted to the printing office of Plantin.

All charts are of identical size and scale. The format being approximately 33 ×
50 cm and the scale about 1:400,000. The river mouths and the harbor entrances
are all expanded and represented on a larger scale. (See Figure 66.) Thus, in navigable river estuaries and harbor entrances there is always ample information on
depths and shoals expressed in soundings in fathoms. This serves to emphasize
that Waghenaer's charts were primarily designed to give information on the nav-
igability of river and harbor entrances. For navigation along the coast, the seaman trusted his experience and the text of the sailing instructions.

The remarkable feature of the charts, however, was the combination of coastline and coastal profile. In reasonable weather, the shipmaster could usually
establish his position by comparing his view of the coast with the coastal profiles
(*opdoeningen*) on the chart. These *opdoeningen* showed conspicuous buildings,
church towers, windmills, and sometimes even beacons. Moreover, he could then

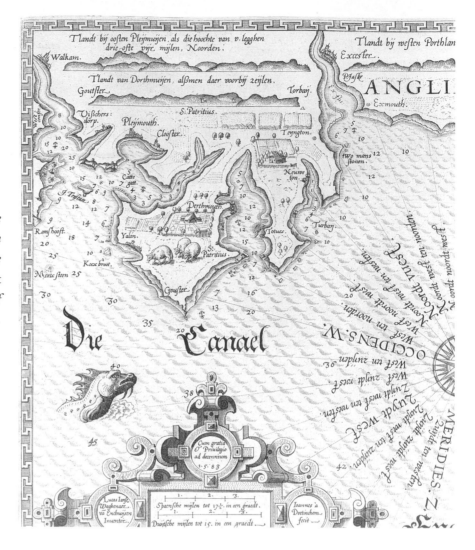

FIGURE 66 *Detail of the "Beschrijvinghe der Zee custen van Engelandt . . ." from the Spieghel der Zeevaerdt (1584–1585). Library of Congress.*

determine from his chart whether he was sailing close to a sandy or rocky coast. Although the Portuguese had previously combined charts with profiles (that is, De Castro's manuscript map of the Red Sea), this technique was perfected by Waghenaer in such a way that for the seaman of his time these new composite charts far surpassed the older ones.

How reliable were the charts? The accuracy of the depiction of the various coastlines varies considerably. The south coast of England, for instance, is very inaccurately drawn. A study by Dr. W. Behrmann shows in graphic form the divergence between the small-scale outline chart in green, the large-scale chart in red, and the actual coastline in black.[16]

The *Spieghel* was published in a number of editions in various languages, closely following one another. For a detailed description of these several editions the reader is referred to C. Koeman's *Atlantes Neerlandici*.[17] With the exception of some minor alterations, the original copperplates were used for all subsequent editions of the *Spieghel*. The English edition, however, was a totally different venture. It was published in London in 1588 without the approval of the author and used a completely new set of plates.[18] The first state of the copperplates had the chart titles and the text accompanying the profiles in Dutch. In the second state, the titles were reengraved with the text in both Dutch and Latin. Adding Latin text for the profiles to the Dutch text, however, did some harm to the simple clarity of the chart picture in the second Dutch edition of 1584 as well as in some of the later ones. The third state shows the number of the plate in both lower margins of the charts. In 1589 when the worn-out plates came into the possession of Cornelis Claesz., they were refreshed and brought up to date. In this new form, the maps appeared in various editions published by Cornelis Claesz. in Amsterdam and Jean Bellere in Antwerp from 1589 until 1605. In the French edition, a translation of the text describing the profiles was printed outside the chart's cadre. Not only the text, but also the chart contents were brought up-to-date according to the latest nautical information.

These adjustments and additions clearly show that Waghenaer intended to perfect his pilot book, as illustrated by the following examples. In the first editions, the banks off the coast of Flanders at Nieuwpoort and Duinkerken were imperfectly drawn. Later editions showed the correct positions of the banks and the addition of a number of soundings. The trend of the Isle of Sark in the early editions was from West to East, but in later editions it changed by 90°. Both of the these changes required only a minor correction of the copperplate. In the case of the Bay of Biscay, however, a completely new copperplate had to be engraved in order to print a new and correct chart.

From the beginning, Waghenaer's *Spieghel der Zeevaerdt* proved to be a bestseller. In its first year of publication, the first part required a second edition. The following year a third edition was published, together with the first edition of the separately issued second part. Waghenaer received from the States of Holland and West Friesland, to whom the second part was dedicated, the considerable amount of 600 Dutch pounds. After 1586, Plantin's son-in-law, Francois van Raphelengen, was responsible for all subsequent editions of the *Spieghel*. Since the 1584 and 1585 editions were published in Dutch only, it was difficult to sell them outside Holland. As early as 1584, perhaps in anticipation of a Latin edition, a Latin text was added to the title page and the charts. In 1586 Van Raphelengen printed, at Waghenaer's expense, the first complete Latin edition, the *Speculum Nauticum*, with the translation by Martin Everaert. (See Figures 67a/b.) The first part is dedicated to Queen Elizabeth of Great Britain and the second part to King Frederik of Denmark. These dedications underline the international character of this edition. In 1588 Van Raphelengen printed a new Dutch edition at the expense of Cornelis Claesz. This time the copperplates were all numbered (third state) and two new charts were added. In 1589 Waghenaer sold his rights to Cornelis Claesz. This Amsterdam publisher worked with Jean Bellere in Antwerp. In 1589 Bellere received the royal privilege from Philip II to publish the *Spieghel* in Latin, Dutch, Spanish, and French.

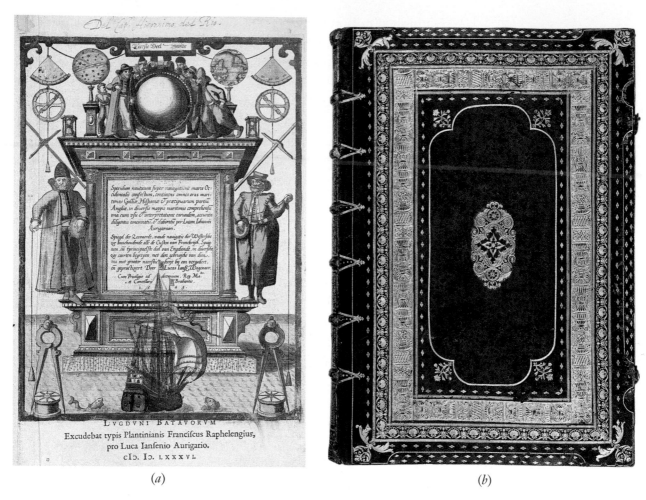

(a)   (b)

FIGURE 67   *Frontispiece (a) and binding (b) of the* Speculum Nauticum *(1586). Library of Congress.*

In that same year a German edition, with a translation by Richard Slotboom, was issued in Amsterdam by Cornelis Claesz. The title page was newly engraved, and the original Spanish title was pasted over with a German title. On the title page, the Enkhuizen flag was superseded by the flag of Amsterdam. The copperplates were refreshed and brought up-to-date. From the original title in Spanish, it can be deduced that a Spanish edition was planned. Apparently this plan was never executed.

Two manuscript charts with Portuguese text are also known to exist. A complete Portuguese edition, however, was not realized.[19] A number of joint editions were published by Cornelis Claesz. and Bellere in Dutch in 1590, 1596, 1597, and 1603; in French in 1590, 1600, and 1605; and one Latin edition in 1591. In all of these editions the verso of the right half of the chart, which was originally kept blank, was printed with historical and topographical information. To the Dutch edition of 1596 with the title *Den Nieuwen Spieghel der Zeevaert* (reissued in 1597) new profiles printed from woodcuts were inserted into the text of the sailing instructions. The text itself was enlarged with text from Waghenaer's *Thresoor*, and new charts, printed from new copperplates, were added. The title page was newly designed. Over the title, there was the mirror flanked by seven shipmasters, the familiar nautical instruments, globes, and a number of inset maps of the Zuyderzee, Helsingor, Lisbon, and Venice.

The *Nieuwen Spieghel* contained a new small-scale chart of Western Europe which was engraved by Baptista van Deutecum in 1592. (See Figure 68.) This chart had already appeared in the Latin edition of 1591 and it was considerably enlarged by adding the Northern European coastline stretching eastward. To this and the following editions, two large-scale charts of the northern part of Norway and Ireland were added. Both were prepared by the famous Dutch pilot Willem Barentsz. and engraved by Pieter van den Keere.

FIGURE 68 *Lucas Jansz. Waghenaer,* Chart of Europe, Spieghel der Zeevaerdt *(1592). Universiteitsbibliotheek, Amsterdam.*

Another edition which should be mentioned is the 1603 edition with the title *Den groten dobbelden nieuwen Spiegel der Zeevaert*. This atlas was considerably enlarged, with a great part of the text from Waghenaer's *Thresoor*, three new charts, plus twelve large-scale charts engraved by Benjamin Wright, all from the same pilot book. All these editions were published legally, except the English edition of 1588 which was pirated from the 1586 *Spieghel* and issued under the title *The Mariners Mirror*. The *Spieghel*'s title page and charts were copied by a team of engravers (Theodor de Bry, Augustine Ryther, Johannes Rutlinger, and Jodocus Hondius), and the English translation was done by Anthony Ashley. Incidentally, Hondius worked in England from 1583 to 1593 when he came into possession of the copperplates for the English edition. After his return to Amsterdam he published another edition in 1605. It was a combination of the charts from the *Mariners Mirror* and a translation of the text of *Den Nieuwen Spieghel* of 1596.

THE *THRESOOR DER ZEEVAERT* (LEYDEN, 1592)

Eight years after the first edition of the *Spieghel*, Waghenaer published his second pilot book which he called *Thresoor der Zeevaert*.[20] Waghenaer had come to realize that the format of the *Spieghel* was too large and unpractical and moreover, that the price was too high for the average seaman. Thus, he decided on a rectangular format, one that was easy to handle and familiar to the seaman. The *Thresoor* contained much more than the *Spieghel* and was in form and content more like the old, trusted rutters, especially in regard to the texts with their numerous coastal profiles. The first edition appeared in 1592 and was printed by Van Raphelengen in Leiden at Waghenaer's expense. This time the title was printed in letter type. The verso, however, was decorated with an engraved emblematic title symbolizing for the seaman the indispensable knowledge stored in a *trezoor* with closed doors. (See Figure 69.) The title on this frontispiece is in Dutch and French, the same as all the chart titles in the pilot book. Following the privileges and the dedication to Prince Maurice is a treatise in which Waghenaer advises the seaman of the errors and faults he is liable to encounter in all pilot books and rutters published by others. The publications of Gover Willemsz. van Hollesloot and Adriaen Gerritsz., two of his rivals, are sharply criticized.

Waghenaer's *Thresoor der Zeevaert* consists of three parts and ends with an appendix. The first part includes a treatise on the art of navigation which is spread over twenty-five chapters. The text is much more elaborate than that in the *Spieghel*. The second and third parts together form the major portion of the pilot book. The second part contains the charts and sailing instructions used for the western, northern, and eastern navigation in twenty-one sections. These sections include 166 pages of sailing instructions and twenty large-scale coastal charts. Throughout the text there are numerous profiles like those usually found in the older rutters. Each chapter on sailing instructions has charts

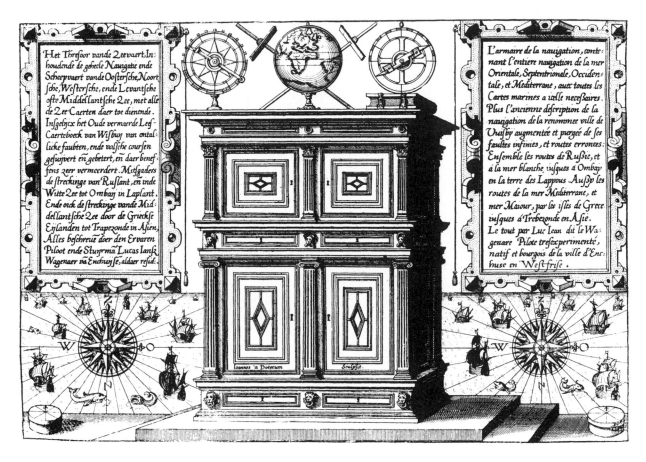

FIGURE 69 *Second frontispiece of Lucas Jansz. Waghenaer's* Het Thresoor der Zeevaert *(1592).*
Maritiem Museum "Prins Hendrik," Rotterdam.

which illustrate the text. In the first edition five of the charts were signed by
Johan van Deutecum, but most of the remaining charts also show the style of
this artist.

The index sheet on which all the charts in the *Thresoor* were plotted clearly
shows the expansion of the Dutch fishing and trading area since 1580. (See Figure 70.) For the first time in a Dutch publication, there were charts and sailing
instructions for navigating the northern part of Scotland, the group of islands to
the north of Scotland, and the White Sea.

Since the third part of the *Thresoor* has its own title, it is quite possible that it
could have been purchased separately. It contains sailing instructions, without
charts, for the western part of the Mediterranean Sea. In this respect, the *Thresoor* was the oldest pilot book with sailing instructions for these waters. It is further proof of the increasing trade in this area and marks the beginning of the
Straetvaart, the trading route through the Strait of Gibraltar. Willem Barentsz.'s
Nieuwe Beschryvinghe ende Caertboeck vande Midlandtsche Zee, published in 1595, is
the oldest printed atlas with full-size charts for navigation in the western part of
the Mediterranean.

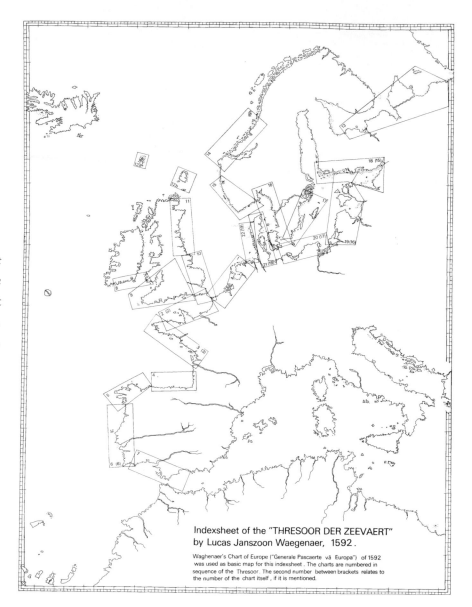

Indexsheet of the "THRESOOR DER ZEEVAERT"
by Lucas Janszoon Waegenaer, 1592.

Waghenaer's Chart of Europe ("Generale Pascaerte vā Europa") of 1592
was used as basic map for this indexsheet . The charts are numbered in
sequence of the Thresoor. The second number between brackets relates to
the number of the chart itself , if it is mentioned.

FIGURE 70 *Index sheet showing the charts preserved in Lucas Jansz. Waghenaer's* Het Thresoor der Zeevaert *(1592). Universiteit, Utrecht.*

The appendix of the *Thresoor* contains ten pages with text on navigation out-side European waters. It is, in fact, a summary of the travels of Drake and Cavendish, with information on the Indies by Dirck Gerritsz., and sailing instructions for the voyage from Holland to the East Indies and return. It ends with the privilege granted to the author by the States General and States of Holland and West Friesland. When comparing the *Spieghel* with the *Thresoor*, it becomes apparent that the sailing instructions for the *Thresoor* are better and more informative. Also, much of Waghenaer's textual information on coasts and waterways presented in the *Thresoor* is not found in the *Spieghel*.

The charts in the *Thresoor* are also quite different. In many cases, the *Spieghel* has more than one chart depicting a given stretch of coastline whereas the *Thresoor* uses only one. The charts are also printed double-pages (c. 19 × 55 cm), and their scale is uniform too, but smaller (c. 1:600,000). As in the *Spieghel*, the river estuaries and harbor entrances continue to be shown on a larger scale. Due to the smaller scale of the publication, however, the coastal profiles have less detail and the inland profiles have disappeared altogether. One improvement, however, is the depth-contour lines in the fairways. In this respect, Waghenaer used Albert Haeyen's *Amstelredamsche zee-caerten* (Leiden, 1585) as an example.[21]

It is not known how well the *Thresoor* sold, but it was four years before a new edition appeared in 1596.[22] Both editions were published by Cornelis Claesz. in Amsterdam. Beginning with the first edition in 1592, the second title page and the titles on the charts were in French as well as in Dutch. A complete French edition, however, only appeared nine years later in 1601 under the title *Thresorie ou cabinet de la route marinesque.* The name of Cornelis Claesz. is not mentioned, but in all probability the work was printed on his presses. The French edition issued in 1606 bore Cornelis Claesz.'s imprint. In general, the contents of the first Dutch editions were the same as those of the first French edition. There are some differences, however, in the later editions: The title page shows, instead of the closed cabinet, an opened *thresoor* from which an experienced and older seaman (Waghenaer?) hands some pilot books to his pupils, the young and inexperienced apprentices. (See Figure 71.) Waghenaer's polemic on the ignorance of his competitors Govert Willemsz. van Hollesloot and Adriaen Gerritsz. has disappeared. In the second part, a chapter on the coast of Barbary has been added and is accompanied by an attractive little map of Tercera (Azores) by Van den Keere. This map is a copy of a map in the *Caert-thresoor* of 1598 and does not reappear in later Dutch editions. The French edition lacks the third part on the coasts of the Mediterranean. Did the publisher assume that the French were better informed about these coasts? It is hard to answer this question. In later Dutch

FIGURE 71 *Frontispiece of the Dutch edition of* Het Thresoor der Zeevaert *(1602). Nederlands Scheepvaartmuseum, Amsterdam.*

editions, however, this section on the Mediterranean appears again. The appendix added toward the end of the volume has been enlarged. To the Dutch edition of 1602, an interesting supplement has been added on the navigation to the East and West Indies. (See Figure 72.) This supplement has twelve pages of text with sailing instructions to Brazil and details of the journey undertaken by Van Neck and Van Warvijck to the Indies from 1598 to 1600. The 1602 and later editions contain a short treatise on the deviation of the compass.

After 1600 the copperplates of the *Thresoor* were so worn that Cornelis Claesz. had to have them reengraved by Benjamin Wright and Josua van den Ende. He also wanted to add new charts including a large-scale chart of the River Thames engraved by Wright. A Latin edition of the *Thresoor* was planned but never realized although two manuscript charts, on vellum, of southern England and the Netherlands with accompanying text in Latin are extant. One of these manuscripts is kept in the H. C. Taylor Collection, Yale University, New Haven. The other copy was recently discovered in the Bibliothèque Nationale in Paris.[23] (See Figure 73.)

Cornelis Claesz. published his last edition three years after Waghenaer's death. This edition has a new title page and the total number of charts increased to

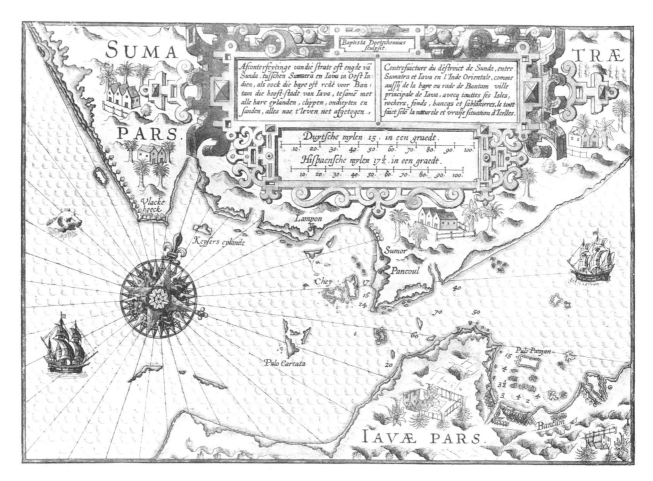

FIGURE 72 *Lucas Jansz. Waghenaer, Chart of Sunda Strait from* Het Thresoor der Zeevaert *(1602). Maritiem Museum "Prins Hendrik," Rotterdam.*

FIGURE 73   *Manuscript chart on vellum covering the coast from Groningen to Flanders, planned for a Latin edition of Waghenaer's* Thresoor. *Bibliothèque Nationale de France.*

thirty. That same year (1609) Cornelis Claesz. died. His death signaled the end of the pilot books by Lucas Jansz. Waghenaer.

One year earlier in 1608, Willem Jansz. Blaeu published his *Licht der Zeevaert*, containing more up-to-date information.[24] It is interesting to note that Blaeu did not use Waghenaer's *Spieghel* as an example but followed the *Thresoor* in format, construction, and chart design.

THE *ENCHUYSER ZEE-CAERT-BOECK*

In 1598 Cornelis Claesz. published Waghenaer's third pilot book.[25] It was a voluminous work in octavo, consisting of some 380 pages. The title was derived from the name of Waghenaer's birthplace. With this book he returned to the familiar format of the old and trusted rutter. The contents, however, were of a completely new conception. It was, in fact, a revised and amended version of the *Thresoor*. The *Enchuyser Zee-caert-boeck* was published as a booklet of modest size for the use of the conservative master who was used to the crude woodcuts of coastal profiles. (See Figure 74.) This was preferred to the cumbersome folio-size volume or a rectangular quarto with large copper-engraved charts, which was difficult to store and use in the modest space of the wheelhouse. It took Waghenaer fourteen years to discover this truth! The publication of the *Enchuyser Zee-caert-boeck* is proof of the unsuccessful endeavors of Waghenaer to stimulate the sale of his earlier pilot books to a certain class of seamen, most of whom preferred the

FIGURE 74 *Frontispiece of Lucas Jansz. Waghenaer's* Enchuyser Zee-caert-boeck *(Amsterdam, 1598). Nederlands Scheepvaartmuseum, Amsterdam.*

more direct printed sailing instructions illustrated with woodcuts of coastal pro-files rather than the still-faulty chart. In the *Enchuyser Zee-caert-boeck*, there were only two small-scale charts of Enkhuizen and the Zuyderzee, which were without any value for navigation and were merely included by Waghenaer as a courtesy to his birthplace.

The book begins with the title page, a dedication, the preface, and a short introduction to the art of navigation. The following 347 pages are divided into some 159 chapters, which include sailing instructions and coastal profiles for the eastern and western navigation and sailing instructions for the sea route to both West Africa and Brazil. The *Enchuyser Zee-caert-boeck* was issued in second and third editions in 1601 and 1605 respectively. Today it is one of the rarest speci-mens of Waghenaer's pilot books and is found only in a very few collections.

WAGHENAER'S LEGACY

With the publication of these three printed pilot books, each of a different size, Waghenaer created a milestone in the development of Western European navigation. For his contemporaries and for the next generation of seafarers as well, these books were a decisive influence.[26] The series started with the memorable folio-size publication of his *Spieghel der Zeevaerdt* (1584–1585), followed eight years later by the *Thresoor der Zeevaert* (1592). The latter was a book of a different format (oblong quarto) with newly compiled charts and more important, coastal profiles inserted in a far better written text than found in the *Spieghel*. The series ended in 1598 with the *Enchuyser Zee-caert-boeck*, which brought Waghenaer back to the original idea of the rutter. With this series of pilot books in various editions and languages, Waghenaer marked the beginning of Dutch dominance in marine cartography, which lasted until the end of the seventeenth century.[27]

Waghenaer's wide knowledge of navigation and his practical sense of recording this information on charts and in writing did not bring him wealth. Nevertheless, he helped the Dutch merchants and ship owners achieve their wealth and power, because his pilot books provided for the safe navigation of their ships. Although he died in 1606 a poor man in his birthplace of Enkhuizen, he left a splendid legacy in his pilot books and other works, and remains an important figure to modern-day historians of cartography.

NOTES

1 This event has been commemorated by an exhibition devoted to Waghenaer, held in the Zuiderzeemuseum of his native town Enkhuizen in the summer of 1984. See *Lucas Jansz. Waghenaer van Enckhuysen. De maritieme cartografie in de Nederlanden in de zestiende en het begin van de zeventiende eeuw* (Enkhuizen, 1984, 135pp., with English summaries).

2 C. P. Burger, "Oude Hollandse zeevaert-uitgaven," *Tijdschrift voor boek- en bibliotheekwezen*, 6 (1908): 119–137 and 245–261; 7 (1909): 1–17, 49–60, 123–132, and 157–172; 8 (1910): 255–262.

3 A bibliography is given by C. Koeman in volume 4, *Celestial and Maritime Atlases and Pilot Books*, of his *Atlantes Neerlandici* (Amsterdam: Theatrum Orbis Terrarum, 1970), pp. 12–13. The edition of 1541 by Jan Jacobsz. was published in facsimile by E. J. Brill (Leiden, 1885).

4 A facsimile and description of the Antwerp manuscript rutter was done by J. Denucé and D. Gernez under the title *Het Zeeboek* (Antwerp, 1936).

5 C. P. Burger, "Oude Hollandsche zeevaart-uitgaven. Het grote zeekaartboek van Govert Willemsz." *Tijdschrift voor boek- en bibliotheekwezen*, 9 (1911): 69–79; Koeman, *Atlantes Neerlandici*, 4:517–518. A prominent place in the series of pilot guides is held

by a Dutch manuscript rutter which was discovered recently by the author in the Biblioteca National in Madrid. The manuscript encompasses some twenty-four charts and coastal views (25.8×56.6 cm each) in pen and ink, some accompanied by nautical sailing instructions. It provides a picture of the European mainland between the Gulf of Finland and the Bay of Biscay. For more details, see G. Schilder, "A Dutch Manuscript Rutter: An Unique Portrait of the European Coasts in the Late Sixteenth Century," *Imago Mundi* 43 (1991): 1–13.

6 C. P. Burger, "Oude Hollandsche zeevaert-uitgaven. 'De Zeevaert' van Adriaen Gerritsz," *Het Boek* (1913), pp. 113–128.

7 B. van 't Hoff, "Jan van Hoirne's Map of the Netherlands and the 'Oosterscher Zee' Printed in Antwerp in 1526," *Imago Mundi* 11 (1954): 136.

8 A full-size reproduction was made by A. W. Lang in his *Historisches Seekartenwerk der Deutschen Bucht* (Neumünster, 1969), plate 1. The same author wrote a monograph about this chart in his *Die "Caerte van Oostlant" des Cornelis Anthonisz. 1543. Die älteste gedruckte Seekarte Nordeuropas und ihre Segelanweisung* (Bremerhaven: Ernst Kabel Verlag, 1986).

9 J. Keuning, "Cornelis Anthonisz. Zijn Caerte van Oostlant, zijn Onderwijsinge van der Zee en zijn Caerte van die Oosterse See," *Tijdschrijft van het Koninklijk Nederlandsch Aardrijkskundig* Genootschap 57 (1950): 687–714, and "Cornelis Anthonisz," *Imago Mundi* 57 (1950): 51–65.

10 C. Koeman, "Lucas Janszoon Waghenaer: A Sixteenth-Century Marine Cartographer," *The Geographical Journal* 131 (1965): 202–217, and *The History of Lucas Janszoon Waghenaer and his Spieghel der Zeevaerdt*. Introduction to the facsimile edition by Elsevier/Sequoia (Amsterdam-Lausanne, 1964). G. Schilder, "The Chart of Europe in Four Sheets of 1589 by Lucas Jansz Waghenaer," *Theatrum Orbis Librorum. Liber Amicorum Presented to Nico Israel on the Occasion of his Seventieth Birthday*. Edited by T. Croiset van Uchelen, K. van der Horst, and G. Schilder (Utrecht: HES Publishers, 1989), pp. 78–93.

11 The following copies have been identified: one each in the Universiteitsbibliotheek, Amsterdam; Rijksarchief, Haarlem; and the Bibliothèque Nationale, Paris; one in a Dutch private collection and one in the Taylor Collection, Yale University.

12 This statement is also proved by Waghenaer's letter to Francois Maelson, dated May 7, 1591. See C. Koeman, *The History of Lucas Jansz. Waghenaer*, pp. 28–29.

13 See C. Koeman's introduction and facsimile edition quoted in note 10. See also R. A. Skelton, "Bibliographical Note" to the facsimile edition of the *Spieghel der Zeevaerdt, 1584–1585* (Amsterdam: Theatrum Orbis Terrarum, 1964).

14 I am indebted to my colleague Marc Hameleers, who provided the index sheet for Waghenaer's *Spieghel* as well as for Waghenaer's *Thresoor*.

15 C. Koeman, "Bibliographical Note" to the facsimile edition of Willem Barentsz., *Beschryvinghe ende Caertboeck vande Midlandtsche Zee, 1595* (Amsterdam: Theatrum Orbis Terrarum, 1970).

16 W. Behrmann, *Über die niederdeutschen Seebücher des fünfzehnten und sechzehnten Jahrhunderts* (Hamburg, 1906), map 7.

17 Koeman, *Atlantes Neerlandici,* 4:477–501.

18 R. A. Skelton, "Bibliographical Note" to the facsimile edition of Lucas Jansz. Waghenaer, *The Mariners Mirrour, London, 1588* (Amsterdam: Theatrum Orbis Terrarum, 1966).

19 Armando Cortesão and Avelino Teixeira da Mota, *Portugaliae Monumenta Cartographica* (Lisbon, 1960), p. 367.

20 R. A. Skelton, "Bibliographical Note" to the facsimile edition of Lucas Jansz. Waghenaer, *Thresoor der Zeevaert, 1592* (Amsterdam: Theatrum Orbis Terrarum, 1966).

21 D. Gernez, "Les Amstelredamsche zeecaerten d'Albert Haeyen," *Compas d'Or. Bulletin de la Societé des Bibliophiles Anversois* (1934), pp. 3–30.

22 For a bibliography of the *Thresoor,* see Koeman, *Atlantes Neerlandici,* 4:502–512.

23 Bibliothèque Nationale de France, MSS Lat. Nouv. Acq. 2313. 40 pp. text and 2 charts on vellum, each 42 × 83 cm: (1) *Descriptio terrarum atque marinarum partium regiones. Embdanae, finite locorum Groningiae, Frisiae tam orientalis et occidentalis quam transmarinae Waterlandiae, Hollandiae, Zelandiae, Flandriae . . .* (2) *Decriptio orarum septemtrionalium Angliae, nec non mirabilium arenarum ac pulvinorum ante littus Londinense, Herwitsense, Jermudense et litense iacentium . . .*

24 R. A. Skelton, "Bibliographical Note" to the facsimile edition of Willem Jansz. Blaeu, *The Light of Navigation, Amsterdam, 1612* (Amsterdam: Theatrum Orbis Terrarum, 1964).

25 Koeman, *Atlantes Neerlandici,* 4:513–516.

26 D. Gernez, "The Works of Lucas Janszoon Waghenaer," *The Mariners Mirror* 23 (1937): 332–350.

27 For a detailed bibliography of Waghenaer's pilot books, see Koeman, *Atlantes Neerlandici,* 4:469–516.

Power and Legitimation in the English Geographical Atlases of the Eighteenth Century

JOHN BRIAN HARLEY

> . . . *power does not merely impinge on science and scientific knowledge from without. Power relations permeate the most ordinary activities in scientific research. Scientific knowledge arises out of these power relations rather than in opposition to them. Knowledge is power, and power knowledge.*
>
> —Joseph Rouse, *Knowledge and Power: Toward a Political Philosophy of Science* (Ithaca: Cornell University Press, 1987), 24.

A publication of the Center for the Book in the Library of Congress is an appropriate place to explore the history of the geographical atlas in its wider political, social and cultural context. Both the specific topic I have selected to write about—the way social power intersects cartographic knowledge—and the approach I have adopted—drawing from social theory and the philosophy of science to interrogate my evidence—is in sympathy with the spirit of *L'histoire du livre.* Indeed, it will be recalled that in *The Coming of the Book,*[1] often regarded as the seminal text of a new historicism in bibliographical interpretation, one of the objectives of Lucien Febvre and Henri-Jean Martin was to establish the role in society of the "Book as a Force for Change."[2] While the analysis of power has not been an explicit concern in the new historical bibliography—for example, the word does not appear in the index of Elizabeth L. Eisenstein's classic study of *The Printing Press as an Agent of Change*[3]—there are recent signs of a new radical awareness. Thus D. F. McKenzie was able to speak in 1985 not only of "Bibliography and the sociology of texts," but also to extend his argument to "nonbook texts," including maps, and above all to recognize that maps "may . . . express ideological meanings" and "function as potent tools for political control."[4] It is equally hard to conceive of a study of the atlas which does not come to terms in some way with the power relations within cartography which do much to structure both its form and its historical significance as a graphic text. The old aphorism that knowledge is power will accordingly be explored in the context of the English geographical atlases of the eighteenth century.

This essay does not seek to make a general case for the effects of power in cartography[5] but to examine how the structure of social power in a particular historical society influenced the production of knowledge and its mode of representation in the geographical atlases produced in England in the eighteenth century. The argument will be presented in three stages. First, the nature of power as it affected the geographical knowledge contained in atlases will be scrutinized and a new distinction drawn between internal and external power within cartography. Then, the patrons of atlas making—the holders of power in English society—will be identified and the links established between them and the small group of craftsmen who produced the geographical atlases. Finally, the influence of power on cartographic representation in the atlases is examined and suggestions made as to how the atlases may have influenced aspects of group consciousness, or *mentalité*, in eighteenth-century England. It will be argued that while the atlas makers were attempting to produce scientific maps of *territorial* space, they were also ineluctably generating images of *social* space which, far from being value free or objective images from the so-called Age of Reason, were subjective, partisan and rhetorical delineations. Yet it was through these partisan, social configurations, as much as through any factual representation of landscape, that the atlases became a force in history.

EXTERNAL AND INTERNAL POWER IN CARTOGRAPHY

I owe my understanding of the distinction between external and internal power to Joseph Rouse's recent book on *Knowledge and Power*.[6] I have freely adopted his discussion of science in general to the particular case of cartographic knowledge, but the argument requires some initial generalizations about its workings in cartography. External power is often written about by historians of cartography. Individuals, such as a monarch or a minister of the Crown, state institutions, and the institutionalized Church, employ power to initiate a program of mapping for administrative or military purposes.[7] The annals of atlas making alone contain numerous such instances. Political activities, involving what Foucault called the exercise of "juridical power,"[8] have always exerted a marked influence on the organization and practice of cartography. Moreover, as well as in the matter of state sponsorship—in setting up national surveys, for example—juridical power was also used to impede the dissemination of cartographic knowledge. Policies of censorship or secrecy are woven into the history of atlas making as frequently as in that of other forms of cartographic activity.[9] In all these contexts external power is that which was usually centralized, and thus imposed from above. It was usually manifest in acts of deliberate policy. It was exercised discontinuously to meet particular needs and situations. At the same time, it was directed towards particular mapmakers and to the creation of particular cartographic products.

In contrast, the idea of a power internal to cartography stresses that power is not separate from knowledge. It is an integral part of the practices that create knowledge and of the way maps—as a particular form of knowledge—work in society. It is universal, being found wherever maps are made, but equally it creates a local knowledge dependent on context. The focus of inquiry, therefore, shifts from the place of cartography in a juridical system of power to the political effects of what cartographers do when they make maps.[10] We find that cartographers cease to be "nonpolitical agents" in society, above or beyond politics. Inasmuch as power traverses the everyday workshop practices of mapmaking, the atlas maker—albeit often unwittingly—was inevitably concerned with the manufacture of power. The key to this internal power lies in the nature of the cartographic processes. Compilation, generalization, classification, formation into hierarchies, and standardization of geographic data, far from being mere neutral technical activities, involve power/knowledge relations at work. Just as the disciplinary institutions described by Foucault—prisons, schools, armies, factories—serve to normalize human beings,[11] so too the workshop of the mapmaker can be seen as normalizing the phenomena of place and territory in creating a sketch of a made world that society desired. The power of the surveyor and the mapmaker was not generally directly exercised over individuals but over the knowledge of the world made available to people in general.[12]

Internal power is thus clearly different from external power in form and nature. Internal power is local and decentralized rather than being centralized and concentrated; it suffuses the practices of all cartographic workshops rather than being targeted only at the projects of state patronage. As it acts through the cartographic workshop, internal power is not necessarily consciously exercised; its practice is taken for granted, unlike the deliberate acts of externally applied power. Yet these differences between internal and external power do not obscure the fact that power relations penetrate the interstices of cartographic practice and representation. Maps may be read as texts of power/knowledge no less than other fabricated systems of signs.

The trade practices of the English atlas maker can be fitted into this interpretation of power/knowledge. By the eighteenth century, the internal logic of printed cartography—what we are defining here as its internal power—was already well established. Indeed, printed maps share the wider characteristics of the "logic of print" which Marshall McLuhan long ago identified as abstraction, uniformity, repeatability, visuality, and quantification.[13] The consequence of these tendencies was that the technology of mapmaking

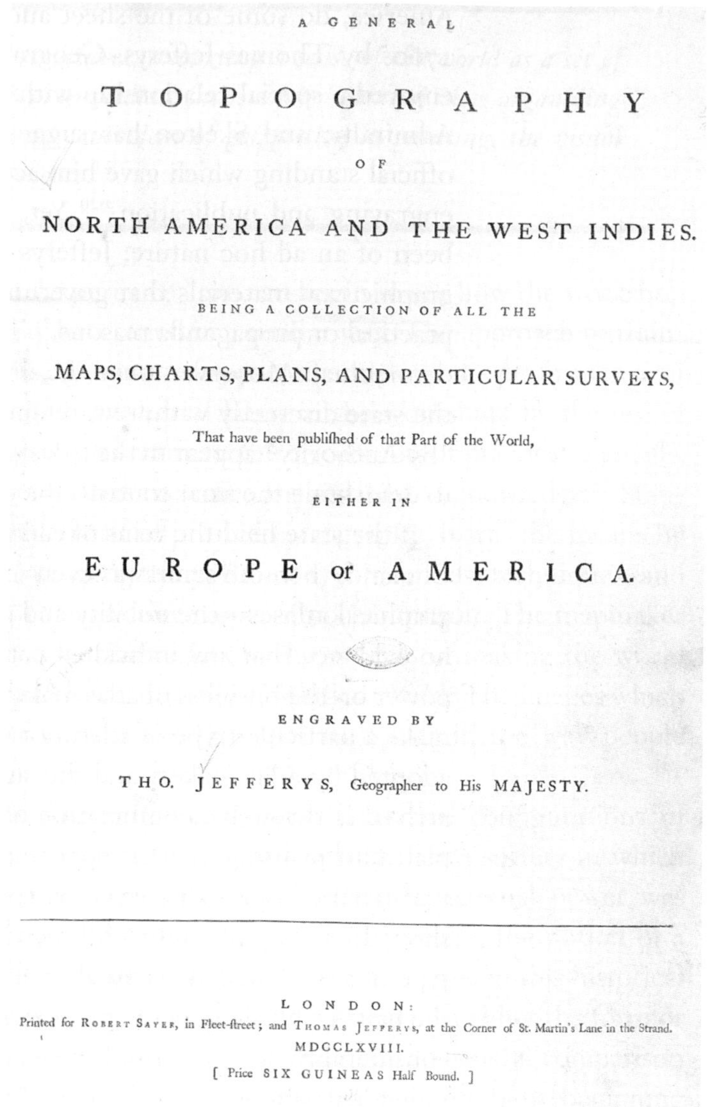

A GENERAL

TOPOGRAPHY

OF

NORTH AMERICA AND THE WEST INDIES.

BEING A COLLECTION OF ALL THE

MAPS, CHARTS, PLANS, AND PARTICULAR SURVEYS,

That have been publifhed of that Part of the World,

EITHER IN

EUROPE or AMERICA.

ENGRAVED BY

THO. JEFFERYS, Geographer to His MAJESTY.

LONDON:
Printed for ROBERT SAYER, in Fleet-ftreet; and THOMAS JEFFERYS, at the Corner of St. Martin's Lane in the Strand.
MDCCLXVIII.
[Price SIX GUINEAS Half Bound.]

FIGURE 75 *The atlas epitomized: title page from* A General Topography of North America and the West Indies . . . *(London: T. Jefferys, 1768). Library of Congress.*

able design, and an awareness of the market, were so enshrined in craft practices and advertised in widely circulating models of what an atlas should look like, that they represent nothing less than a received geography of power. New surveys and raw material arriving in the workshop were processed in the light of the logic of this defined canon. They were accorded, unchallenged, the standard treatment and—not surprisingly—emerged as standardized new maps.

The origin of these graphic stereotypes can be traced back to the sixteenth century, when the epistemological principles of measurement and classification were first indoctrinated into English atlas making.[24] By the eighteenth century, the descendants of these first stereotypes were as much the product of social as of technical factors. Mapmakers were guided by a broad consensus about matters of class, status and ethnicity, sharing the views of their patrons. Elsewhere, or in other periods in England, a cartography of protest can be discerned[25] but few eighteenth-century atlas makers seem to have questioned the social and political order of their world or to have perceived their own craft as a social practice. On the contrary, the more they followed received cartographic practice, the more they were, if inadvertently, reinforcing and reciprocating the dominant social configuration of their age. Their atlases are at once cultural texts and visible models of the social relationships of eighteenth-century England. In this way, power is both implicit and explicit in the mapmakers' projection of an external geography onto the map page. The atlas maker approached his data with hard-headed expectations about the world he was mapping and a clear understanding of the rules of cartography by which the map image was to be produced—rules, such as those of social status, consistent with the rules of society at large. This is the process by which it revealed a terrain of internal power, as clearly delineated in implied social relationships as the engraved lines of rivers and mountain chains in the map image.

PATRONS AND ATLAS MAKERS

In the context of the commercial mapping of eighteenth-century England, the atlas patrons were the agents by which external social power, exchanged through the mapmaker and a standardized technology, entered the atlases to become an interiorized form of power/knowledge. Such a study of the atlas *within* society—as opposed to one in which the atlas is removed from society for minute technical or bibliographical analysis—requires its own special approach. It becomes as important to reconstruct the social divisions and power relations within society as it is to understand the technical processes of mapmaking. We have, therefore, to identify these patrons of eighteenth-century English atlas cartography and to show how they were brought into a close historical and geographical relationship with those who were engaged in the trade of making and selling maps.

Although the precise nature of the English social structure in the eighteenth century—its profile, changing character, and class tensions—have been the subject of much debate,[26] its basic anatomy is sufficient to show how power intersected the geographical knowledge reproduced in the atlases. English society in this period was arranged into a series of marked social divisions, each division having its own symbols of power, snobbery, and wealth. Despite a rigid hierarchy, one social historian has described eighteenth-century English society as a "one-class society," meaning that there was only one major class—comprising the strata of nobility, gentry, clergy, and the professional groups—who possessed a national consciousness of its own existence and influence.[27] Whatever the shortcomings of this diagnosis in historical sociology, it is a useful concept to explain some of the stereotyped images of the atlases, which do indeed appear to mirror the preoccupations of this dominant class in society.

Another major characteristic of English social structure in this period is the extent to which political power was derived from landed wealth. England's elite has been described as "a tight, privileged ring of landowners," while the nation resembled a "federal republic of country houses."[28] Nearly half the cultivated land in eighteenth-century England was owned by some five thousand families. At the apex of this domination, "four hundred families, in a population of some seven or eight million people, owned nearly a quarter of the cultivated land."[29] It is this relation between land and political power, and within which political power was used to protect property, which serves to frame the history of the atlas. Whether at the scale of the English country or of the overseas empire, maps were perceived as reinforcing the patterns of territorial ownership, and it is this potential which helps to explain both which geographical features were emphasized in the atlases and how these representations became a force in society.

Even a cursory inspection suggests that the patrons of English geographical atlases were likely to have been drawn from these upper ranks of society, the landowning class at large. Such groups represented perhaps no more than five percent of the total population yet they exerted a political and cultural hegemony disproportionate to their numbers. Just as was the case with the high art of the period, with its literature, and with its performed music and opera, so too the geographical atlases were regulated and made fashionable by the landed sector of English society. The fact that the sale price of a larger geographical atlas exceeded the average weekly wage of an artisan[30] likewise confirms a form of knowledge whose social distribution was heavily concentrated.

Several historical sources exist to link this social structure to the actual readership of the atlases, and from both sides of the mapmaker patron divide. As far as the map sellers were concerned, they regularly promoted the atlases to catch the eye of their patrons. In advertisements in the London newspapers, it was often the nobility and the gentry who were flattered into buying atlases, often by stressing features of particular interest to their class.[31] Similarly, in atlas dedications—both to the work in general and to the individual maps which comprised them—it is the nobility and gentry who are singled out, in addition to royalty, for attention. It is not by accident (as it will be shown) that coats of arms were so common a form of decoration on these maps.[32]

Even more central to our argument is the extent to which the atlases were actually purchased by those for whom they were intended. Here there is the evidence from the contents of individual libraries,[33] from book auction catalogs, and from subscription lists printed in the atlases themselves. The London auction lists are the subject of existing studies which confirm the regular purchase of geographical atlases by the nobility, gentry, and professional groups.[34] But it is the subscription lists, available for a dozen or so eighteenth-century English atlases, which provide the richest data for sociostructural analysis of map readership.[35] An analysis is given below of two of the surviving lists. It is a means of linking social structure to atlas production, and it also shows how cartography was caught up in an intricate network of wider power relations.

The first example is afforded by John Senex's *A New General Atlas*, published in London in 1721.[36] Naming himself in the Preface as Geographer to the Queen, he commended "... the usefulness of a Book of this sort to Nobleman, Gentlemen, Commanders by Sea and Land, Divines, Lawyers, Physicians, and Merchants."[37] Eight categories of prospective reader were identified by Senex,[38] headed by "Sovereigns, with their Ministers" and ending with "Husbandmen, with Ordinary Mechanicks." For some reason, Senex made a special appeal to the last group. "This Science is necessary," he wrote, "for all Ranks of men, from the Prince to the Peasant" but we should not allow this egalitarian sentiment to distract us from the reality of his readership. Also in the preliminaries of the atlas, 1061 subscribers, identifying rank and title, are enumerated. (See Figure 76.) Table 1 is a simple analysis of this list. While it cannot reflect the many fine gra-

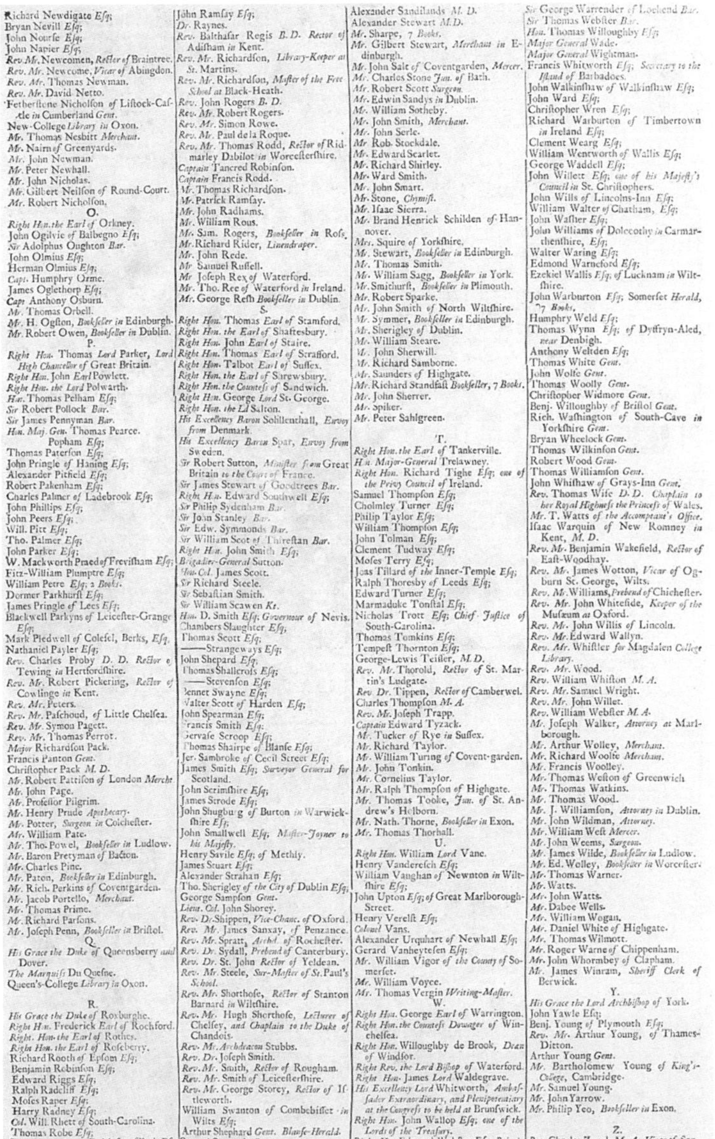
Richard Newdigate Esq;
Bryan Nevill Esq;
John Nourse Esq;
John Napier Esq;
Rev. Mr. Newcomen, Rector of Braintree.
Rev. Mr. Newcome, Vicar of Abingdon.
Rev. Mr. Thomas Newman.
Rev. Mr. David Netto.
Fetherstone Nicholson of Listock-Castle in Cumberland Gent.
New-College Library in Oxon.
Mr. Thomas Nesbitt Merchant.
Mr. Nairn of Greenyards.
Mr. John Newman.
Mr. Peter Newhall.
Mr. John Nicholas.
Mr. Gilbert Neilson of Round-Court.
Mr. Robert Nicholson.
O.
Right Hon. the Earl of Orkney.
John Ogilvie of Balbegno Esq;
Sir Adolphus Oughton Bar.
John Olmius Esq;
Herman Olmius Esq;
Capt. Humphry Orme.
James Oglethorp Esq;
Capt Anthony Osburn.
Mr. Thomas Orbell.
Mr. H. Ogston, Bookseller in Edinburgh.
Mr. Robert Owen, Bookseller in Dublin.
P.
Right Hon. Thomas Lord Parker, Lord High Chancellor of Great Britain.
Right Hon. John Earl Powlett.
Right Hon. the Lord Polwarth.
Hon. Thomas Pelham Esq;
Sir Robert Pollock Bar.
Sir James Pennyman Bar.
Hon. Maj. Gen. Thomas Pearce.
Popham Esq;
Thomas Paterson Esq;
John Pringle of Haning Esq;
Alexander Pitfield Esq;
Robert Pakenham Esq;
Charles Palmer of Ladebrook Esq;
John Phillips Esq;
John Peers Esq;
Will. Pitt Esq;
Tho. Palmer Esq;
John Parker Esq;
W. Mackworth Praed of Frevisham Esq;
Fitz-William Plumptre Esq;
William Petre Esq; 2 Books.
Dormer Parkhurst Esq;
James Pringle of Lees Esq;
Blackwell Parkyns of Leicester-Grange Esq;
Mark Pledwell of Colesel, Berks, Esq.
Nathaniel Payler Esq;
Rev. Charles Proby D. D. Rector of Tewing in Hertfordshire.
Rev. Mr. Robert Pickering, Rector of Cowlinge in Kent.
Rev. Mr. Peters.
Rev. Mr. Paschoud, of Little Chelsea.
Rev. Mr. Symon Pagett.
Rev. Mr. Thomas Perrot.
Major Richardson Pack.
Francis Panton Gent.
Christopher Pack M. D.
Mr. Robert Pattison of London Mercht
Mr. John Page.
Mr. Professor Pilgrim.
Mr. Henry Prude Apothecary.
Mr. Potter, Surgeon in Colchester.
Mr. William Pate.
Mr. Tho. Powel, Bookseller in Ludlow.
Mr. Baron Pretyman of Bacton.
Mr. Charles Pine.
Mr. Paton, Bookseller in Edinburgh.
Mr. Rich. Perkins of Coventgarden.
Mr. Jacob Portello, Merchant.
Mr. Thomas Prime.
Mr. Richard Parsons.
Mr. Joseph Penn, Bookseller in Bristol.
Q.
His Grace the Duke of Queensberry and Dover.
The Marquiss Du Quesne.
Queen's-College Library in Oxon.
R.
His Grace the Duke of Roxburghe.
Right Hon. Frederick Earl of Rochford.
Right. Hon. the Earl of Rothes.
Right Hon. the Earl of Roseberry.
Richard Rooth of Epsom Esq;
Benjamin Robinson Esq;
Edward Riggs Esq;
Ralph Radcliff Esq;
Moses Raper Esq;
Harry Radney Esq;
Col. Will. Rhett of South-Carolina.
Thomas Robe Esq;
Tho. Strangeways Robinson of York Esq
Thomas Robinson of Rookby Esq;
John Ramsay Esq;
Dr. Raynes.
Rev. Balthasar Regis B. D. Rector of Adisham in Kent.
Rev. Mr. Richardson, Library-Keeper at St. Martins.
Rev. Mr. Richardson, Master of the Free School at Black-Heath.
Rev. John Rogers B. D.
Rev. Mr. Robert Rogers.
Rev. Mr. Simon Rowe.
Rev. Mr. Paul de la Roque.
Rev. Mr. Thomas Rodd, Rector of Ridmarley Dabilot in Worcestershire.
Captain Tancred Robinson.
Captain Francis Rodd.
Mr. Thomas Richardson.
Mr. Patrick Ramsay.
Mr. John Radhams.
Mr. William Rous.
Mr. Sam. Rogers, Bookseller in Ross.
Mr. Richard Rider, Linendraper.
Mr. John Rede.
Mr Samuel Russell.
Mr Joseph Rex of Waterford.
Mr. Tho. Ree of Waterford in Ireland.
Mr. George Resh Bookseller in Dublin.
S.
Right Hon. Thomas Earl of Stamford.
Right Hon. the Earl of Shaftesbury.
Right Hon. John Earl of Staire.
Right Hon. Thomas Earl of Strafford.
Right Hon. Talbot Earl of Sussex.
Right Hon. the Earl of Shrewsbury.
Right Hon. the Countess of Sandwich.
Right Hon. George Lord St. George.
Right Hon. the Ld Salton.
His Excellency Baron Sohllenthall, Envoy from Denmark.
His Excellency Baron Spar, Envoy from Sweden.
Sir Robert Sutton, Minister from Great Britain to the Court of France.
Sir James Stewart of Goodtrees Bar.
Right Hon. Edward Southwell Esq;
Sir Philip Sydenham Bar.
Sir John Stanley Bar.
Sir Edw. Symmonds Bar.
Sir William Scot of Thirestan Bar.
Right Hon. John Smith Esq;
Brigadier-General Sutton.
Hon. Col. James Scott.
Sir Richard Steele.
Sir Sebastian Smith.
Sir William Scawen Kt.
Hon. D. Smith Esq; Governour of Nevis.
Chambers Slaughter Esq;
Thomas Scott Esq;
——Strangeways Esq;
John Shepard Esq;
Thomas Shallcross Esq;
——Stevenson Esq;
Bennet Swayne Esq;
Walter Scott of Harden Esq;
John Spearman Esq;
Francis Smith Esq;
Gervase Scroop Esq;
Thomas Shairpe of Hanse Esq;
Jer. Sambroke of Cecil Street Esq;
James Smith Esq; Surveyor General for Scotland.
John Scrimshire Esq;
James Strode Esq;
John Shugburg of Burton in Warwickshire Esq;
John Smallwell Esq; Master-Joyner to his Majesty.
Henry Savile Esq; of Methly.
James Stuart Esq;
Alexander Strahan Esq;
Tho. Sherigley of the City of Dublin Esq;
George Sampson Gent.
Lieut. Col. John Shorey.
Rev. Dr. Shippen, Vice-Chanc. of Oxford.
Rev. Mr. James Sanxay, of Penzance.
Rev. Mr. Spratt, Archd. of Rochester.
Rev. Dr. Sydall, Prebend of Canterbury.
Rev. Dr. St. John Rector of Yeldean.
Rev. Mr. Steele, Sur-Master of St. Paul's School.
Rev. Mr. Shorthose, Rector of Stanton Barnard in Wiltshire.
Rev. Mr. Hugh Shorthose, Lecturer of Chelsey, and Chaplain to the Duke of Chandois.
Rev. Mr. Archdeacon Stubbs.
Rev. Dr. Joseph Smith.
Rev. Mr. Smith, Rector of Rougham.
Rev. Mr. Smith of Leicestershire.
Rev. Mr. George Storey, Rector of Istleworth.
William Swanton of Combebisset in Wilts Esq;
Arthur Shephard Gent. Blanse-Herald.
Samuel Symonds Gent.
Mr. William Smith Merchant.
Alexander Sandilands M. D.
Alexander Stewart M. D.
Mr. Sharpe, 7 Books.
Mr. Gilbert Stewart, Merchant in Edinburgh.
Mr. John Salt of Coventgarden, Mercer.
Mr. Charles Stone Jun. of Bath.
Mr. Robert Scott Surgeon.
Mr. Edwin Sandys in Dublin.
Mr. William Sotheby.
Mr. John Smith, Merchant.
Mr. John Serle.
Mr Rob. Stockdale.
Mr. Edward Searlet.
Mr. Richard Shirley.
Mr. Ward Smith.
Mr. John Smart.
Mr. Stone, Chymist.
Mr. Isaac Sierra.
Mr. Brand Henrick Schilden of Hanover.
Mrs. Squire of Yorkshire.
Mr. Stewart, Bookseller in Edinburgh.
Mr. Thomas Smith.
Mr. William Sagg, Bookseller in York.
Mr. Smithurst, Bookseller in Plimouth.
Mr. Robert Sparke.
Mr. John Smith of North Wiltshire.
Mr. Symmer, Bookseller in Edinburgh.
Mr. Sherigley of Dublin.
Mr. William Steare.
Mr. John Sherwill.
Mr. Richard Samborne.
Mr. Saunders of Highgate.
Mr. Richard Standfast Bookseller, 7 Books.
Mr. John Sherrer.
Mr. Spiker.
Mr. Peter Sahlgreen.
T.
Right Hon. the Earl of Tankerville.
Hon. Major-General Trelawney.
Right Hon. Richard Tighe Esq; one of the Privy Council of Ireland.
Samuel Thompson Esq;
Cholmley Turner Esq;
Philip Taylor Esq;
William Thompson Esq;
John Tolman Esq;
Clement Tudway Esq;
Moses Terry Esq;
Joas Tillard of the Inner-Temple Esq;
Ralph Thoresby of Leeds Esq;
Edward Turner Esq;
Marmaduke Tonstal Esq;
Nicholas Trott Esq; Chief Justice of South-Carolina.
Thomas Tomkins Esq;
Tempest Thornton Esq;
George-Lewis Teissier, M. D.
Rev. Mr. Thorold, Rector of St. Martin's Ludgate.
Rev Dr. Tippen, Rector of Camberwel.
Charles Thompson M. A.
Rev. Mr. Joseph Trapp.
Captain Edward Tyzack.
Mr. Tucker of Rye in Sussex.
Mr. Richard Taylor.
Mr. William Turing of Covent-garden.
Mr. John Tonkin.
Mr. Cornelius Taylor.
Mr. Ralph Thompson of Highgate.
Mr. Thomas Tooke, Jun. of St. Andrew's Holborn.
Mr. Nath. Thorne, Bookseller in Exon.
Mr. Thomas Thorhall.
U.
Right Hon. William Lord Vane.
Henry Vanderesch Esq;
William Vaughan of Newnton in Wiltshire Esq;
John Upton Esq; of Great Marlborough-Street.
Henry Verelst Esq;
Colonel Vans.
Alexander Urquhart of Newhall Esq;
Gerard Vanheytesen Esq;
Mr. William Vigor of the County of Somerset.
Mr. William Voyce.
Mr. Thomas Vergin Writing-Master.
W.
Right Hon. George Earl of Warrington.
Right Hon. the Countess Dowager of Winchelsea.
Right Hon. Willoughby de Brook, Dean of Windsor.
Right Rev. the Lord Bishop of Waterford.
Right Hon. James Lord Waldegrave.
His Excellency Lord Whitworth, Ambassador Extraordinary, and Plenipotentiary at the Congress to be held at Brunswick.
Right Hon. John Wallop Esq; one of the Lords of the Treasury.
Right Hon. Edward Webster Esq; Principal Secretary to the Ld Lieut. of Ireland.
Sir George Warrender of Lochend Bar.
Sir Thomas Webster Bar.
Hon. Thomas Willoughby Esq;
Major General Wade.
Major General Wightman.
Francis Whitworth Esq; Secretary to the Island of Barbadoes.
John Walkinshaw of Walkinshaw Esq;
John Ward Esq;
Christopher Wren Esq;
Richard Warburton of Timbertown in Ireland Esq;
Clement Wearg Esq;
William Wentworth of Wallis Esq;
George Waddell Esq;
John Willett Esq; one of his Majesty's Council in St. Christophers.
John Wills of Lincolns-Inn Esq;
William Walter of Chatham, Esq;
John Washer Esq;
John Williams of Dolecothy in Carmarthenshire, Esq;
Walter Waring Esq;
Edmond Warneford Esq;
Ezekiel Wallis Esq; of Lucknam in Wiltshire.
John Warburton Esq; Somerset Herald, 7 Books.
Humphry Weld Esq;
Thomas Wynn Esq; of Dyffryn-Aled, near Denbigh.
Anthony Weltden Esq;
Thomas White Gent.
John Wolfe Gent.
Thomas Woolly Gent.
Christopher Widmore Gent.
Benj. Willoughby of Bristol Gent.
Rich. Washington of South-Cave in Yorkshire Gent.
Bryan Wheelock Gent.
Thomas Wilkinson Gent.
Robert Wood Gent.
Thomas Williamson Gent.
John Whishaw of Grays-Inn Gent.
Rev. Thomas Wise D. D. Chaplain to her Royal Highness the Princess of Wales.
Mr. T. Watts of the Accomptant's Office.
Isaac Warquin of New Romney in Kent, M. D.
Rev. Mr. Benjamin Wakefield, Rector of East-Woodhay.
Rev. Mr. James Wotton, Vicar of Ogburn St. George, Wilts.
Rev. Mr. Williams, Prebend of Chichester.
Rev. Mr. John Whiteside, Keeper of the Musæum at Oxford.
Rev. Mr. John Willis of Lincoln.
Rev. Mr. Edward Wallyn.
Rev. Mr. Whistler for Magdalen College Library.
Rev. Mr. Wood.
Rev. William Whiston M. A.
Rev. Mr. Samuel Wright.
Rev. Mr. John Willet.
Rev. William Webster M. A.
Mr. Joseph Walker, Attorney at Marlborough.
Mr. Arthur Wolley, Merchant.
Mr. Richard Woolfe Merchant.
Mr. Francis Woolley.
Mr. Thomas Weston of Greenwich
Mr. Thomas Watkins.
Mr. Thomas Wood.
Mr. J. Williamson, Attorney in Dublin.
Mr. John Wildman, Attorney.
Mr. William West Mercer.
Mr. John Weems, Surgeon.
Mr. James Wilde, Bookseller in Ludlow.
Mr. Ed. Wolley, Bookseller in Worcester.
Mr. Thomas Warner.
Mr. Watts.
Mr. John Watts.
Mr. Dabee Wells.
Mr. William Wogan.
Mr. Daniel White of Highgate.
Mr. Thomas Wilmott.
Mr. Roger Warne of Chippenham.
Mr. John Whormbey of Clapham.
Mr. James Winram, Sheriff Clerk of Berwick.
Y.
His Grace the Lord Archbishop of York.
John Yawle Esq;
Benj. Young of Plymouth Esq;
Rev. Mr. Arthur Young, of Thames-Ditton.
Arthur Young Gent.
Mr. Bartholomew Young of King's-College, Cambridge.
Mr. Samuel Young.
Mr. John Yarrow.
Mr. Philip Yeo, Bookseller in Exon.
Z.
Rev. Charles Zouch M. A. Vicar of Sandal Magna.

FIGURE 76 *The patrons of atlas cartography: list of subscribers. John Senex,* A New General Atlas *(London: D. Browne, 1721). Library of Congress.*

TABLE 1   Social Status of Subscribers to Senex's *A New and General Atlas . . .* 1721

Recorded status in subscriber list*	Number of subscribers		Percent
1. Noblemen (includes Dukes, Earls Marquess's, Viscounts, Barons) and Spiritual Lords (Archbishops and Bishops)	100 } (Nobility)		10
2. Baronets and Knights	62		
3. Esquires	330 } (Gentlemen)		41
4. Gentlemen	34		
5. Clergymen	105		10
6. "Professions"† (MDs, Lawyers, Merchants, Military Officers, etc.)	120		11
7. "Non-Gentry" (includes Yeomen, Husbandmen, Tradesmen, and Craftsmen)	296		28
Totals‡	1047		100

* These categories are adapted from the discussion in Peter Laslett, *The World We have Lost: Further Explored,* 3d ed. (London: Methuen, 1983), including Table 2, p. 38. Categories 1–6 provide approximately three-quarters of the subscribers (72%).

† The term is Laslett's.

‡ Not all subscribers are identified by rank and occupation; the total number listed is 1061.

dations and nuances of contemporary English social structure, it nevertheless serves to underline how the subscribers to Senex's *Atlas . . .* were drawn largely from groups in whose hands economic and political power was concentrated. Indeed, the alphabetical listings are a roll call of honorific titles. They enable us to locate the atlas patrons among the greater and minor nobility and, above all, from that class known as the gentry. While the designations do not always permit us to distinguish between those who were primarily landowners from those with other definite occupations—such as clergymen, court officials, diplomats, lawyers, merchants, military officers, schoolmasters and dons—there is no doubt that their common interest, and the class identity postulated by Laslett, lay in the possession of landed property. That such a class dominated atlas patronage is confirmed by the coats of arms engraved after the subscriber lists. (See Figure 77.) These were designed to single out those subscribers with the right to bear arms and it is significant that well over half (728) of the subscribers to Senex's *Atlas . . .* came from the mainly landed families which possessed such a right.

The dominance of the landowners as atlas patrons must, however, be approached cautiously. During the eighteenth century their relative importance, numerically if not in terms of power, was slipping with the rise of an urban and industrial bourgeoisie. Even in Senex's *Atlas . . .* of 1721—published at a time when Laslett's supposed one-class society was at its zenith—twenty-six percent of

FIGURE 77 *Subscribers' coats of arms: Senex,
A New General Atlas (London, 1721). Library
of Congress.*

the subscribers did not belong to the gentry or nobility. In London especially, but also in the larger towns, a readership was growing for maps from the rising commercial and craft groups and among the artisan mathematical practitioners whose fortunes were enhanced by the expansion of agriculture, commerce, and industry.[39] Thus, even among Senex's subscribers, we find occupations such as those of apothecary, architect, bookseller, draper, goldsmith, limner (painter), mathematical-instrument maker, printer, watchmaker, and writing master.

By the late eighteenth century the numerical importance of these groups as patrons of cartography had further increased. More atlases were being published and some were cheaper in price. Maps in general were sharing the reality, by 1790, of "a well-developed print society," as compared with a century earlier.[40] Such was the background for our second example, Cary's *New and Correct English Atlas* (1787).[41] This includes a list containing approximately the same number of subscribers as Senex's *Atlas...*, but Table 2 shows a striking difference in the social composition of the readership. The relative importance of the nobility had declined from ten to three percent and that of the gentry had dropped, less markedly, from forty-one to thirty-six percent. Clergymen remained a stable group of atlas buyers. Most outstanding was the rise of the "nongentry" subscribers to over forty percent in Cary's atlas. Even if these two atlases are not representative of eighteenth-century atlases as a whole,[42]—or that Cary's was a smaller and cheaper work—the differences nevertheless alert us to the possibility of a changing relationship between social structure and cartography.

In attempting to understand how power becomes internal to cartographic practices, we also have to consider the context of mapmakers in their articulation of that power. The English geographical atlas of the eighteenth century can be seen as "the deposit of a social relationship."[43] On one side of the relationship were, as we have seen, the patrons of the atlas—a readership drawn predominantly from one class who purchased the atlases and recommended them to others in their circle. On the other side, there was the mapmaker who made the atlas or at least supervised its making. The balance of power in eighteenth-century England lay with the patron rather than with the craftsman who supplied his needs. Mapmakers and map sellers were located well down the hierarchy of social power. This meant that mapmaking could never be an autonomous enter-

TABLE 2   Social Status of Subscribers to Cary's *New and Correct English Atlas* (1787)

Recorded status in subscriber list*	Number of subscribers		Percent
1. Noblemen	39	(Nobility)	3
2. Baronets and Knights	27		
3. Esquires	396	(Gentry)	35.7
4. Gentlemen	—		
5. Clergymen	158		13
6. Miscellaneous† (MDs, Lawyers, Merchants, Military Officers, etc.)	44		4.5
7. "Non-Gentry"	520		43.8
Totals	1184		100.0

* For comparative purposes these groups are derived from Laslett (1983) as in Table 1 although the divisions, reflecting a configuration from the late seventeenth century, were increasingly inappropriate to English society by the end of the eighteenth century.
† The term is Laslett's.

prise, especially for the atlas makers who were aiming a relatively expensive product at a quality market, and who could not hope to be entirely free and independent agents. Directly and indirectly, like most craft practitioners, the atlas maker's livelihood lay in the palms of the Great.[44]

By identifying the position of the atlas maker in eighteenth-century society we can begin to understand how their maps came to adopt and to reinforce the dominant social values of their patrons. Indeed, there would have been several reasons why the cartographic tradesmen may have been especially responsive to their patrons' social world and to their particular class's constructions of geographical knowledge. For one thing, atlas makers never formed a strong or cohesive craft group. At any one moment throughout the eighteenth century only a handful of named individuals—the Bowles family, the Bowens, Ovary, Dury, Dunn, Faden, Gibson, Jefferys, Kitchin, Moll, Sayer and Senex—never more than a dozen or so, were dominant in this specialized form of geographical publishing. While their output may appear at first sight to be prolific, a closer look shows how they borrowed their cartography freely from a limited, and usually outdated, stock of original maps. Trading copperplates between publishers, they also engaged in serial publication and took shares in each others' atlases.[45] As their contemporaries realized, the trade was largely driven by the market rather than by any sustained notion of a "scientific" geography.[46] In such a publishing climate, we may suppose that the atlas makers had to be especially sensitive to the traditional values of their patrons as well as to changes of fashion in the print trade as a whole.

In fact, the term "atlas maker," as we apply it to the eighteenth century, is the creation of modern cartobibliography. The production of maps in eighteenth-century England (as at other times) was a manifold process requiring the work of editor, draftsmen, engraver, printer, map colorer, publisher and seller. In practice, these functions were sometimes combined into one workshop, but in other instances they were separated. More alien still to eighteenth-century eyes would have been our modern notion (which only emerged in nineteenth-century England) of the specialist atlas maker. Even the most specialized mapmakers diversified their businesses into a wide range of other publications. Bowen, Jefferys, and Kitchin, for example, while styling themselves as "Geographers" and holding privileges to supply members of the royal household with maps, engaged in other branches of engraving, publishing and print selling.[47] Thomas Kitchin published "hieroglyphicks" and other political prints;[48] Thomas Jefferys and Robert Sayer had a line in prints other than the strictly geographical;[49] and later in the century, Robert Sayer, while issuing specialist atlas catalogs was also a major publisher in other branches of the graphic arts.[50] For other "atlas makers," moreover, the geographical atlas was even more of an incidental line of business. Thomas and John Bowles, for example, may have been better known as publishers of prints of social satires than as map publishers.[51] Thus, in John Bowles's 1753 "Catalogue of Maps, Prints, Copy Books, &c.," we read that "Merchants for

Exportation, Gentlemen for Furniture, Shop-keepers to sell again, May be furnished with the greatest Variety of Maps and Prints, at the lowest Prices".[52] Bowles' phrase, "the greatest variety of maps and prints," reminds us to place the geographical atlas in the wider world of the graphic arts. Bowles and Son ran a wholesale and retail business selling sheet maps in various formats, but they also stocked a range of prints of different sizes and subjects. Historical, sporting, architectural, moral, religious, naval and military prints, perspective views, writing and drawing books, mezzotints—all passed through their hands. Only a small section of their 1753 Catalogue was devoted to "Books of Maps" (that is, atlases) and these were mixed in the stock with texts on architecture and on practical geometry and items such as "Gentleman's Guides" and "Pocket Companions."

The significance of such diversity is that there were many conduits from the wider world into the atlas maker's workshop. Far from being an esoteric craft, such cartography was borne along by the wider currents of social and political attitudes which flowed through English society. Atlas production in eighteenth-century England, linked both to the general expansion of the graphic arts and to the wider fields of geographical and historical publishing, was particularly well placed to articulate the social construction of geographical knowledge favored by its patrons.

The proximity of eighteenth-century atlas making to the seats of national power in London also reinforced this tendency. That production and distribution was overwhelmingly concentrated in the capital is well known, but its significance for the patronage of cartography needs to be stressed. While surveying skills were widely diffused in Great Britain and to a lesser extent in the overseas colonies, most of the map and atlas compilation, editing, engraving, printing, and publication—in common with the book and print trades—was concentrated in London.[53] For atlas production this domination may have been a nearly total one[54] and it brought cartographers and patrons into potentially close proximity. London-based institutions such as the Court, Parliament, the departments of State, the law courts, the great chartered companies, as well as the social round, all drew the landed gentry away from the shires for at least part of the year. If the mapmaker only occasionally met his patron face-to-face, he would have been constantly reminded of his existence and of the need to manipulate knowledge to serve his interests. The eminences of social power were never far away from the map sellers' shops of St. Pauls and the Strand.

The mapmaker working in London also had easy access to a geographical knowledge already structured by power. The source materials of geographical atlases reveal their compilers as in tune not only with events in the domestic sphere impinging on their craft—the enactment of Parliamentary legislation relating to canals and turnpike roads, to take just one example—but also with military struggles in the European theater and, increasingly, with the national saga of the British overseas empires in North America, Asia, and the Pacific.[55]

After the defeat of France in the Seven Years War (1756–1763), England's supremacy over the seas and imperial trade was greatly enhanced. Her hold on the non-European world was tightening and English geographical discovery, the events of which were often given prominence on new maps, was constantly serving colonial schemes. London became an *entrepôt* and clearinghouse for the geographical knowledge of a far-flung territorial system. (See Figure 78.)

For the social history of the English atlas, its position at a crossroads of knowledge is a matter of considerable importance. The atlas maker had access—albeit sometimes indirectly or at several removes—to the geographical intelligence, including maps, which filtered into London through diplomatic, military, naval, and mercantile channels.[56] Located in an increasingly cosmopolitan city, the cartographer was being exposed to those ideas, political attitudes, ethnic stereotypes, cultural values and ideological convictions which permeated not just maps but a burgeoning knowledge industry in general.[57]

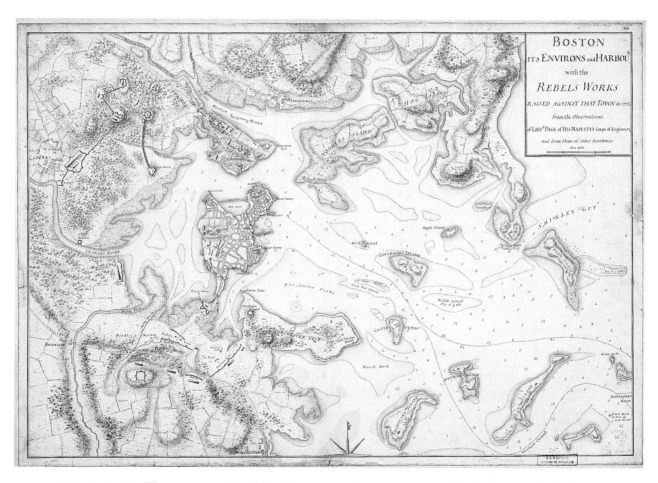

FIGURE 78   *The raw materials of the atlas: manuscript maps.* Boston, its Environs and Harbour with the Rebels Works . . . from the Observations of Lieut. Page of His Majesty's Corps of Engineers . . . *(1775). Library of Congress.*

REPRESENTATIONS OF POWER

We can now turn to see how power is represented in the maps of the atlases and try to gauge its influence. The argument focuses on the unarticulated aspects of power in the atlas, that is to say on the hidden agenda of social power which operates on the reader as an unconscious force and through the symbolic meaning of the image as much as through the literal facts of geography. In the discussion of historical influence, I am less concerned with the practical ways in which the atlases were used in the exercise of power—for administrative, diplomatic, military, propaganda, or surveillance purposes, all of which were well documented in the eighteenth century—than with the way the atlas maps worked to structure social attitudes and to support a preexisting geography of power relations. These tendencies—both of representation and of influence—will be illustrated in relation to the ideology in maps found in two groups of English geographical atlases: first, the county or regional atlases of England and Wales; and second, the general or universal atlases published before American independence. In the case of the latter, the discussion will be confined to examples of maps of North America.

County Atlases

Despite the continuing expansion of the English overseas world in the eighteenth century, the horizons of the majority of Englishmen were limited to the countrysides and towns of which they had direct experience. In practice, the county was the focus of the lives of the English nobility and gentry. It was through the county administrative and legal systems that regional patronage and power were exercised. It was within a county framework, too, that social power circulated, with the leading families arranged in their own county hierarchies and closely linked by ties of marriage and property.[58] The gentry may have held land in more than one county, or have visited London and Bath in the season, but it was to their own counties that they returned and to which they felt the strongest loyalty. Much of the popularity of the county atlas—as of other works of county history and topography—rested on this county/gentry association. From the first publication of Saxton's atlas in 1579, the bonding of county atlas and county society was one of the active factors in the regionalization of English society. By the eighteenth century, the county atlas—in its many formats—had become entrenched as the dominant form of native English atlas publication.

But the county atlas/county society relationship was more than a matter of custom, format, and trade. Consensus and reciprocity between publisher and reader extended into the content and design of the maps. By 1700, the mapmakers had accumulated over a century's experience in pleasing their clients. Many features of seventeenth-century atlases—as well as some of the copperplates themselves—passed into the new century with no more than cosmetic modification.[59] Throughout the eighteenth century, county atlases remained markedly conservative in the way they represented the class interests of their clients. Genuflections to rank and power are found in the decoration of each map, in its dedications, and in features such as lists of the "seats of nobility." The coats of arms of county nobility, towns or institutions were a particularly common addition to county maps and atlases before 1750.[60] John Warburton made a point of advertising the provision of engraved coats of arms as the hallmark of his county maps. These would serve for "Persons of Distinction most of which are descended or enjoy Lands," he wrote snobbishly, "as an Index to shew the present Possessors of every individual Village, Castle, or Seat."[61] Even utility atlases, those designed for travelers, such as John Owen's roadbook *Britannia Depicta* (a combination of strip maps showing the roads and small county maps), were often dressed with features such as "The Arms of the Peers of this Realm who derive their Titles from places lying on, or near the Roads" and, to register the power of the established state religion, "The Arms of all ye Bishopricks & Denaries, their foundation, Extent, Yearly-Value, Number of Parishes &c."[62]

The general fashion for coats of arms was past by the middle of the century but confirmations of the structure of English society continued to be provided. In the atlases produced by Bowen and Kitchin these included dedications to the Lords Lieutenant of each county; marginal lists of "Seats of the Nobility and Gentry"; dates, going back to the Norman conquest, for those holding the rank of Earl; lists of Bishops ("Since the Reformation"); and dates of ancient borough charters.[63] (See Figure 79.) This sort of historical information, whether added to the map itself or given in an accompanying text,[64] reflects in part the atlas makers' perception of the rise of antiquarian interests among the nobility and gentry in eighteenth-century England.[65] But it is also open to ideological interpretation. Coats of arms or engravings of cathedrals in the corners of maps may be read as emblems of power, transferring authority into the space of the map.[66] Likewise, an affirmation of antiquity can be seen as an act of unconscious legitimation, a symbol of social cohesion, and a displaying of the roots of institutions and hierarchical domination as a justification of their survival to the present time.[67]

So much for the atlas in its general format and decoration. Turning now to the maps themselves, it is not difficult to see how they also had been made to suit the rights and priorities of the patron class. From 1750 onward, the county atlas maps were derived from more detailed original surveys,[68] but even so they continued to portray a decidedly partial view of the landscape of England and Wales. Social eminences such as country houses were surveyed as much as natural landmarks. The compilation of each map had clearly involved not only judgments about how things were in the landscape but also about the way the dominant group in society believed they ought to be. The beliefs and values of the nobility and gentry had thus structured a way of seeing, a way of surveying, and a way of interpreting the world so that the map became an image of their domination.

For instance, the boundaries of administrative units of jurisdiction and taxation—the county and the hundred—were always stressed. So too were the bor-

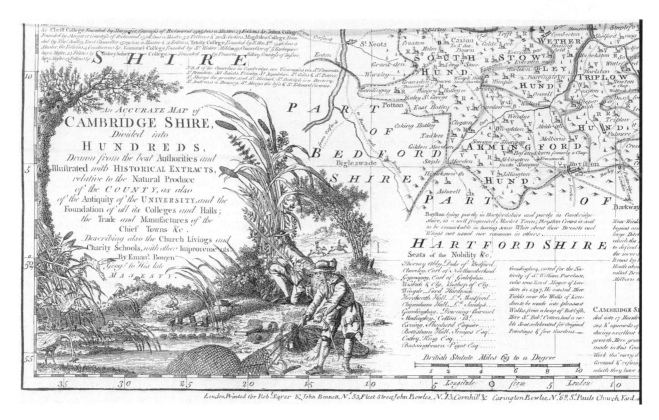

FIGURE 79 *The atlas as social proclamation: detail showing seats of nobility, etc., in Cambridgeshire. Emmanuel Bowen,* The Royal English Atlas *(London: C. Bowles, 1778). Library of Congress.*

oughs, from the courts of which justice was dispensed or which sent members to the Parliament at Westminster to represent the interests of this one national class and to enact its legislation. Similarly, the action and living space of the gentry and clergy was underlined on the maps, which served to confirm their social authority. The "seats," or houses, of gentlemen together with their parklands are especially prominent. (See Figure 80.) Rectories, vicarages, and curacies were included as emblems of the social power of the established church, not just as records of the livelihood of a large group of subscribers. The content of the atlas maps did not, of course, remain unchanged throughout the century. In line with the growing percentage of subscribers to Cary's 1787 atlas who were associated with trade and manufactures, the image of some of Cary's atlas maps also began to reflect the care taken to locate the investment opportunities of this class in commercial and industrial enterprises. Coal mines, canals, turnpike roads, commons and heaths in process of enclosure, expanding towns and suburbs were all entered into maps as symbols of the new wealth. But it is the rise of new masters rather than a decline of power that these late-eighteenth-century maps portray. Instead of the old landscape of a predominantly landowning society, we detect in the new maps signs of a strengthening agrarian and industrial capitalism, that of the so-called agricultural and industrial revolutions.

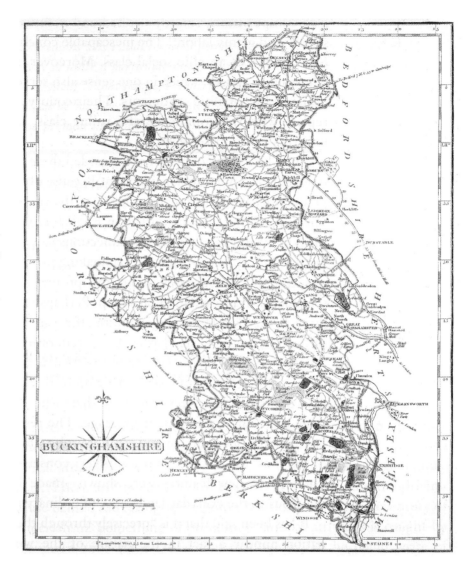

FIGURE 80 *The atlas as gentrified landscape: parklands in Buckinghamshire. John Cary, New and Correct English Atlas (London: J. Cary, 1787). Library of Congress.*

As witnesses of the social order of Georgian England, the cartographic silences in the county atlas maps are as eloquent as the features that are mapped. Atlas maps, just like the English landscape paintings of the same period, idealized the countryside. They sought, if unwittingly, to hide the reality of rural poverty.[69] The only hint that another social class perhaps existed in England is the newly introduced sign for "charity schools."[70] Although individual parklands on late-eighteenth-century maps are crowded with the designs of landscape gardeners such as Capability Brown, beyond the wall of the park, where men and women toiled in the fields, the map landscape is often quite empty. No awkward manifestations of backwardness are shown. There are no map signs for poverty or squalor, and the bland washes of the map colorer denote a green and pleasant land. Even where there are vignettes of industrial activity on a map, it is sometimes only the tools of trade that are displayed while the workers themselves are either hidden from view or are presented in ideal-

English nation against all other nations. Thus Moll could end the introduction to the *Atlas Minor* (1729) with a flourish: "the *British* Nation has no Superior upon the Globe, and the King of *Great Britain* no Equal."[78] In the concluding part of this essay, it will be shown how such attitudes were manifest in representations of North America in these world atlases.[79] As in the case of the county atlases, we shall focus on how cartography exerts power by legitimation rather than with how maps were a vital instrument in the practical management of colonial and imperial enterprises.[80] All that has to be borne in mind is that, given the colonial context, a different set of power relations was at work in the case of the American maps. An English social structure was transplanted into some of the North American colonies but, as the atlases reveal, power struggles between different European nations for overseas territory and, more unequally, the power relations between European and non-European peoples also play their role in producing the map image.

Until the War of Independence, the thirteen North American colonies were the jewel in the English imperial crown. While in all general European atlases the nations of Europe tended to be allocated space disproportionate to their size in the world,[81] in the atlases of the London cartographers, North America and the West Indies assumed increasing prominence throughout the eighteenth century. Even in the earlier atlases of Moll,[82] Senex, and Bowen, published before the French and Indian War (1756–1763), these colonies began to be highlighted for a domestic readership. After 1755, drawing on French sources and on a series of detailed maps of the individual English colonies,[83] the London atlas makers, notably Thomas Jefferys and his successors, began to produce detailed regional atlases for the North American and West Indian theaters of colonial activity. Some of these works, such as Jefferys's *A General Topography of North America and the West Indies* (1768) (see Figure 75), appeared before the beginning of the War of Independence but, in other instances, such as *The American Atlas*, *The North American Atlas*, and *The West India Atlas*, published between 1775 and 1777,[84] they were clearly rushed out by the owners of the copperplates as a deliberate attempt to cash in on the topicality of the mounting military and political crisis in the continent. Yet, whatever the changing historical or bibliographical context, it is the ideological repetitiveness of the images on the maps of North America which allows generalization about the way the world atlases manufactured and disseminated power.

In the eighteenth century, atlas making was already under the influence of a Science of Geography whose productions were unabashed handmaidens of imperialism.[85] On the American maps, this ideology is found in the wording of title pages, in dedications, and in the motifs for cartouches and other marginal emblems. Titles increasingly contain allusions to "British Dominions and Settlements throughout the World." Even if these imperial territories were not yet painted red, the British Empire had already appeared on the map, carrying with it implications of inevitability and right. "A Map of the British Empire, in

North America," included in Thomas Jefferys's *The American Atlas* (1776) displays a note which states "The British Empire in North America contains . . . ": then it lists "The Hudsons Bay Company's Territories," "Canada or the Province of Quebec," followed by the individual colonies and then by "The Reserved Lands." The inventory-like arrangement of this table is striking.[86] It is in fact an inventory of the overseas property of the English crown. The function of the atlas maker was to inscribe its boundaries as legitimate and permanent. To strengthen the authority of representation, supporting allusions to international treaties appear on some maps. For instance, following the Treaty of Paris (1763), which gave England practically all North America east of the Mississippi as well as Canada, the relevant articles of the "Definitive Treaty" were engraved on maps, as if to confirm these extended bounds of the English empire.[87] (See Figure 81.)

Yet it would be wrong to imply that North America was no more than a fief of the English crown. The same notions of status and proprietorship as those in the English county atlases can be found in the maps of America but they are applied to American society. Thus we find that the map of Pennsylvania in Jefferys's *American Atlas* is dedicated to "Thomas Penn and Richard Penn Esquires" (note the inclusion of their mark of social rank) as the "True and Absolute Proprietaries & Governors of the Province of Pennsylvania."[88] Even if this is a special case, these are key words: True, Absolute, Proprietaries, and Governors belong to the language of authority in eighteenth-century English. They epitomized the rele-

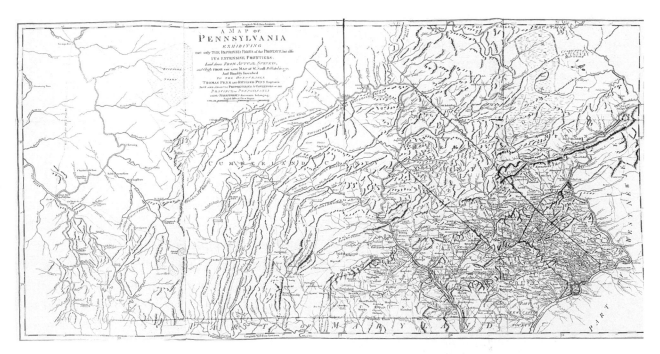

FIGURE 81   *The atlas as colonial territory: W. Scull's map of Pennsylvania, 1775.*
American Atlas *(London: T. Jefferys, 1782). Library of Congress.*

vance of the concepts of right and of land ownership, held in an English county by a nobility with legal privileges, to the colonial world.

Many of the decorative features in the cartouches of English maps of North America reinforce these statements of power relations. The cartouche is the *pictura loquens* of cartography. Like the emblematic title page or frontispiece, it serves to abstract and epitomize some of the meaning of the work as a whole. A cartouche may thus be decorative, illustrative, programmatical, propagandist, doctrinal or controversial.[89] All these elements recur in the English atlases of the eighteenth century but I am concerned here with how certain motifs are an integral part of the political rhetoric of the map as a whole. The King's coat of arms appeared on maps of America in the general atlases just as it had been nailed to trees on the ground as a mark of colonial sovereignty.[90] Other motifs such as the English crown, the national flag, or the coats of arms of English noblemen who were also colonial officials, are reminiscent of the emblemata of the county atlases. Equally recognizable to many patrons would have been the expression of royal power in George Willdey's map of North America. This was dedicated "To his Sacred & Most Excellent Majesty George by the Grace of God King of Great Britain . . ."[91] The cartouche contains the standard emblems for North America. Above this is a portrait of the King, with crown and laurels. It is held over the landscape beneath by allegorical figures of Mercury and an angel. Thus, in Willdey's cartouche, English sovereignty, the cult of the crown, Anglican theology (in which traditional doctrines of the divine right of Kings persisted), and imperial commerce were firmly tied to the soil of America.

On other maps, the cartouches are used to develop a visual vocabulary of colonial exploitation by making them specific to America. A recurrent message is the cornucopia that the continent had become: various maps are decorated with the beaver, with hogshead of tobacco, with sugar cane and with codfish. Ships with their sails furled stand in calm estuaries ready to convey this wealth back to the mother country. Such engravings tell us that the land of America belongs to the Euro-Americans and that sovereignty led to an appropriation of the wealth of the land. Even seemingly innocent cartouches may have reinforced these assumptions. The scene below Niagara Falls in the inset to Moll's "Beaver Map" is often reproduced.[92] (See Figure 82.) At first glance, it might merely suggest an interest in natural history, or that the fur trade was a source of wealth to some of the atlas patrons. Yet a closer look shows an absence of people and especially, of the native Americans upon whom the fur trade depended. In the final analysis, unless the beavers are intended as a symbol for the hard-working Europeans, it is just as likely that it was this negative aspect, the absence of people, which entered the reader's consciousness as any of the images of natural history or the fur trade. Such images, associated with the representation of the territory on the map, and becoming part of the process of persuasion and mythmaking, rendered legitimate the holding of English colonies in America.

The Cataract of NIAGARA, some make this Water-Fall to be half a League while others reckon it no more than a hundred Fathom.

A View of ye Industry of ye Beavers of Canada in making Dams to stop ye Course of a Rivulet, in order to form a great Lake, about wch they build their Habitations. To Effect this; they fell large Trees with their Teeth, in such a manner as to make them come Cross ye Rivulet, to lay ye foundation of ye Dam; they make Mortar, work up, and finish ye whole with great order and wonderfull Dexterity.

FIGURE 82   *The beaver inset. Herman Moll,* A New and Exact Map of the Dominions of the King of Great Britain on ye Continent of North America *(London, 1715). Library of Congress.*

It is true that many of these map emblems were added with little conscious thought by the atlas maker. But the fact remains that they served to further strengthen the perception of power relations between Europeans and non-Europeans. By the eighteenth century, the English colonies in North America had already been engaged in a long and bitter encounter with both native Americans and with the Africans in the New World. Popular images of this encounter, repeated in map cartouches and linked to the cartographic representation and symbolism of territory, helped to stereotype and to universalize the institutions they record. The cartouches confirm that the principal English encounter with

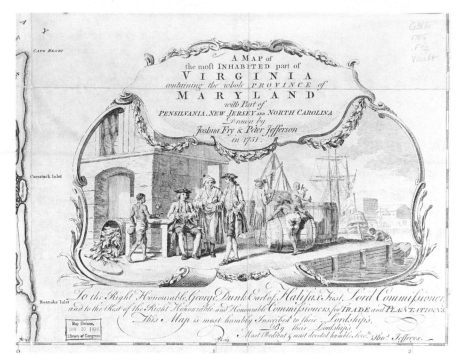

FIGURE 83 *Cartouche in Joshua Fry and Peter Jefferson, A Map of the Most Inhabited Part of Virginia Containing the Whole Province of Maryland . . . (London: T. Jefferys, 1755). Library of Congress.*

African slaves was in the West Indies,[93] but that slave owning also extended throughout the thirteen colonies is brought home by Fry and Jefferson's map of Virginia of 1754.[94] The cartouche on this map shows a wharf scene. It is a silent parable of class relations in mid-eighteenth-century Virginia. (See Figure 83.) The first tier of power lies in the dedication to the Earl of Halifax, the chief colonial official in England. His imprimatur served to enhance the authority of the map. At the next tier, the plantation owner is shown seated. Below him are ranged men loading tobacco. Finally, beneath them all, are the Black laborers and the Black boy who is serving a glass of wine to the plantation owner.

Whites and Indians were frequently depicted in cartouches in clearly indicated relations of superiority and inferiority. Many of the eighteenth-century motifs were inherited from earlier centuries of colonial rule. The lifestyle of the Indian was represented as that of a "savage," often naked, emphasizing that in the European view, "the adoption of clothing symbolized the development of law, authority and power . . . whereas the naked Amerindian represented the state of nature."[95] The judgment that Indians could not be given the same rights as those who had attained the maturity of civility thus provided a justification for taking their land. To denigrate the indigenous population still further, on some eighteenth-century maps, Indians were represented as cannibals or monkeys with human heads.[96] While such images may not have been deliberately intended to inspire racial propaganda in our modern sense, they certainly would have consolidated European attitudes toward the Indian, dividing the North American population into the "other" and "they" as opposed to "us" and "we."[97] Even at best they were always shown subject to the settlers: the Indian stood by while the

European was the principal actor. On one map a suitably-tamed Indian is shown stroking a representation of the British lion.[98] Or in the iconography of the Revolutionary period, a Tory fights an American patriot while the Indian—always the loser—is depicted showing fear and apprehensiveness in case the protection of his colonial masters was withdrawn. Such were the prophecies of power which would run wherever colonies extended on the map.

The symbolism in Benjamin West's 1771 painting of "Penn's Treaty with the Indians"—a map is held by one of the group of colonists—is apt.[99] Yet such colonial maps were more than legal instruments enforcing Indian land treaties, more than strategic documents in colonial wars with the French, and more than a tool in the settled areas to divide the farmland or plat the city. They exercised power in other ways too. The maps in the general atlases—like those in the county atlases—entered power relations the way they standardized North American geography, erected social hierarchies in its landscape, and selectively omitted or emphasized features on the maps. For America as for England, the cartographic process was also the processing of power. Workshop techniques enabled the mass production of maps (in relative eighteenth-century terms) and, as private tradesmen, the English atlas makers used commerce to return these politically constructed geographies to those that held power.

This sort of cartographical circuit in power relations enabled a power/knowledge to be disseminated in such a way that it could be used to reinforce or to challenge earlier configurations of power. The most visible example of such a circuit in the preindependence period is the way English atlas makers championed national claims at a continental scale. In the run-up to the French and Indian War, both the French and English used maps as weapons of international propaganda or to sway domestic public opinion to support military action. It was the English mapmakers, however, who may have gone furthest—with or without direct patronage—in arbitrarily extending the boundaries of the thirteen colonies on their maps west toward the Mississippi. Yet, the increasingly ritualized depiction of these claims also shows the need to distinguish between external and internal power in cartographic representation. The ostensible mark of external power is that territorial claims were made on behalf of the nation, accompanied by partisan endorsements. The initial formulation of these claims, and their communication to the mapmakers, were probably deliberate acts of policy by a few leading colonial strategists who were using the atlases to promote their cause, but whose power was still located outside the workshop. At some point, however, these representations of power were internalized in cartographic practice. Diffused between a number of London mapmakers, external power became internal power. The English atlas maker could not take independent initiatives in choosing how particular configurations of colonial power were standardized, made more persuasive, or popularized in smaller-scale atlases.

During the eighteenth century these transfers of power were enacted on many occasions as the political realities changed or as new information became available. Ownership was constantly redefined or extended. Already, in the early eighteenth century, Moll's maps were annotated with anti-French propaganda. Maps by Morden and Senex claimed for England large parts of New France such as the Niagara peninsula of what is now Ontario, Canada. French maps were variously criticized for depicting their "political system of encroachment upon the territories of other nations," or as "an arbitrary Fiction, false and unjust,"[100] as the English atlas makers redrafted geography with bold sweeps of the burin to proclaim a manifest destiny of colonial expansion in North America. (See Figure 84.) The zeal of some cartographers for the national cause went beyond the demands of patronage. They added their own polemics to the power they derived. Thomas Jefferys, in particular, was an active agent rather than a pawn in the power relations of colonialism. In one sense he could be described as the mouthpiece for

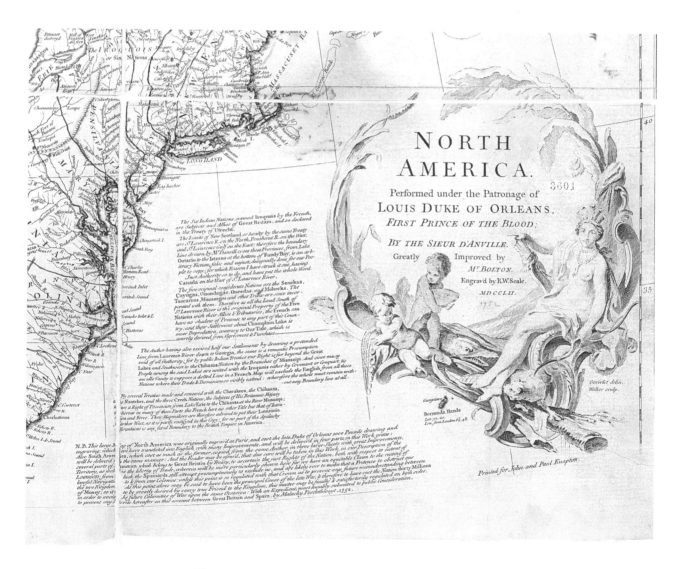

FIGURE 84   *The atlas as political propaganda: Solomon Bolton's* North America . . .
(London: printed for John and Paul Knapston, 1752). Library of Congress.

Pitt's imperial strategies but in another he had also set himself up as the leading cartographic champion of his country's claims. In 1755, for example, on his *Map of North America From the French of Mr. D'Anville* he had included the argument that "The French are intruders into Canada, part of Cabots discovery and have no Right but by Treaties."[101] By overstating the authority for the claim as well as by expanding its boundaries, the map had been manipulated to enhance its rhetoric. Jefferys had deliberately used the power of the atlas—as well as the armory of his workshop practices—to support the cause of imperial expansion.

Power did not have to be deliberately exerted, however, either by the cartographer or through the patron, for it to be effective. The depiction of the ordinary geography of North America in the atlases—the patterns of place-names, settlements, roads and local administrative boundaries—illustrates this content forcibly. Like the landscapes of the English county atlases the geography of North America on the maps of the general atlases is a geography with a hidden agenda. The maps of the thirteen colonies in the larger atlases are preeminently a record of colonial self-interest. They are an unconscious portrait of how successfully a European colonial society had reproduced itself in the New World. As maps of a new environment, they granted reassurance to settlers by reproducing the symbolic authority and place-names of the Old World. Some local administrative boundaries had been settled by the "King in Council." On the map of the "Island of St. John" in Jefferys's *American Atlas*, Kings County, Queens County, and Princes County are found adjacent to each other. Such loyalty to English social structure appears in innumerable instances.

Looking at the maps of the eastern seaboard, we find it is as if the Europeans had always lived there. (See Figure 78.) In representing place, time had also been inserted into the landscape. If we forget geography for a moment, then it is possible to imagine oneself reading not maps of the New World but from an atlas of *English* counties. True, these American maps are emptier, but in settled areas it is the framework of a European geography that has taken shape. Wherever British influence was strong, as in New England, the names on the land constantly remind us of this coincidence.[102] Or again, on Jefferys's map of New England, place-names are derived from English or Scottish toponymy, from the personal names of British settlers or from allusions to English nobility or the heroes of some English cause. (See Figure 85.) Everywhere the maps served to emphasize the structures and consequences of colonialism on the land, reminding readers that the courthouses dispensed an English system of justice in its colonies, that the roads and trackways linked the New World settlements to the outposts of Empire trade, that the forts were there to defend the colonies, and even that the routes of navigation on charts served to facilitate His Majesty's ships. Not least, the atlas maker was helping construct a colonial history. Where historical events were recorded on the maps, they related to English discoveries, to English victories, to the surrender of native American peoples, to some atrocity committed by Indians, or to the defeat of England's colonial rivals such as the Dutch or the

FIGURE 85 *The atlas as England recreated: the colony of Connecticut from* A Map of the Most Inhabited Part of New England . . . *(London: T. Jefferys, 1755). Library of Congress.*

French.[103] It became an act of colonial promotion to encourage the portrayal of a landscape that was familiar and not hostile to English eyes. The map was inviting settlers. There were few obstacles in the paper landscape that would have seemed insurmountable.

The historical force of these carefully standardized maps may have been greater in a new society than in the old society portrayed in the English county atlases. Their power was as much psychological as practical. Their images were a metaphor for control. They made the new land believable. The wilderness was tamed on paper before the wilderness itself had been encountered. Space shrank. In the minds of administrators and settlers, the distant land was made domestic and the unknowable conquerable. Maps often ran ahead of the settled frontier, preceding the axe and the plough. Eastern North America was recolonized on paper by Europeans before it was recolonized on the ground.

The same maps were also the subliminal charters of colonial legitimation. As in the case of maps of the English landscape, English maps of the New World exercised power through the categories of their omissions. These silences applied especially to Indian civilization. We ask ourselves, where are the traces of Indian occupation on the land? At best they are only randomly preserved on the maps but, more often than not, as the frontier moved west, the traces of an Indian past were dropped altogether from the image. Although some maps mark "Indian houses and Plantations" and "English Plantations" separately,[104] more often than not, where Indian villages are identified or their nations named, it is usually on the margins of the European settlement, where they served as a guide to the fur trade, to military deployment or ultimately to colonial appropriation. With the exception of the survival of the Indian names for natural features, such as rivers, lakes, and mountains, the maps seldom represented an Indian geography mapped in its own right and they were never a means of preserving ethnic integrity. Many eighteenth-century mapmakers preferred blank spaces to a relict Indian geography. This was defended on the grounds that it was good scientific practice to avoid mapping what could not be verified. Yet the ideological implications of the silence about Indian geography cannot be overlooked. It lent unwitting support to the legal doctrines of *terra nullis* and *vacuum domicilium*, which, since the earliest days of the colonies, had featured among the grounds for acquiring land title and assuming political jurisdiction. The English in particular believed that Indian land awaited their immediate settlement because it was vacant.[105] There is a moral neutrality about a blank space which is easily divided and ruled. In the end, we find it hard to believe that the Indians had ever lived on the land. The act of mapping had transformed what was being described and had given it new meanings and potentialities.

CONCLUSION

In this essay I have sought to deconstruct some map images in eighteenth-century English atlases. By this I mean that they have been interpreted in terms of their effects as a representation of power rather than as representations of the topographical reality of the English or American landscapes in the eighteenth century. The social power in question had become internal to cartography and was manufactured in its own workshop practices. It was in these workshops that the link with one reality was transformed and a new reality created. These processes are comparable to those of scientific procedures in the laboratory. The atlas maker disciplined and ordered geographical information, the grids and graticules of the map providing a framework of systematic domination. Through selection, classification, standardization, and the creation of mappable hierarchies, the atlas maker made mapped geography a more robust form of knowledge. By different means—regular mapping, decorative iconography, and textual glosses on maps—social power was represented. As a text of power rather than as a map of physical topography, it mattered less whether the image was a technically accurate representation of a landscape or an original rather than a plagiarized image. More important, it should be believable. It mattered that it represented power in ways which coincided with the values of contemporary society. Power relations such as the rights of the crown, the deferential ranking of power within English society, and the inherent superiority of the English over other nations and especially non-Europeans, were all as important to cartographic practice as they were to other forms of knowledge in eighteenth-century England.

Once impregnated with power, cartographic knowledge worked through society in a number of ways. It worked both consciously and subliminally. It never operated alone but always in conjunction with other forms of knowledge and representation. Nevertheless, by its focus on the power relations both inherent and manifest in landscape and territory, it played a distinctive role in the social configuration of the age. Maps worked principally through legitimation. By representing territorial power relations as a normal part of the world, they enabled the status quo to be more easily accepted. The repetition of similar images through a succession of atlases strengthened this acceptance. In a society where many, even among the upper classes, lacked first-hand experience of other places, the map could become the only reality. Though divorced from the world on the ground, it acquired a mythic authority. As knowledge by force of tradition, its representations were more difficult to subvert, and indeed, many maps in the atlases had extraordinarily long lives which were independent of change in the world itself. The making and reading of maps, by constantly recycling a normalcy in power relations is akin to a ritual, a ritual performed with knowledge and linked to attitudes and emotions widely held and expressed in English society. These included an attachment by the patrons to their own class and nation, a love of ownership and property, a bellicose chauvinism, and a tendency to despise the savages. Representing these emotions through maps tended not only to reinforce them but to associate them with ever wider geographical areas.

The answer to the initial question as to how were the atlases a force for change in society always depends on the context of power relations. In England itself, the county atlases tended toward conservatism and reaction and they helped to maintain the long-standing hegemony of a broad ruling class. In the North American colonies, however, the maps operated decisively in favor of the new society of Euro-Americans and at the expense of the Indians. Yet for both areas the atlas makers had produced a discourse of power. Even where the true nature of its dialectic was hidden from contemporaries, we can be sure that its reality was always socially constructed.

ACKNOWLEDGMENTS

In the four years since this paper was originally presented in a preliminary form in Washington D.C., I have accumulated more debts than I can hope to properly acknowledge. In preparing this new version for publication, however, I am especially indebted to Howard Deller, Ellen Hanlon, and Sarah Wilmot for bibliographical assistance and to Dalia Varanka who has supplied me with some new examples of cartouches on North American maps. For making valuable comments on a draft of the essay I am also particularly grateful to James R. Akerman, Catherine Delano Smith, Matthew Edney and Barbara McCorkle, and to John Wolter and his staff in the Geography and Map Division of the Library of Congress for help with selecting illustrations and in other editorial matters.

NOTES

1 Lucien Febvre and Henri-Jean Martin, *L'apparition du livre* (Paris: Edition Albin, 1958); English edition, *The Coming of the Book: The Impact of Printing, 1450–1800*, new ed., ed. Geoffrey Nowell-Smith and David Wootton, trans. David Gerard (London: NLB, 1976).

2 Ibid., p. 248.

3 Elizabeth L. Eisenstein, *The Printing Press as an Agent of Change: Communications and Cultural Transformations in Early Modern Europe*, 2 vols. (Cambridge: Cambridge University Press, 1979).

4 D. F. McKenzie, *Bibliography and the Sociology of Texts. The Panizzi Lectures* (London: The British Library, 1986), esp. 34–39. I share his view that Arthur H. Robinson and Barbara Bartz Petchenik, *The Nature of Maps: Essays toward Understanding Maps and Mapping* (Chicago: University of Chicago Press, 1976), 43, were fundamentally wrong when they wrote "the two systems, map and language, are essentially incompatible." Unfortunately, even in the history of cartography, it has led (in the words of McKenzie, 37) to a view of maps as solely "silent, visual, spatial, and a-temporal."

5 For a general discussion see J. B. Harley, "Maps, Knowledge and Power," in *The Iconography of Landscape*, eds. Denis Cosgrove and Stephen Daniels (Cambridge: Cambridge University Press, 1988), 277–312.

6 Joseph Rouse, *Knowledge and Power: Toward a Political Philosophy of Science* (Ithaca: Cornell University Press, 1987).

7 Recently, see James R. Akerman and David Buisseret, *Monarchs, Ministers, and Maps: A Cartographic Exhibit at the Newberry Library* (Chicago: Newberry Library, 1985).

8 Michel Foucault, *Power/Knowledge: Selected Interviews and Other Writings, 1972–1977*, ed. Colin Gordon, trans. Colin Gordon, Leo Marshall, John Mepham, Kate Soper (New York: Pantheon Books, 1980), 88; see also Rouse, *Knowledge and Power*, 209–210.

9 J. B. Harley, "Silences and Secrecy: The Hidden Agenda of Cartography in Early Modern Europe," *Imago Mundi* 40 (1988): 111–130.

10 Rouse, *Knowledge and Power*, 17–24.

11 Ibid., 213–226.

12 An analogy may be drawn here between the "construction of microworlds" in the scientific laboratory and the construction of geographical knowledge in the cartographer's workshop. In both cases the key is standardization: Rouse, *Knowledge and Power*, 95–125. On the effect of standard tools, techniques and procedures on the creation of scientific knowledge, see also Jerome R. Ravetz, *Scientific Knowledge and Its Social Problems* (Oxford: Clarendon Press, 1971), 194–202.

13 Marshall McLuhan, *The Gutenberg Galaxy* (Toronto: University of Toronto Press, 1962), passim. Quoted in Alvin Kernan, *Printing Technology, Letters and Samuel Johnson* (Princeton, New Jersey: Princeton University Press, 1987), 50; I find Kernan's whole discussion of "Print Logic," 48–55, particularly helpful to my understanding of atlas cartography.

14 Kernan, *Printing Technology*, 51.

15 The trade practices of the eighteenth-century cartographic workshop still have to be fully constructed but on engraving and printing maps see Coolie Verner, "Copper-plate Printing," in *Five Centuries of Map Printing*, ed. David Woodward (Chicago: The University of Chicago Press, 19751), 51–75.

16 Josef W. Konvitz, *Cartography in France, 1660–1848. Science, Engineering, and Statecraft* (Chicago: The University of Chicago Press, 1987), 3–4, compares the development of geographical mapping in England and France in this respect.

17 William Gerard De Brahm, *Report of the General Survey in the Southern District of North America*, ed. and with an introduction by Louis De Vorsey, Jr. (Columbia: University of South Carolina Press, 1971), 3–6.

18 J. B. Harley, "The Origins of the Ordnance Survey," in *A History of the Ordnance Survey*, ed. W. A. Seymour (Folkestone: Dawson, 1980), 1–20; J. B. Harley and Y. O'Donoghue, "The Ordnance Survey Becomes a Map Publisher, 1801–1820," in ibid., 67–78.

19 For details see H. G. Fordham, *John Cary: Engraver, Map, Chart and Print-Seller and Globe-Maker, 1754 to 1835* (Cambridge: Cambridge University Press, 1925); reprinted Folkestone: Dawson, 1976.

20 R. A. Skelton, *James Cook Surveyor of Newfoundland. Being A Collection of Charts of the Coasts of Newfoundland and Labradore, &c. Drawn From Original Surveys Taken by James Cook and Michael Lane. London, Thomas Jefferys, 1769–1770*. With an Introductory Essay by R. A. Skelton (San Francisco: David Magee, 1965), 7.

21 J. B. Harley, "The Bankruptcy of Thomas Jefferys," 35–37.

22 Hodson, *County Atlases*, xi.

23 For example, the earliest of these, *A General Topography of North America and the West Indies* (1768), published by Sayer and Jefferys and consisting of 100 maps on 109 sheets was described as "a collection of all the maps, charts, plans, and particular surveys that have been published of that part of the world, either in Europe or America"; it was issued with both a French and English title page and contents. In general, how-

ever, the composite atlas was declining in the English map trade after 1700 and was to disappear around the middle of the nineteenth century.

24 For a fuller discussion see Harley, "Silences and Secrecy," 119–120.

25 A cartography of protest against established power relations is an accepted part of present-day cartography. A recent prototype, originally published in one-sheet form by the Society for Human Exploration, is *The Nuclear War Atlas* (Victorianville, Quebec: The Society, 1982); it was republished as William Bunge, *The New World Atlas* (New York: Blackwell, 1988). Other recent examples of cartography as protest include Michael Kidron and Ronald Segall, *The New State of the World Atlas* (New York: Simon and Schuster, 1984); Joni Seager and Ann Olson, *Woman in the World: An International Atlas* (New York: Simon and Schuster, 1986) and Barbara Gimla Shortridge, *Atlas of American Women* (New York: Macmillan, 1987).

26 See, for example, the diversity of interpretation expressed by Peter Laslett, *The World We Have Lost: Further Explored*, 3d ed. (London: Methuen, 1965, 1983); Harold Perkin, *The Origins of Modern English Society 1780–1880* (London: Routledge & K. Paul; Toronto: University of Toronto Press, 1969); R. S. Neale, *Class in English History, 1680–1850* (Oxford: Blackwell, 1981), esp. Chapter 3; Roy Porter, *English Society in the Eighteenth Century* (London: Penguin Books, 1982); L. Stone and J. C. F. Stone, *An Open Elite? England, 1540–1880* (Oxford: Clarendon Press; New York: Oxford University Press, 1984); J. C. D. Clark, *English Society, 1688–1932. Social Structure and Political Practice During the Ancien Régime* (Cambridge: Cambridge University Press, 1985).

27 Laslett, *The World We Have Lost*, 1983, 22–52.

28 Porter, *English Society*, 69, 78.

29 Raymond Williams, *The Country and the City* (London: Chatto and Windus, 1973), 60.

30 This type of analysis still has to be undertaken for English cartography, but the raw material exists in price data on atlases in trade catalogs and in standard series of wage data. On the former see the interim list by Antony Griffiths, "A Checklist of Catalogues of British Print Publishers, c. 1650–1830," *Print Quarterly* 1 (1984): 4–22; on the latter see Mitchell and Deane, Abstract of *British Historical Statistics* (Cambridge: Cambridge University Press, 1962) and J. E. Thorold Rogers, *Six Centuries of Work and Wages. The History of English Labour*, with a new Preface by G. D. H. Cole (new ed.) (London: Allen and Unwin, 1949).

31 For examples of these advertisements, which appear throughout the eighteenth century, see Sarah Tyacke, *London Map-sellers, 1660–1720* (Tring, Hertfordshire: Map Collector Publications, 1978) and Donald Hodson, *County Atlases of The British Isles Published after 1703*, vol. 1, *Atlases Published 1704 to 1742 and their Subsequent Editions* (Tewin, Hertfordshire: Tewin Press, 1984).

32 The general European practice of displaying coats of arms in atlas maps was already common by the mid seventeenth century; in the English atlases the fashion was at its height in the early eighteenth century.

33 See, for example, John Harrison, *The Library of Isaac Newton* (Cambridge: Cambridge University Press, 1978), who records that Newton, as well as some seventy-six books relating to voyages, travel and geography, owned a copy of Senex's *The English Atlas* (1714) and Moll's *A New Description of England and Wales . . .* (1724); his library as a whole comprised 2,100 volumes at the time of his death. Also R. A. Harvey, "The Private Library of Henry Cavendish (1731–1810)," *The Library*, Sixth Series, 2 (1980): 281–292; as well as many books of travel and voyages, Cavendish had collected maps, plans, and surveys, comprising 656 sheets bound together in six giant volumes, each measuring 22 × 16½ inches.

34 J. B. Harley and Gwyn Walters, "William Roy's Maps, Mathematical Instruments, and Library: The Christie's Sale of 1790," *Imago Mundi* 29 (1977): 9–22; J. B. Harley and Gwyn Walters, "English Map Collecting, 1790–1840: A Pilot Survey of the Evidence in Sotheby Sale Catalogues," *Imago Mundi* 30 (1978): 31–53. References to atlases can also be found among *Sale Catalogues of Libraries of Eminent Persons*, 12 vols., Gen. ed. A. N. L. Munby (London: Mansell With Sotheby Parke-Bernet Publications, 1971–1974). Volume II, *Scientists*, ed. and introduced by H. A. Fiesenberger (London, 1975), has references to atlases. The whole topic of eighteenth-century English map ownership requires a systematic study.

35 They are listed in F. J. G. Robinson and P. J. Wallis, *Book Subscription Lists: A Revised Guide* (Newcastle upon Tyne: Harold Hill & Son for The Book Subscription List Project, 1975); occasional typewritten supplements have been issued. Advance subscription was a standard way of financing book publication in the eighteenth century but though it was widely employed in financing the English county surveys of the period it was not generally used for atlas publication. On the county surveys see, for example, J. B. Harley, *William Yates' Map of Lancashire, 1786* (Historic Society of Lancashire and Cheshire, 1968), 48. Paul Laxton, *250 Years of Mapmaking in the County of Hampshire*, Introduction to a collection of facsimiles (Lympne, 1976), on Isaac Taylor's map of that county.

36 John Senex, *A New General Atlas, . . . Containing a Geographical and Historical Account of all the Empires, Kingdoms, and Other Dominions of the World* (London, 1721).

37 Ibid., Preface.

38 The following categories given in Senex's *Introduction* provide an eighteenth-century perspective on the value of maps, not least where questions of power relations are involved: "Sovereigns, with their Ministers . . . find it necessary for Civil Government; and particularly for understanding the Interests, Extent, Situation, Wealth and Strength of their own Dominions, and those of their neighbors"; "Generals, and other Commanders of Armies, find this Study absolutely needful for directing their Marches, Encampments, Fortifications, &c."; "Divines find it no less necessary, for understanding several Religions of the World"; "'Tis no less useful to the Gentlemen of the Long Robe, for knowing the Laws and Customs of all Nations"; "It is equally necessary to Physicians, for knowing the several Conditions and Diseases of People; and what Provision the bountiful Hand of Providence has made for the Preservation

& Cure of Mankind"; "Historians, Poets and Philosophers cannot be ignorant of it for no part of history, or even so much as a Gazette, can be understood without it"; "Above all, it is useful to Merchants and Sailors, for Directing them in their Commerce or Navigation"; "nor can Travellers by Sea or Land be without it . . ."; and "Nay, the very Husbandmen, with ordinary Mechanicks, and their Families, must be convinc'd of its Usefulness to inform them of the Quality and Product of the Soil which Mankind lives upon . . ."

39 On the increasing number of mathematical practitioners in the eighteenth century, which drew interested persons from all layers of society, see E. G. R. Taylor, *The Mathematical Practitioners of Hanoverian England, 1714–1840* (Cambridge: Cambridge University Press, 1966).

40 For this wider context to atlas history see Terry Belanger, "Publishers and Writers in Eighteenth-century England," in *Books and their Readers in Eighteenth-Century England*, ed. Isabel Rivers (London: St. Martin's Press, 1982), 5–25.

41 John Cary, *Cary's New and Correct English Atlas, being a new Set of County Maps from actual Surveys, etc.* (London, 1787).

42 For example, the smaller atlases like the geography texts in octavo were aimed at a more general market than the larger folio atlases for which the readership was more restricted. One of the problems in generalizing about English atlas cartography is that there is no cartobibliography of the world atlases or of atlases in general. Driven by the collector interest, emphasis has been placed on bibliographies of county atlases or of the maps of individual counties. Work on the world atlases is a desideratum for future research.

43 Michael Baxendall, *Painting and Experience in Fifteenth-Century Italy: A Primer in the Social History of Pictorial Style* (Oxford: Clarendon Press, 1972), 1.

44 Porter, *English Society*, 86.

45 The most scholarly analysis of the practices of the eighteenth-century London atlas trade is that of Hodson, *County Atlases*, vol. 1. For a discussion of a particular atlas, see *The Royal English Atlas. Eighteenth-Century County Maps of England and Wales by Emanuel Bowen and Thomas Kitchen*, with an introduction by J. B. Harley and Donald Hodson (Newton Abbot: David & Charles Ltd., 1971).

46 See, for example, the comment of Richard Gough, *British Topography*, 2 vols. (London, 1780), 1, xvi that "As to the several sets of county maps professing to be drawn from the *latest* observations, they are almost invariable copies of those that preceded them." A high level of plagiarism was also characteristic of the English geographies in the same period.

47 For the complexity of the eighteenth-century London print trades with which atlas making was intermeshed, see H. M. Atherton, *Political Prints in the Age of Hogarth* (London, . . . 1974), esp. Chapter 1, "Printshops of London and Westminster," and Chapter 2, "Of Prints and Their Makers."

48 Ibid., 8; the term "hieroglyphicks" refers to the use of hieroglyphic emblems in the design of the prints.

49 Mary Pedley. "Gentlemen Abroad: Jefferys and Sayer in Paris," *The Map Collector*, no. 37 (1986), pp. 20–23; for Sayer's print stock in this period, see also Robert Sayer and John Bennett, *Catalogue of Prints for 1775* (London: reprinted by Holland Press, 1970).

50 Robert Sayer, *Atlases, Both Ancient and Modern, Books of Maps, Surveys, and Catalogue of Single Maps, of all the Empires, Kingdoms, States, &c. in the Universe* (London, 1788); *Catalogue of Pilots, Neptunes, and Charts, Both General and Particular, for the Navigation of All the Seas and Coasts of the Universe* (London, 1787); *Catalogue of New and Interesting Prints Consisting of Engravings and Metzotintos of Every Size and Price, Likewise Paintings on Glass, Books of Architecture & Ornaments, Penmanship, &c. &c. &c.* (London, 1786).

51 Atherton, *Political Prints*, 5.

52 For locations of Bowles' and other eighteenth-century trade catalogs, see Griffiths, "A Checklist of Catalogues of British Print Publishers, c. 1650–1830."

53 John Feather, *The Provincial Book Trade in Eighteenth-Century England* (Cambridge: Cambridge University Press, 1985), Chapter 1, "London and the Country," 1–11.

54 Unlike the eighteenth-century geographies, for example, which were also published in Edinburgh, Glasgow, Montrose, Dublin, Eton, Oxford, and Manchester.

55 See, for example, the discussion of one atlas maker's geographical sources in J. B. Harley, "The Bankruptcy of Thomas Jefferys: An Episode in the Economic History of Eighteenth-Century Mapmaking," *Imago Mundi* 20 (1966): 27–48.

56 For examples, see Ibid., 33–41; the manuscript "Catalogue of Drawings & Engraved Maps, Charts and Plans; the Property of Mr. Thomas Jefferys, Geographer to the King, 1775," Manuscript list in the Collections of the Royal Geographical Society, London, contains almost 200 items for North America and the West Indies alone.

57 On the increasing cosmopolitanism of eighteenth-century London, with many implications for the growth of geographical knowledge, see Thomas M. Curley, *Samuel Johnson and the Age of Travel* (Athens: The University of Georgia Press, 1976), esp. Chapter 1, "Johnson's Lifetime, 1709–1784: The Age of Travel," 7–46; on the growing English knowledge of the world, see also P. J. Marshall and Glyndwr Williams, *The Great Map of Mankind: British Perceptions of the World in the Age of Enlightenment* (London: Dent. 1982). The same point is borne out by E. A. Reitan, "Expanding Horizons: Maps in the *Gentlemen's Magazine*, 1731–1754," *Imago Mundi* 37 (1985): 54–62.

58 Porter, *English Society*, 70–71; see also J. V. Beckett, *The Aristocracy in England, 1160–1914* (Oxford: Blackwell, 1986), esp. Chapters 3 and 10 for fuller details of the ties of marriage and property in English county societies.

59 This is most fully documented in Hodson, *County Atlases*. Until the publication of later volumes of Hodson's work, we have to rely on older bibliographies such as

Thomas Chubb, *The Printed Maps in the Atlases of Great Britain and Ireland. A Bibliography, 1579–1870* (London: E. J. Burrow, 1927) or on the cartobibliographies of individual counties for which Donald Hodson, *The Printed Maps of Hertfordshire, 1577–1900* (London: Dawsons, 1974) also provides a model.

60 In England, heraldic art may be said to have reached its maturity by the fourteenth century: see Anne Payne, "Medieval Heraldry," 55–59, *Age of Chivalry: Art in Plantagenet England, 1200–1400*, ed. Jonathan Alexander and Paul Binski (London: Royal Academy of Arts in association with Weidenfeld and Nicolson, 1987). During the Middle Ages an important task of the heralds at tournaments had been the receipt, the certification, and the display (nailing up) of a participant's coat of arms and this custom survived at tournaments until Elizabethan times: see Alan Young, *Tudor and Jacobean Tournaments* (New York: Sheridan House, 1987), 46.

61 Quoted in Hodson, *County Atlases*, 171.

62 Ibid., 78–95. The atlas was reissued in many editions down to the 1760s. A facsimile was published as *Britannia Depicta or Ogilgby Improved* by Emanuel Bowen (Newcastle upon Tyne: Frank Graham, 1970) with an Introduction by J. B. Harley.

63 This type of marginal note was systematically added to Emanuel Bowen and Thomas Kitchen, *The Royal English Atlas: Being a New and Accurate Set of Maps of all the Counties of South Britain, Drawn from Surveys, and the Best Authorities . . . By Emanuel Bowen, Geographer to His Late Majesty, Thomas Kitchen, Geographer, and Others. The Whole Comprised in Forty-four Sheet Maps* (London, c. 1763).

64 See, for example, *England Displayed. Being a New, Complete, and Accurate Survey and Description of the Kingdom of England, and Principality of Wales . . . By a Society of Gentlemen . . . Revised, Corrected, and Improved, by P. Russell, Esq; and . . . Mr. Owen Price* (London, 1769). In this case, the small county maps—derived from John Rocque's *The Small British Atlas*—served as illustrations to a topographical and historical text rather than providing an atlas in the usual sense.

65 See *The Old Series Ordnance Survey Maps of England and Wales. Scale: 1 Inch to 1 Mile. A Reproduction of the 110 Sheets of the Survey in Early State in 10 Volumes, Vol. 3, South-Central England*. Introduction by J. B. Harley and Yolande O'Donoghue, pp. xxii–xxx, "The Birth of Archaeological Cartography."

66 For other examples of this process, see Harley, "Maps, Knowledge and Power," 296–298.

67 For insights into the use of the past in this way, see Eric Hobsbawm, "Introduction: Inventing Traditions," in *The Invention of Tradition*, ed. Eric Hobsbawm and Terence Ranger (Cambridge: Cambridge University Press, 1983), 1–14.

68 J. B. Harley, "The Remapping of England, 1750–1800," *Imago Mundi* 19 (1965): 56–67.

69 See John Barrell, *The Dark Side of Landscape: The Rural Poor in English Painting, 1730–1840* (Cambridge: Cambridge University Press, 1980).

70 Charity Schools were supported by endowments or subscriptions given by the philanthropically inclined. They were intended to teach the "Three Rs" to children of the "lower classes" who would not need Latin and other subjects taught in the grammar schools: see Mary G. Jones, *The Charity School Movement: A Study of Eighteenth-Century Puritanism in Action* (Cambridge: Cambridge University Press, 1938).

71 In the vignette for Northumberland in the *Royal English Atlas*, for example, three coal workers are seated on piles of coal, one smoking a pipe. For examples of such tendencies in the art of the period, see Hugh Prince, "Art and Agrarian Change, 1710–1815," in *The Iconography of Landscape*, ed. Denis Cosgrove and Stephen Daniels (Cambridge: Cambridge University Press, 1988), 98–118.

72 Maurice Bloch, "Symbols, Song, Dance and Features of Articulation: Is Religion an Extreme Form of Traditional Authority?" *European Journal of Sociology* 15 (1974): 79; quoted in David I. Kertzer, *Ritual, Politics, and Power* (New Haven: Yale University Press, 1988), 40.

73 Emile Durkheim, *The Elementary Forms of the Religious Life* (1915), trans. Joseph Swain (Glencoe: Free Press, 1974) argued that through ritual people project the secular sociopolitical order in which they live onto a cosmological plane. It is through ritual that people symbolize the "system of socially approved 'proper' relations between individuals and groups." See the discussion in Kertzer, *Ritual, Politics, and Power*, 37.

74 Kertzer, *Ritual, Politics, and Power*, 40, notes that standardization "along with its repetitive nature, gives ritual its stability." See also Hobsbawm, "Introduction: Inventing Traditions," 1, where " 'Invented tradition' is taken to mean a set of practices, normally governed by overtly or tacitly accepted rules and of a ritual or symbolic nature, which seek to inculcate certain values and norms of behavior by repetition, which automatically implies continuity with the past."

75 Kertzer, *Ritual, Politics, and Power*, 40.

76 Samuel Johnson, Dedication for George Adams's *Treatise on the Globes* (London, 1766); quoted in Curley, *Samuel Johnson*, 12.

77 Examples abound, but see, for example, Charles Theodore Middleton, *A New and Complete System of Geography* (London, 1778), which presents a view of Europe not only advanced in culture, but dominant over the world. The frontispiece shows allegories of the four continents presided over by an angelic Europe with a verse beneath which develops the theme:

> Europe *by Commerce, Arts, and Arms obtains*
> *The Gold of Afric, and her Sons enchains,*
> *She rules luxurious* Asia's *fertile Shores,*
> *Wears her bright Gems, and gains her richest Stores.*
> *While from America thro' Seas she brings*
> *The Wealth of Mines, and various useful things.*

Reproduced in Margarita Bowen, *Empiricism and Geographical Thought from Francis Bacon to Alexander von Humboldt* (Cambridge: Cambridge University Press, 1981), 170. Apart from the picturing of Great Britain as the delight, envy, and mistress of the world, the English geographies were particularly racist in their descriptions of Africa. For example, in the Preface to William Guthrie's *A New System of Modern Geography* (London: printed for C. Dilly and G. G. and J. Robinson, 1795), it is concluded that "In Africa the human mind seems degraded below its natural state. To dwell long on the manners of this country . . . would be disgusting to every lover of mankind."

78 H. Moll, *Atlas Minor* (London, 1729).

79 Much of the argument could be applied to other continents. For the role of geographical knowledge in the European construction of colonial power relations, see Edward W. Said, *Orientalism* (London: Penguin Books, 1985), esp. 215–219, but referring to the nineteenth-century use of geography.

80 For an early example of practical uses involving the creation of an atlas for English colonial administration in North America at the beginning of our period, see Jeanette D. Black, *The Blathwayt Atlas*, vol. II, *Commentary* (Providence, RI: Brown University Press, 1975). The extent to which the colonial government for North America used maps is also indicated by the maps in the records of the "Lords of Trade and Plantations," a body which was abolished in 1782: Ralph B. Pugh, *The Records of the Colonial and Dominions Offices* (London, PRO Handbook no. 3, HMSO, 1964), 5–6. These maps are listed in Peter A. Penfold, ed., *Maps and Plans in the Public Record Office*, 2, *America and West Indies* (London: HMSO, 1974), passim.

81 James R. Akerman, "National Geographical Consciousness and the Structure of Early World Atlases," paper presented at the Eleventh International Conference on the History of Cartography, Ottawa, Canada, July 1985.

82 On Moll, see Dennis Reinhartz, "Herman Moll, Geographer: An Early Eighteenth-century European View of the American Southwest," in *The Mapping of the American Southwest*, eds. Dennis Reinhartz and Charles C. Colley (College Station: Texas A&M University Press, 1987), 18–36; an Appendix to the volume, pp. 79–83 is a "Selected Cartobibliography of the Works of Herman Moll Depicting the American Southwest" and, in effect, provides a list of the geographical atlases by Moll relevant to this chapter. The popularity of Moll's atlases—along with voyages, travels, and other geographical works—is suggested by Frederick Bracher, "The Maps in Gulliver's Travels," *Huntingdon Library Quarterly* 8 (1944): 60–64.

83 For a description of these maps, see William P. Cumming, *British Maps of Colonial America* (Chicago: The University of Chicago Press, 1974), esp. Chapters 1 and 2; see also Seymour I. Schwartz and Ralph E. Ehrenberg, *The Mapping of America* (New York: Harry N. Abrams, 1980), esp. Chapters 6 and 7.

84 For lists of the maps in these regional atlases and in some of the other eighteenth-century English atlases depicting North America, see P. L. Phillips, *A List of Geo-*

graphical Atlases in the Library of Congress, vols. 1–4 (Washington, D.C.: Government Printing Office, 1909–1914), passim; reprinted Amsterdam: Theatrum Orbis Terrarum, 1967.

85 Bowen, *Empiricism and Geographical Thought*, 169.

86 "A Map of the British Empire in North America." By Samuel Dunn, Mathematician, improved from the Surveys of Capt. Carver; sheet 8 in Thomas Jefferys, *The American Atlas or, a Geographical Description of the Whole Continent of America* (London: Sayer and Bennett, 1776).

87 For example, "A Map of the Whole Continent of America . . . with a Copious Table Fully Showing the Several Possessions of Each European Province & State, as Settled by the Definitive Treaty Concluded at Paris, Feby. 10th, 1763" in Thomas Kitchin, *A General Atlas* (London, editions 1773–1793). The boundary is also marked and the treaty referred to in the map of North America in the same atlas: "An Accurate Map of North America Describing and Distinguishing the British and Spanish Dominions on this Great Continent, According to the Definitive Treaty . . ."

88 "A Map of Pennsylvania Exhibiting Not Only the Improved Parts of that Province, but also its Extensive Frontiers: Laid Down from Actual Surveys, and Chiefly from the Late Map of W. Scull Published in 1770," sheet 20 in Jefferys, *The American Atlas*.

89 This reading is adapted from Karl Josef Holtgen, *Aspects of the Emblem. Studies in the English Emblem Tradition and the European Context* (Kassel: Reichenberger, 1986), 92.

90 Cornelius J. Jaenen, "Characteristics of French-Amerindian Contact in New France," in *Essays on the History of North American Discovery and Exploration*, eds. Stanley H. Palmer and Dennis Reinhartz (College Station: Texas A&M Press, 1988), 90; other symbolic acts of sovereignty by European powers in North America included planting crosses and burying inscribed lead plates to establish a claim in the face of European rivals.

91 The cartouche is reproduced in Schwartz and Ehrenberg, *The Mapping of America*, 163.

92 Herman Moll, "A New and Exact Map of the Dominions of the King of Great Britain on ye Continent of North America," 1715, published in Moll's *The World Described* (London, 1708–1720).

93 By 1710, there were already 50,000 Black slaves in the American colonies. See James Egert Allen, *Black History Past and Present* (New York: Exposition Press, 1971). See also Larissa Brown, *Africans in the New World, 1493–1834: An Exhibition at the John Carter Brown Library* (Providence, Rhode Island, 1988) for examples of literature and attitudes towards Blacks in the eighteenth century. The Chesapeake region already contained 40,000 Black slaves by 1720: A. Roger Ekirch, *Bound for America: The Transportation of British Convicts to the Colonies, 1718–1775* (Oxford: Oxford University Press, 1988).

94 Joshua Fry and Peter Jefferson, "A Map of the Most Inhabited Part of Virginia, Containing the Whole Province of Maryland with Part of Pennsylvania, New Jersey and North Carolina," 1751. Bibliographical details of the inclusion of this map in various atlases appear in Coolie Verner, "The Fry and Jefferson Map," *Imago Mundi* 21 (1967): 70–94. For the context behind the social structure in the cartouche, see Allan Kulikoff, *Tobacco and Slaves* (Chapel Hill: University of North Carolina Press, 1986).

95 Olive Patricia Dickason, "Old World Law, New World Peoples, and Concepts of Sovereignty," in *Essays on the History of North American Discovery and Exploration*, ed. Palmer and Reinhartz, 60.

96 For a discussion of the origins of this image in art, see H. W. Janson, *Apes and Ape Lore in the Middle Ages and the Renaissance* (London: The Warburg Institute and the University of London, 1952).

97 On the question of the Other with implications for cartographic discourse, see Henry Louis Gates, Jr., ed., *"Race," Writing, and Difference* (Chicago: The University of Chicago Press, 1986); *Europe and its Others*, 2 vols., ed. Francis Barker et al. (Colchester, 1985).

98 A very limp-looking lion or lion hide in the cartouche for D'Anville and Robert, "A New and Correct Map of North America with the West India Islands," 1779: in *A General Atlas Describing the Whole Universe* (London, 1782).

99 Reproduced in Schwartz and Ehrenberg, *The Mapping of America*, 118.

100 "North America. Performed under the Patronage of Louis Duke of Orleans, First Prince of the Blood; By The Sieur D'Anville Greatly Improved by Mr. Bolton . . . 1752. In J. Savary de Bruslans, *The Universal Dictionary of Trade* . . . (London. 1757), vol. 1, plates 1–4. Quoted in Conrad E. Heidenreich, "Mapping the Great Lakes: The Period of Imperial Rivalries, 1700–1760," *Cartographica* 18, no. 3 (1981), 74–109.

101 Thomas Jefferys, "North America from the French of Mr. D'Anville" . . . 1755 in *The Natural and Civil History of the French Dominions* . . . (London, 1760), 134. Quoted in Heidenreich, "Mapping the Great Lakes."

102 On New England names, see Arthur J. Krim, "Acculturation of the New England Landscape: Native and English Toponymy of Eastern Massachusetts," in *New England Prospect: Maps, Place Names, and the Historical Landscape* (Boston: Boston University, The Dublin Seminar for New England Folklife: Annual Proceedings, 1980), 69–88.

103 This emphasis is paralleled in the text of the eighteenth-century English geographies. It is the colonial presence which is usually stressed—what crops settlers raise, what schools they have founded, their churches, towns and villages. I owe this point to Barbara McCorkle.

104 Emanuel Bowen, *A Complete Atlas or Distinct View of the Known World, Exhibited in 68 Maps* (London, 17 . .), map 38, "A New and Accurate Map of Virginia and Maryland."

105 See the discussion in Robert F. Berkhofer, Jr., *The White Man's Indian: Images of the American Indian from Columbus to the Present* (New York: Vintage Books, 1979), 115–126. Francis Jennings, *The Invasion of America: Indians, Colonialism, and the Cant of Conquest* (New York: Norton, 1976), also stresses how the English colonists had rigged rationales as well as legal procedures to favor themselves in land dealings; we can add atlas cartography to the rationale.

PART THREE

Atlases of the Late Eighteenth and Nineteenth Centuries

German Atlas Development during the Nineteenth Century

WOLFGANG SCHARFE

INTRODUCTION

To characterize the phenomenon "atlas," one should consider—besides the standard definitions[1]—the following features. In contrast to a single map, an atlas is formally, as well as with regard to its content, a monolithic, but nevertheless internally manifold entity. An atlas represents at the same time a concept and a commercial product, the price of which determines the number of customers. Finally, an atlas, in the same way as a map, reflects the level and the possibilities of the reproduction technology available at the time of publication. During the nineteenth century the atlas was well known in Germany not only as a form of publication but also with regard to the above-mentioned aspects. The German atlases of this period have their roots in the eighteenth century, while their branches spread into the twentieth century. For this reason we cannot confine our discussion in the historical sense to a century-by-century description. In this contribution the "nineteenth century" will be synonymous with the period between the French Revolution and the First World War.

The eighteenth century roots for subsequent atlas cartography were based in a regime of absolutism, the spirit of enlightenment, and the political and military events which took place during the second half of the eighteenth century. The regime of absolutism had begun and encouraged systematically operated compilations and surveys with regard to quantitative, textual, and spatial information. One of the most important consequences of these efforts in Germany was the publication of Anton Büsching's *Neue Erdbeschreibung* (1754–1792) that popularized geographical thought.[2] The spirit of enlightenment must be seen as a rational impetus with social consequences especially for the middle classes and their educational behavior. The political and military events of the second half of the eighteenth century attracted the attention of and excited almost all Germans. These events started with what could be termed the first real "world war" (1755–1763 in Europe and North America), continued with the independence of the United States from Great Britain, and ended with the French Revolution and its political, military, and social consequences. With these events the spatial consciousness of a great public was awakened.

In the nineteenth century several factors contributed to the dissemination of spatial information in the form of the atlas and its subsequent spread as a broad stream to the urban middle class; later, to the proletariat; and finally to the rural populace. First, modern geography was established in Germany by Alexander von Humboldt and Carl Ritter early in the century. Second, for the first time in history, a large proportion of the German population gained spatial mobility and by this means spatial consciousness (self-stimulated spatial consciousness). The rapidly growing distribution of news; the beginnings and later, the stressing of nationalism; and finally the strong participation of Germans in activities abroad and overseas (exploration, emigration, business, colonial endeavors) stimulated their interest in spatial knowledge (event-stimulated spatial consciousness). In addition, the development of a German national history, which included contemporary events of the nineteenth century, led to activities which focused on local or regional events, the so-called "Heimatkunde" (local history and topography), complementing this outward-looking view. Finally, all of these impulses and developments found their analogies in the contents of education on all levels, especially in the schools. Unlike during the eighteenth century, all children had to attend school and from then on became a commercially relevant group of customers.

The thematic atlases of the nineteenth century, devoted to physical geography, regional geography, ethnology, and human geography, became new components in the atlas market. They reflected the growth of modern geography and thematic cartography, which had to solve problems never seen before. The atlas publishing houses were becoming focal points of scientific geographers and cartographers. (See Figure 86.)

PRINCIPLES AND PROBLEMS OF NINETEENTH-CENTURY ATLAS CARTOGRAPHY

The introduction of Stieler's *Hand-Atlas* of 1816 provided the basis for the nineteenth-century atlas concept.[3] Stieler wanted to create an atlas that combined "a general usefulness with solidity and completeness" and that should serve "as well for instruction as for the daily use for people from all walks of life." For this reason the atlas should have "a handy size, a moderate number of sheets, a certain conformity of projections and scales . . . and a price, as low as possible." By analyzing examples reflecting Stieler's atlas concept, three important components can be recognized: first, the geographic-topographic content; second, the cartographic outline; and last, the reproduction technique.

The quality of the geographic-topographic content depended on current information, which was based on the ability to obtain relatively new information from topographic surveys (especially in Europe), geographic discoveries (Africa,

SYNOPSIS

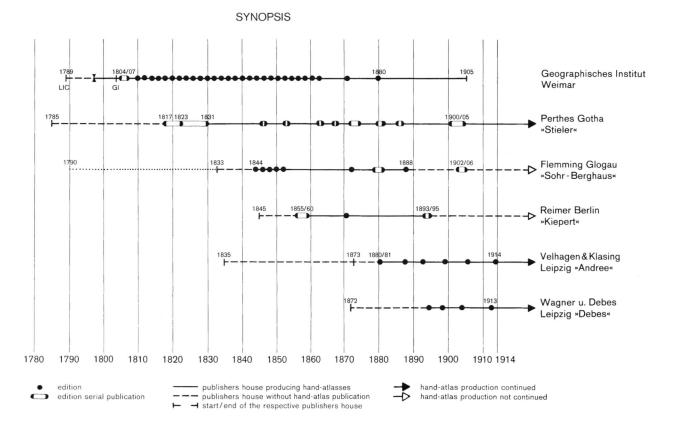

FIGURE 86 *Synopsis.*

Asia, America, and Australia), political and administrative changes (boundaries, territorial names), and the establishment of settlements and lines of communication (streets, railways, canals, transoceanic cables). The necessity of obtaining current information is the very basis of modern atlas editorial work. The nineteenth century was the era of national surveys and the last great geographical discoveries, which extinguished the "horror vacui" on maps. The procedure of gathering together the numerous topographical documents, studying them critically, and making full use of them, has been a perennial challenge for editors and geographers. However, only a few of them were able to face this challenge successfully, with regard to the large financial, organizational, and scientific input which was necessarily required.

The cartographic outline of an atlas is defined by its aim. For the geographic-topographic atlases published in the nineteenth century, the aim was to give a true, detailed, and homogeneous impression of the world. A single map could achieve this purpose only with difficulty because of its small scale or unhandy size. For this reason the surface of the earth had to be partitioned into sheets with different scales. In the majority of the nineteenth-century German atlases, the number of maps increased from edition to edition with the maps of Central Europe and European regions dominating. At first the geographic-topographic atlas was a mirror of the more or less speculative characteristics of the earth, as they had been sketched out by Alexander von Humboldt, Carl Ritter, and Heinrich Berghaus. Since the middle, but more particularly since the third quarter of the nineteenth century, this focus changed considerably. The atlases became more and more topographic compendiums, often including great numbers of geographic names according to Max Eckert, especially for the readers of newspapers.[4] This criticism, even if true, has to be seen in connection with the development of geography during this period. The great atlases could no longer fulfill the demands of modern scientific geography. The geographic focus had changed from macrospaces to microregions, and analytic induction was replacing speculative deduction. By the end of the nineteenth century, the significance and importance of the famous geographic-topographic atlases for scientific geography were substantially reduced.

The third component, the reproduction technique, concerns the graphic detail and the general visual impression of the maps, which often influenced the decision to purchase an atlas. Its economical aspect can be defined by the relation between financial input, number of copies per edition, the simplicity or difficulty of altering the printing plate, and the final atlas price. With regard to the German atlases, the economical aspect is a fundamental one, because all these atlases were produced by private enterprise, necessitating economic success for continuous publication, if not for simple survival.

Although it is impossible to provide a comprehensive account of nineteenth-century reproduction techniques, an example of how a technical innovation influenced price is provided by the well-known Stieler atlas. The Perthes publishers at Gotha preferred copper engraving. This technique produced brilliant map images, but the copperplates and the engraving process were expensive, and the time spent in printing was relatively high. It was easy to correct a copperplate, but the number of perfect copies printed from a single plate—without a special treatment—was limited to about 2,000, over a long time. Around 1840, the price of the Stieler was 17⅓ Thaler. In 1837 electrodeposition was invented by Jacobi in St. Petersburg and by Spencer in Liverpool, which made it easy to produce homogeneous copperplates and to copy the hand-engraved copperplate perfectly. By this technique the number of copies per edition could be increased as needed. On the other hand, while printing one edition the engraver could update the copperplate for the next edition, an advantage for maintaining currency. Perthes, having used electrodeposition since 1845, reduced the prices for Stieler editions by twenty-five percent, and for the single sheets by about thirty-three percent, mainly by increasing the number of copies per edition.

The Great Geographic-Topographic Atlases

During the nineteenth century, more than 1,000 atlases of different types were published in Germany. One of the most significant categories was the "hand-atlas," for which systematic historic and bibliographic research is still in the beginning stages.[5] For that reason, the following contribution cannot be more than a preliminary report.

The "hand-atlas" as a geographic-topographic atlas contains generally or predominantly maps of states, parts of continents, continents, and seas, with each map showing, for the most part, the coastlines, the hydrologic network, the main geomorphologic units, the most important settlements, the main communication lines, and the administrative boundaries. The most detailed maps have scales of about 1:1,000,000. Insets at larger scales are used primarily to illustrate capitals and important sea channels.

Geographisches Institut Weimar   The transition from eighteenth- to nineteenth-century German atlas cartography can be documented most completely by the early history of the Geographisches Institut at Weimar. Within the "Landes-Industrie-Comptoir" (founded in 1789 at Weimar), Friedrich Justin Bertuch established the Geographisches Institut in 1804 that would engage in geographic and cartographic publication. The Institut was equipped with a copper-engraving workshop, a copper printing press, and eventually a lithographic printing press. In 1800, Bertuch became editor of the *Allgemeine Geographische Ephemeriden*, the first German language geographical periodical of high international reputation.[6] After 1797, the "Landes-Industrie-Comptoir" published maps that formed the *Allgemeiner Hand-Atlas der ganzen Erde*, which appeared from the Geographisches Institut (1804–1807) with sixty sheets.[7] (See Figure 87.) The conceptual basis of

FIGURE 87   *Title page*, All-gemeiner Hand-Atlas der ganzen Erde *(Weimar: Verlag des Geographischen Instituts, 1804–1807). Library of Congress.*

this atlas was the geographical compendium of Adam Christian Gaspari, a well-known geographer and educator of the late eighteenth century. This atlas particularly illustrates the connection between the eighteenth and nineteenth centuries. The sheets of the first edition were published initially as single maps, designed by eleven cartographers including representatives of the old cartography, such as Franz Ludwig Güssefeld (see Figure 88), as well as representatives of a new cartographical spirit, such as Friedrich Wilhelm Streit and Adolf Stieler. The early catalogs of the Institut point out that the maps are printed in the "so-called Homannian Size" (68 × 58 cm), indicating that a concession had been made to the eighteenth-century map tradition. On the other hand, the catalogs stressed that all maps "will be corrected continuously according to each geographical discovery and to each political change," which shows that an effort would be made to keep them up-to-date.

The single-sheet publication and the participation of eleven cartographers initially gave this atlas a nonuniform appearance, which was diminished by the increasing preponderance of Carl Friedrich Weiland's contribution. Of the six remaining cartographers, Weiland was the author of more than fifty percent of

FIGURE 88   Charte von den Vereinigten Staaten von Nord-America nebst Louisiana . . .
(Weimar: Verlag des Geographischen Instituts, 1805). Library of Congress.

the maps of the 1823 edition. Ten years later only two cartographers, Weiland and Streit, were still at work, and Weiland designed fifty-eight of the sixty sheets.[8] Weiland's influence on the Weimar atlas, which began in 1817, was terminated when Heinrich Kiepert moved to Weimar (1845–1852) to become the head of the geographic and cartographic activities of the Geographisches Institut. However, even after his return to Berlin, Kiepert tried to oversee the production of the Weimar atlas up to its last edition, the forty-ninth in 1880.[9] During this time, the title of the Weimar atlas changed several times: 1811, *Allgemeiner neuester Hand-Atlas*, respectively, *Allgemeiner Hand-Atlas der ganzen Erde*; 1845, *Allgemeiner Handatlas der ganzen Erde und des Himmels*; and 1871, *Großer Hand-Atlas des Himmels und der Erde*. But this title change did not mean any fundamental change in the atlas concept.

Between 1807 and 1850 the number of sheets in the *Allgemeiner Hand-Atlas* increased from sixty to sixty-three to seventy-two, but was reduced to seventy sheets in the last editions, while the fundamental set of detailed mapped regions and the "Homannian" size did not change substantially from edition to edition. The new maps in the atlas had previously been published as supplements and among them we cannot detect any regional preference. In 1845 the title received the additional, . . . *und des Himmels*, because three maps of stars and planets were integrated. Only the later editions contained a few thematic maps. (See Figure 89.)

Apart from the *Allgemeiner Hand-Atlas*, the Geographisches Institut published a *Handatlas über alle Theile der Erde* with sixty, later sixty-one maps, but also with thirty-four or thirty-five maps, that was devoted to "middle class schools and

FIGURE 89 *Title page,* Hand-Atlas der Erde und des Himmels *(Weimar: Geographisches Institut, 1867). Free University of Berlin.*

HAND-ATLAS

DER

ERDE UND DES HIMMELS.

IN SIEBZIG BLÄTTERN.

ZWEIUNDVIERZIGSTE AUFLAGE.

BEARBEITET

VON

D.R. H. KIEPERT, C. GRÄF, A. GRÄF UND D.R. C. BRUHNS.

WEIMAR,
GEOGRAPHISCHES INSTITUT.

readers of newspapers."[10] Despite the use of Handatlas in the title, the reduced size, the reduced scales, and the low price (10 Thaler in comparison to 20 Thaler for the "great" *Hand-Atlas*) demonstrate that this atlas cannot be described as a "hand-atlas" but rather as a "family atlas," which of course has its own history. After 1845 the smaller version of the great atlas contained many supplementary maps according to the location of customers in northern and southern Germany, Prussia, Austria, Scandinavia, and Russia. In addition to these hand-atlases, the Geographisches Institut was the editor of school atlases, celestial atlases, historical atlases, regional "topographic military" atlases, globes, geographic textbooks and manuals, and travel books.

The leading characters on the cartographic scene during the most brilliant and successful period at Weimar were the aforementioned Bertuch, followed by Streit, Weiland, and last Kiepert. By the middle of the nineteenth century the importance of the Geographisches Institut slowly declined for several reasons. In 1852 Kiepert returned to Berlin without leaving an equally skilled successor in Weimar; the Institut ownership changed repeatedly without financial improvement and without technical renewal; the competition in the atlas market and generally in the geographic market increased. The last edition of the *Allgemeiner Hand-Atlas* appeared in 1880 (second issue 1882), and in 1905 the Geographisches Institut at Weimar ceased to exist after a productive period of 100 years.

Justus Perthes at Gotha and the Stieler   The Stieler atlas was born with the alliance between the publisher Justus Perthes and the administrative expertise of Adolf Stieler. Perthes founded a publishing house in 1785 and began by editing the court almanac of Gotha and a famous necrology. About 1800 Perthes began publishing geographic books. Stieler was a self-educated man in the fields of geography and cartography. His first mapping efforts were encouraged by Freiherr v. Zach and were published in 1797 by the Geographisches Institut at Weimar. Perthes first contacted Stieler in 1805 when Stieler drew a map of Germany which was to be included in a book edited by Perthes. The first atlas that Perthes published appeared in 1809: *Hand-Atlas über alle bekannte Länder des Erdbodens . . .* by Johann H. G. Heusinger, with some twenty-four maps.[11] In spite of the title this atlas did not belong to the hand-atlas type as mentioned above, but must be considered as an early attempt at regional classification by very simple physical features. The concept of the atlas was below standard and its topography had an archaic level; thus, this enterprise totally failed.

Near the end of 1814 or the beginning of 1815, Stieler wrote down his concept for a new atlas and sent it to Perthes. He noted that as special elements of innovation in comparison with atlases already published, each map of the new atlas should show the names of the author and engraver and should be accompanied with an explanatory text describing the map sources. Perthes agreed, and in April 1816, the atlas entitled *Hand-Atlas über alle Theile der Erde nach dem neuesten Zustande und über das Weltgebäude* was officially announced.[12] (See Figure 90.) At this

FIGURE 90 *Title page, Hand-Atlas über alle Theile der Erde nach dem neuesten Zustande . . . (Gotha: Justus Perthes, 1817–1823). Free University of Berlin.*

time the atlas was comprised of some fifty maps, each having a size of 35 × 29 cm. In 1817, the first part of the atlas was published, the last part in 1823. Most of the maps had been drawn by Stieler, the others by C. G. Reichard. While editing the 1823 issue, the atlas concept was extended by publishing five supplementary parts with twenty-five maps (1823–1831/34). (See Figure 91.) Thus, the first complete edition of the Stieler contained seventy-five maps in all. For lack of copper engravers at Gotha, the maps had to be given to engravers in Weimar and Berlin.

The first Stieler edition would not have won an award for the elegance of its map engraving. However, its great advantage was and would be for a long time to come the permanent revision and renewal of the contents of the maps. This attribute of the Stieler atlas became its main characteristic throughout the century. Between 1834 and 1879 (first through seventh editions), 197 totally new maps were drawn and engraved. The basis for permanent revision was that qualified geographers and cartographers were available to face this challenge and that the publisher was willing to take the financial risk. The different members of the Perthes family never

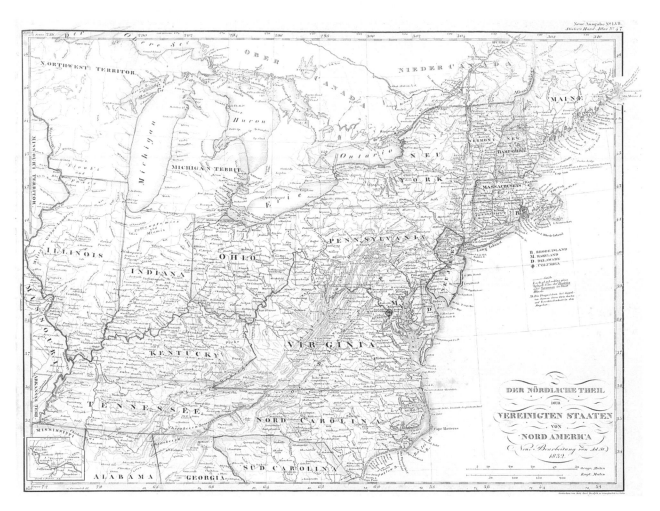

FIGURE 91   *"Der nördliche Theil der Vereinigten Staaten von Nord America. 1832,"* Hand-Atlas über alle Theile der Erde nach dem neuesten Zustande . . . *(Gotha: Justus Perthes, 1834). Library of Congress.*

hesitated to promote the atlas in every possible way and they succeeded in employing outstanding persons for the atlas work. During the lifetime of Adolf Stieler, several scholars joined the Gotha team as map authors, among them the former Prussian captain Friedrich von Stülpnagel and the well-known geographer Heinrich Berghaus. After Stieler died in 1836, it was Stülpnagel who replaced him and continued the Stieler map tradition. From the second to the fourth editions (1845/47–1862/64), Stülpnagel created more than fifty percent of the maps. In this period, the number of maps per edition increased from seventy-five (first edition) to eighty-three (second/third editions, 1845/47–1852/54) and finally to eighty-four (fourth/fifth editions, 1862/64–1866/68).

Both scientifically and economically, the Stieler atlas was a great success. For this reason other publishers tried to share this success by mere plagiarism—a source of continuous complaint. In the long run, however, plagiarism had no chance, and moreover, the Perthes publishers were both flexible and clever. In

1830 and in 1834, they edited two smaller issues of the Stieler atlas containing thirty-one and sixty-three maps, which were compiled for customers with lower budgets. Because of this, the high quality of the general input, and the lack of copper engravers, all complete editions appeared as serial publications and could be bought sheet by sheet.

The early Stieler editions showed a preponderance of geographic-topographic maps, but few if any thematic maps. This feature formed a part of the Perthes' Stieler concept, which concentrated on publishing the geographic-topographic maps in the Stieler atlas and publishing thematic maps (as well as regional maps) separately, in special atlases, or as map series.

During the first half of the nineteenth century, the volume of spatial information increased enormously, reflecting new surveys and discoveries. The efficient compilation of the Stieler atlas depended to a high degree on the engagement of geographers, who although certainly known to Perthes, were not closely linked to the publisher and did not live in Gotha. Bernhardt Perthes I (1821–1857) tried to found a new organization by forming a geographic establishment that would become the absolute center of German and European geography and cartography. He succeeded in winning over August Petermann who moved to Gotha to realize the bold project. Petermann had been trained in cartography by Heinrich Berghaus in his "Geographische Kunstschule" at Potsdam before he went to Great Britain for several years, busied himself in cartographic affairs and was engaged as a promoter of the African and polar regions discoveries. One of Petermann's first activities in 1855 was the founding of the *Mittheilungen aus Justus Perthes' geographischer Anstalt* . . . that continued the explanatory texts to the Stieler maps and the short-lived attempt of Heinrich Berghaus to create a geographical periodical.[13] The *Mittheilungen* . . . , the only German periodical in this line, was not linked to any of the several scientific geographical societies. Within a few years it grew to be the most important German-language geographical periodical and at the same time mirrored the Stieler atlas development which was also headed by Petermann. In this period Perthes introduced the electrodeposition technique, as mentioned above, and concentrated all the technical branches of his establishment, whether in his own house or at Gotha and its vicinity, which previously had been widespread over the country. By these steps the publisher was able to train the rising generation of geographers and cartographers as well as others in the technical branches within its own establishment and according to his ideas.

Although the Stieler concept did not change, Petermann and his team tried to answer the geographic development of regional specialization with large-scale maps in several sheets which were integrated into the atlas or appended to it by request. By this means the number of maps increased from eighty-four (fifth edition, 1866–1868) to ninety (sixth edition, 1871–1875) and ninety-five (seventh/eighth editions, 1879/82–1888/91) (see Figure 92), and finally one hundred (ninth edition, 1900–1905). The eighth edition, the first to contain a gazetteer,

FIGURE 92 *Title page, Adolf Stieler's Hand-Atlas über alle Theile der Erde . . . (Gotha: Justus Perthes, 1882). Free University of Berlin.*

was the last atlas reproduced by monochrome copper printing with hand coloring, the technique used since 1817. This technique had become too costly; in 1885 almost ninety employees were engaged in coloring. This process was superseded by polychrome transfer printing, which had already been used to print the Andree atlas. At Gotha this change in printing was introduced in the ninth edition and its following ten issues up to 1914.

Thus, the nineteenth-century development of the Stieler atlas can be divided into four periods, the first three being 1816–1836, the Stieler period; 1836 to about 1860, the Stülpnagel period; and up to the 1880s, the Petermann period. Within the Petermann period, modern geography had its real takeoff, reflected in the establishment of numerous chairs of geography at German universities, and the increased competition from the Flemming and Reimer hand-atlases.

After Petermann's death in 1878, the fourth Stieler period began. It was not dominated by an outstanding leader but was characterized by the teamwork of about ten highly qualified geographers and cartographers who had received part of their cartographic education from Petermann within the Perthes' establishment, but were also already skilled academically. Among them were Carl Vogel and Hermann Habenicht, the most important authors of the eighth and ninth editions, and Hermann Haack, who succeeded them and continued the Stieler up to 1940 (1945).

During the 123-year (1817–1940) history of the Stieler atlas, some ten complete and two incomplete editions in German and other languages were published. In addition, numerous issues intermediate to the editions were produced.

This excellent work became the longest lived, the most well known and above all the most successful German hand-atlas of the nineteenth century.

The Sohr-Berghaus Atlas Unlike the other hand-atlas sites, which were already well known as capitals or by their outstanding commercial activities, Glogau in lower Silesia became common knowledge because of the Flemming publishing house and its cartographic products.

In 1833, the young bookseller Carl Flemming, who was born near Leipzig, bought a publishing house at Glogau where he initially published popular booklets and almanacs. The decisive years for the beginning of Flemming's cartographic branch were 1839 and 1844. In 1839, the cartographer Friedrich Handtke, aged 24, joined the publishing house, and in 1844, the first edition of the *Vollständiger Hand-Atlas der neueren Erdbeschreibung über alle Theile der Erde* was published, edited by Dr. Karl Sohr.[14] (See Figure 93.) That same year, Flemming also bought the *Reymann'sche Karte*, the most famous, privately compiled and produced general map of nineteenth-century Germany.[15] Both enterprises became the basis for the cartographic success of the Glogau publisher.

In the present stage of research, one aspect of the history of this atlas is most mysterious. In all editions of the *Vollständiger Hand-Atlas*, the name Sohr was placed on the frontispiece, but no map was ever signed by Sohr nor could any biographical information about Dr. Karl Sohr be found. Heinrich Berghaus, who knew the German cartographic scene in detail, wrote a letter to Perthes at Gotha in November 1847 in which he mentioned that Sohr must be an imaginary name. If Berghaus was correct—and there is no reason to distrust him—Flemming had

FIGURE 93 *Title page,* Vollständiger Hand-Atlas der neueren Erdbeschreibung über alle Theile der Erde . . . , *ed. Dr. K. Sohr. (Glogau and Leipzig: C. Flemming, 1844). Library of Congress.*

invented an academic phantom to give his atlas the appearance of high scientific quality in order to promote its sale.

At first the atlas appeared with eighty sheets, the relatively high number of sheets compensating for the relatively small size of the maps (37 × 28 cm). The most important authors of this edition were Handtke with thirty-eight maps and the Prussian engineer-lieutenant A. Theinert with twenty-one maps. In 1846 and 1847, two different supplementary volumes were published of which the latter, containing 110 maps, became part of the next edition. The fourth edition of 1849 to 1850 had only eighty-two maps, many of them revised by Heinrich Berghaus, whereas the fifth edition, published repeatedly between 1852 and 1865, contained some one hundred fourteen maps.[16] Because of this, the period up to 1865 must be considered as an experimental stage in developing the atlas concept. However, the rapid sequence of editions of the atlas and the different types of supplements prove that the flexibility of the publishers and the sale of the atlas must have been excellent. In contrast to Weimar and Gotha, Flemming introduced lithography as the reproduction technique for the atlas but was not able to achieve the graphic and cartographic splendor of copper engraving.

The sixth edition, published after 1872, constituted a new atlas with one hundred maps, of which ninety-two had been revised to a large extent, newly lithographed and reproduced by polychromatic printing. Sohr-Berghaus on the frontispiece had become a signature, while Handtke was now named as the person responsible for the atlas.[17] (See Figure 94.) The seventh (1878) and eighth (1888) editions were published with only minor revisions in comparison to the sixth edition, but the culmination of the Handtke atlas had passed. In 1878 Carl Flemming died and was followed by Friedrich Handtke the next year. The Flemming publishers and the "Hand-Atlas" lost their powerful leaders and the publishing house was sold in 1888. By this time some 100,000 copies of the Glogau atlas had been sold.

The new owners of Flemming continued to edit cartographic products, but they failed to win a successor equal to Handtke and by this means continue this great atlas. In 1902 the cartographer Alois Bludau started the serial publication of a new atlas for which he used the signature Sohr-Berghaus, but four years later this attempt had to be abandoned.

Reimer at Berlin and the Kiepert Atlas   By the end of the eighteenth century, a considerable private cartography had begun in the Prussian capital, Berlin. It was continued and intensified in the nineteenth century by Daniel Friedrich Sotzmann, Daniel Gottlob Reymann, Ferdinand August von Witzleben, F. B. Engelhardt, K. W. von Oesfeld, F. W. von Etzel, and later by Heinrich and Hermann Berghaus. Furthermore, from the beginning of the nineteenth century, the cartographic activities of the Prussian General Staff and the outstanding geographic influence of Humboldt and Ritter were also present in Berlin. Because of this, many maps, school atlases, and regional atlases were published, including

FIGURE 94 *Title page*, Sohr-Berghaus Hand-Atlas über alle Theile der Erde ... *(Glogau: Carl Flemming, 1877). Free University of Berlin.*

the first national atlas, the *Administrativ-statistischer Atlas vom Preußischen Staate* in 1827 to 1828.[18]

However, during the first half of the nineteenth century no Berlin publisher dared risk competition with the already well-known hand-atlases from Weimar, Gotha, and Glogau. Only Dietrich Reimer, since 1845 owner of a book and map shop and since 1847 owner of a publishing house that still exists in Berlin today, took a decisive step. In 1852 he called Heinrich Kiepert back to Berlin, guaranteeing him favorable financial remuneration. Moreover, the Prussian capital offered better possibilities for the realization of Kiepert's scientific projects: contact with the scholars at the University of Berlin.

Until his death, Heinrich Kiepert compiled more than 450 maps, map series, wall maps, atlases, and globes, mostly edited by Reimer. Among these was the first edition of the *Neuer Hand Atlas über alle Theile der Erde,* with a map size (54 × 42 cm) that was similar to the size of the Weimar atlas.[19] The reproduction process for the forty atlas maps became difficult because there was not a sufficient number of copper engravers available at that time in either Berlin or in all of Germany. Regardless of the intention of Kiepert and Reimer to reproduce the whole atlas by copper engraving, several maps had to be lithographed and some of them even had to be sent to Nuremberg, Munich, and Stockholm in order to finish the first atlas edition in time. Consequently, the graphical image of the first editions of the Kiepert atlas seemed nonuniform and also somewhat rough where the work had been completed in a hurry.

Problems had already risen in the stage of gathering and selecting the geographical sources. In the commentary to the first atlas edition, Kiepert explained that a single scholar would be overwhelmed if he tried to evaluate all the sources, published maps and books, and especially statistics in regard to their actual value. Nevertheless, the energetic Heinrich Kiepert designed all the maps in the first and second editions, whereas for the third edition—in 1893 he was seventy-five years old—Kiepert's son Richard took over a part of the map design while Paul Lippert and M. Busemann wrote the statistical commentary.

The first edition of the *Neuer Hand-Atlas* was printed repeatedly. In 1871 the second edition with forty-five maps was published. The low quality of reproduction of the first edition maps encouraged Kiepert to revise fourteen (thirty-five percent) of them for the second edition. In spite of this corrective procedure, several poorly designed sheets remained, primarily where the relief representation was not separated from the other graphic elements of the black plate. Kiepert's reply to this criticism was that changing the relief representation would be the same as destroying all the plates, and consequently, an economic disaster. The second atlas edition was printed at least four times (probably eight times). The third edition was issued as a serial publication, 1893–1896, with the title *Grosser Hand-Atlas.*[20] Although this edition also contained forty-five maps, the price had been reduced. Again, eleven maps had been totally renewed, but the atlas concept did not change.

The third edition was the last. Heinrich Kiepert died in 1899. His son Richard, who had become a specialist in the field of historical geography, was not able to continue the atlas. The publisher, Reimer, presumably was handicapped economically and could not redesign the atlas to conform with the Stieler, Andree, or Debes. Because of this, the Kiepert atlas was not able to compete with its rivals successfully. After Kiepert's death, Reimer never produced a similar atlas.

In view of the history of this hand-atlas, the enterprise must be considered as essential; but the limitation of only one author, although highly skilled and experienced, and the lack of a real financial commitment by the publisher could not bring about a long-term success. When Albrecht Penck wrote an article about the German hand-atlases in 1911, he never mentioned the Kiepert atlas.[21]

The Andree Atlas The Velhagen & Klasing publishing house was founded at Bielefeld in 1835 and began by issuing literary and theological publications, schoolbooks, and periodicals. In 1864, Velhagen & Klasing established a branch in the burgeoning metropolis of Leipzig, to which was added in 1873 a Geographische Anstalt headed by Richard Andree. Among other atlases of different types, the first part of the *Allgemeiner Hand-Atlas* was published in 1880, the completed first edition with eighty-nine maps one year later.[22] By 1876 Andree had already published a school atlas and in 1877 in cooperation with Oskar Peschel the *Physikalisch-statistischer Atlas des Deutschen Reiches.*[23] Some years later the Putzger *Historischer Atlas* and the Droysen *Allgemeiner Historischer Atlas* strengthened the cartographic output of this branch of Velhagen & Klasing.[24]

By the beginning of the First World War, six German editions of the Andree atlas had appeared. (See Figure 95.) Also Swedish, French, English, Italian, Austrian, and Danish editions had been published. This was perhaps the widest range

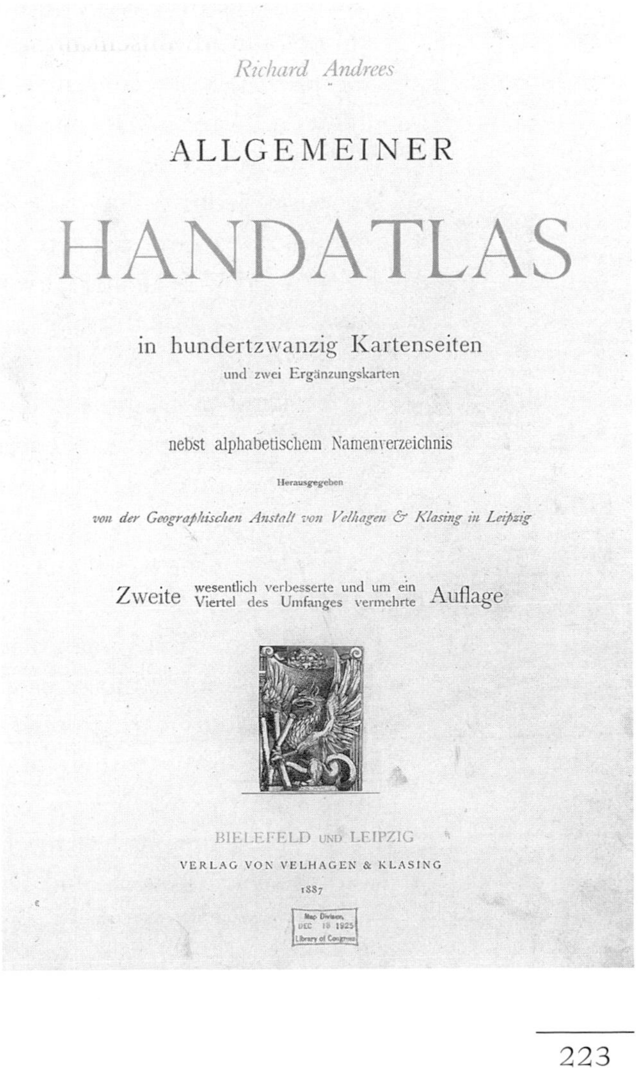
Richard Andrees

ALLGEMEINER

HANDATLAS

in hundertzwanzig Kartenseiten

und zwei Ergänzungskarten

nebst alphabetischem Namenverzeichnis

Herausgegeben

von der Geographischen Anstalt von Velhagen & Klasing in Leipzig

Zweite wesentlich verbesserte und um ein Viertel des Umfanges vermehrte Auflage

BIELEFELD UND LEIPZIG

VERLAG VON VELHAGEN & KLASING

1887

Map Division, DEC 18 1925 Library of Congress

FIGURE 95 *Title page,* Richard Andrees Allgemeiner Handatlas . . . *(Bielefeld and Leipzig: Velhagen & Klasing, 2d ed., 1887). Library of Congress.*

of distribution among all atlases of this type and it was as successful as the Stieler. Moreover, the second and third editions were published in two issues, the fourth in five, and the fifth in six issues, thus giving a total of seventeen editions and issues between 1881 and 1914. Each issue differed from the preceding one not only by corrections and new details but mostly by the addition of new maps.

Two major aspects characterized the development of the Andree atlas in this period. First, the number of sheets and maps grew, edition by edition, in spite of the relatively high number of maps included in the first edition and in spite of a map size of 49 × 36 cm.

Edition	Year	Number of Sheets	Number of Maps (without insets)
1st	1881	96	86
2nd	1887	122	107
3rd	1893	142	98
4th	1899	186	132
5th	1906	207	150
6th	1914	224	170

The reduction of the number of maps between the second and the third editions was the result of changing single-sheet maps into double-sheet maps. Second, the atlas concept changed repeatedly. The second edition contained eighteen more maps than the first one (see Figure 96), but really some thirty-three maps had been renewed, whereas the number of thematic maps had been decreased from twenty-two to thirteen. The third edition contained only one thematic map, but again thirty-three maps had been newly designed or newly integrated into the atlas. From the third to the fourth edition, the number of maps increased by thirty-four, but sixty-four maps were really new, among them thirty thematic maps. Albert Scobel, editor since the fourth edition, augmented the fifth and sixth editions considerably. The numbers of geographic-topographic and thematic maps included were also increased. (See Figure 97.) Between 1899 (fourth edition) and 1914 (sixth edition), almost every year saw a new Andree issue. This success was based on the large number of maps that showed a considerable part of the world in a much more detailed fashion than in any other hand-atlas. Additionally, the Geographische Anstalt of Velhagen & Klasing was headed by excellently skilled men like Richard Andree (died 1912), Albert Scobel (died 1912), and Ernst Ambrosius whose efforts were effectively supported by a team of about twenty cartographers and about thirty lithographers. Among the Velhagen & Klasing cartographers, special mention must be made of Dr. Ernst Friedrich, who qualified in 1901 as university lecturer with his inaugural dissertation about thematic cartography, and to G. Jungk, E. Umbreit, R. Köcher, A. Thomas, H. Mielisch, and Dr. E. Ambrosius who created the majority of the Andree maps. There also were geographers and cartographers such as Dr. A. Bludau, P. Bosse, A. Brandrupp, and O. Herkt who worked at the same time on the

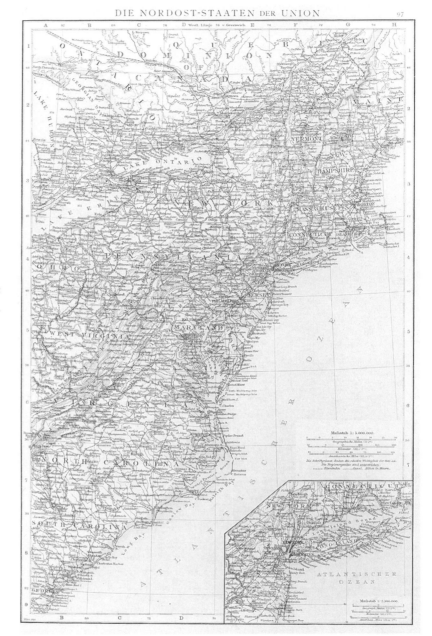

FIGURE 96   *"Die Nordost-Staaten der Union,"* Richard Andrees Allgemeiner Handatlas . . . *(2d ed., 1887). Library of Congress.*

hand-atlases of Velhagen & Klasing, Flemming, and Wagner and Debes. Finally, one of the reasons for the success of the Andree atlas was its low price, lower than the price of the Stieler.

In spite of the relatively large number of geographers, cartographers, and lithographers who worked on the Andree atlas, it showed a cartographic uniformity beginning with its first edition. The Stieler atlas also succeeded in achieving this uniformity but not before the ninth edition in 1905. Moreover, the Andree atlas contained, since the 1899 edition, maps with contour lines, in contrast to the usual relief representation by hachures, and more than fifty thematic maps. The Debes showed similar features, the Stieler did not. In spite of the German eco-

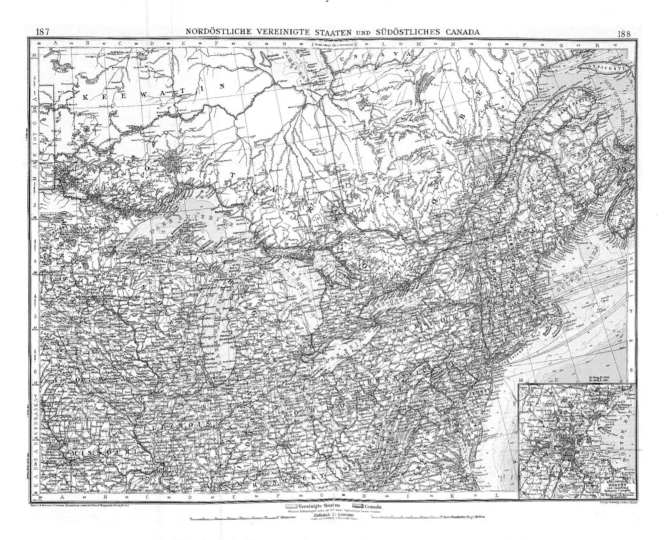

FIGURE 97   *"Nordöstliche Vereinigte Staaten und Südöstliche Canada,"* Richard Andrees
Allgemeiner Handatlas . . . *(5th ed., 1906). Library of Congress.*

nomic problems that rose during and after the First World War, the Andree atlas
was continued up to 1937 without any considerable change.

The Debes Atlas   Despite the fact that there was already strong competition
between the Stieler, the Andree, the Kiepert, and the Sohr-Berghaus atlases, a new
hand-atlas was published by Wagner and Debes in 1894 to 1895 at Leipzig. The
initiative for this atlas was taken by Ernst Debes, who was trained in cartography
by August Petermann at Gotha and was initially occupied with drawing maps for
Baedeker's guidebooks. In 1872, Debes and Wagner founded a publishing house
and a Geographische Anstalt where they began to produce school atlases, wall
maps, and maps edited by other publishers. The outstanding success of their
work—the school atlas was published in some fifty editions between 1882 and
1906—encouraged them to begin to design a hand-atlas in 1884.[25] This atlas was

characterized by a relatively low number of sheets and maps (first edition, fifty sheets with fifty-nine maps; third edition, fifty-two sheets with sixty-one maps) but not an extraordinarily large map size (Debes size, 48 × 36 cm); a very clear map image, not overprinted by a proliferation of names; and a constancy in concept. Between 1894 to 1895 and 1913, four editions of the Debes atlas were published (first edition, 1894 to 1895; second, 1898; third, 1905; fourth, 1913) and moreover, like the Andree atlas, several intermediate issues.[26] (See Figure 98.)

In comparison with the Stieler and the Andree, the success of the Debes atlas, although clearly limited, was made possible by recruiting a team of highly qualified geographers and cartographers. By this means, Wagner and Debes succeeded in continuing their atlas after 1918; since 1935, the Debes atlas has been published as *Columbus-Weltatlas*.[27]

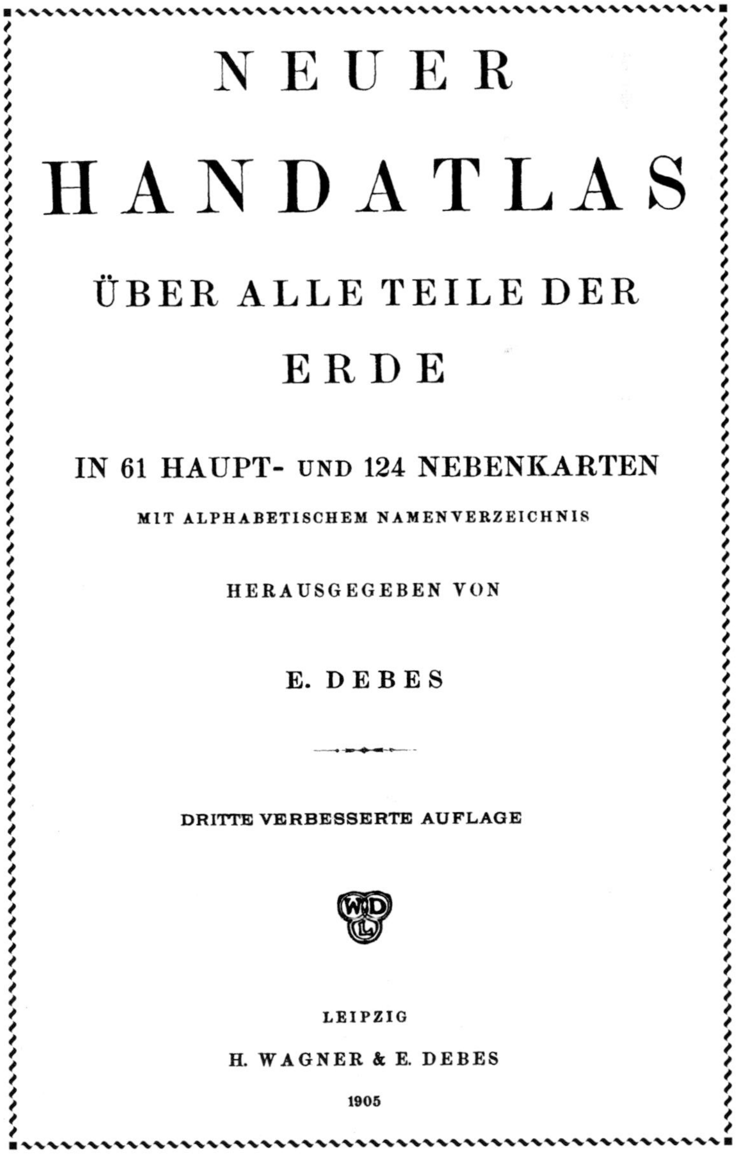

FIGURE 98 *Title page*, Neuer Handatlas über alle Teile der Erde ... *(Leipzig: H. Wagner & E. Debes, 1905). Free University of Berlin.*

NEUER

HANDATLAS

ÜBER ALLE TEILE DER

ERDE

IN 61 HAUPT- UND 124 NEBENKARTEN

MIT ALPHABETISCHEM NAMENVERZEICHNIS

HERAUSGEGEBEN VON

E. DEBES

DRITTE VERBESSERTE AUFLAGE

LEIPZIG

H. WAGNER & E. DEBES

1905

Thematic Atlases

This survey of German hand-atlases would remain incomplete without mention of two important thematic hand-atlases, both edited by Perthes at Gotha. The first was the *Physikalischer Atlas*, encouraged by Alexander von Humboldt in 1827 and realized by Heinrich Berghaus between 1838 and 1848. This atlas was the first attempt to visualize by thematic maps the results of nineteenth-century geography, which was in a stage between speculation and more perfect knowledge. The first edition of the *Physikalischer Atlas* contained ninety maps and was soon followed by the second, published between 1849 and 1852.[28] In spite of the high price of 34⅓ Thaler, this atlas was more than a scientific and economic success. It must be considered, on the one hand, as proof of the efficiency of the newborn science of geography and on the other hand, as one of the earliest great challenges for thematic cartography. The *Physikalischer Atlas* was the real cartographic supplement to Humboldt's *Kosmos*, although in 1851 to 1854 Traugott Bromme published the *Atlas zu Alex. v. Humboldt's Kosmos* with forty-two maps, partly copied or derived from the Berghaus atlas.[29] With the lower price of 8 Thaler, the atlas was destined for wider distribution. In a clearer way than the German geographic-topographic atlases of this period, the Berghaus *Physikalischer Atlas* became the model for similar publications in other countries. Between 1886 and 1892, the third edition of the *Physikalischer Atlas* was edited by Hermann Berghaus, Heinrich Berghaus's nephew, but this edition with contributions from twelve highly skilled scholars was a totally new atlas reflecting the progress of geography by the middle of the nineteenth century.[30]

At the same time in the field of history, a real giant was created by Karl von Spruner, a Munich military officer who eventually became a general and aide-de-camp of the King of Bavaria. Between 1837 and 1853, the *Historisch-geographischer Hand-Atlas* was published, containing 118 maps in three parts, based on the concept that "each historic map should fulfill for the respective period the same requirements as an excellent geographic map for modern times."[31] The most remarkable feature of this atlas was its third part, which was devoted to the history of Asia, Africa, America, and Australia at a time when the common consciousness of European people was focused mainly upon their own continent.

CONCLUSION

Both of these thematic atlases highlight some general features of the German atlases in the nineteenth century. First, all the great hand-atlases had been created by the favorable alliance between a resolute private publisher and a highly qualified geographer, both aware of the mistakes of the past as well as of the possible future role of the atlas. But this alliance, with an awareness of the future of a hand-atlas, was based primarily on the personal engagement of the respective scholar. This strong connection between a work and its originator in the field of private atlas cartography cannot be compared to the official government surveys of the time that were for the most part characterized by anonymity.

Second, this contribution has singled out almost artificially the hand-atlases from the environment of other cartographic publications, edited by the same publishers. Generally, the hand-atlas was the scientifically based flagship of a more or less numerous and powerful fleet of minor general atlases, school atlases, and maps of different types. The authors of the hand-atlases had considerable influence on the features of the other cartographic publications in the same way they did for the hand-atlases.

Finally, we should not forget that, as in our time, an atlas, with its varied maps has been a medium for spatial communication. The range of that communication depends on the quality of the sender's information and the number of recipients. Therefore, the nineteenth century hand-atlases were documents of the first order. With regard to the socially important consequences in the field of instruction, especially of primary and secondary school teaching, the development of German hand-atlases in the nineteenth century was only the first but, nevertheless, a most important and decisive step in the evolution of atlas publishing.

NOTES

1   See International Cartographic Association, Commission II, ed. *Multilingual Dictionary of Technical Terms in Cartography* . . . (Wiesbaden: Franz Steiner Verlag, 1973).

2   *Neue Erdbeschreibung* (Hamburg, 1754–1792, 11 vols.). A biography of Büsching and a brief bibliographical accounting of this multivolume, multiedition work are found in Manfred Büttner and Reinhard Jäkel, "Anton Friedrich Büsching, 1724–1793," *Geographers: Biobibliographical Studies*, ed. T. W. Freeman (London: Mansell Publishing Ltd., 1982), vol. 6, pp. 7–15.

3   The earliest edition of this atlas in the Library of Congress is Adolf Stieler, *Hand-Atlas über alle Theile der Erde nach dem neuesten Zustande und über das Weltgebäude* (Gotha: Justus Perthes, 1834).

4   Max Eckert, *Die Kartenwissenschaft; Forschungen und Grundlagen zu einer Kartographie als Wissenschaft* (Berlin and Leipzig: Vereinigung wissenschaftlicher Verleger, W. de Gruyter, 1921–1925, 2 vols.).

5   A very useful bibliographic reference work has recently been published: Jürgen Espenhorst, *Andree, Stieler, Meyer & Co. Handatlanten des deutschen Sprachraums (1800–1945) nebst Vorläufern und Abkömmlingen im In- und Ausland. Bibliographisches Handbuch* (Schwerte: Pangaea Verlag, 1994).

6   *Allgemeine geographische Ephemeriden* (Weimar: Verlag des Landes-Industrie-Comptoirs, [etc.], 1798–1816, vols. 1–51). Superseded by *Neue allgemeine geographi-*

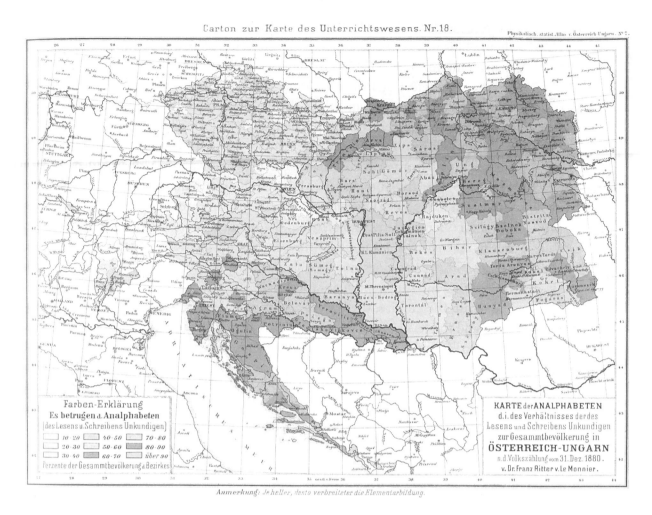

FIGURE 100   *Map depicting the regional variation of illiteracy within Austria-Hungary. J. Chavanne et al.,*
Physikalisch-statistischer Hand-Atlas von Oesterreich-Ungarn *(Vienna: Hölzel, 1887). Library of Congress.*

Freisauff's *Ektypographischer Schul-Atlas für Blinde* (Ectypographic school atlas for
the blind, Vienna, 1837), containing fifteen maps that were executed in elevated
print so that the blind could feel the outline, relief, and symbols with their fin-
gers; and Franz Raffelsperger's *Austria. Erster typometrischer Atlas* (Austria. First
typometric atlas, Vienna, 1841–1842) with fifteen maps in typographic reproduction.[5] The larger number of atlases in use at that time came, however, from other
parts of Germany, primarily from Gotha where atlases by Stieler and others were
published. (See essay by Scharfe in this volume.)

AUSTRIAN ATLASES BETWEEN 1860 AND 1918

Beginning in the late 1850s, commercial cartography in Austria had a resurgence.
Subsequently Austrian atlas production experienced, in connection with other
factors, a renaissance. Four types of atlases can be distinguished.

Large-Sized World Atlases ("Hand-Atlas")

The world atlas of a larger format, the so-called "Hand-Atlas," was seldom represented in the production of Austrian atlases because of the excellent works of this kind from Germany (Stieler, Andree, and others), which presented an overwhelming competition.

The only Austrian atlases of this kind produced were:

1. Joseph von Scheda's and Anton Steinhauser's *Hand-Atlas der neuesten Geographie* (Hand-atlas of the newest geography) from the Viennese publishing house Artaria and Company, containing twenty-four topographical maps (1868–1877), which were relatively late examples of copperplate engraved atlas sheets (see Figure 101), and fifteen plates of thematic maps (1870–1881), mainly of the physical world, in chromolithographic reproduction (see Figure 102).

2. The *Volks-Atlas* (People's atlas, 1888) with 100 pages of maps and an index, from the publishing house Adolf Hartleben (Vienna), whose

FIGURE 101 *Example of copper-engraved, topographic maps as published in J. Scheda and A. Steinhauser,* Hand-Atlas der neuesten Geographie *(Vienna: Artaria & Co., 1873–1879). Library of Congress.*

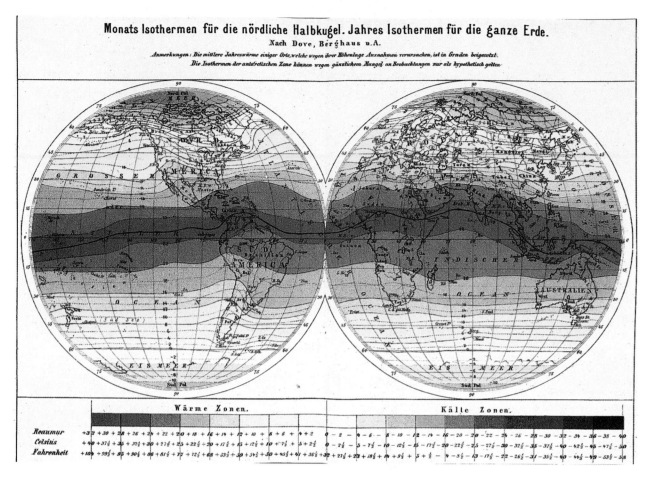

FIGURE 102 *Example of chromolithographic, thematic map, showing world temperature distribution. J. Scheda and A. Steinhauser,* Hand-Atlas der neuesten Geographie *(Vienna: Artaria & Co., 1873–1879). Library of Congress.*

quality could not compete with the leading German products mentioned earlier, but was widely used in the Habsburg Monarchy due to its comparatively low price.[6] Prior to World War I several editions of different sizes (between 40 and 126 pages of maps) and correspondingly different prices appeared,[7] as well as an edition with nearly 500 pages of text and 1,000 illustrations.[8]

3. The *Ottův zeměpisný atlas* (Otto's geographical atlas), which was published in the Czech language by the Prague publishing house J. Otto with thirty-eight plates of maps, begun in 1901 and ended shortly after World War I.

Thematic Atlases of Austria-Hungary

Three Austrian thematic atlases are remarkable because they provide a good picture of the physical geography and, additionally, information about the very different economic and social conditions within the state. First is the *Atlas der Urproduction Oesterreichs* (Atlas of the primary production of Austria, Vienna: R. v. Waldheim, 1878), edited by Joseph R. Lorenz von Liburnau. The thirty-one plates of maps plus four plates of diagrams and several pages of text treat mainly the natural basis of agriculture, agricultural production and forestry, as well as mining and metallurgy.[9] In contrast to the first atlas, which is limited to the primary economic activities in the Austrian half of the Habsburg Monarchy, is the *Physikalisch-statistischer Hand-Atlas von Oesterreich-Ungarn* (Physical-statistical hand-atlas of Austria-Hungary), which was edited in the Viennese publishing house Eduard Hölzel between 1882 and 1887 by Joseph Chavanne in cooperation with renowned Austrian scholars. (See Figure 100.) It encompasses the entire state and includes other topics as well in twenty-five plates of maps and extensive explanations, most particularly focusing on the population with its strong ethnic, religious, educational, and other differences.[10] This work is not only the first large sized and only comprehensive thematic atlas of the Austro-Hungarian Monarchy, but one of the earliest national thematic atlases as well. The third work, a special atlas, is Gustav Freytag's *Reise- und Verkehrs-Atlas von Österreich-Ungarn und den angrenzenden Ländertheilen einschliesslich der Balkan-Halbinsel* (Travel and traffic atlas of Austria-Hungary and the adjacent areas including the Balkan peninsula, Vienna: G. Freytag & Berndt, 1896) with forty smaller-sized plates of maps. In addition to the usual transportation maps with detailed presentations of the railway and post-route lines including stations and their intermediate distances, the atlas contains several remarkable isoline maps of Austria-Hungary and Central Europe (related to Vienna). As a whole, the maps form a cartographic railway guide from which distances, fares, lengths of journeys, the routes of express and luxury trains, as well as trains with dining cars and sleepers can be determined.[11]

School Atlases

School atlases compose by far the largest group, constituting about four-fifths of all Austrian atlases published during the late nineteenth and early twentieth centuries. As far as can be determined, about 200 atlases were published for use at schools during the fifty-five years from 1860 to 1914, including greatly enlarged editions, revised and redrawn editions, and editions or versions in languages other than German.

For a long time, geography had played a subordinate role in the Gymnasium (Austrian grammar schools) and Bürgerschulen (a four-year school comparable to junior high school), as a mere appendix to the teaching of history. At the primary schools, it was not taught at all until the beginning of the 1870s. Only through the reform of the grammar schools from 1849 to 1854 and then through the basic reorganization of the elementary schools or Volksschulen and the Bürgerschulen from 1869 to 1874 did geography become a separate subject. It was taught from third grade to eighth grade (from the age of eight to fourteen years). In 1851 the first chair of geography at an Austrian university was established in Vienna. In 1908–1909 geography became a subject in the upper grades of the Gymnasium or Mittelschule from the ninth grade on.

This strong increase in the importance of geography teaching in the Austrian schools, mainly in the very numerous general schools, elementary and Bürgerschulen, stimulated the production of school atlases, since the publishers could count on a much larger market. Although there were some Austrian atlases for schools in existence before 1875, such as B. Kozenn's *Geographischer Schul-Atlas* (Geographical school atlas) for grammar schools (1st ed., 1861) or A. Steinhauser's very remarkable *Atlas für die erste Stufe des geographischen Unterrichts in den österreichisch-deutschen Schulen* (Atlas for the first stage of geographical instruction at the Austrian-German schools, 1865–1869),[12] the prevailing number of atlases used in schools came from Germany. Because geography teaching in Germany had received greater attention at a much earlier time, not only the general atlases but also most school atlases were of an internationally leading standard. Accordingly, it was difficult for the Austrian publishers to enter into competition with the German products, and despite partial state subsidy, it took some time before the Austrian school atlases gained almost complete control of the home market.

It must be noted that the Austrian atlas publishers gradually improved the quality of their products. In the 1890s, in most cases, the standard of the best German atlases was reached. They took into account the variety of Austrian schools by publishing regional issues for elementary schools, where the treatment of the surrounding country of the capital city and the respective province or "Kronland" was a central aspect of geography teaching. In some cases there were up to eleven regional issues. Further, they published special atlases or atlas editions for the different types of schools—for elementary schools (differentiated into schools concentrating all levels in one to three classes and four to six classes), Bürgerschulen, grammar schools, military schools, teacher-training colleges, commercial schools, and so on. Finally, but especially important, they published issues or editions for schools with teaching languages other than German. Since almost two-thirds of the population of Austria (Austrian half of the Habsburg Monarchy) had a mother tongue different from German, atlas editions or issues in non-German languages gradually gained more importance and kept pace with the continual growth of the Austrian educational system. The first and, until 1918, by far the most numerous of these editions or issues appeared in the Czech language, with Czechs constituting almost a quarter of the Austrian population.[13] (See Figure 103.) There were, for example, fifteen Czech editions of Kozenn's atlas for grammar schools published prior to World War I (in comparison, the original issues of Kozenn's atlas in German reached forty-two editions in the same period).[14] In addition to the Czech editions there were also several in Polish, Croat, Italian (see Figure 104), and Slovene, and until the 1870s, also in Hun-

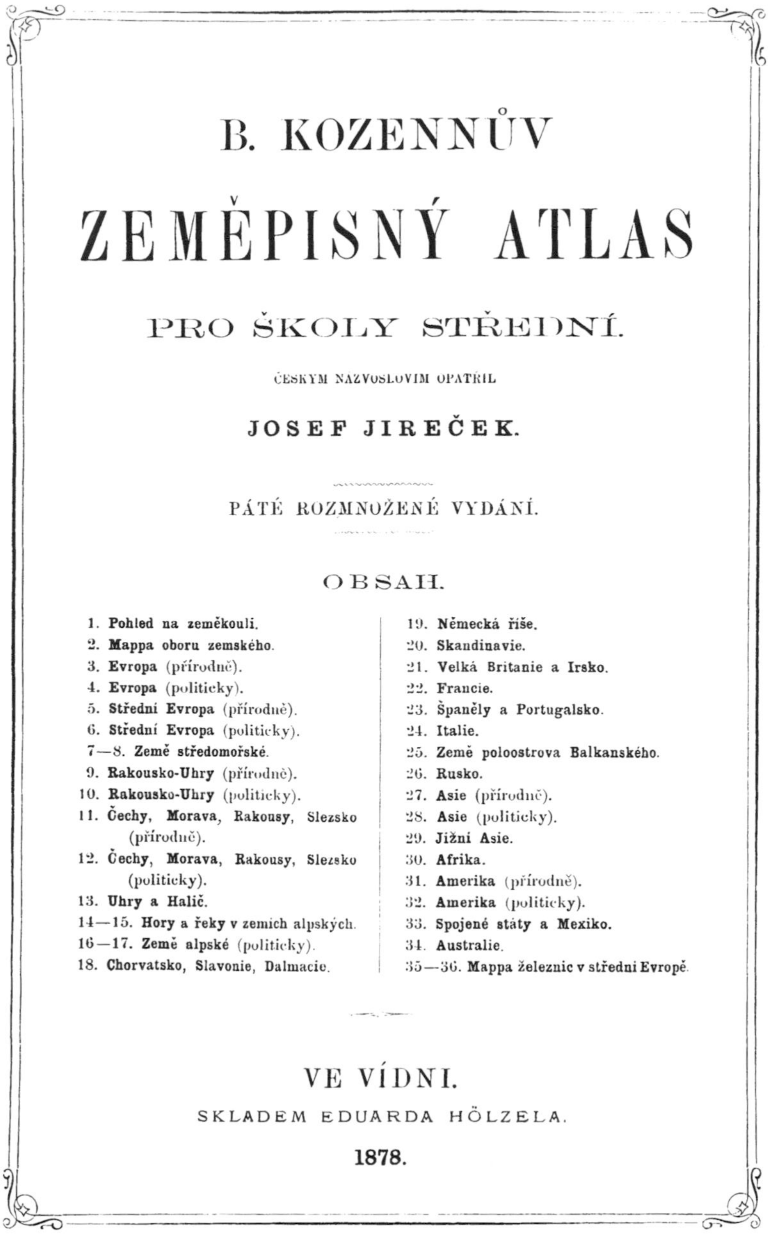

FIGURE 103 *Title page for Czech edition of B. Kozenn's school atlas. B. Kozennův Zeměpisný atlas . . . , 5th ed. (Vídeň [Vienna]: Hölzel, 1878). Library of Congress.*

B. KOZENNŮV

ZEMĚPISNÝ ATLAS

PRO ŠKOLY STŘEDNÍ.

ČESKYM NAZVOSLOVIM OPATRIL

JOSEF JIREČEK.

PÁTÉ ROZMNOŽENÉ VYDÁNÍ.

OBSAH.

1. Pohled na zeměkouli.
2. Mappa oboru zemského.
3. Evropa (přírodně).
4. Evropa (politicky).
5. Střední Evropa (přírodně).
6. Střední Evropa (politicky).
7—8. Země středomořské.
9. Rakousko-Uhry (přírodně).
10. Rakousko-Uhry (politicky).
11. Čechy, Morava, Rakousy, Slezsko (přírodně).
12. Čechy, Morava, Rakousy, Slezsko (politicky).
13. Uhry a Halič.
14—15. Hory a řeky v zemich alpských.
16—17. Země alpské (politicky).
18. Chorvatsko, Slavonie, Dalmacie.
19. Německá říše.
20. Skandinavie.
21. Velká Britanie a Irsko.
22. Francie.
23. Španěly a Portugalsko.
24. Italie.
25. Země poloostrova Balkanského.
26. Rusko.
27. Asie (přírodně).
28. Asie (politicky).
29. Jižni Asie.
30. Afrika.
31. Amerika (přírodně).
32. Amerika (politicky).
33. Spojené státy a Mexiko.
34. Australie.
35—36. Mappa železnic v středni Evropě.

VE VÍDNI.

SKLADEM EDUARDA HÖLZELA.

1878.

garian.[15] All of these editions were derivations of the original editions in the German language and were, from the cartographic point of view, either completely or in some cases almost identical to them. They differed principally only in the language of the maps (toponymy, titles, legends, etc.) and of the text (title page, table of contents, preface, explanatory notes). Some original school atlases in non-German languages also appeared, but mostly of a smaller volume for elementary schools. These were predominantly atlases in Czech and mainly from publishers in Prague.[16] Especially after 1900, there were also occasional editions in Polish (see Figure 105),[17] and in the Ukrainian (Ruthenian) language and characters.[18] In this context, an atlas which was published by the Armenian Mechi-

FIGURE 104 *Title page for Italian edition of B. Kozenn's school atlas*, Atlante geografico ad uso delle scuole medie . . . *(Vienna: Hölzel, 1905). Library of Congress.*

tarist Monastery in Vienna deserves mention. With twenty-one maps, it was probably the first printed, general school atlas in the Armenian language and characters.[19]

There were five principal establishments which published larger numbers of school atlases:

1. Eduard Hölzel (Vienna and Olmütz/Olomouc, later Vienna): atlases for grammar schools from 1861 onward (see Figure 99),[20] then for elementary schools and for Bürgerschulen,[21] for military schools and for teacher-training colleges,[22] and also historical school atlases.[23] Many of these atlases were published in non-German versions also, predominantly in Czech but also in Hungarian, Polish, Croat, Italian, and Slovene.

2. Artaria and Company (Vienna): atlases for grammar schools (from 1865 onward), elementary schools and Bürgerschulen,[24] as well as for commercial schools (from 1892 on).[25]

3. K.k. Hof- und Staatsdruckerei (Imperial state press, Vienna): atlases for elementary schools (from 1879 onward) and for Bürgerschulen,[26] as well as for grammar schools (from 1883 on);[27] a few of them also in Czech versions.

FIGURE 105 *Map of North America from Polish school atlas. E. Romer, Atlas geograficzny (Lwów: Nakl. Towarz. Naucz. Szkół Wyższ., 1908). Library of Congress.*

4. Friedrich Tempsky (Prague, then Vienna and Prague, later only Vienna): atlases for elementary schools and Bürgerschulen (from 1884 onward),[28] as well as for grammar schools (from 1897 on);[29] some of them in Czech and Italian versions.

5. Gustav Freytag and Berndt (Vienna): atlases for elementary schools and for Bürgerschulen (from 1893 onward),[30] later for grammar schools[31]; a few of them also in Czech, Polish, and in Italian versions. Some other publishing houses edited few or only one school atlas; for instance, Carl Gerold, Jacob Dirnböck, and Alfred Hölder in Vienna[32] or I. L. Kober, Antonín Felkl, V. Neubert, and A. Haase in Prague.[33]

While the quality of the first Austrian school atlases ranked, in some cases, quite considerably below the German atlases, by the 1890s, the Austrian school atlases had reached a very high level, paralleling the steep upward trend of Austrian commercial cartography. They compared favorably with the internationally leading German products both in content and didactics as well as in technical-aesthetical execution. Quite a few innovations, which had been developed in Austria, especially in relief representation, were incorporated.[34] The following works

Krakow, 91,000 inh., 8%; Plzeň/Pilsen, 68,000 inh., 14%; Czernowitz, 68,000 inh., 52%; Pressburg (Bratislava), 66,000 inh., 52%; Temesvár, 53,000 inh., 52%; Pécs/Fünfkirchen, 44,000 inh., 17%; Ljubljana/Laibach, 36,000 inh., 15%.

3 See Johannes Dörflinger, "The first Austrian world atlases: Schrämbl and Reilly," *Imago Mundi* 33 (1981): 65–71. Dörflinger, *Die österreichische Kartographie im 18. und zu Beginn des 19. Jahrhunderts unter besonderer Berücksichtigung der Privatkartographie zwischen 1780 und 1820.* vol. 1: *Österreichische Karten des 18. Jahrhunderts* (Vienna, 1984), pp. 159–270.

4 Among others: *Atlas des Österreichischen Kaiserthums. Atlas de l'Empire Autrichien* (Vienna, 1805) with forty large folio plates of maps, and *Allgemeiner Hand-Atlas der ganzen Erde* (Vienna, 1807) with twenty-five large folio plates of maps (later enlarged), respectively Joseph Dirwaldt's *Allgemeiner Hand-Atlas* (Vienna, 1816) with twenty-seven plates of maps (edition of 1820 with fifty-three plates). See Dörflinger, *Die österreichische Kartographie im 18. und zu Beginn des 19. Jahrhunderts.* vol. 2: *Österreichische Karten des frühen 19. Jahrhunderts* (Vienna, 1988).

5 Other atlases were, for example: Franz Fried's *Atlas der neuesten Geographie für Jedermann und jede Schulanstalt* (Vienna: Artaria & Co., 1825) with twenty-four plates of maps (later enlarged to thirty-six plates, editions up to the 1870s); J. G. Schmidtfeldt's small *Taschen Atlas über alle Theile der Erde* (Vienna: T. Mollo, 1831) with thirty-one plates of maps in pocket format; Václav Merklas's *Malý příruční atlas wšech částí země* (Prague, 1846) with twenty-seven plates of maps; Friedrich Simony's *Kleiner Schul-Atlas für den Elementar-Unterricht* (Vienna, 1854) with seven maps.

6 Second edition, 1892; 5th ed., 1911, 125 pages of maps.

7 *Universal-Handatlas*, 1891–1892, 126 pages of maps and index. *Kleiner Hand-Atlas über alle Theile der Erde*, 1892, 60 pages of maps; 2d ed., 1911. *Kleiner Volks-Atlas*, 1896, 40 pages of maps; 2d ed., 1911, 41 pages of maps. The maps for all these editions were made by the Viennese cartographic firm G. Freytag and Berndt.

8 *Die Erde in Karten und Bildern*, 1889, 63 pages of maps.

9 The atlas was also published in two separate parts: agriculture and forestry (25 plates), mining and metallurgy (10 plates).

10 Collaborators were Vinzenz von Haardt, Anton Kerner von Marilaun, Joseph R. Lorenz von Liburnau, Franz von Le Monnier, Carl Sonklar von Innstätten, and Franz Toula.

11 A small-sized thematic atlas of Austria-Hungary in the Czech language was published by Václav Křížek in 1873, *Atlas statistický rakousko-uherské říše* (Statistical atlas of the Austro-Hungarian empire) (Prague: I. L. Kober) with twenty-three plates of maps and thirteen plates of diagrams; the maps include themes such as climate (precipitation, temperature), geology, mineral baths, population density, ethnography, religions, mining, railways, schools, crimes, taxes, and so forth. By 1862–1864, a remarkable economic atlas of Bohemia, with twelve large-sized maps, was published by Anton Leo Hickmann, *Industrial-Atlas des Königreiches Böhmen* (Prague: H. Mercy).

12 See notes 20 and 24.

13 See Ludvík Mucha, "Český zeměpisný atlas světa v letech 1835–1960," *Sborník Pedagogického institutu v Praze. Přírodní vědy* 1 (1961): 375–430; Ludvík Mucha, "České historické atlasy," *Sborník Československé společnosti zeměpisné* 66 (1961): 239–251.

14 See Ludvík Mucha, "Česká vydání Kozennových školních zeměpisných atlasů," *Acta Universitatis Carolinae. Geographica* (1971): 119–134.

15 See notes 20, 21, 23, 26, 28–30.

16 For instance, atlases by Antonín Tille, Jan Lepař, Emanuel Hercík, Rudolf Knaus, Antonín Mikolášek, Emil Rác, and especially Josef Brunclík. See notes 13 and 33.

17 Eugeniusz Romer's *Atlas geograficzny* (Lwów, 1908) with ten pages of maps. The maps were lithographed and printed in the Military Geographical Institute, Vienna.

18 Myron Korduba's *Geografičnyj atljas* (Kolomyja, 1913) with twenty-four pages of maps.

19 Astwacatur Awagian's *Atlas gam ašarhaċuiċ dachdagk i bedas askaïn tabroċaċ* (Atlas or maps representing the world for use of the national schools) (Vienna, 1857; 2d ed., 1860).

20 Blasius Kozenn's *Geographischer Schul-Atlas für die Gymnasien, Real- und Handels-Schulen der österreichischen Monarchie* (1st ed., 1861, 31 maps), which became the most widely spread atlas for grammar schools in the Austrian half of the Habsburg Empire, reached forty-two editions prior to World War I. From the 1860s to the 1890s, small and large editions were published. After several revisions and enlargements, it was completely revised by Vinzenz von Haardt and Friedrich Umlauft from 1876 to 1882, *B. Kozenn's geographischer Schul-Atlas für Gymnasien, Real- und Handelsschulen,* 27th ed., 1882, fifty maps; 31st ed., 1887, fifty-nine maps; and in 1897 the widely revised 37th edition appeared in a larger format, *B. Kozenns geographischer Atlas für Mittelschulen* by V. v. Haardt and W. Schmidt (84 maps on 56 plates); 39th ed. (1901), by Haardt, Schmidt, and F. Heiderich; 40th ed. (1906) to 42d ed. (1910, 79 maps and 211 insets on 52 plates) by Heiderich and Schmidt. Czech versions appeared from 1875 onward (first by Josef Jireček, *B. Kozennův Zeměpisný atlas pro školy střední;* later by Jindřich Metelka, *B. Kozenna Zeměpisný atlas pro střední školy,* with fifteen editions up to World War I); Polish versions from 1879 on (by Bronislaw Gustawicz, *B. Kozenna Atlas geograficzny dla szkół średnich*); Croat versions from 1887 on (by A. Dobrilović and P. Matković, *Kozenov geografijski atlas za srednje škole;* later by H. Hranilović); Italian version (from 1904 on, by Michele Stenta, *B. Kozenn Atlante geografico ad uso delle scuole medie*).

21 Atlases for elementary schools, for example, by C. F. Baur (*Elementar-Schul-Atlas für Volksschulen,* 1874, 10 maps; versions in Czech and Croat) and by V. v. Haardt (*Geographischer Atlas für Volksschulen,* 1879, 12 maps; versions in Czech, Polish, and Italian, later also in Slovene). Atlases for Bürgerschulen, for example by V. v. Haardt (*Geographischer Atlas für Bürgerschulen,* 1885, 30 maps) and by A. E. Seibert (*Atlas für Bürgerschulen und mehrclassige Volksschulen,* 1902, 19 maps).

pean publishing companies and, as far as atlases were concerned, any ruling family, eminent person, or important library obtained copies of French, Dutch, and German works, whose wide distribution was witnessed by the presence of a considerable number of these works in Italian libraries and archives.[13] In addition, Italian authors sought foreign firms who had the interest and skill to publish their works; for example, the scientist Ferdinando Marsigli used publishers in Holland.[14] The famous *Theatrum Sabaudiae*, the most important collection of topographical images and views of Savoy and Piedmont, was published in Holland, although the drawings and relief representation were all made by native Italian engineers and topographers.[15]

Political and economic conditions in Italy during the first half of the eighteenth century were not favorable to the autonomous and competitive production of atlases, which was based on high technology, dexterity in the practice of engraving, and commercial daring.[16] Only in the second half of the eighteenth century, in particular in the 1770s, when a few chalcographical and publishing firms reached the apex of their expansion, and when the negative economic tendencies of the early part of the century were over, could the atlas be produced in Italy.

The forerunner of this new interest in atlas production was the publisher Giovambattista Albrizzi, who published an atlas in two volumes in 1740 and 1750 respectively.[17] (See Figure 114.) The geography text was basically copied from Nicolas Sanson and the maps from those of Isaak Tirion and Guillaume De L'isle. The name of the latter appears in the illustrated frontispiece. This publisher, however, only made a profit on the plates he engraved for the Italian edition of the geographical-historical work by the English publisher Thomas Salmon, which appeared in Venice in twenty-six volumes between 1731 and 1762.[18]

Because of the fame of the atlases of Didier and Gilles Robert de Vaugondy,[19] Francesco and Paolo Santini,[20] publisher and engraver respectively, published an *Atlas Universel* which copied a large number of the maps originally found in the Robert de Vaugondys' atlas of 1757.[21] The maps came from numerous authors: the Frenchmen Rigobert Bonne, Jean Janvier, and Jean Baptiste Bourguignon D'Anville; the German Johann Baptist Homann and his heirs; and several Italian cartographers whose works were used mainly for the new regional maps of Italy.

It is strange that the Santinis were not among the subscribers of the Robert de Vaugondys' atlas, and nothing has been found in the archives concerning letters of agreement between the Robert de Vaugondys and the Santinis.[22] Though the atlas was not a slavish reproduction of the French edition—new and different maps were added—the frontispiece was faithfully copied from the *Atlas Universal* of 1757. (See Figure 115.) Furthermore, the Santinis used the same size and languages as the original. Probably, the minor changes and the addition of a few different maps—it is worth noting that each map bore the name of the author—saved the Santinis from the accusation of plagiarism. Among the novelties included were the recent three-sheet maps of the State of the Church by

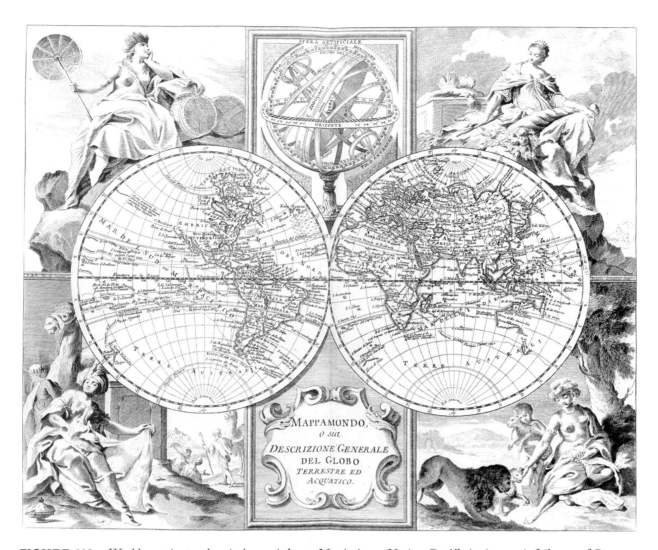

FIGURE 114 *World map in two hemispheres,* Atlante Novissimo *(Venice: G. Albrizzi, 1740). Library of Congress.*

Ruggero Boscovich, and many more Italian maps "dressées sur les lieux." All the maps were engraved and published between 1775 and 1780 and collected in two volumes by Domenico Baratti, who did not sign the copperplates.[23]

The Santinis did not have very good luck with the atlas; they were probably overwhelmed by expenses, especially the cost of the copperplates.[24] Since the atlas was sold on June 22, 1781 to Giuseppe Remondini,[25] first editions with the Santinis imprint are very scarce.[26]

Remondini, whose popular images were sold throughout Europe, was an audacious and bold publisher in Bassano and Venice. The extraordinary growth of the Bassanese firm has been thoroughly studied in the last few years.[27] In the second half of the eighteenth century, under the direction of Giuseppe the second, the Remondinis became one of the first industries in Europe to produce printed paper. From colored wallpaper,[28] which is supposed to be their invention, to holy and popular images, to the finest printing, their works covered the full range of

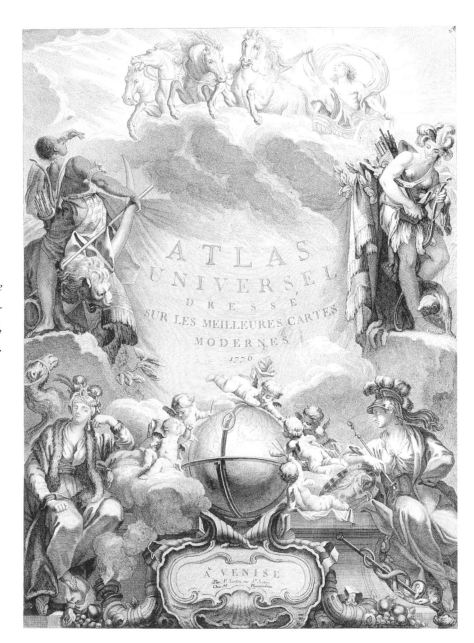

FIGURE 115 *Frontispiece from Paolo Santini,* Atlas Universel *(Venice: Remondini, 1776). Library of Congress.*

printing. The Remondinis, in a strikingly modern business sense, enlarged their activity by acquiring paper mills, spinning mills, landed estates, and a foundry for producing printing types and borders. They also opened a workshop for training young engravers.[29] With such policies, the firm became independent of the mood of the market and controlled production from the raw materials to the finished product. According to Giuseppe Remondini, the atlas was a good business, and as it has been noted, "it was an authentic sales success."[30] The atlas was reprinted in 1784, adding eight plates to the first volume and four to the second. "Chez Remondini" was engraved on the frontispiece of each map.[31]

The Remondini acquisition of Santini's copperplates occurred in the same year that Antonio Zatta was printing his impressive four-volume atlas and only a few months after the announcement of the atlas by Giovanni Antonio Rizzi-Zannoni. Giuseppe Remondini, with this timely acquisition, took advantage of the increasing interest in atlases, which was inspired by the contemporary atlases of Zatta, a scholarly publisher, and by Rizzi-Zannoni, who was a world-renowned scientist.

The first volume of Zatta's atlas appeared in 1778.[32] That the conflict between these two publishers must have been very fierce, becomes apparent in reading the introduction to Zatta's atlas, called "Saggi preliminari di geografia," which was reprinted in the second volume in 1782 with minor changes. It was a fight among giants in the publishing world where the prize was an audience consisting of academies, universities, schools, scholars, collectors, and merchants. It was a fight for economic domination.

Zatta's atlas was intended to be appended to Anton Fredrich Büsching's *Geography*,[33] for which he received a fifteen-year copyright from the Venetian Senate in 1773. In the "Saggi preliminari di geografia," which introduced the atlas, the unknown compiler (or compilers) pointed out that "in our beautiful and cultured part of Europe, it was a long time before we felt the need of an atlas,"[34] and he proceeded to criticize all the other contemporary works. Furthermore, the compiler, making no reference to the Santinis, commented that some recent undertaking "put down the Nation, by placing a foreign language before our mother tongue."[35] The Santinis' atlas was written in French!

In order to discredit the Santinis' name, Zatta crudely attacked the Robert de Vaugondys' work, making reference to a faulty entry on recent discoveries in North America (appearing in 1774). The compiler of the "Saggi" wrote, "we are far from giving him any credit, on the contrary we will not allow it;"[36] and a few lines later he wrote "we do not approve what has been done by that French geographer in the mentioned map."[37] In a footnote to the "Tavola delle longitudini e latitudini," taken from the data of the *Academie des Sciences* of Paris (1775), the author (which is likely Zatta) very haughtily tells his readers, should they find differences between his maps and others, the first could serve "di *emendazione* [italics are not mine] alle carte delli medesimi ed altri autori (to *emend* the maps by other authors)."

Among the novelties of Zatta's atlas was the first appearance in Italy of the new islands discovered in the Pacific and the first Italian printed map of New Zealand (1778): "we have only copied it, but we are the first to communicate such an interesting map to Italy, and that's our boasting."[38] (See Figure 116.)

Before dismissing Zatta's four-volume atlas, which remains one of the most important ever produced in Italy, it should be noted that he took great care in executing the atlas, not only in engraving the maps but in the composition of the text. In fact, in 1773, the Senate gave the copyright and permission to Zatta "under the condition that the text be well printed, on good paper, perfect margin, and accurate corrections, and the above mentioned maps [i.e., the atlas] be finely engraved." In the text of the "Saggi preliminari," Zatta made extensive use of his

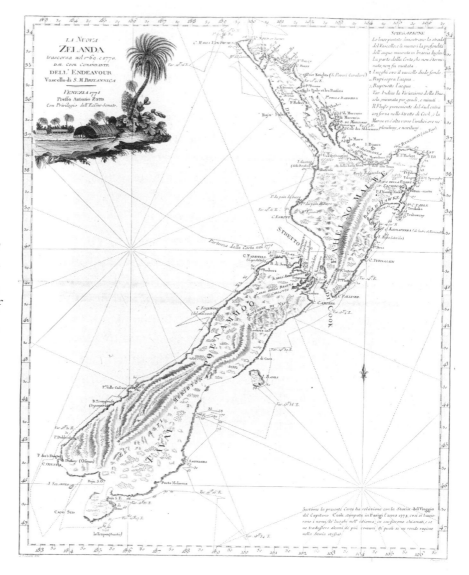

FIGURE 116 *Map of New Zealand from* Atlante Novissimo *(Venice: A. Zatta, 1779–1785). Library of Congress.*

famous printing types and borders for framing the text and decorating the titles.[39] (See Figure 117.)

He again used his borders as a decoration in his minor school atlas.[40] In that period, the number of simplified and smaller atlases produced for teaching geography must have been very high even though this is difficult to prove, because only a very few examples have survived. We may infer the size of the market from the number of editions of the small atlas by Zatta to which Remondini gave a prompt response and to the *Nuovo atlante portatile*, also printed in Venice by Giacomo Storti.[41] In the foreword, we learn that there were other atlases for teaching geography to young boys,[42] since the author (again unknown, as in Zatta's "Saggi preliminari") tried to explain why his method and his maps were better than the others. There was indeed a ruthless competition! It appears that all these small atlases followed French-language examples.[43]

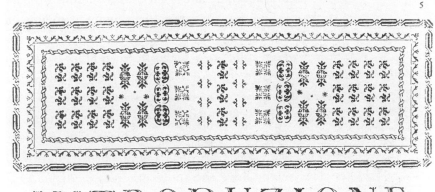

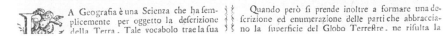

Example of typography used for borders in Atlante Novissimo (Venice: A. Zatta, 1779–1785). Library of Congress.

FIGURE 117

The *Encyclopédie* and the Birth of the Geographical Discipline

The "Age of Reason" interest in geography and the reform of the educational system which passed from private and clerical hands to those of the state,[44] were two factors which influenced the renewed interest in atlas making in the second half of the eighteenth century. In this respect, the Republic of Venice made the foremost contribution with the publication of the enlarged and improved edition of the *Encyclopédie*.[45] This great undertaking began as early as 1783 and has been defined as "the most magnificent work" printed by the Tipografia del Seminario in Padova.[46]

The Italian edition of the *Encyclopédie*, though printed in French, was quite different from the French edition. It was especially improved from the Italian point of view. Italian editors were aware that "Frenchmen generally do not pay any attention to anything that is not French."[47] They also made reference to very recent events such as the terrible earthquake in Calabria in 1783 and the "rouineuse guerre" between Great Britain and its American colonies.

Completely rejected is Zatta's opinion on Didier Robert de Vaugondy, who is cited as a collaborator of the *Encyclopédie*, a work which "a la mérite d'être très exacte."[48] Zatta, in order to destroy the scientific validity of the atlas published by the Santinis, had dared to write that Didier Robert de Vaugondy was not a reliable scholar.

The Padova edition assisted the birth of geography as a scientific and autonomous discipline. The editors expanded on the narrow opinion of d'Alembert who "relegue d'émblée la Géographie à l'ombre del'Histoire."[49] Masson de Morvilliers, in the introduction to geography in the Padova edition, is said to have been astonished "de l'espace d'indifférence qu'on a eu jusq'ici pour cette science dans nos maisons d'instruction."[50]

Finding longitude accurately, which was the great problem of oceanic navigation; the use of astronomy in solving problems of position and area of lands; and
the birth of geodesy were among the factors which contributed to the elevation
of geography to a scientific role. This role was not expanded in subsequent
years. In 1789 and 1790, the *Atlas de Géographie Moderne* was published, two
years after the French edition by Rigobert Bonne and Nicolas Desmarest.[51] The
atlas presented, in 140 maps, a current image of the world. An appendix, with
nineteen maps, was entirely devoted to the new discoveries in the Pacific; the
strait between Tasmania and Australia (now Bass Strait) was about to be
unveiled, since the shore line was depicted as an interrupted line for the first

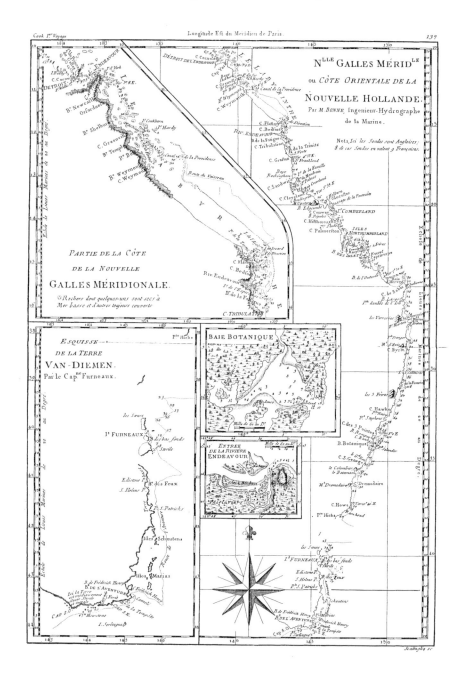

FIGURE 118 *Maps of Australian coastline from* Atlas Encyclopédique *(Padua, 1789–1790). Author's Collection.*

time. (See Figure 118.) Though not comparable with Zatta's fresh engravings, the atlas of the *Encyclopédie* was the most up-to-date atlas produced in Italy to that time.

Rizzi-Zannoni's Project and the End of Venetian Primacy

Rizzi-Zannoni's project to publish a political, nautical, and military atlas deserves special mention, although the project did not lead to any engraved maps and was abandoned a few months after the issue of its "Manifesto."[52] The atlas, as revealed in the "Manifesto," represents the most ambitious project ever planned in Italy and the forerunner, in some respects, of the Philippe Vandermaelen and Adolf Stieler atlases. (See Figure 119.) It should be noted that as late as 1927, the Touring Club Italiano published an atlas which was worthy of comparison with the projected atlas by Rizzi-Zannoni.

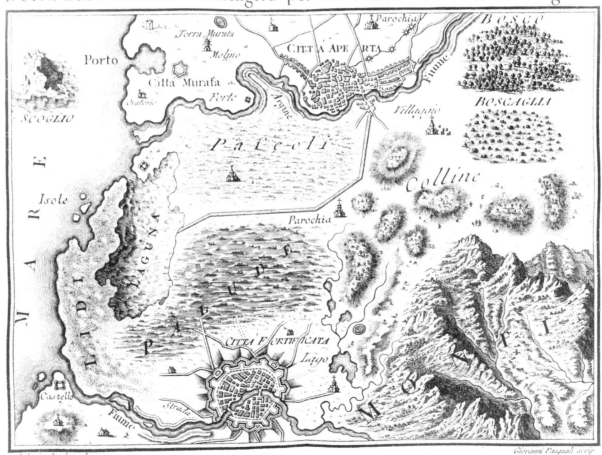

FIGURE 119 *Sample plate from the "Manifesto" for G. A. Rizzi-Zannoni's projected* Atlante Geografico *(1781). Biblioteca Marciana, Venice.*

The "Manifesto" was published in order to describe the atlas and gather subscriptions, because of the cost of engraving the copperplates. The atlas was planned for more than 200 plates in the imperial sheet size (60 × 80 cm). The name of the publisher is not known, but the subscriptions were received by some book dealers and printers, who were acknowledged at the end of the prospectus.[53] They probably established an association in order to share the risk and the cost of the undertaking.[54]

It was the intention of the author to make an atlas as complete as possible by gathering into one work celestial, terrestrial, nautical, and historical maps—a sort of geographical encyclopedia. The work was really planned for the Livorno edition of the *Encyclopédie* "project which was abandoned for several reasons, that are useless to record here."[55] The author also announced the insertion of mineralogical maps and made reference to those by J. E. Guetard which "may well throw light on the natural history of the earth."[56] For the use of navigation, he also planned to publish a map of magnetic declination following a map by James Dodson.[57] A few sheets of geographical description were also supplied at the end of the section of maps devoted to a specific region.[58]

The author of the "Manifesto" spoke of the "great number of islands scattered in the vastness of the Pacific Ocean,"[59] and analyzed the contemporary production of maps and atlases. Nevertheless, he complained that such useful aids had not stirred geographers to renew their production or to produce an atlas which was better than the others.

The atlas was addressed, in the words of the author, to "sovereigns and their ministers in any field of public administration and to soldiers, merchants, travellers, and philosophers."[60] The first sheets of the atlas, related to the State of the Church and Tuscany, were planned to be issued in the month after the "Manifesto" was circulated (i.e., April 1781). It is likely that Rizzi-Zannoni's move to Naples forced the publishing company to give up the atlas. Further references will be made to Rizzi-Zannoni and the effect his move to Naples had on the renewal of geographical culture in southern Italy.

The end of the Republic of Venice in 1797 marked the decline of printing activity in that city. Cultural influence also moved from France to Austria at that time and in general, to the German-speaking world. Venice was ceded to Austria in 1806. In the first two decades of the nineteenth century, we find only one other edition of the *Atlas Universel* by Remondini (1804) and a badly engraved small atlas by Giovanni Valerio Pasquali (1810) who probably profited from his experience in working on the Rizzi-Zannoni atlas.[61]

In 1829, an interesting atlas finally appeared in Venice, the *Atlante Universale del Globo* edited by Giuseppe Dembsher. (See Figure 120.) Unfortunately, no information was found regarding Dembsher. The atlas was similar to those by Adolf Stieler and Christian G. Reichard, who were authors of the first edition of the famous *Stieler's Hand Atlas.*[62] It was issued by the Tipografia di Alvisopoli which took its name from the utopian city founded in 1800 by Alvise Mocenico,

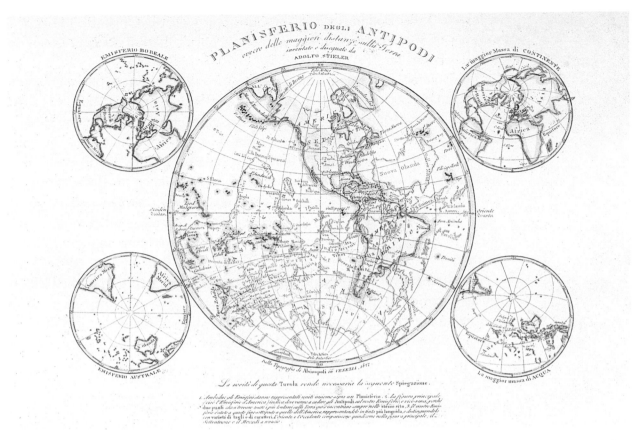

FIGURE 120 *Planispheres of the antipodes from the 1816 original by A. Stieler, as published in Guiseppe Dembsher,* Atlante Universale del Globo *(Venice: Tipografia di alvisopoli, 1829). Author's Collection.*

a Venetian noble. He intended to give substance to the illuministic dream of a free city where industrial and agricultural firms joined with intellectual activities. The printing press in Alvisopoli was one of the most active in Venice in the first half of the century. In an outstanding monograph devoted to the publications of Alvisopoli the atlas was not mentioned.[63]

The calligraphical title of the atlas was lithographed by Deye, while the plates were printed from copperplate engravings which were beautifully hand colored in the original Stieler fashion. Maria Rocchetti, a woman engraver, signed two of the maps.[64] In Venice, it was not uncommon to find women active as engravers from the second half of the eighteenth century.

HISTORICAL ATLASES—GEOGRAPHICAL ATLASES

The relation between history and geography which was so clearly expressed in the views of the encyclopedists, and the renewed education system, lead to a new historical atlas. The last classic atlas published in Italy, which followed the antiquarian fashion, was published in Rome in 1774.[65] It was in Latin and was taken

269

from the 1764 London edition of Christoph Cellarius's historical atlas. The authors of the Roman edition were the scholars Giovan Battista Ghigi and Francesco Tirolio.[66]

The volume opened with two beautiful frontispieces, one of which was an etching in the peculiar style of Giovambattista Piranesi, then still alive and active. (See Figure 121.) His "Antichità Romane" certainly influenced the designer Giuseppe Barberi,[67] who produced a miscellaneous work from them. The Italian edition includes some additions to the London one; among the thirty-five maps was a map of the Americas accompanied by an "Additamentum de novo orbe" by Corrado Schwartz. Francesco Jacquier, a professor of mathematics, wrote ten pages on "De origine et progressu Geographiae." The atlas ended with a note by Ruggero Boscovich, describing an ancient anemometer found in the Via Capena in 1753.

After the revival of ancient Rome as expressed in this edition of the Cellarius work, historical atlases developed in two different ways. On the one hand, the most common one, geographical atlases included a percentage of historical maps varying from fifteen to twenty percent of the whole work. These were generally

FIGURE 121 *Frontispiece from* Christophori Cellarii Geographia Antiqua *(Rome, 1774).*
Author's Collection.

modern maps supplemented by historical data. They were included in virtually all the general atlases up to the first half of the nineteenth century.

On the other hand, an original product was produced mainly for school purposes and provided maps, tables, historical text, and diagrams. The prototype was found in the historical atlas by Emmanuel Dieudonné, Earl of Las Cases (called "Le Sage"), published in Paris in 1803.[68] The first Italian edition was in French and appeared in Florence in 1807,[69] followed in 1813 by the Italian translation enlarged with a few maps and printed again in Florence.[70]

In 1826, two Italian-language editions followed. One was published in Naples by the "Stamperia Reale" (Royal Printing Office), the other in Venice by the publisher Tasso. The Neapolitan one bore a lithographed frontispiece by Lorenzo Bianchi and Domenico Cuciniello[71] and followed the structure of the original French edition where maps were interspersed with diagrams and text, while the Venetian one separated the maps from the printed text. In the latter, the maps reached the largest number ever to appear in this kind of atlas, more than twenty-four. In 1840, the Venetian edition was completed by adding a longer text without maps.[72]

An interesting later product, following the Le Sage tradition, was printed in Capolago (Italian Switzerland) by the Frenchman J. de Mancy.[73] It is an historical atlas which relates to the 1830 and 1831 Polish revolution. The place of the edition was possibly invented due to the political content of the atlas.[74] It was a token of friendship from France to the Polish people of which, as the author reminds us, 200,000 died "for France in Europe, in Africa, and in America." Among the chapters can be found a "patriotic feeling of Polish women."

Another type of historical atlas, which could hardly be called an atlas, although it bears the name, was the *Nuovo atlante storico* by Leonardo Cacciatore,[75] published in Naples in the years 1825 and 1827. The author accompanied the text with figures, maps, and reproductions of coins. In other words, he only used images as an aid to the reader.

THE BEGINNING OF ATLAS PRODUCTION IN MILAN

Only nineteenth-century atlases are recorded for Milan. This is a result of the city's increasing importance when, with the aid of the French army, it first became the capital of the "Repubblica Cisalpina," later (1805) the Kingdom of Italy. In Milan, as had happened in Naples, the establishment of a topographical office created interest in geography and related map production. The topographical office also became an efficient school for map engravers.

A few years after the settlement in Milan of the Bureau Topographique (1796), which was a branch of the Depôt de la Guerre, Paris, there appeared an interesting universal atlas published by Carlo Antonio Barbiellini.[76] The atlas, including forty-nine maps of different sizes, accompanied the thirteenth volume of the *Nuova geografia universale*, published a few years earlier. The work was dedicated

Rossi was an author born in Parma but no mention is made in the biography of his geographical efforts.[85]

Other atlases, apart from the topographical activity of the Istituto Geografico Militare, were published by Camillo Vacani, Carlo Rossari, and Stanislao Stucchi. The first appended sixteen maps, which were published in atlas form, to his historical work on the war in Spain.[86] In his maps we find, for the first time in Italy, an extensive use of contour lines in depicting the mountainous areas. Rossari issued a small atlas in 1824,[87] and the engraver-publisher Stucchi printed an atlas, with twenty-six folio maps, in 1826, the largest ever engraved in Milan.[88]

THE ATLAS MARKET IN GENOA

Genoa did not provide original contributions to the growing production of atlases in Italy, but it did supply Italian and foreign markets with charts and nautical atlases. The market for the charts was definitely favorable since Genoa, whose maritime activity had its roots in the Middle Ages, was one of the most active seaports in the Mediterranean.

Only a few atlases were published in Genoa, most of them being slavish reproductions of French atlases. One was the famous *Recueil* of the Mediterranean ports by Joseph Roux, which was printed in Genoa in 1779, fifteen years after the Marsiglia edition.[89] The second was a maritime atlas with charts of the Mediterranean by Jacques Nicolas Bellin.[90] Both atlases were published by Yves Gravier, who had the plans reengraved and added his imprint on the frontispiece.

Apart from this limited activity as atlas publisher, Yves Gravier had a substantial business in atlas and chart sales. From Gravier's catalog dated 1818,[91] we learn that in his establishment, sailors and merchants could find charts of any corner of the world. Genoa was an international market, and through Gravier's bookshop, it contributed to the dissemination of French nautical atlases and charts all over the world.

Thus far, no naif atlas published in Genoa in the period has been found; however, some regional atlases should be expected as a consequence of the many surveys made by the republic during the eighteenth century.[92] No atlas published in Turin in the late eighteenth and early nineteenth centuries has been found, although atlases were produced at that time. For instance, the Abbot Salvatore Lirelli proposed at the end of 1780s an atlas of Europe, of which two maps, numbered twenty-nine and thirty, were found in 1789.[93] There is currently no evidence that the atlas was completed, although further study in the Turinese archives and libraries may provide an answer.

ATLASES IN TUSCANY

In Tuscany, atlas production, although limited in the past, began to attract attention in the last quarter of the eighteenth century. Not only Florence, the capital, but Siena and Livorno were part of this new geographical interest.

In Siena, the general atlas published by Vincenzo Pazzini Carli was engraved by many artists active in the period between 1788 and 1800.[94] The atlas has more than 100 quarto maps, clearly and neatly engraved with nice, discreet decorations around the titles.

The same publishers had already printed in 1788, as a possible basis for the atlas, a letter of criticism by Bartolomeo Borghi of a map by Zatta.[95] In the booklet, Borghi, an esteemed geographer who was the editor of the atlas, addressed severe words to Zatta, who is described as "a respectable printer and chalcographer, but not a geographer at all."[96] This was another sign of the great rivalry among publishers and geographers at that time. Borghi tried to denigrate the scientific contents of Zatta's map of European Turkey by discussing faulty longitudes and boundaries, but certainly, no more vehemently than Zatta did against the atlases of Santini and Remondini. Borghi published the letter for people who "unfortunately spent the exceeding sum of seven Lire for acquiring a useless sheet."

Borghi was also the author, in the second decade of the nineteenth century, of the most important Florentine atlas, consisting of 137 maps and thirty-five pages of introduction.[97] (See Figure 123.) The atlas was highly successful and

FIGURE 123   *Portrait of Bartolomeo Borghi*
in his Atlante Generale *(Florence, 1819).*
Library of Congress.

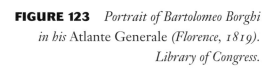

was published in the several editions, the fourth appearing in 1835.[98] The Borghi atlas remained an unsurpassed model for many other lesser and larger works.

Another eighteenth-century Florentine atlas should be cited because, among other things, it reflected the contemporary taste for refined pocket objects of noble ladies and gentlemen. It was a small pocket atlas (7 × 10 cm) by Giovanni de Baillou and Agostino da Rabatta.[99] (See Figure 124.) This atlas, due to its size, might be of little interest if the authors had not paid attention to the "very recent exploration of Captain James Cook in the South Sea, and in the Australis Pole, as well as the explorations by Russians and other explorers in the North and North-west part of the America." It is interesting to consider that Cook's voyages in the search of the Australian continent occurred in the years 1776 through 1778. At that time, of course, there was no telegraph for broadcasting news! In the same year in which Zatta published his map of New Zealand, another map of the islands appeared in Italy. The pocket atlas by Baillou and Rabatta reminds us on

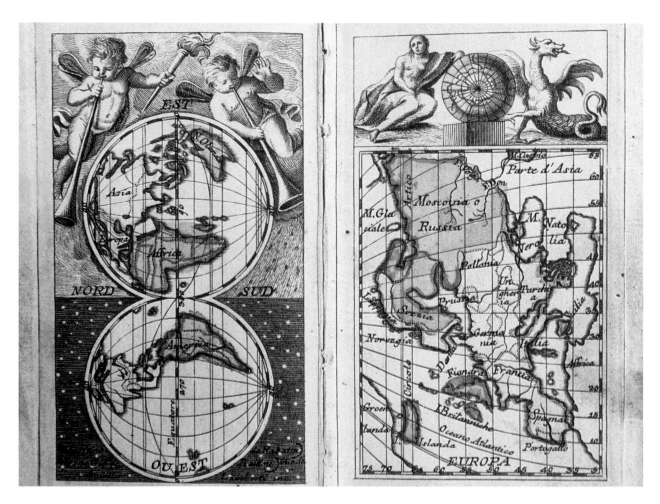

FIGURE 124 *Two plates from pocket atlas,* Nuovo Atlante Generale *(Florence: Giovanni de Baillou & Agostino da Rabatta, 1779). Pietro Crini Collection, Florence.*

one hand of the *Atlas Géographique* by Rizzi-Zannoni published in Paris in 1762,[100] which was a fine example of the lady's pocket-size atlas, and on the other of geographical playing cards, close to the atlas in size and with a mixture of images and text.

Livorno had an unusual history of typographical activity during the eighteenth century, since it was the seaport of the Granducato, with extensive and continuous contact with many European countries. Trade in Livorno was in foreign hands; the English, Spanish, and Dutch had formed a very active corporation in the city. The abbot Coyer wrote in 1776, "La franchise de son port y attire une foule de navigateurs qui font sa fortune et la leur."[101] In 1777, the same year that the French edition of the *Encyclopédie* appeared in Livorno,[102] the publisher Masi produced an *Atlante dell'America*,[103] responding to the worldwide interest in the Revolutionary War in the English colony.[104] (See Figure 125.) The maps were taken from the *Gazettiere Americano*[105] published by Marco Coltellini in 1763 and were not, for the time, particularly accurate. Nevertheless, the idea of preparing

FIGURE 125 *Port of Boston in* Atlante dell'America *(Leghorn: Masi, 1777). Library of Congress.*

277

and was made with concern for its scientific validity. It remained the only one published in Rome before the unification of Italy.[115]

Unusual among the interesting contents are the gores for making celestial and terrestrial globes, which are included at the beginning of the atlas. They are the only printed gores that appeared in Italian atlases during this period.[116] A description of the method for drawing gores and constructing globes appeared in the first chapter, "Introduzione generale allo studio della geografia," published together with the first volume. Since it was used in the contemporary production of atlases, the unknown compiler of the introduction widely discussed the sources, which were adopted in compiling the maps.[117]

THE KINGDOM OF NAPLES

Atlases from Geometrical Surveys: Maritime and Regional Atlases

In southern Italy, then the Kingdom of Naples, as in northern Italy, people experienced the same atmosphere of renewal. This reached its climax, as far as education and schools were concerned, with the expulsion of the Jesuits in 1767,[118] which led to a reorganization of the university and the high school in 1777.[119]

A turning point in the geographical culture of southern Italy was the foundation of the Officina Topografica in 1781.[120] The development of the Officina will not be discussed because of the author's recent studies on this subject, which led to an exhibition covering the entire production of the topographical institutions in Naples.[121] We may only mention its most spectacular publications, many of which are included in the atlas collection of the Library of Congress: the *Atlante marittimo* (see Figure 127) and the *Atlante geografico*, both related to the Kingdom of Naples.[122] They were models for all subsequent foreign and Italian maps and atlases on the Kingdom of Naples, such as the pocket atlas dedicated to the queen in 1813 by Celestino Ricci, which followed the eighteenth-century tradition of ladies' atlases, and Gennaro Bartoli's atlas of the provinces of the Kingdom, which appeared after the establishment of new internal boundaries in 1816.[123]

In the same years in which Rizzi-Zannoni was working in the geodetical survey of the Kingdom, among the first endeavors of its kind in Italy, an older atlas of the provinces appeared, reusing the seventeenth-century geographical knowledge of southern Italy. In the *Accuratissima delineazione* published by Terres, the copperplates engraved in 1692 were reissued after adding only the main roads.[124] It was the last attempt to publish poor cartographical material in Naples!

Also worthy of mention is a maritime atlas of the Mediterranean by the Filetis (father and son), who were seamen and authors of books on the art of navigation, all printed in Sicily around the first decade of the nineteenth century. Both served as directors of the Nautical Institute in Palermo.[125] No complete copy of the

FIGURE 127 *Title page of first part*, Atlante Marittimo *(Naples: G. A. Rizzi-Zannoni, 1792). Library of Congress.*

atlas, which was composed of eleven sheets, is known to exist. A loose sheet is reproduced here for the first time. (See Figure 128.) Fileti (we do not know which one) made use of the best authorities for drawing his maps. At the beginning of the nineteenth century, his central map of the Mediterranean was definitely superior to other contemporary French and English charts. The atlas was only recorded in an old catalog of the Officio Topografico library in Palermo.[126]

General Atlases

General atlases of the eighteenth century were very scarce in Naples. Editions of Paolo Petrini's atlas were published initially in 1700 and reprinted up to the end of the century, with only the dates in the title of each map changed. The only new atlas was the one appended to a geographical dictionary printed by Terres, whose maps, after Sanson and Gilles Robert de Vaugondy, were not always bound sepa-

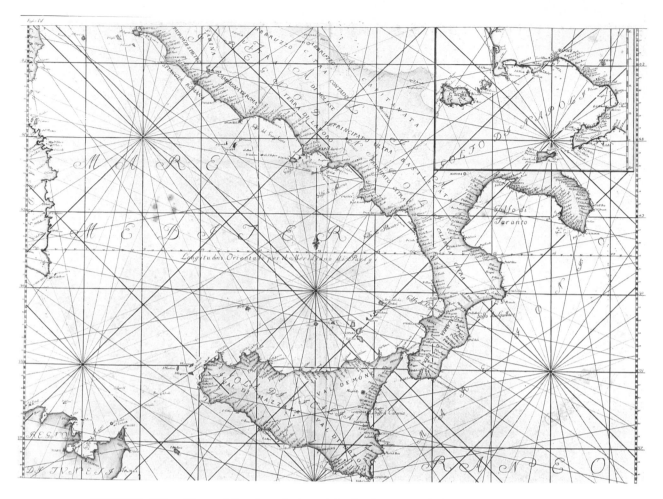

FIGURE 128   *Chart of Southern Italy and Sicily*, Carte Piana del Mare Mediterraneo
(*Palermo: Giovanni Fileti, 1802*). *Author's Collection.*

rately in order to make up an atlas, but were quite often inserted in the volumes of text.[127]

An attempt to publish a general atlas was made in 1813 when the Gabinetto Letterario translated the 1812 edition of Pierre Lapie's atlas.[128] This French edition, which was published for the military school and lyceum, was adopted immediately in Naples because of French rule in the Kingdom. Although not too pretentious, it was a good work, finely engraved by local artists who were active in the topographical service and involved daily in map engraving.[129] The Lapie atlas provided Naples with a very up-to-date work which was published in several editions up to 1847.[130] The first edition of the atlas may be related to the foundation of the Scuola Politecnica which followed the French model of education.[131]

In the 1840s, Naples produced a general atlas by Benedetto Marzolla, who was highly praised for the quality of his lithography and for his care in choosing the best references. Marzolla brought cartographical lithography in Naples to its highest expression.[132]

Atlases and Lithography: A Neapolitan Record

A turning point which also marks the end of this study is the introduction into Naples, and then into Italy, of the lithographic process applied to maps. The first experiments so far recorded were made in Naples in the Officio Topografico as early as 1818 under the direction of Ferdinando Visconti.[133] As revealed in unpublished archival records, the Stamperia Militare was established in 1817,[134] and at the beginning of the 1820s, the military printing office obtained a lithographic press. In the same year, a contemporary observer wrote that "the military printing office is among the most beautiful in the capital."[135]

The head of the Litografia Militare, officially founded in 1823, was Luigi Bardet di Villanova, an army officer and author of the first Italian treatise on lithography, the only one strictly concerned with cartographical applications.[136] The first lithographed Neapolitan atlas was titled *Portolano delle coste della penisola di Spagna*, and included maps dated from 1823 to 1826.[137] (See Figure 129.) The

FIGURE 129 *Title page from first lithographed Neapolitan atlas,* Portolano delle coste della Penisola di Spagna *(Naples: Reale Litografia Militare, 1825). Author's Collection.*

name Litografia Militare already appeared on the maps. In a short time, lithography had gained a firm position in the Tipografia della Guerra, due to the effort of the active director.

The Litografia Militare also published, in 1824, single maps in two sheets of some ports in the Mediterranean—Gibraltar, Cartagena, and Toulon. In 1829 and 1830, there appeared a few maps after Adrien Hubert Brué, which may have belonged to an atlas which was never completed.

In general, lithography in the 1820s gained a strong foothold in Naples and several lithographers started working in topography as well as in geography.[138] After the *Portolano*, an important contribution to atlas making was made by Benedetto Marzolla, a soldier-geographer and lithographer, who published the national atlas of the Kingdom of Naples between 1828 and 1831, the most scientific and the finest lithographed atlas ever produced in Italy.[139]

AUTHORS AND ENGRAVERS

Considering the lack of bibliographical and biographical information that was apparent at the beginning of this study, it is surprising to observe how extensive Italian atlas production was during the last quarter of the eighteenth century and the first decades of the nineteenth century, prior to the introduction of lithography in Italian printing. During this critical period, when there was a growing interest in geography and the dissemination of geographic information resulting from new discoveries in the Pacific Basin and the changing political situation in Europe and the Americas, some forty atlases, including more than 1,800 maps, were published in Italy. While this atlas production was greatest in Venice, there were also numerous titles published in five other Italian cities—Milan, Genoa, Florence, Rome, and Naples. In total, over seventy authors and engravers were involved in this atlas production. Based on the information discovered in this study, it has been possible to compile a bibliography of the atlases and short biographies of the people involved, which have been issued in another publication.[140]

NOTES

1 See the introduction by F. Barberi in the exhibition catalog, *Arte della stampa 1734–1799* (Naples, 1980), p. 9.

2 G. Morazzoni, *Il libro illustrato veneziano del Settecento* (Milan, 1943).

3 N. Vianello, *La tipografia di Alvisopoli e gli annali delle sue pubblicazioni* (Florence, 1957).

4 M. Infelise, *I Remondini di Bassano* (Bassano, 1980), p. 107.

5 O. Baldacci, "Introduzione ad una mostra di atlanti antichi," and M. La Corte, "Catalogo di atlanti dei secoli XVI–XVIII," both in *Mostra di Tolomei e di atlanti antichi*

(Rome, 1967), pp. 41–93 and 95–136 respectively. See also, Baldacci, "Atlanti geografici e atlanti storici in biblioteche della Puglia e della Basilicata (Saggio per un catalogo da estendersi a tutta l'Italia)," in *Atti del XIX Congresso Geografico Italiano* (Como, 1964), 3: 421–432.

6 V. Valerio, *Atlanti napoletani del XIX secolo (1806–1860)* (Naples, 1980). In this work, thirty-three atlases are described in detail, with the list of their maps and some thirty illustrations.

7 In the five-page biography of Luigi Bossi, by L. Sebastiani, in *Dizionario biografico degli italiani*, there is no mention of his geographical atlas. In the many works devoted to the Venetian engravers, there is, with few exceptions, no cartographical work attributed to them.

8 P. Lee Phillips, *A List of Geographical Atlases in the Library of Congress*, vols. 1–4 (Washington, 1909–1920); and the addition by C. E. Le Gear, vols. 5–9 (Washington, 1958–1992); *National Maritime Museum: Catalogue of the Library*, the third volume in two parts is devoted to "Atlases and Cartography" (London, 1971); *The A. E. Nordenskiöld Collection in the Helsinki University Library*, compiled by A. M. Mickwitz and L. Miekkavaara, three volumes (Helsinki, 1979–1984).

9 There is no mention of Italy's role in W. W. Ristow's outstanding study, "Lithography and Maps, 1796–1850," in *Five Centuries of Map-Printing*, edited by D. Woodward (Chicago, 1975), pp. 77–112.

10 A. Bertarelli, *Le stampe popolar italiane* (Milan, 1974), with an introduction by C. Albrici.

11 I do not agree with the rather theological translation made by D. Woodward in his "The Techniques of Atlas Making," *The Map Collector*, no. 18 (1982), p. 2. Apart from an erroneous transcription of the original title, I do not find the call of the biblical creation; on the contrary, it is a sound appeal to a technical approach to the structure of the world (de fabrica mundi) and to the representation (fabricati figura).

12 On the work of Coronelli, see the still-outstanding work by E. Armao, *Vincenzo Coronelli, cenni sull'uomo e la sua vita. Catalogo ragionato delle sue opere-lettere-fonti bibliografiche-indici* (Florence, 1944). On the sources used by Coronelli in compiling these works, see E. Armao, *Il 'Catalogo degli autori' di Vincenzo Coronelli. Una bibliografia geografica del '600* (Florence, 1957).

13 For a sample of Roman institutions, see M. La Corte, *Catalogo di atlanti dei secoli XVI–XVIII* (Rome, 1967), pp. 95–136.

14 Marsigli's most important works were published in Amsterdam and The Hague, namely: *Histoire Physique de la Mer* (1725) and *Danubius Pannonico-mysicus* (1726). On Marsigli's activity, see F. Farinelli, "Multiplex geographia Marsili est difficilissima," in *I materiali dell'Istituto del le Scienze* (Bologna, 1979), pp. 63–74, with bibliographical notes.

15 For up-to-date and detailed studies on this undertaking, see the scholarly papers accompanying the facsimile reproduction of the two volumes edited by L. Firpo and

published by the historical city archive of Torino in the years 1983 and 1984. The beautifully printed volumes are now available on the market.

16 For a general account of the state of the art of printing in the eighteenth century, see G. Morazzoni, *Il libro illustrato veneziano del Settecento* (Milan, 1943) and M. Infelise, *I Remondini di Bassano* (Bassano, 1980), in particular chapter six, pp. 163–194.

17 There is no mention of the atlas in Morazzoni's work in which Albrizzi's activity is widely shown. It has escaped many authors that the decoration of the world map of the atlas was drawn by G. B. Piazzetta and was engraved by G. Giampiccoli. The title of the atlas is: *Atlante novissimo che contiene tutte le parti del mondo, nel quale sono esattamente descritti gl'imperi, le monarchie, stati, repubbliche ec.* (Venice, 1740), 2 vols. The dedication is addressed to Andrea Capello, who was Venetian ambassador in Vienna, to whom the fourth volume of the Salmon history had already been dedicated. A copy is in the Library of Congress (Phillips no. 594). Albrizzi was also publisher of some of Coronelli's geographical works.

18 Information about the Italian edition of the T. Salmon work is in *Arte della stampa 1734–1799* (Naples, 1980), pp. 33–34 and in *Vicenza città bellissima, iconografia vicentina a stampa dal XV al XIX secolo* (Vicenza, 1984). The dates reported in the above-mentioned volumes are in conflict with my own findings.

19 The article "Géographie," which appeared in the *Encyclopédie . . .* in 1757, was written by the Robert de Vaugondys. It is not known if it was the father Gilles or the son Didier, who had already produced in 1755 the "Essai sur l'histoire de la géographie," which was reprinted in 1757 as an introduction to the atlas of 108 maps. See N. Broc, *La géographie des philosophes. Géographie et voyageurs français au XVIIIe siècle* (Paris, 1975), p. 250.

20 Almost nothing is known about the Santinis (were they brothers or perhaps cousins?). Only Francesco signs the plates in full as a publisher: "chez François Santini, Rue St. Justine près la dite Eglise." Tooley in his *Dictionary of Mapmakers* (Tring, 1979), p. 559, gives him a French origin probably due to the language used in his atlas. Baldacci in his works (referred to in note 5) calls the other Pietro, as did G. Morazzoni, *Catalogo del fondo cartografico queriniano* (Venice, 1959), in which he follows the *Catalogo ragionato delle carte geografiche esistenti nella cartoteca dell'Istituto di geografia della R. università di Bologna*, edited by D. Albani (Bologna, 1943). However, the name of P. Santini is definitely "Paolo" as it appeared in archival records referred to in G. Moschini, *Dell'incisione in Venezia* (Venice, 1924): 156, and R. Gallo, *L'incisione nel '700 a Venezia e Bassano* (Venice, 1941), p. 16. Other works referring to Paolo Santini were kindly suggested by Laura Sitran Gasparrini, of the Biblioteca Marciana in Venice; they are: E. Cicogna, *Saggio di bibliografia veneziana* (Venice, 1847), n. 4968, and G. Moschini, *Della letteratura veneziana* 3 (Venice, 1806).

21 On the Robert de Vaugondys' atlas, see Mary Sponberg Pedley, "The Subscription List of the 1757 'Atlas Universel'," *Imago Mundi* 31 (1979): 66–77, and "New Light on an Old Atlas: Documents Concerning the Publication of the 'Atlas Universel' (1757)" *Imago Mundi* 36 (1984): 48–63.

22 I am obliged to Mary Sponberg Pedley for the information communicated in a letter (February 29, 1984) containing the list of Italian subscribers to the *Atlas Universel*.

23 A copy of this first edition is in *The A. E. Nordenskiöld Collection in the Helsinki University Library*, 2:263–268. The Library of Congress and the National Maritime Museum have a later edition by Remondini (see note 31). The title of the atlas is *Atlas Universel dressé sur les meilleurs cartes modernes* (Venice, 1776), vol. I, index, with sixty maps; vol. II, index, with sixty-three maps; no engravers signed the maps.

24 A document cited by R. Gallo, *L'incisione nel '700 a Venezia e a Bassano* (Venice, 1941), p. 17, sheds light on the difficulties Santini encountered in his relations with the engraver Baratti.

25 Gallo, *L'incisione*, p. 16, from which we learn that the sum of 33,000 Italian lire was paid for the acquisition of the copperplates.

26 Paolo Santini published two more atlases in the following years: in 1783, the *Atlas portatif d'Italie à l'usage des voyageurs, comprenant toutes les villes, et autres lieux par les quels l'on passe de post en post avec leurs distances respectives*, with seven maps and three tables (Library of Congress, Phillips no. 3059), and in the years 1788–1793, the *Atlas portatif à l'usage des colleges pour servir a l'intelligence des auteurs classiques. Dedié à l'Academie de Padoue*, with sixty-three maps. This atlas was compiled by Grenet who was professor at Lisieux and author of the *Atlas portatif* (1779–1782), and other works on ancient and modern geography. The author of the map was Rigobert Bonne. The Library of Congress possesses a French edition with forty-four maps (Phillips no. 288). Another French edition appeared in 1785 with sixty-five maps, an edition copied by Santini. See Reiss and Auvermann, *Catalogue of Auction* (October 1984), vol. 31, no. 3305.

27 M. Infelise, *I Remondini di Bassano* (Bassano, 1980), provides a scholarly survey on the economic and social aspects of the Remondini's affirmation. See also G. M. Zilio, "L'arte della Stampa," in *Storia di Bassano* (Bassano, 1980), pp. 271–310, and A. Bertarelli, "La remondiniana di Bassano Veneto. Contributo alla storia della calcografia in Italia," in *Emporium* (1928), pp. 358–369.

28 S. Di Giacomo, "La stamperia Remondini di Bassano e le carte di Varese," in *Emporium* (1924), pp. 19–35. A great number of woodblocks for wallpapers and popular images and a rich collection of engravings from the Remondinis are kept in the Museo Civico di Bassano. I thank the direction of the Museo for the kind assistance during my visit there in August 1984.

29 M. Infelise, *I Remondini di Bassano* (Bassano, 1980), pp. 104–105.

30 G. M. Zilio, "L'arte della Stampa," in *Storia di Bassano* (Bassano, 1980), p. 306.

31 The Atlas was reissued in 1804, "a Venice chez Joseph Remondini & fils," with several maps added. A copy preserved in the Museo Civico in Bassano, contains a map of England in four sheets, after Kitchin, dated 1799. A few maps were embellished with frontispieces (added to the maps from small copperplates with the title) in imitation of Zatta. A copy of the Remondini issue is in the Library of Congress (Phillips

no. 647), and in the *National Maritime Museum Catalogue of the Library*, among "French Atlases," pp. 335–337. A complete list of Remondini's geographical copperplates may be found in the catalogs listed in *Vicenza città bellissima, Iconografia vicentiana a stampa dal XV al XIX secolo* (Venice, 1984), pp. 396–397.

32 The title of the atlas is: *Atlante novissimo, illustrato ed accresciuto sulle osservazioni, e scoperte dei più celebri e recenti geografi, che ora per la prima volta si produce* (Venice, 4 volumes): vol. I (1779), frontispiece + xvi pages + 50 pages + 6 pages + 70 maps; vol. II (1782), 49 maps; vol. III (1784), 52 maps; vol. IV (1785), 44 maps. The atlas was published in several editions up to the end of the century. The Library of Congress has the edition, with maps whose dates vary from 1779 to 1799 (Phillips no. 651). The copy described in F. Wawrik, *Berühmte Atlanten* (Dortmund, 1982), pp. 250–255 is missing a fourth volume, and is a mixture of first and later editions.

33 The work by Anton Fredrich Büsching (1724–1793) had a good reputation in Italy and was printed in several cities. Before Zatta's edition, there was *Nuova Geografia all'altezza Reale di Pietro Leopoldo*, published in Florence by Stecchi and Pagani in the 1770s. An account of Zatta's edition of Büsching may be found in his *Avviso apologetico* (Venice, 1780), which is kept in the Biblioteca Apostolica Vaticana (R. G. Miscellanea A.58–21), and is cited in A. P. Frutaz, *Le carte del Lazio* (Rome, 1972), 1:98.

34 "Saggi preliminari di geografia in cui compendiosamente si contengono gli elementi di questa scienza," fifty numbered pages, published in 1777 and reprinted in the 1780s. The phrase is quoted from page 45.

35 Ibid., p. 45.

36 Ibid., p. 48.

37 Ibid., p. 49.

38 Ibid., p. 49.

39 D. B. Updike, *Printing Types. Their History, Form and Use* (Cambridge: Harvard University Press, 1937), 2d edition, reprinted by Dover in 1980, vol. I, pp. 174–175 and figures 133 and 134.

40 The title is *Nuovo Atlante* followed by the list of plates. The first appearance of this atlas is in *Catalogo delle stampe in rame, carte geografiche; e musica, che si trovano vendibili nella calcografia di Antonio Zatta e figli* (Venice, 1790), p. xxi. The title used in the catalog is *Atlante portatile geografico . . . ad uso della* gioventù studiosa (to be used by the studious youth) in 20 maps. The Library of Congress has a second edition (1799) with twenty-four maps (Phillips no. 6014), and an identical copy marked as a third edition (1800, Phillips no. 695).

41 Remondini's atlas is titled *Atlas Géographique dressé sur les meilleurs cartes de ces derniers tems, à l'usage des écoles, et de toute la jeunesse des deux sexes* (Venice, 1801), sixty maps. The atlas is described in Remondini's catalog *Libri e collezioni di stampe pubblicate negli anni 1800 e 1801. Dalli Signori Giuseppe Remondini, e figli di Venezia* (Venice, 1801), pp. 1–2. The title of Storti's atlas is *Nuovo atlante portatile ovvero metodo facile per apprendere in breve la geografia* (Venice, 1796), xii pages, 312 pages,

twenty-four maps. The permission to print given to Francesco Andreola was dated February 7, 1794.

42 For a general discussion on the reform of teaching during the eighteenth century, see D. Balani and M. Roggero, *La scuola in Italia dalla controriforma al secolo dei Lumi* (Turin, 1976), in particular, chapter five, pp. 143–157 with bibliography, and chapter six, pp. 173–197.

43 I found an *Atlas des enfens ou methode nouvelle, courte facile et demonstrative, pour apprendre la géographie* (Amsterdam, 1760), with twenty-two maps, and an *Atlas des enfens ou nouvelle methode pour apprendre la géographie* (Lyon, 1784), with twenty-four maps. An Italian translation of the latter was referred to in the foreword of Storti's atlas.

44 D. Balani and M. Roggero, *La scuola in Italia dalla controriforma al secolo dei Lumi* (Turin, 1976), p. 176: "the organization of the absolute state led the sovereigns to transform the religious and charitable aims of the school into new political and social objectives." Furthermore, Masson de Morvilliers in his *Discours sur la Geographie* (Padova, 1785), p. xiv, expressed well the aversion to the clerical methods in the instruction: "Nous aimerons [he wrote] autant un genre d'éducation qui fôrmat des hommes pour la société, et nous donnât des citoyens, que des jeunes pedans, qui croient tout savoir parce qu'ils peuvent reciter en grec et en latin des morceaux de Démosthene et de Tite-Live."

45 The editions of the French *Encyclopédie* came after the Italian translation of the *Chambers' Cyclopaedia*, which appeared in Naples in the years 1747–1754.

46 G. Bellini, *Storia della Tipografia del Seminario di Padova, 1684–1938* (Padova, 1938), in which the author discusses in detail the Padova edition of the *Encyclopédie*. Bodoni printing types were proposed to be used, and Rizzi-Zannoni was asked to write the portion related to geography. In an interesting work by R. Almagià, "Padove e l'Ateneo padovano nella storia della scienza geografica," *Rivista Geografica Italiana* (Florence, 1912), pp. 465–510, no reference is made to the important contributions of Padovani geographers to the edition of the *Encyclopédie*. The study does provide insight into the status of the discipline of geography at the time of the publication. Almagià fails to acknowledge that Giuseppe Toaldo (1729–1797), who was a professor of geography and astronomy, was one of the Italian editors for the *Encyclopédie*.

47 It is taken from the "Advertissement des editeurs de Padoue" in the volume *Géographie Moderne*, published in 1785. On the contemporary criticism of the Encyclopédie, see N. Broc, *La géographie des philosophes* (Paris, 1975), pp. 250–256, and the general survey by F. Venturi, *Le origini dell'Enciclopedia* (3d ed., Turin, 1977).

48 Masson de Morvilliers, "Discours sur la Géographie," in *Géographie Moderne* (Padova, 1785), p. xii.

49 N. Broc, *La géographie des philosophes* (Paris, 1975), p. 250; on the ambiguity of geography in the encyclopedists, see also pp. 251–256 and M. Quaini, "L'Italia dei cartografi," *Storia d'Italia* (Turin, 1976), 6:20–21, and G. Natali, *La geografia e l'opera degli enciclopedisti francesi* (Bologna, 1922).

50 Masson de Morvilliers, "Discours sur la Géographie," in *Géographie Moderne* (Padova, 1785), p. xiv.

51 *Atlas Encyclopedique, contenant la géographie ancienne, et quelques cartes sur la géographie du Moyen Age, la géographie moderne, et les cartes relatives à la géographie physique* (Padova, 1789 and 1790), vol. I, 72 pages, 69 maps; vol. II, 122 pages, 71 maps. The maps were all engraved by Alessandro Scattaglia. The Library of Congress has no copy of the Padova edition, but has two copies of the original French atlas (Phillips no. 666 and 667), from which the Padova edition was derived. The number, order, and design of the maps are exactly the same.

52 "Manifesto dell'edizione di un nuovo atlante geografico, nautico, politico e militare del Sig. Gio. Antonio Rizzi-Zannoni," Venice, March 17, 1781, consisting of thirty-two numbered pages and a sample of the engraving. The copy, which is kept in the Biblioteca Marciana (Misc. 2040.6), was first referred to by A. Blessich, "Un geografo italiano del secolo XVIII. Giovanni Antonio Rizzi-Zannoni (1736–1814)" in *Bollettino della Società Geografica Italiana* (Rome, 1898), fasc. I, II, IV, IX, XI. I express my thanks to the Director of the Marciana Library and to Laura Sitran Gasparrini for the opportunity to study this interesting document.

53 The subscriptions were collected in Venice by Giovan Battista Pasquali, Gasparo Storti, Tommaso Bettinelli, and Simon Occhi. The copperplates were engraved in "Sª Sofia in ruga de' due Pozzi" under the direction of Giovanni Valerio Pasquali.

54 Page 32 of the "Manifesto" reads: "the way of subscription allows the Company the possibility to relieve some of the expenses. . . ."

55 It is taken from a footnote in the first page of the "Manifesto." The first volume of the Livorno encyclopedia was published in 1770 and the last volume (33d) appeared in 1779; see T. Iermano, *Intellettuali e stampatori a Livorno tra '700 e '800* (Livorno, 1983), pp. 13–27, with useful bibliography on the Tuscan editions of the *Encyclopédie*.

56 "Manifesto" (Venice, 1781), p. 14.

57 Ibid., p. 28.

58 Briefly, the atlas includes the following numbers of plates: eight for ancient history; one for the Middle Ages; two for the planispheres; an unspecified number for the Americas as the dimension "depends on the destiny of the American affairs"; twenty for Asia; eight for Africa; twelve for England; eight for Sweden and Norway; twelve for Russia; six for Poland; ten for Spain and Portugal; twelve for France; thirty for Germany and Holland; four for the Ottoman empire; six for Naples; four for Rome; six for the Piedmont; twelve for Venice; three for the Italian islands; one for Italy as a whole; thirty nautical charts; one for the magnetic declination; and sixty-six geographical descriptions.

59 "Manifesto" (Venice, 1781), p. 3.

60 Ibid., p. 8.

61 *Piccolo atlante geografico* (Venice, 1810); it contains twenty-seven maps which are listed in the catalog *Carte Geografiche e vedute* (Florence, 1975), p. 6, of the Gonnelli bookdealer.

62 *Atlante universale del globo compreso in XVIII carte elegantemente intagliate in rame, tratto dall'originale tedesco pubblicato in Gotha da C. G. Reichard ed A. Stieler e perfezionato con l'aggiunta delle più recenti scoperte* (Venice, 1829). The dates on the maps vary from 1826 to 1829. Each map has an explanatory sheet, but only three maps are signed by the engravers M. Zuliani and Maria Rocchetti. Rocchetti is mentioned in G. Moschini, *Dell'incisione in Venezia* (Venice, 1924), p. 178, but her cartographic activity is not. A copy of this unusual atlas is in the Querini Stampalia library in Venice; see G. Mazzariol, *Catalogo del fondo cartografico queriniano* (Venice, 1959), p. 144.

63 N. Vianello, *La tipografia di Alvisopoli e gli annali delle sue pubblicazioni* (Florence, 1957). The first two chapters help to explain the economic and political situation of Venice at the end of the eighteenth century, and the transfer of power from Venice to Milan in the first decades of the nineteenth century. The fall of the market as a consequence of Napoleonic war, and the beginning of German world-cultural influence is also explained, pp. 9–12. Failure to mention the atlas does not detract from this interesting work.

64 Her full name is Marietta Minio Rocchetti. See note no. 62.

65 The title is *Christophori Cellarii geographia antiqua in compendium redacta, novis praefationibus nunc exornata a Francesco Tirolio et Joanne Baptista Ghisio communi sumpta atque labore, amplioribus tabulis aucta et accuratioribus catalogis locupletata* (Rome, 1774), thirty-five maps and twenty-six pages of text. A copy is in the library of the Società Geografica Italiana, to which I am indebted for the opportunity I was given to study the atlas. A first reference to the work appeared in G. Marinelli, *Saggio di cartografia della regione veneta* (Venice, 1881), no. 1167. The atlas was also listed in M. La Corte, *Catalogo di atlanti dei secoli XVI–XVIII* (Rome, 1967), p. 134.

66 The noble G. B. Ghigi was also author of a map of Sicily in four sheets published in Rome in 1779. For activity of Ghigi, see A. P. Frutaz, *Le carte del Lazio* (Rome, 1972), 1:93 and table no. 200. Ghigi also published a book of *Rime* which appeared in Naples in 1787. Nothing was found about F. Tirolio.

67 The drawing represents the Coliseum and other ancient Roman buildings, adorned by martial decorations and panoplies. The engraver was Camillo Tinti, whose engravings are listed in *Catalogo generale dei rami incisi al bulino e all'acquaforte posseduti dalla Regia Calcografia di Roma* (Rome, 1883), and C. A. Petrucci, *Catalogo generale delle stampe tratte dai rami in cisi posseduti dalla Calcografia Nazionale* (Rome, 1953), p. 120.

68 The Library of Congress possesses the first edition (Phillips no. 124).

69 *Atlas historique cronologique géographique et genealogique par M. A. Le Sage avec corrections et additions* (Florence, 1807). The atlas has thirty-five sheets with nineteen maps

among diagrams. The engravers were G. Canacci and G. Giarre, both active in Forence.

70 *Atlante storico geografico genealogico e cronologico* (Florence, 1813), with thirty-six sheets.

71 *Atlante storico geografico genealogico e cronologico* (Naples, 1826), with a lithographed frontispiece, forty pages, and eighteen maps. Dates vary from 1823 to 1826. The Library of Congress has a copy (Phillips no. 126). The atlas has been described by V. Valerio, *Atlanti Napoletani del XIX secolo (1806–1860)* (Naples, 1980), pp. 28–29 and figure 4. Another edition "con notabili miglioramenti fattivi dietro le più recenti edizioni e nella presente accresciuti" was published in Naples in 1836. It appeared in a catalog by the bookdealer L. Regina, *Catalogo di cartografia meridionale* (Naples, 1982), p. 66, with the frontispiece reproduced.

72 *Atlante storico, geografico, genealogico, cronologico e letterario* (Venice, 1826), with 24 maps and 8 + 183 pages. The text, which appeared in 1840, bears the title *Atlante storico, letterario, biografico, archeologico dai secoli omerici ai nostri giorni*, 2 + 223 pages only. A review of the atlas appeared in G. Bertocci, *Repertorio bibliografico delle opere stampate in Italia nel secolo XIX* (Rome, 1880), 1:79–80.

73 *Atlante storico-politico e statistico della Polonia* (Capolago, c. 1832), with one sheet and seven maps of Poland in the years 1768, 1772, 1793, 1795, 1807, 1809, and 1815. The first page is titled "Quadro istorico delle rivoluzioni nazionali di Polonia (Metodo di Le Sage, C.te di Las Casas), par J. De Mancy." A copy can be found in the Biblioteca Nazionale in Rome (9 Banc. 5.3).

74 M. Parenti, *Dizionario dei luoghi di stampa falsi, inventati o supposti* (Florence, 1951). On page 45, the author mentions four works printed in Milan and Modena between 1834–1850 with the Capolago imprint.

75 The first volume of the atlas was published in Naples, by the Società Filomatica in 1825, with 355 pages and thirty-one tables of images; the second volume was published by Tremater in 1827, with 250 + 75 pages and forty-three tables. A biography of L. Cacciatore was appended to the second volume in 1827. The atlas was well accepted by the public and had several editions. The second edition was published in Naples in 1828 by Tremater, followed by several editions published in Florence in three volumes beginning in 1831.

76 *Atlante della geografia antica e moderna, cosmografica, fisica, topografica, di commercio e d'industria, politica, statistica, ethografica ed istorica di tutte le parti del mondo* (Milan, 1807), with forty-nine maps, title, dedication, and index. No information was available on Barbiellini who also published in Milan in 1806 *Nuova descrizione geografica dell'Italia antica e moderna*. A Barbiellini family was active in Rome between 1749 and 1790: see *Il libro romano del Settecento, la stampa e la legatura* (Rome, 1959), pp. 42–44, but it is not known if a component of the Roman family moved to Milan toward the end of the eighteenth century.

77 The publisher included a list of map engravers and their places of activity. We find: Marco di Pietro active in Rome; Saverio Chianale active in Turin; Giuseppe Bonatti

of Bassano; the Bordiga brothers with Guiseppe Caniani; Bertolotti and Giovanni Boggi active in Milan.

78 G. Vancouver, *A Voyage of Discovery to the North Pacific Ocean . . .* , *and Performed in the Years 1790, 1791, 1792, 1793, 1794 and 1795* (London, 1798), three volumes with eighteen maps; there is also a folio atlas containing sixteen charts of Vancouver's discoveries.

79 *Atlante ad uso del nuovo dizionario geografico di L. R. Formiggini* (Milan, 1814). The atlas was sold by the book dealers Ferdinando Artaria and Giovanni Bernardoni. Unfolded, the six maps measure 55 × 77 cm.

80 In the Biblioteca Nazionale in Rome, there is an atlas titled *Atlante scelto di carte geografiche, politiche e fisiche prospetti astronomici, oro-idrografici e storici composto di 40 fogli grandi*, published in Rome by Gaspare Ardin, who only collected single maps by various authors. The map of the Americas, which is that engraved by Bordigas, still bears the name "Luigiana" though the date was changed into 1856. Other maps are from Stanislao Stucchi in Milan and Giovani Battista in Turin.

81 *Novissimo atlante geografico in tavole XXII per la studiosa gioventù* (Milan, 1819).

82 *Nuovo atlante universale della antica e moderna geografia dei signori Arrowsmith, Poirson, Sotzman, Lapie, D'Albe, Malte-Brun ed altri accreditati autori e per la parte antica dei signori D'Anville e Bonne* (Milan, 1824), thirty-nine pages, thirty-seven maps. The Library of Congress has a copy (Phillips no. 743). The atlas also includes a list of subscribers. From the introduction we learn that in 1822 there appeared a "Manifesto" for gathering subscriptions.

83 See the biography by L. Sebastiani in *Dizionario biografico degli italiani*.

84 *Nuovo atlante di Geografia universale in 52 carte compilazione ridotta ad uso degli italiani, riveduta ed ampliata per opera del Cav. Luigi Rossi* (Milan, 1820), xx pages, 150 pages, fifty-two maps, of which eighteen are double maps. A copy is in the Library of Congress (Phillips no. 739).

85 A biography of Rossi is in *Dizionario biografico universale* (Florence, 1845–1846), 4:953. I have to thank Mr. Antonio Fuortes in Milan, who drew my attention to this biography.

86 Among the works of the Istituto Geografico Militare is the *Carta di cabotaggio del mare Adriatico*, published in the years 1822–1824 in twenty sheets, with title and a sheet of geographical positions of landmarks and seven sheets of views. A portolan accompanying the atlas was published in 1830. The title of Vacani's atlas is *Atlante topografico militare per servire alla storia delle campagne e degli assedi degl'italiani in Ispagna dal 1808 al 1813 ricavato dagli antichi documenti e da nuove ricognizioni eseguite nel corso della guerra* (Milan, 1822), with sixteen maps. A copy is in the Library of Congress (Phillips no. 3130). On Vacani's life, see G. Ferrario, *Sulla vita e le opere del generale del genio Barone Camillo Vacani. Autobiografia con completamento* (Milan, 1862).

87 *Nuovo atlante di geografia moderna, dedicato a S.E. il Signor Conte Giulio di Strassoldo compilato da Carlo Rossari, . . . e riveduto nell'inclito I.R. Istituto Geografico Militare*

(Milan, 1824). Although no copy of this atlas was found, a copy should be in the Marciana Library in Venice; see G. Marinelli, *Saggio di cartografia della regione veneta* (Venice, 1881), p. 318, no. 1558.

88 *Grande atlante universale di geografia moderna secondo i principi di Malte-Brun nuovamente disegnato ed inciso dall'incisore geografo Stanislao Stucchi* (Milan, 1826), twenty-six maps with dates from 1822 to 1827. A copy is in the Library of Congress (Phillips no. 748).

89 *Recueil des principaux plans, des ports, et rades de la Mer Méditerranée, extraits de ma carte en douce feuilles dediée a Mons.gr le Duc de Choiseul Ministre de la guerre et de la marine par son humble serviteur* (Genoa, 1779), 123 charts. A full description of the maps is found in *The A. E. Nordenskiöld Collection* (Helsinki, 1981), 2:245–246. One copy is also recorded in the National Maritime Museum; see the *Catalogue of the Library* (London, 1971), 3:320. A new enlarged edition appeared in 1804 titled *Recueil de 163 des principaux plans des ports et rades de la Méditerranée, dont 40 on été dernièrement publiés par J. J. Allezard, et plusieurs des autres corrigés* (Genoa, 1804). This copy appeared in "Wertvolle Buecher Dekorative Graphik," Reiss and Auvermann auction, October 31, 1984, no. 3330.

90 *Atlas Maritime* (Genoa, 1802), with thirty-seven maps mainly of the Mediterranean coast, which were taken from earlier editions of *Le Neptune François* and the *Hydrographie François*. A copy of the Genovese edition is in National Maritime Museum, *Catalogue of the Library* (London, 1971), 3:258.

91 *Catalogue des livres français qui se trouvent chez Yves Gravier Imprimeur-Libraire à Gênes* (Genoa, 1818), p. 90. I am indebted for this information to the kind attention of Mrs. Norma Dallai in Genoa, to whom I express my warmest thanks. Among the atlases recorded in the catalog under the heading "Cartes Géographiques et hydrographiques" is the impressive five-volume atlas *Le petit atlas maritime* by N. Bellin (1764) with 580 maps, and the two volumes of *Le Neptune Oriental* by De Mannevillette (1745–1775).

92 One of the most important, which remained in manuscript, is the "Pianta delle due Riviere" by Matteo Vinzoni (finished in 1758); see M. Vinzoni, *Pianta delle due Riviere della Serenissima Repubblica di Genova divise ne' commissariati di sanità*, edited by M. Quaini (Genoa, 1983), with a fairly good reproduction of thirty-five maps of the atlas.

93 On his project, see "Introduzione allo studio della geografia," appearing in the Cassini's atlas (Rome, 1792), p. 20; and A. Mori, *La cartografia ufficiale in Italia e l'Istituto Geografico Militare* (Rome, 1922), p. 12, whose information basically comes from H. M. A. Berthaut, *Les ingénieurs géographes militaires* (Paris, 1903), 1:371, 374, which is useful for understanding Lirelli's activity as head of the topographical office and astronomical observatory in Turin.

94 Since all the copies known to me are missing the frontispiece, it is likely that a title was never printed. There is a copy in the Library of Congress (Phillips no. 669). Two

more copies are recorded in the *Union Catalog,* 67:188, with "title page and tables of contents in ms." The engravers of the 102 maps were Agostino Costa, Giovanni Silvestrini, Bartolomeo Borghi, Giovanni Valerio Pasquali, Giovanni Garti d'Alibrandi, Filippo Conti, and Giuseppe Bonatti.

95 "Lettera del Sig. arciprete Bartolommeo Borghi al Sig. avvocato Lodovico Coltellini di Cortona, sopra la carta geografica pubblicata da Antonio Zatta e Figli col titolo, Parte dell'Impero Ottomano, che confina con gli Stati Austriaco, e Veneto, ec." (Siena, 1788).

96 From the "Introduzione allo studio della geografia," appearing in Cassini's atlas (Rome, 1792), p. 20, where the priest tells us of recent atlases which deserve our attention.

97 *Atlante generale dell'Ab: Bartolommeo Borghi corredato di prospetti istorici-politici-civili-naturali di ciascheduno stato* (Florence, 1819). The dates on the maps vary from 1816 to 1819. The atlas was sold in issues which were printed by different publishers: Niccolò Carli (1816–1817), Giovanni Marenigh (1818–1819), Guglielmo Piatti (1819), and Stamperia Granducale (1819). In the frontispiece, there appeared the name of the last publisher who was Aristide Parigi. The engravers were Canacci, Poggiali, and the Giarre workshop in addition to Agostino Costa, who also engraved maps for Pazzini and Carli atlas. The authors of the description were B. Borghi, Giulio Bertolini, Agostino da Rabatta, Luigi Parigi, and Zanobi Zucchini. A copy is in the Library of Congress (Phillips no. 735).

98 This edition was published by Vincenzo Batelli e figli, in Florence.

99 *Nuovo atlante generale metodico ed elementare tascabile per lo studio della geografia ed istoria antica, e moderna arricchito di varie carte delle nuove scoperte* (Florence, 1779), ninety-six sheets and a sheet of keywords. The only known copy belongs to the Società Geografica Italiana and was first mentioned in M. La Corte, *Catalogo di atlanti dei secoli XVI–XVIII* (Rome, 1967), p. 134. The atlas is unknown to the literature on Baillou: see F. Inghirami, *La storia della Toscana compilata ed in altre epoche distribuita* (Fiesole, 1843), pp. 157–159; and H. M. A. Berthaut, *Les ingenieurs géographes militaires (1624–1831)* (Paris, 1902), 2:380; and A. Mori, *La cartografia ufficiale in Italia e l'Istituto Geografico Militare* (Rome, 1922), p. 61. A very recent biography by N. Carranza appeared in the *Dizionario biografico degli italiani,* but the atlas is not mentioned. Nothing was found on Agostino da Rabatta, who collaborated twenty-five years later on the atlas by Borghi (see note no. 97).

100 *Atlas géographique contenant la mappamonde et les quattre parties avec les differents états d'Europe* (Paris, 1762), frontispiece, title, thirty-one maps. The volume measures 12 × 7 cm. The atlas is worthy of mention, though printed in Paris by Lattre, since the author was the famous Italian astronomer and geographer Rizzi-Zannoni.

101 Abbe Coyer, *Voyage in Italie* (Paris, 1776), pp. 136–137, letter dated Livorno, November 17, 1763; quotation taken from T. Iermano, *Intellettuali e stampatori a Livorno tra '700 e '800* (Livorno, 1983), p. 27.

102 On the Livorno edition of the *Encyclopédie*, see L. Servolini, "L'edizione livornese della celebre enciclopedia di Diderot e D'Alembert," in *Accademie e Biblioteche d'Italia* (Rome, 1941), 15:1–5, and the recent work by T. Iermano, *Intellettuali e stampatori a Livorno tra '700 e '800* (Livorno, 1983), pp. 13–28, where the author also discusses the two Tuscan editions of the *Encyclopédie* (Lucca, 1756–1771 and Livorno, 1770–1779) paying attention to the historical-economical context. Iermano's work provides a more detailed bibliography on the two undertakings.

103 *Atlante dell'America contenente le migliori carte geografiche, e topografiche delle principali città, laghi, fiumi, e fortezze del nuovo mondo con una succinta relazione dei diversi stabilimenti europei in quella parte del globo, e principalmente dei luoghi, che servono adesso di teatro alla presente guerra fra i coloni inglesi, e la Madre Patria* (Livorno, 1777), forty-four maps. The Library of Congress has a copy of this atlas (Phillips no. 1167); see also, *The A. E. Nordenskiöld Collection* (Helsinki, 1979), 1:4–5, where the atlas is fully described.

104 On the Revolutionary War appeal, especially the Italian reaction to the War, see F. Venturi, *Settecento riformatore* (Turin, 1984), 4:3–145.

105 The Library of Congress has a copy of the parent work of the *Atlante d'America* (Phillips no. 1167). I have inspected a copy in the National Library of Naples and went through the 236 pages of text. The engravers of the plates were: Veremondo Rossi, Violante Vanni, Andrea Scacciati, Giuseppe Pazzi, and G. M. Terreni.

106 For the story of this lesser-known edition signed by Remigio Pupares (a pseudonym of Giuseppe Ramirez), see F. Venturi, *Settecento riformatore* (Turin, 1984), 4:5.

107 See his study in this volume.

108 *Recueil de 163 des principaux plans des ports et rades de la Méditerranée, dont 40 on été dernièrement publiés par Jean Joseph Allezard ancien captain de marine* (Livorno, 1817). This is the same as the Genoa edition of 1804 (see note no. 89). A new edition with the addition of ". . . 16 des meilleurs captains anglais" appeared in 1833. For the first, see National Maritime Museum, *Catalogue of the Library*, 3:321; for the latter, see *Carte Geografiche e Vedute* (Florence, 1975), catalog of the book dealer Gonnelli, p. 12.

109 A. Zuccagni Orlandini, *Atlante Geografico, fisico, e storico del Granducato di Toscana* (Florence, 1832), facsimile edition by the Cassa di Risparmio di Firenze (Florence, 1974); L. Serristori, *Saggio di un atlante statistico dell'Italia* (Vienna, 1833); F. C. Marmocchi, *Atlante di Geografia Universale* (Florence, 1838). In the latter, a great number of maps by Borghi were reissued.

110 See A. Grizzuti, "Appunti su Giovanni Maria Cassini e le sue opere geografiche," *Studi Romani* (Rome, 1971), pp. 400–409, where the author in a short study treats in depth Cassini's life and activity; and A. P. Frutaz, *Le carte del Lazio* (Rome, 1972), pp. 99–100 and 113.

111 Referred to in Grizzuti, p. 406, no. 12.

112 *Nuovo atlante geografico universale delineato sulle ultime osservazioni* (Rome: Calcografia Camerale), vol. I (1792), 55 maps; vol. II (1797), 70 maps; vol. III (1801), 57 maps. The Library of Congress has a copy (Phillips no. 670).

113 *Catalogo generale dei rami incisi al bulino e all'acquaforte posseduti dalla Regia Calcografia di Roma* (Rome, 1883), pp. 70 and 71, with the prices of single sheets and complete volumes. Also useful for the historical survey of the copperplates collection are pages iii–x. See also the last catalog on the collection by C. A. Petrucci, *Catalogo generale delle stampe tratte dai rami incisi posseduti dalla Calgografia Nazionale* (Rome, 1953), in which the author gives a useful list of engravers with biographical data.

114 Taken from "Introduzione generale allo studio della geografia," Cassini's atlas (Rome, 1792), p. 20.

115 On the state of school in the period in the State of the Church, see D. Balani and M. Roggero, *La scuola in Italia dalla controriforma al secolo dei lumi* (Turin, 1976), pp. 104–107 and 184–185; and S. Bucci, *La scuola italiana nell'ete napoleonica* (Rome, 1976), pp. 127–146.

116 On the Cassini's globes, see the old but still-outstanding work by M. Fiorini, *Sfere terrestri e celesti di autore italiano oppure fatte o conservate in Italia* (Rome, 1899), pp. 442–444. Fiorini is the father of the study on old globes and as early as 1899 provided Italy with a complete catalog of its holdings on celestial and terrestrial globes.

117 We know that the author of the geographical introduction to the atlas was Girolamo Pongelli "padre somasco," as Cassini was; see A. Grizzuti, pp. 407–408.

118 On the conflict between laity and church during the eighteenth century, see the outstanding third volume by F. Venturi, *Settecento riformatore* (Turin, 1976), in particular the "Prefazione," pp. xi–xiv and the chapter devoted to Naples, pp. 163–184. On the school in Naples, see A. Zazo, *L'istruzione pubblica e privata nel napoletano (1767–1860)* (Città di Castello, 1907).

119 For a survey on scientific institutions and schools in Naples between the eighteenth and nineteenth centuries, see F. Amodeo, "Gli istituti d'istruzione scientifici a Napoli intorno al 1800," in *Atti dell'Accademia Pontaniana*, vol. 34 (Naples, 1905); and D. Balani and M. Roggero, *La scuola in Italia dalla controriforma al secolo dei lumi* (Turin, 1976), in particular pp. 143–157, with bibliography.

120 On Rizzi-Zannoni's life and activity, see the authoritative work by A. Blessich, "Un geografo italiano del secolo XVIII: Giovanni Antonio Rizzi-Zannoni (1736–1814)," *Bollettino della Società Geografica Italiana* 35 (1898): 12–23, 56–69, 183–203, 452–466, 523–537, to whom all the following researches are more or less indebted. A few additions are in A. Mori, *La cartografia ufficiale in Italia e l'Istituto Geografico Militare* (Rome, 1922), pp. 86–92. For new approaches and information coming from archival records and direct inspection of all of the works by Rizzi-Zannoni, see V. Valerio, "A Mathematical Contribution to the Study of Old Maps," in *Imago et Mensura Mundi*, *Proceedings of the IX International Conference in the History of Cartography, Pisa, Florence, Rome 1981* (Rome, 1985), 2:489–496, and V. Valerio, "La cartografia napoletana tra il secolo XVIII e il XIX. Questioni di storia e di metodo," in *Napoli Nobilissima* (Naples, 1981), pp. 171–179.

121 V. Valerio and G. Alisio, editors, *Cartografia napoletana dal 1781 al 1889* (Naples, 1983), in particular the description of the exhibits by V. Valerio, pp. 120–167.

with 178 lithographed views. See A. Negro Spina, *L'incisione napoletana dell'Ottocento* (Naples, 1976), pp. 93–103.

139 The title is *Atlante corografico storico e statistico del Regno delle Due Sicilie eseguito litograficamente, compilato e dedicato a S. M. Ferdinando II* (Naples, 1832), twenty-two maps whose dates vary from 1828 to 1832. On Marzolla, see V. Valerio, *Atlanti napoletani*, pp. 30–33, 44–46, 71–78, and 97–106, with bibliography.

140 Since this article was written, the author has prepared an updated list of atlases, authors, and engravers, which has been published as "Italian Atlases and Their Makers, 1770–1830," *The Map Collector*, no. 45 (Winter 1988), pp. 10–18.

Early American Atlases and Their Publishers

WALTER W. RISTOW

Only a modest number of maps, charts, and plans were compiled and published in the English colonies in America prior to 1776. Not until the United States was almost a decade into its independence, however, was an atlas produced by an American publisher. Beginning with the first American atlases, which were published in 1790s, this essay provides a bibliographic survey of the major world, American, and related reference atlas series that were published or had their inception in the United States prior to the Civil War. Particular attention is devoted to the publishing networks that were established, highlighted by biographical insights about the compilers, engravers, and publishers who were involved in the production of these early American cartographic publications.[1]

MATHEW CAREY AND OTHER EARLY ATLAS PUBLISHERS

The pioneer atlas printer and publisher was Mathew Carey, a native of Dublin, who immigrated to Philadelphia in 1784. Carey initially focused his efforts on newspapers and magazines, but he turned to monograph and book publishing in 1792. Two years later his first cartographic publication, *A General Atlas for the Present War*, was issued. The atlas, which illustrated theaters of conflict in the French Revolutionary Wars, reprinted seven maps from the 1785 London publication, *Atlas to Guthrie's System of Geography*. All were redrafted, probably by Samuel Lewis, and engraved by three American engravers, William Barker, Joseph T. Scott, and Cornelius Tiebout.

Aimed more directly at the American market was *The General Atlas for Carey's Edition of Guthrie's Geography Improved*, which was published in 1795. The popularity in England and the United States of *Guthrie's Geography*, or *A New System of Modern Geography* was readily apparent to Carey; the *General Atlas* was his response. The forty-five maps in the atlas include twenty-two which were not in the 1795 London edition. A number of the maps were redrafted, most of them by Samuel Lewis, but also including several by Amos Doolittle. Engraving was contracted to nine different engravers, most of them in Philadelphia, but also embracing craftsmen in Boston, New Haven, and New York City. Cartographic publishing was but a small segment of Mathew Carey's business and it thus was inexpedient for him to have draftsmen and engravers in his permanent employ. Operating on a small budget was also an inducement to job out the various steps in atlas production.

In the interest of economy and to make the widest possible use of each map, Carey, as Harley has reported, "became a master in the art of packaging the same maps for reissue in several of his publications."[2] Thus, his *American Atlas*, also published in 1795, includes sixteen maps of individual states that are also found in *The General Atlas*. Carey's *American Atlas*, which has a total of twenty-one maps, is generally recognized as the earliest atlas of the United States. A second edition of the atlas, published in 1809, has twenty-six maps.

Carey's *General Atlas*, published in six or more editions between 1796 and 1818, drew liberally from the aforementioned atlases for its maps. The same cartographic sources supplied maps, in reduced formats, for Carey's *American Pocket Atlas* in editions dated 1796 to 1814, and in Carey's *Minor Atlas*, of which there are 1802 and 1810 editions.

Carey's *American Atlas* inspired several similar works. In 1796 John Reid published in Philadelphia *The American Atlas* by William Winterbotham. Similar in size and format to Carey's *American Atlas*, Winterbotham's was published as an accompaniment to his *An Historical Commercial and Philosophical View of the United States*. The atlas has twenty-one plates including a plan of the newly laid out city of Washington, D.C. Benjamin Tanner engraved nine of the maps, five are credited to D. Martin, two to D. Anderson, and one each to John Roberts and John Scoles. There are no engraving credits on two of the maps.

Also dated 1796 is Joseph Scott's *An Atlas of the United States Containing a Large Sheet Map of the Union*. It was published in Philadelphia by Frank and Robert Bailey. Scott's small-format atlas has a fold-in map of the United States and eighteen state maps. All nineteen maps were initially included in Scott's *United States Gazetteer*, which was published in 1795.

Samuel Lewis, who drafted maps for several Carey publications, also contributed to other early American atlases. Of particular interest is *A New and Elegant General Atlas*, which Lewis compiled in collaboration with Aaron Arrowsmith of London. The first edition, including sixty-three maps, was published in 1804 by John Conrad of Philadelphia and related firms in Baltimore, Norfolk, and Washington. The 1805 edition of the Arrowsmith-Lewis atlas contains this title-page note: "Intended to accompany the Improved Edition of Morse's Geography, and equally well calculated to be used with any former edition, with his gazetteers, or any other geographical work."

The American Geography, compiled by the Boston Congregational minister, Jedidiah Morse, and first published in 1789, went through a number of editions during the next four decades. Early editions were criticized for the small number and poor quality of map illustrations. Morse had, as early as 1796, invited Lewis to prepare maps for his geographies, but apparently nothing came of this. Lewis subsequently seems to have made arrangements with Arrowsmith to collaborate on the *New and Elegant General Atlas*, and beginning with the 1805 edition, represented it as a supplement to Morse's geographies. The 1805, 1812, and 1819 editions of the Arrowsmith-Lewis atlas were published in Boston by Thomas and Andrews.

Foreign maps in the *New and Elegant General Atlas* were apparently drawn by Arrowsmith and his assistants. All the maps of American states were compiled and drafted by Samuel Lewis. Both series of maps were engraved in the United States. Following the precedent set by Mathew Carey, preparation of the copperplates was contracted to a number of engravers, among them David Fairman, William Harrison, Jr., William Hooker, William Kneass, Alexander Lawson, Thomas Marshall, Joseph Seymour, and Benjamin Tanner.

John Melish

John Melish, a native of Glasgow, Scotland, significantly advanced American cartographic publishing during the second decade of the nineteenth century. Following studies at the University of Glasgow, Melish engaged in textile enterprises. Official travel took him to the West Indies in 1798 and to the eastern United States in 1806 to 1807. Because of unfavorable commercial and political relations between Great Britain and the United States, Melish's textile business deteriorated. In 1811, therefore, he severed his commercial and personal ties with Scotland, and immigrated to the United States. Intending to engage in farming, Melish traveled extensively in the settled areas of the country as well as beyond the Appalachians to ascertain the most favorable agricultural regions. During his travels, Melish compiled detailed and perceptive notes. This information, along with records of his earlier travels, was assembled and published in 1812 in a two-volume work entitled *Travels in the United States*. In the preface to volume one, Melish wrote: "As I have always considered books of travel to be very defective when unaccompanied by maps, I have spared no labour, nor expense, to have a good set of maps to illustrate this work. They have been drawn with great care from the best materials to which I could get access, aided by much local information, and the engraving has been executed by the first artists in Philadelphia."[3] The two engravers who prepared plates for the *Travels* maps were John Vallance and Henry S. Tanner. Melish would have subsequent associations with both. The map of the United States, which Tanner engraved, is believed to be his first professional cartographic contribution.

It is not clear whether Melish was trained in map compilation and drafting or if he was self-taught. At any rate, the eight maps he prepared for the *Travels* volumes apparently directed him to a career as mapmaker and publisher. His first contribution to atlas cartography was *A Military and Topographical Atlas of the United States; Including the British Possessions & Florida*, which was published in 1813. (See Figure 130.) It brought together a *Map of the Seat of War in North America*, a *Map of the Southern Section of the United States*, and a *Map of the American Coast, from Norfolk, Virginia to Newport, Rhode Island*, all of which were previously issued as separates, and several of the maps which first appeared in the *Travels* volumes. Henry S. Tanner engraved all but one of the atlas maps. *A Military and Topographical Atlas* was sufficiently successful to induce Melish to publish an enlarged and revised edition in 1815, after the war was terminated.

Following precedents set by Mathew Carey and Samuel Lewis, Melish's next atlas venture had a direct English derivation. In collaboration with John Val-

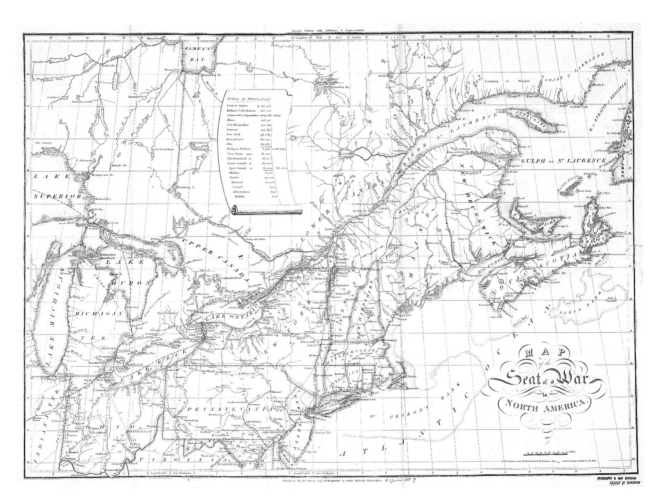

FIGURE 130 *"Map of the Seat of War in North America," from John Melish's* A Military and Topographical Atlas of the United States *(Philadelphia, 1813). Library of Congress.*

lance and Henry S. Tanner, he published, in Philadelphia, *A New Juvenile Atlas and Familiar Introduction to the Use of Maps*, which was printed by G. Palmer in 1814. An "Advertisement" on the verso of the title page acknowledges that "this work was originally published in London, by Laurie.and Whittle, celebrated map publishers . . . In the present edition, the maps and geography of the latest London edition have been carefully revised and improved; and the American part has been much altered, in consequence of the revolutions that have taken place in that quarter." A noteworthy addition is a map of the United States, which was drawn by Melish and engraved by Henry S. Tanner. The latter engraved five of the ten maps; four were prepared by John Vallance and one by James Thackara. In addition to the Advertisement previously noted, there is, on the verso of the title page, a list of thirteen works published by John Melish, most of which are cartographic. Included in the list are the *Travels* volumes and several of the maps that were subsequently published in *A Military and Topographical Atlas*.

In 1813, John F. Watson of Philadelphia published *An Atlas . . . of Ancient Geography intended as an accompaniment to Robert Mayo's A View of Ancient Geography and Ancient History*. The atlas includes eight maps and a chronological historical chart. Three of the plates were engraved by James Thackara, three by Henry S. Tanner, and two by John Vallance. One map has no engraving credit. Watson also published an 1814 edition of the atlas of ancient geography, with no apparent changes or additions. A third edition of the atlas, dated 1815, was published by "John Melish No. 49 South Third Street." It contains the same group of maps found in the two Watson editions.

By 1815, John Melish was firmly established as a cartographical and geographical publisher. He was the first American to focus exclusively on these specialized subjects. During the next five or six years Melish was busily engaged in compiling a large map of the United States, the first edition of which was published in 1816, and an official map of the state of Pennsylvania. His previous associates, Henry S. Tanner and John Vallance, engraved the copperplates for the United States map, and Benjamin Tanner, Henry's older brother, engraved the Pennsylvania map, which was published in 1822. Melish printed only one hundred copies of the United States map at a time, and revised and updated the copperplates between printings. Because of this practice, twenty-four variant states of the map, published between 1816 and 1823, have been identified.

Occupied as he was with these two maps and a large world map, which he published in 1817, Melish found little time to devote to atlas compilation and publishing after 1815. A list of Melish publications, dated 1818, includes a *Universal School Atlas*, with eight maps. The Library of Congress has no copy of this atlas, which may have been a revision of *A New Juvenile Atlas*.

John Melish did anticipate publishing an atlas of the United States. In his *A Geographical Description of the United States*, first published in 1816 as an accompaniment to his map of the United States, Melish wrote,

FIGURE 132   *View of Niagara Falls and Natural Bridge of Virginia, inset on map of North America, in Tanner's New American Atlas (Philadelphia, 1823). Library of Congress.*

Folio four, distributed to subscribers late in 1822, was limited to a large four-sheet map of North America, which Tanner registered for copyright May 27, 1822. Below the title cartouche, on the lower left sheet, there is an illustration embracing both the Natural Bridge of Virginia and a view of Niagara Falls. (See Figure 132.)

The fifth and last folio included maps of the following states, Pennsylvania and New Jersey, Kentucky and Tennessee, North and South Carolina, Georgia and Alabama, Illinois and Missouri, and Florida. All were registered for copyright August 20, 1823. Folio five also included an elaborately engraved title page, an index of all the maps, and a comprehensive "Geographical Memoir" of more than seventeen large folio pages. The lengthy title reads *A New American Atlas Containing Maps of the Several States of the North American Union Projected and drawn on a Uniform Scale from Documents found in the public Offices of the United States and State Governments and other Original and Authentic Information,*

FIGURE 133 *Title page of Tanner's New American Atlas (Philadelphia, 1823). Library of Congress.*

by Henry S. Tanner, Philadelphia: Published by H. S. Tanner, 1823. An engraving, illustrating the "First Landing of Columbus in the New World," decorates the title page. (See Figure 133.)

The "Geographical Memoir" is a particularly valuable feature of the atlas. By summarizing the source material consulted in compiling the maps, Tanner assembled a comprehensive inventory of the major cartographic resources available at that time. The Memoir is patterned in part upon John Melish's *Geographical Description of the United States*, which similarly listed compilation source materials.

Tanner's *New American Atlas* set a standard for such publications in the United States, and it was accorded favorable reviews in this country as well as in Europe. In the April 1824 issue of *The North American Review*, Jared Sparks expressed the view that

The All-American County Atlas: Styles of Commercial Landownership Mapping and American Culture*

MICHAEL P. CONZEN

The industrial revolution in the early nineteenth century brought lithographic printing to the New World and ushered in the first era of inexpensive mass-produced graphic art in America.[1] In so doing it also democratized cartography and allowed imaginative entrepreneurs to combine mapping, landscape sketching, and portraiture with traditional textual printing to evolve a classic new publication form—the illustrated county landownership subscription atlas—that enjoyed enormous popularity from its invention in 1861 to its transformation after 1876 into a more utilitarian publication. During its first hurrah, well over 300 decorative county atlases were produced, and the genre in all its ultimate permutations has swelled to well over 5,000 titles. In its initial heyday, the American county atlas fused the pride of material possession, social status, and the needs of business advertising and land transfer with the civic goals of building community. It graphically reflected and fostered, at a local scale, a general belief in what is an ordered life of material abundance and personal freedom.[2] The enormous success of the illustrated county atlas affirms its significant role in defining and promoting the ideals and methods by which Americans extended a settled landscape across the continent and sought identity within it. Such a role was particularly notable in an era of mass migrations, economic transformation, and regularly contested social values.

* The research on which this essay is based has received Fellowship support from the U.S. National Endowment for the Humanities and the Newberry Library, Chicago, and this support is gratefully acknowledged.

mon book form for presenting maps, but this was for world, national, and state compilations—not previously thought of for a county map. Perhaps the response to the Berks County publication was so positive that Bridgens saw the opportunity to make the article less bulky and include more incidental information, such as business advertisements and other local nonmap information between the pages of separated township maps. The experiment succeeded, since there was a further edition issued in 1862. The business notices—graphic renderings of business cards, in effect—show a similarity to those crowded together on Joshua Scott's 1858 revised edition of his *Map of Lancaster County*, a neighboring county; such crowding may have helped nudge Bridgens toward the atlas form as an answer to wall-map congestion and expandability. Two years later Bridgens gave Lancaster County the atlas treatment, similar in design to the earlier one, but thereafter he seemed to run out of steam, producing only one further county atlas almost a decade later.[24] Nevertheless, other minds were focussed on Bridgens's innovation and the publishing of this new form—the county atlas—was taken up by a small, alert group of surveyors who had crossed paths with Fagan while making county maps for Smith in New York state during the 1850s, namely, the Beers family.

THE EASTERN MODEL

Three young men in their early twenties, Silas N. Beers, his brother Daniel G. Beers, and their cousin Frederick W. Beers, came from a farming and small village background in Newtown, in western Connecticut.[25] They were recruited into local mapmaking in New York during the late 1850s by their former village academy teacher, J. Homer French, to help carry out R. P. Smith's dream of county surveys that would lay the foundation for a newly accurate state map of New York.[26] That notable goal was reached in 1860, and the Beers boys, set loose but now with a professional occupation, sallied forth to map counties further afield in the northeastern states. By 1864 they were in their midtwenties and they took up the atlas concept with enthusiasm. They formed the nucleus of a small, cohesive group—the "Newtown connection"—that shaped the county atlas into a saleable and durable mapping form.[27]

Silas and Daniel Beers jointly published thirteen atlases between 1864 and 1867, mostly in New York, beginning with Jefferson County. Since the vast majority of county wall maps they had been associated with had been engraved and printed in Philadelphia, it was natural to take their atlas business there. Frederick Beers entered the atlas field a year later and teamed up initially with his cousins' brother-in-law, Beach Nichols, also of Newtown, to make county atlases, first in western Pennsylvania and Ohio, and then in New York, New Jersey, and New England. Having spent his adolescence in Brooklyn helping his father in his gold-pen shop in Manhattan, Frederick Beers set up headquarters in New York, though he likewise sent his atlas work to Philadelphia for manufacture.[28] Within five short years no less than forty-six county atlases had been produced by this group and their backers in the northeastern states and Ohio. (See Figure 148.) Thus, by 1869 there had emerged a characteristic type of county atlas, which might be considered to represent an "eastern model." It owed its content, structure, and appearance to the skills and market perceptions of a small group of young men from Connecticut with Philadelphia business connections. This model is important, because it set a mold that subsequent atlas makers followed, seemingly with blind faith, as the atlas craze spread westward, until it clashed with a more elaborate, less restrained "western model," that sprung from the special conditions of the Middle West and with which it was to coexist in uneasy balance as the atlas phenomenon swept on for another decade.[29]

What propelled these county atlases through the countryside were their packaging and their marketing. The essential features of the eastern county atlas consist of pages of individual town or township maps, at scales usually approximating one inch to the mile, that show the layout of the general landscape: its rivers,

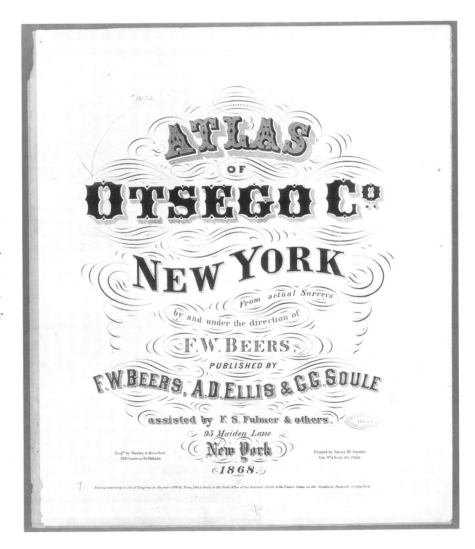

FIGURE 148 *Characteristic title page of an early Beers atlas. Frederick W. Beers,* Atlas of Otsego Co., New York *(New York: F. W. Beers, A. D. Ellis & G. G. Soule, 1868), Library of Congress.*

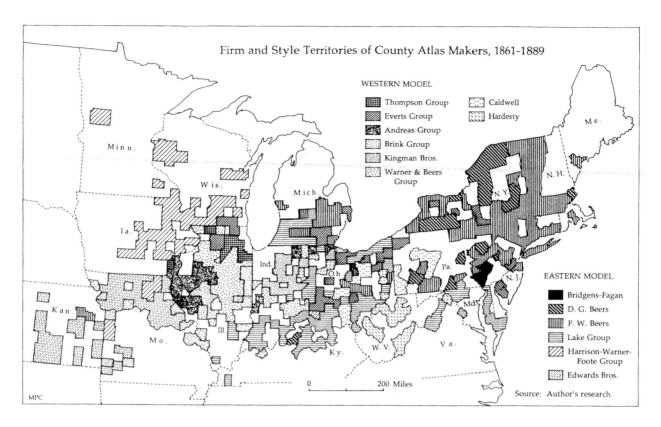

FIGURE 161 *Regional mosaic of entrepreneurial coverage: firm and style territories of county mapmakers, to 1889.*

tion publication, people had to be pressed into purchasing it. Once they owned one of their county, the immediate market was used up, and the publishers could only survive by pressing on into "unatlased" regions. Thus, while the Beers' atlases had largely exhausted the northeastern states by 1876, the genre was able to continue by serving markets along the margins of the Great Plains and south of the Ohio River, until the fertile fields of counties with prosperous yeomen and small-town merchants ran out. (See Figure 145.)

There was another sign, however, that the bubble could not last. The nation's centennial in 1876 brought forth a presidential suggestion that communities everywhere could fittingly observe the nation's anniversary by organizing the publication of local histories.[56] To what extent this idea had its origins in the splashy county atlases, which by the end of 1875 numbered around 300 nation-wide, requires further study. Atlases that gave only limited space to the facts of local history were obviously not the only form that such histories could take. To be sure, town, county, and city histories without maps or elaborate illustrations already existed in a number of localities. What is incontrovertible, however, is the fact that 1876 marks a distinct slackening in the production of county atlases—indeed an emphatic halt in well-worked areas—and a conspicuous turn to mass-produced county history books without maps. The call for local history was answered by not a few local historical societies, county commissioners, and assorted amateurs, but they were soon far outpaced by large metropolitan firms that compiled formulistic histories, many hundreds of pages in length and often padded with reprintings in full of state laws, constitutions, presidential lives, and the like, that were produced to cash in on the wide interest and approbation. The majority of these firms were the atlas companies of the previous year.[57] Suddenly, maps were superfluous, sacrificed to the gods of verbosity (at half a cent a word for the personal biographies that were to swell the rear of the volumes!), and with this the publishers' chameleon became the mass-produced county history.

The illustrated county atlas enjoyed an amazing and brief period of unquestioned popularity between 1870 and 1876, but it did not vanish altogether. In fact it solidified a continuing role for county landownership mapping that has lasted to the present—if in vastly simpler form. The county atlas produced two mutations. One was its transformation into a "county history," the other its transformation into a "plat book." With some publishers, like Andreas, the change to text-only county histories was sharp and immediate.[58] With others, the detailed township maps and village plans disappeared, but the lithographic views and portraits remained, and even the nearly atlas-sized, physical format was retained, at least for a while. On the atlas side, some publishers such as Hardesty, Lake, B. N. Griffing, and a few others kept the illustrated atlas going well into the 1880s, while others such as Warner and Foote maintained the more spartan "eastern model" county atlas right through the end of the century. It was this company, in fact, that since 1878, had quite accurately named their volumes "plat books" rather than atlases.[59] By the 1890s, George A. Ogle had joined their ranks, having apprenticed briefly with Warner and Foote in Minneapolis in the late 1880s, and his innovation was to give the plat books of his mentors a thoroughly professional orientation and appeal to that rising corps of county officials—assessors, engineers, judges, recorders, and surveyors, as well as the contractors, bondsmen, and insurers with whom they did business—all of whom could use accurate local geographical information in readily accessible cartographic form. Ogle's "standard atlases" fostered what can be termed the "neo-professional" period of county atlas production, but this period ushers in developments reflecting new dynamics and requires another context for interpreting their true economic and cultural meaning.[60]

THE INTERPLAY OF ATLAS TYPES IN THEIR SOCIAL CONTEXT

Commercial cadastral mapping on a regional scale, as represented in these county atlases, is a genuinely American historical achievement. Mapping of landownership at the county level was attempted in no other country so early in the modern industrial era, and even later not under private aegis. Its prodigious development in the United States and Canada can be attributed to the demands for business-related information on landholding that speculators, developers, and

44 This first appeared on the *Map of Jackson County, Iowa* (Geneva, Illinois: Thompson and Everts, 1867).

45 These are examined in Conzen, "County Landownership Map in America," pp. 17–19.

46 Regan, *Beers Family*, ibid., p. 112; *Commemorative Biographical Record of Fairfield County, Connecticut* (Chicago: J. H. Beers and Company, 1899), pp. 990–992.

47 It is unclear whether Andreas was influenced by Augustus Warner's 1869 Coles County atlas, given the even earlier midwestern atlas experiments already noted. More tellingly, Andreas's atlases were different from the outset.

48 For a full treatment of this development, see Michael P. Conzen, "Maps for the Masses: Alfred T. Andreas and the Midwestern County Atlas Trade," in *Chicago Mapmakers: Essays on the Rise of the City's Map Trade*, edited by Michael P. Conzen (Chicago: Chicago Historical Society for the Chicago Map Society, 1984), pp. 47–63.

49 Full details of his financial experiences are given in Conzen, "Maps for the Masses," ibid.

50 On the county atlas trade in Ontario, see Lillian R. Benson, "The Illustrated Historical Atlases of Ontario, with Special Reference to H. Belden & Co.," in *Aspects of Nineteenth-Century Ontario: Essays Presented to James J. Talman*, edited by F. H. Armstrong et al. (Toronto: University of Toronto Press, 1974), pp. 267–277.

51 From the *Prospectus* of Messrs. Beers & Co. for an illustrated historical work about Johnson County, Indiana, printed in full in the *Franklin Democrat*, January 30, 1880, as quoted in John V. Bergen, "Maps and Geographical Data in Johnson County History: Principal Publications Relating to 19th Century Johnson County, Indiana," in *Atlas of Johnson County Indiana, 1820–1900*, compiled and edited by John V. Bergen (Franklin, Indiana: Johnson County Historical Society, 1983–1984), p. 335.

52 Editorial in the *Franklin Democrat*, January 7, 1881, as quoted in Bergen, ibid., p. 336.

53 Following his triumphal superintendency of Andreas's great Minnesota state atlas. See Walter W. Ristow, "Alfred T. Andreas and his Minnesota Atlas," *Minnesota History* 40 (1966): 120–129; and Conzen, "Maps for the Masses," p. 54.

54 Caldwell appears as a teacher, aged 23, in his father's farm household in the 1860 Federal Census of Ohio, Manuscript schedule, Trenton Township, Delaware County, p. 88.

55 See [Harrington] *How 'Tis Done*, pp. 55–76; and Conzen, "Maps for the Masses," pp. 53–58.

56 Kammen, "American Revolution Bicentennial and the Writing of Local History," p. 187.

57 Andreas has been credited with being possibly the first entrepreneur to grasp the commercial potential of the "packaged" county history. He created and headed H. F. Kett and Company, the earliest of the "assembly line" local-history publishing firms,

and its successor, the Western Historical Company. See Conzen, "Maps for the Masses," pp. 58–60. Other publishers who made the transition from atlases to histories included L. H. Everts, Thompson and West, W. R. Brink, H. R. Page, Howard Belden, J. H. Beers, the Kingman brothers, O. L. Baskin, D. J. Stewart, D. W. Ensign, F. W. Beers, and H. H. Hardesty. On Brink, see Raymond and Betty Spahn, "Wesley Raymond Brink, History Huckster," *Journal of the Illinois State Historical Society* 58 (1965): 117–138. The Spahns describe Brink's shift to county histories, but failed to see its general import. The atlas origins of the most prolific county history publishers will be treated in more detail in the author's forthcoming monograph.

58 In his case bankruptcy encouraged a complete redefinition of his business interests and his visible product. See Conzen, "Maps for the Masses," p. 58.

59 Beginning with their "plat books" of Houston and Olmsted Counties, Minnesota.

60 An outline of this altered phase is offered in Conzen, "County Landownership Map in America," pp. 23–26.

PART FOUR

Atlases of the Late Nineteenth and Twentieth Centuries: The Future of the Atlas

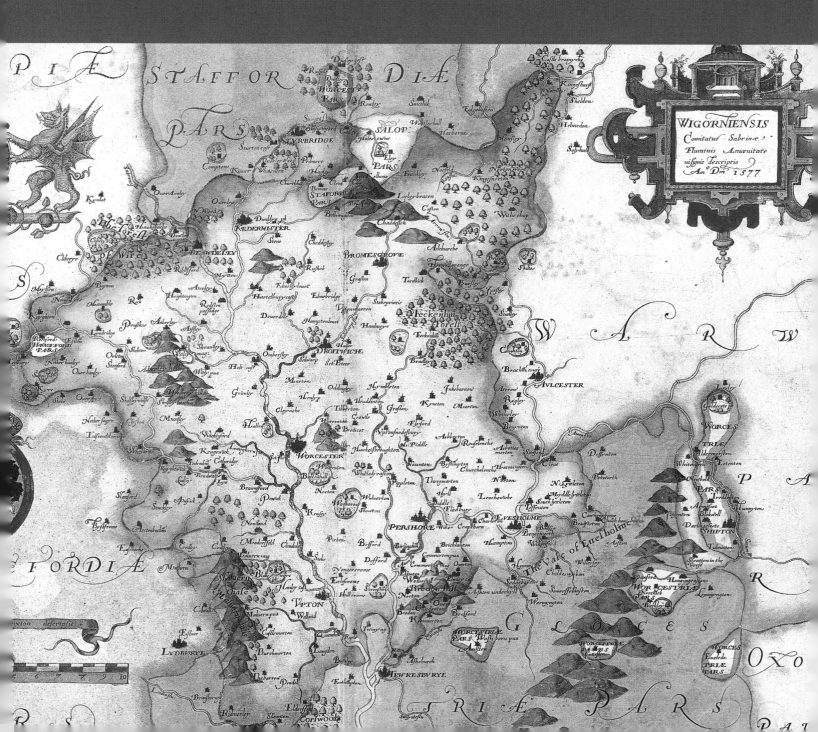

The Rise of the National Atlas*

MARK MONMONIER

The national atlas is largely a twentieth-century phenomenon. Yet the informational roots of the generally comprehensive, officially sanctioned single-country atlas would appear to lie in the development, principally during the nineteenth century, of national surveys and scientific and other scholarly societies that promoted the systematic collection of topographic and geographic information upon which a national atlas is based. Indeed, the national atlas may be viewed as the inevitable systematic publication of institutionally collected geographic knowledge. The national atlas also plays a second, and perhaps more important, role as a symbol of nationhood, national unity, or national pride. The roots of this iconic function extend deep into the sixteenth century, when advances in printing made the atlas practicable as a national symbol.

A PROBLEM OF DEFINITION

An attempt to trace the rise of the national atlas is confounded by the need to define what a national atlas is, and what it is not. Not every volume with "national atlas" in its title merits consideration, and not every atlas worth considering advertises itself as "national." The most often cited criteria are presented in the 1960 report of the International Geographical Union's Commission on National Atlases, chaired by Prof. K. A. Salichtchev.[1] According to the Salichtchev Commission, a national atlas would do the following:

1. Cover a single country, or nation.
2. Provide a variety of thematic maps based on scientific data and covering the physical, economic, demographic, and cultural-historical geography of the country.
3. Receive the enthusiasm and support of the nation's scientific organizations and government agencies.

*   This paper was previously published in *Cartographica* 31 (1994): 1–15.

map was considered by one reviewer as "extraordinarily effective" and in close agreement with a map of the value of agricultural raw material.[42] Its title page proudly announces that the *Atlas* was presented to the International Geographical Congress, held in 1928 at Cambridge, where its editor, Hussein Sirry Bey, also delivered a paper on "The New Atlas of Egypt."[43]

The title page also clearly announces the existence of the atlas (see Figure 175) "by command of his majesty, King Fouad I" and omits any reference to continued ties to Britain, which administered Egypt as a protectorate from 1914 to 1922, and stationed troops there until the Anglo-Egyptian treaty of 1936. Yet in the late 1920s, the Survey of Egypt still employed a number of British subjects in influential positions. Non-Egyptians compiled the orographic, geologic, meteorological, and economic maps, and shared editorial responsibility with Egyptians. The postcolonial influences that underlie the splendid cartography might not have been completely beneficial. According to the Salichtchev report, the *Atlas* neglects irrigation and other topics important to economic development, and omits maps of commerce, finance, cultural problems, and other subjects "likely to be embarrassing to colonialism and feudalism."[44]

Yet, a decade later, the *Atlas of Egypt* must have been of great value to the country's German and Italian invaders. In the era before satellite remote sensing, a

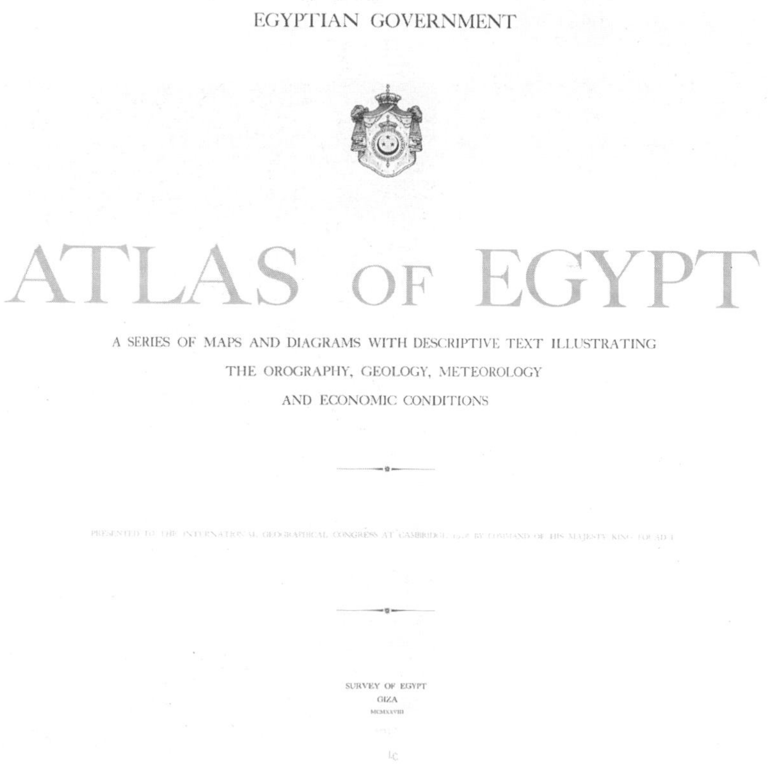

EGYPTIAN GOVERNMENT

ATLAS OF EGYPT

A SERIES OF MAPS AND DIAGRAMS WITH DESCRIPTIVE TEXT ILLUSTRATING
THE OROGRAPHY, GEOLOGY, METEOROLOGY
AND ECONOMIC CONDITIONS

SURVEY OF EGYPT
GIZA

FIGURE 175 *Title page of the* Atlas of Egypt *(1928). Library of Congress.*

comprehensive, detailed national atlas could be as much a military liability in the hands of any enemy during war as an asset for its citizens during peace.

Perhaps the most militarily sensitive national atlas was the *Bolshoi Sovietsky Atlas Mira* (Great Soviet Atlas of the World), begun in 1933 by a decree of the Central Executive Committee requiring the cooperation of all scientific institutions.[45] (See Figure 176.) This monumental work, which involved a staff of 175 cartographers, was divided into two volumes, published in loose-leaf binders in 1937 and 1939, respectively. Volume I consisted of eighty-three plates containing over 100 world and continent maps and eighty-five plates of almost 100 maps addressing the Soviet Union, European Russia, and other important subregions. Symbolic of Marxist ideology, economic themes predominated, but the *Great Atlas* more than adequately addressed physical and historical geography. Its detailed two-page 1:15,000,000-scale politico-administrative map included a chart portraying the complex Soviet system of administrative regions. American

ПРОЛЕТАРИИ ВСЕХ СТРАН, СОЕДИНЯЙТЕСЬ!

БОЛЬШОЙ

СОВЕТСКИЙ

·АТЛАС

МИРА

FIGURE 176 *Title page of Volume I of the* Great Soviet Atlas of the World *(1937).* *Library of Congress.*

I

МОСКВА

1937

26 See Herman R. Friis, "Statistical Cartography Prior to 1870," pp. 130–131; and Fulmer Mood, "The Rise of Official Statistical Cartography in Austria, Prussia, and the United States, 1855–1872," *Agricultural History* 20 (1946): 209–225. Mood describes Meitzen's atlas and the several forms in which it was published between 1869 and 1871 (ref. pp. 213–216).

27 Mood, "Rise of Official Statistical Cartography," pp. 216–217.

28 Edwards disputes Mood's charge. See Edwards, "Walker's 1870 *Statistical Atlas*," pp. 26–37.

29 Société de géographie de Finlande, *Atlas de Finlande* (Helsingfors: F. Tilgman, 1899).

30 Hugh Robert Mill, "Finland and Its People," *Geographical Journal* 15 (1900): 145–149.

31 "Review of *Finland As It Is*, by Harry de Windt (London: John Murray, 1901)," *Geographical Journal* 18 (1902): 274.

32 International Geographical Union, Commission on National Atlases, "National Atlases," pp. 3–5.

33 A brief editorial comment precedes a review reprinted from *Revue Générale des Sciences*. See Gustave Regelsperger, "The Atlas of Finland: A Model Geographical Work of a Little Known but Interesting Country," *Scientific American Supplement* 78 (October 3, 1914): 218–219.

34 J. G. Bartholomew, *The Survey Atlas of Scotland* (Edinburgh: Edinburgh Geographical Institute, 1912). Also see "Atlas of Scotland," *Scottish Geographical Magazine* 27 (1911): 263; and "The Survey Atlas of Scotland," *Scottish Geographical Magazine* 28 (1912): 381–382.

35 *A Survey Atlas of England and Wales*, designed by and prepared under the direction of J. G. Bartholomew. (Edinburgh: John Bartholomew and Co., 1903). Also see E. A. Reeves, "Survey Atlas of England and Wales," *Geographical Journal* 25 (1935): 82–83.

36 *Atlas of Canada*, prepared under the direction of James White (Toronto: Department of the Interior, 1906).

37 Richard Groot, "Canada's National Atlas Program in the Computer Era," *Cartographica*, monograph no. 23 (Toronto: University of Toronto Press, 1979), pp. 41–52.

38 Daniel S. C. Mackay, "James White: Canada's Chief Geographer, 1899–1909," *Cartographica* 19 (Spring 1982): 51.

39 "Atlas of Canada," *Scottish Geographical Magazine* 23 (1907): 448.

40 Postcolonial and other national atlases supported with technical assistance to a developing country might reflect the political objectives of the technically superior nation as well as economic topics such as plantation agriculture of particular concern to foreign investment capital. See Leont'yev, "National Atlases," pp. 114–116.

41 *Atlas of Egypt: A Series of Maps and Diagrams with a Descriptive Text Illustrating the Orography, Geology, Meteorology, and Economic Conditions* (Giza: Survey of Egypt, 1928). In the early nineteenth century, Egypt was the scene of one of the more inten-

sive colonial-mapping efforts, under Napoleon Bonaparte. A cartographic product that long survived Napoleon's defeat in 1801 was the skillfully prepared *Atlas de l'Egypte*, published in 1828. See Anne Godlewska, "Conquest and Cartography: The Napoleonic Mapping of Egypt," *The Map Collector*, no. 24 (September 1983), pp. 2–9.

42 Eugene Van Cleef, "The Atlas of Egypt," *Geographical Review* 19 (1929): 342–343.

43 Hussein Sirry Bey, "The New Atlas of Egypt," *Proceedings*, Twelfth International Geographical Congress, Cambridge, 1928, pp. 105–107.

44 International Geographical Union, Commission on National Atlases, "National Atlases," p. 8.

45 *Bolshoi Sovietskiy Atlas Mira* (Great Soviet Atlas of the World), directed by V. E. Motylev (Moscow: Scientific Editorial Institute of the Great Soviet World Atlas, volume I in 1937 and volume II in 1939).

46 George B. Cressey, "First Volume of the Soviet World Atlas," *Geographical Review* 28 (1938): 527–528. Cressey also lamented the lack of an English translation of titles and legends, and vowed to "see that something is made available in mimeographed form." He fulfilled this promise; see *Great Soviet World Atlas, Volume I* (titles and legends only, in English), translated by Andrew Perejda and Vera Washburne under the direction of George B. Cressey (Ann Arbor, Mich.: Edwards Brothers, 1940).

47 Leonard S. Wilson, "Present Status of 'The Great Soviet World Atlas' in the United States," *Annals of the Association of American Geographers* 37 (1947): 67–72. The Soviet effort to recall the atlas was apparently highly effective. A 1944 review praising volume I maintained that volume II was not yet published. See "The Great Soviet World Atlas," *Scottish Geographical Magazine* 59 (1944): 105.

48 This observation appeared in the *Geographical Review*, which had reviewed a number of national atlases, starting with the *Geographical and Statistical Atlas of Poland* (1916, 1921) in 1921. See "National Atlas of Italy," *Geographical Review* 30 (1940): 340–342. No author is identified.

49 This list is based on a review article by the map curator at the American Geographical Society. See Ena L. Yonge, "National Atlases: A Summary," *Geographical Review* 47 (1957): 570–578. Yonge refers to fourteen national atlases reviewed previously in the *Geographical Review* and provides a cursory assessment of several others. She mentions atlases in preparation in Canada, Israel, and New Zealand, and includes the loose-leaf national atlas begun for the United States in 1956 by the National Academy of Sciences. To her list of twenty-six national atlases, the author has added the first edition of the *Atlas of Canada* (1906).

50 J. Drecka, H. Tuszynska-Rekawek, and Stanislaw Leszczycki, *National Atlases: Sources, Bibliography, Articles* (Warsaw: Institute of Geography, Polish Academy of Sciences, 1960). The bibliography of 130 single-country atlases includes thirty-six atlases designated by an asterisk as appearing to meet the essentials of the criteria established by the Salichtchev Commission. Leszczycki, under whose direction the bibliography was compiled, was a member of the Commission. The preface mentions

the small number of atlases "corresponding fully" with the Commission's criteria, but asserts that ". . . the authors of this bibliography came to the conclusion that it was perhaps worth while to include some other atlases which have certain features in common with those of the national atlases, and can—in a way—form substitutes for them" (p. 5).

51 The list is a xeroxed collection of facsimiles of cards in the catalog of the Geography and Map Division of the Library of Congress. It was compiled by Patrick E. Dempsey, and is dated May 21, 1980. To the eighty-two national atlases in the list, the author has added the *Atlas of Egypt* (1928).

52 Membership in the United Nations, for example, has risen from 51 in 1945 to 151 in 1978. United Nations, Department of Public Information, *Everyone's United Nations*, 9th ed. (New York: United Nations, 1979), p. 7.

53 The data for the cumulative-frequency graph reflect reviews of atlases, not atlases reviewed; a comparative review of two national atlases, for example, would be counted twice. The compilers apparently canvassed geographical journals in Polish libraries and selected only "critical reviews," not mere announcements. See Drecka, Tuszynska-Rekawek, and Leszczycki, *National Atlases*, p. 4. The author has not attempted to verify the completeness of this list. A number of early reviews not in the list have been encountered.

54 A historical-bibliographic analysis of cartographic books, journals, and bibliographic aids indicates that "cartographic literature in all formats has been increasing at an exponential rate." See John A. Wolter, "The Emerging Discipline of Cartography" (Ph.D. diss., University of Minnesota, 1975), p. 281.

55 The map reflects nine published atlases and nine atlases "in production," including the loose-leaf *National Atlas of the United States* begun in 1956. Also included, but barely visible, is Israel. It was compiled from a map and discussion in Union Geographique Internationale, *Atlas Nationaux*, pp. 50–53. The map omits eleven atlases identified in the IGU report as "in preparation." The base map for figures 179 and 180 shows international boundaries recognized for the late 1970s.

56 Countries with national atlases, but barely visible on the map because of their small size include Denmark, Costa Rica, Cuba, Honduras, Panama, Salvador, Israel, and the Philippines.

57 Countries with national atlases, but barely visible on the map because of their small size include Denmark, Luxemburg, Israel, Malaysia, Lebanon, the Philippines, the Bahamas, Jamaica, Guatemala, British Honduras, and Cuba. Included in the Library of Congress list but preempted on the map by the symbol for the larger nation are national atlases for Latvia and Wales.

58 Edward Imhof, ed., *Atlas der Schweiz* (Wabern-Bern: Eidgenössischen Landestopographie, 1965–1978).

59 James R. Anderson, "The National Atlas of the United States of America," *Cartographica*, monograph no. 23 (Toronto: University of Toronto Press, 1979), pp. 35–39.

60 Irish National Committee for Geography, *Atlas of Ireland* (Dublin: Royal Irish Academy, 1979).

61 Harold Carter and H. M. Griffiths, eds., *National Atlas of Wales* (Cardiff: University of Wales Press for the Social Science Committee, Board of Celtic Studies, University of Wales, 1980).

62 Norman Nicholson considers the 1960s and 1970 the "age of regional atlases," in contrast to the "age of national atlases" during the 1920s and 1930s. See N. L. Nicholson, "The Evolving Nature of National and Regional Atlases," *Bulletin*, Geography and Map Division, Special Libraries Association, no. 94 (December 1973), pp. 20–25, 63.

63 For example, an announcement of a 1957 Executive Order authorizing a standard series of thematic sheets produced by Federal agencies maintains that ". . . the United States has never had a national atlas . . ." See "National Atlas of the United States," *Bulletin*, Geography and Map Division, Special Libraries Association, no. 28 (April 1957), p. 9. The editor of the later, successful effort acknowledged the loose-leaf National Atlas initiated during the 1950s but made no mention of Walker's work. See Arch C. Gerlach, "The National Atlas of the United States of America," *The Cartographer* 2 (May 1965): 35–36. Obviously Salichtchev alone cannot be faulted for having overlooked the 1874 *Statistical Atlas*.

64 Mark S. Monmonier, "DIDS: A De Facto National Atlas," *Bulletin*, Geography and Map Division, Special Libraries Association, no. 132 (June 1983), pp. 2–7.

Twentieth-Century Children's Atlases: Social Force or Educational Farce?

HENRY W. CASTNER

INTRODUCTION

Research in cartographic communication has increased our concern in map design for factors relating to map users: their information needs; their experience; the ways in which they process graphic images; and so forth. As a result, we have developed a rich vocabulary to describe the various levels of map use. Distinctions are made between map viewers, map readers, map users, and map percipients[1] and between the processes of map reading, map analysis, and map interpretation.[2] These three processes are of particular interest in this paper. Simplistically, map reading involves using a map as one uses a dictionary—to look up some particular piece of information. Map analysis involves breaking down the map image through map reading in such a way that it is possible to describe it and to generate new information from it. Then, and only then, can map interpretation apply to that description other information that gives it meaning.

Presumably, in cartographic and geographic education, we wish to train students in all these aspects and levels of map use, whether they are using "manuscript,"[3] printed, or electronic images. From an examination of a sample of twentieth-century-printed children's atlases, many held in the Library of Congress, an assessment has been made of how these educational materials have historically addressed these various educational goals. In other words, how children's atlases have introduced mapping and, to a lesser extent, geographic concepts to children.

BACKGROUND

Certainly the reference sections of atlases implicitly ask young children to look up a variety of things. It would be regrettable if the impression were given that

that is all one can do. There is also some evidence that we assume children are capable of interpretative activities. For example, this quote from 1922 is typical.

These maps show surface temperatures for January and July; . . . isobars and prevailing winds . . . the winter six months of rain . . . the summer six months of rain; the annual precipitation; the natural vegetation; a relief map showing the great plains and the great highlands; and, finally, a population density map. In this series the student can read *[my emphasis] lessons in cause and effect; for example, from hot summers and scant rain, to deserts and sparse human occupation . . . In short, all sorts of geographic causal relations can be read out of this series of maps, a valuable series in the fundamentals of geography.*[4]

I suggest that children can only do this if they have considerable additional information at their disposal. Then these maps may illustrate something we already know: The causal relations are not self-evident in the graphic images themselves. More succinctly and twenty-eight years later from the same publisher, we read:

To read a map well, you have to do more than know the different map symbols . . . You must be able to visualize things for which the symbols stand . . . After you have learned to read maps very well, you can imagine what a shore line is like at any particular place.[5]

To illustrate, a typical atlas plate often provides information on economic activities in the form depicted in Figure 182.[6] With study, it is probably obvious that there is a relationship between the occurrence of the two fish-processing plants and the fact that commercial fishing takes place in most of the surrounding lakes. However, the occurrence of the gold, silver, and copper mines has nothing to do with any other factors shown on this map or on any other map in the atlas. Neither the position of the Canadian shield nor the structural geology in this area is shown. Thus, we can easily question students on where there are such mines, but not why they are there, unless we assume that the children in the classroom (the map users) have the requisite experience to supply the necessary geologic information with which to address the "why" questions.

Another plate in the same atlas shows patterns of land use in several Canadian cities by categories of residential, commercial, industrial, institutional, transportation, and parks (including cemeteries).[7] For children in grades four to six, the intended users of this atlas, one wonders how they might go about comparing the shapes, sizes, or structures of these different cities. Certainly the relative

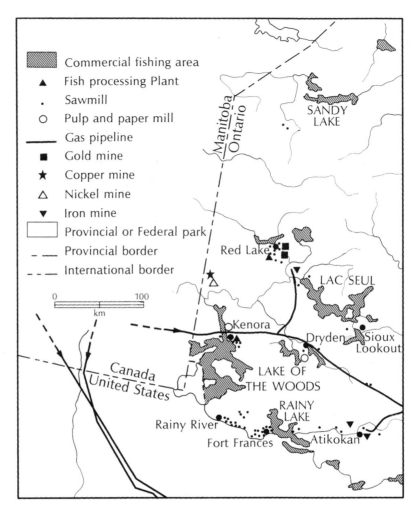

FIGURE 182 *Portion of a map of Northern Ontario after that from a children's atlas.*

sizes, shapes, and distances of the classed areas from the center of the city are significant dimensions describing the morphology of urban places. Can we expect children in these grades to have a command of these measurement procedures unless we provide them? The abstractness of the map classes would, in addition, probably make any analysis meaningless.

To those who have disciplined viewing habits or who already know the answer to an analytical question, a map pattern simply verifies what we already know—it is self-evident. In the case of an unfamiliar map (see Figure 183), we carefully follow the coastline, process the relative density of symbols, or sample the place-names, so as to match our analysis with other information or mental templates at our disposal. In this case, establishing the northwest-flowing river as the Angara, the delta as that of the Selenga, the small north-flowing rivers below the lake as evidence of the Krebet Khamar Daban, and observing the longer latitudinal than longitudinal extent are clues that help to identify the body of water as Lake Baikal in south central Siberia.[8] If the young map users do not have this other knowledge, or a sufficient inventory of geographic names and images in memory, then

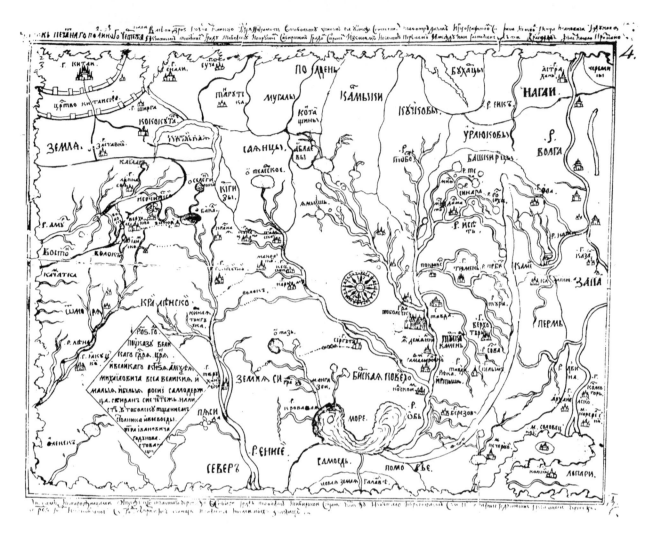

FIGURE 183 *Plate 145 from Remezov's* Khorograficheskaya Kniga *(1697).*
Houghton Library, Harvard University.

how can they possibly use the map in the same way we do? They may only be able to say that "it looks funny."

Thus, what may have been given relatively little attention in school atlases is the teaching of skills in map analysis. By this I mean the various ways in which we visually summarize or break down the graphic image. This may range from simply recognizing various shapes of, configurations or linkages to counting the number of, or measuring the extent of, certain map elements. These kinds of determinations are basic to building concepts of classification and regionalization; and to any teaching strategy that encourages hypothesis generation and testing. We have tended to make great claims about the accuracy and valid content of maps, but we have never made much of an attempt to help people deal with their structure and complexity or hidden biases.[9]

This concern with analysis comes at a time in our history when the computer is becoming more and more a part of cartography and education. Interesting comparisons can be made between a hand-drawn personalized collection of maps drawn at the end of the seventeenth century by Semyon Remezov, which includes the previous "unfamiliar" image of Lake Baikal (see Figure 183), and the modern electronic atlas, which is increasingly a part of the scene.[10]

Semyon Remezov was a district draftsman, land surveyor, and contractor in Tobol'sk, Western Siberia. He was under general orders to produce maps of the various Siberian townships and a general map of all Siberia. This meant that he had to collect materials that were available to him in Tobol'sk. He did this by pasting copies of maps into an oblong book, 30 by 195 cm, and cutting them where necessary to fit this format.[11] The book, known as the *Khorograficheskaya Kniga*, is held in the Houghton Library, Harvard University. It contains maps at various scales, mostly of river basins, which are undoubtedly copies of other maps previously brought to Tobol'sk.

Remezov continued to collect maps, for we know of two other collections: the *Chertezhnaya Kniga Sibiri*, now in the Lenin Library, Moscow; and the *Sluzhebnaya Chertyozhnaya Kniga*, held in the Leningrad Public Library. Except for the *Chertezhnaya Kniga Sibiri*, which was made specifically for A. A. Winius, the State Secretary at the *Sibirskyy prikaz*, all these maps were made for Remezov's own use and interest in fulfilling his mandate. Presumably he enjoyed this work for they are exquisitely drawn and beautifully rendered in pleasing colors and symbolization.

One can surmise, then, that their creation was aimed at collecting place information about Siberia for the day when he would once again be called upon to produce some special maps, such as the general map. Their design requirements, however, were minimal other than to provide the satisfaction gained from their execution. Presumably the technical skills employed by Remezov are no more sophisticated than those needed to *produce* pleasing graphics from the new electronic atlases. Further, and more important, the skills required in their *use* are not unlike those required in the use of their manuscript and printed predecessors. Thus we may have come full circle in terms of making information available in a personalized way. (See Figure 184.) While the form of the image will have changed, we are developing new computer systems that have among their most saleable qualities the opportunity for an individual to interrogate their associated data banks and create a personalized image, unique in its information content, symbolization, and design.

At this point, the distinction should be made between interrogation skills that arise out of the way information may be held in electronic storage, and those that are applied to the graphic image itself. The former set of skills has to do with data analysis, that is, asking the most revealing questions about the data sets. Their successful application would seem to depend upon an understanding of the possible interrelationships between the various and perhaps quite diverse components of information held in a data bank and upon skills in the application of

IV.

Typische Landschaft aus Oberösterreich.

Bad Ischl im Salzkammergut. Ausblick gegen NO. Im Vordergrunde das Kesseltal
von Ischl. Haupttal der Traun, Seitental am Mitter-Weißenbach. Bewaldetes Berg-
land. Kahle, steilwandige Felsenlandschaft des Höllengebirges im Hintergrunde.
Aufnahme Photoglob, Zürich.

FIGURE 188 *Two images of Bad Ischl from Rothaug's 1912* Geographischer Schulatlas *showing an oblique photograph above a map of the area at a scale of 1:100,000. The area in the photograph is depicted in the map in the lighter tones.*

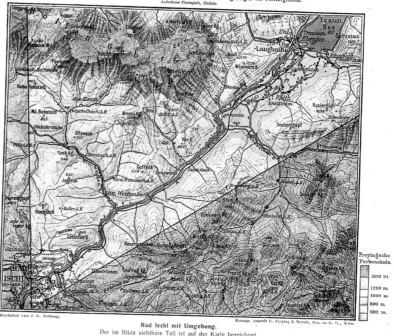

Bad Ischl mit Umgebung.
Der im Bilde sichtbare Teil ist auf der Karte bezeichnet.
Maßstab 1 : 100.000.

age in the distance than in the foreground. In addition, the problem of rotation[17] is illustrated by the comparison of the familiar and concrete oblique photograph with the abstract map constructed from a point of view overhead. No specific example of this comparative presentation was found in any of the sample atlases; a variation of the technique was used five times in one of the Provincial atlases in the comparative group.[18]

As was noted, an inordinate amount of attention seems to have been paid to projection theory, particularly on the derivation of different projections. In contrast, in the sample set, very little attention has been paid to aspects of projections that users need to evaluate when they interpret different maps. Figure 189, from an atlas of 1847, could be used as a tool to evaluate the relative distortion of areas on different map projections. In addition, if the squares are arranged to coincide roughly with their relative geographic positions, they would represent

VIEW OF THE COMPARATIVE MAGNITUDES OF THE OCEANS, SEAS, ISLANDS,
AND CONTINENTAL DIVISIONS OF THE GLOBE

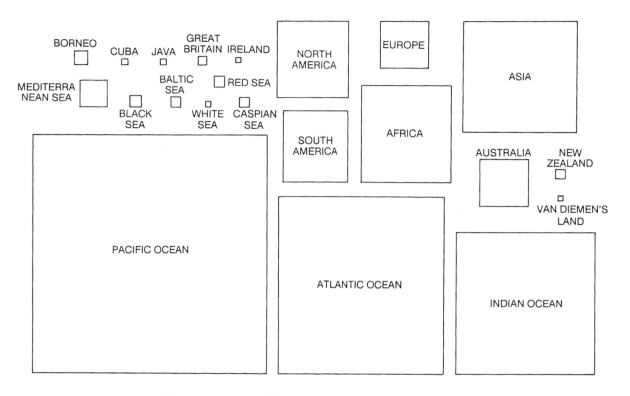

FIGURE 189   *The areas of the world's oceans, continents, and islands after an 1847 atlas.*[19]
Frontenac County Schools Museum, Kingston, Ontario.

the prototype cartogram. This would provide a useful transitional-educational step between projection theory and the mapping of behavioral or attitudinal regions that we associate with mental maps and behavioral geography. Another illustration from this same 1847 atlas (see Figure 190) provides an important example of projection use.[20] Centering a stereographic projection on both London and its antipode in the South Pacific suggests that projections can be usefully focused on any point on the earth, not just on those along the equator. The modest calculation of antipodal points is, in itself, a useful test of whether or not a student actually understands the mathematics of the system of latitude and longitude.

Telling students about the formal structure of maps (their conventional symbols, scale bars, north arrows and grids, for example) is not equivalent to teaching them what decisions went into the selection and placement of information on the map. Neither does it help them to know how to process the resultant complex graphic image in order to visualize all those things the teacher presumably sees in the map.

The Natural History of the Atlas: Evolution and Extinction*

BARBARA BARTZ PETCHENIK

". . . I could not help philosophizing that life will always remain a gamble, with prizes sometimes for the imprudent, and blanks so often to the wise."

—Jerome K. Jerome, *My Life and Times*

INTRODUCTION

The facts about the development of the atlas as a form in which spatial knowledge takes on substance are reasonably well known. What matters in looking at the future of the atlas, however, is not so much the evolution of the form but an understanding of the needs it has developed to meet. How this relationship between the atlas-producing and atlas-using elements of our culture has evolved, and what the future character of this relationship is likely to be is the subject of this paper.

---

* This essay was previously published in *Cartographica* 22 (1985): 43–59 along with two other related essays by the author, which were originally presented as talks at other conferences in 1984. Grouped together under the general title, "Value and Values in Cartography," the other two essays were "Maps, Markets and Money: A Look at the Economic Underpinnings of Cartography," pp. 7–19, and "Facts or Values: Basic Methodological Issues in Research for Educational Mapping," pp. 20–42.

between one-half and two-thirds of the adult driving population would, if they had a choice, prefer written itineraries or sets of driving instructions to maps when they need information to assist them in finding their way to a novel destination.

When we use almost any map, we can or do derive from it knowledge of distinctly different types, although we are probably not often conscious of this fact. In reading a road map, for instance, we are in fact, primarily trying to construct a set of verbal driving instructions—"I must go out on the Edens Expressway to the Lake Street exit, where I turn right," and so on. At another level some users (not all, as Thorndyke and Stacsz have shown clearly)[5] can acquire from a road map an overall image of the arrangement of routes and places such that in the future they have fewer needs to refer to specific directions, and (more important) new destinations can be found without much recourse to specific verbal information. In other words, maps serve as sources of specific facts or propositions, often verbal or numerical in form, and also as sources of comprehensive images, of arrangements and distributions.

Many maps are made without a clear recognition of this fact, and indeed I believe that some maps are not even made primarily to serve as knowledge sources of either type. To illustrate in concrete terms the great diversity of motives that can shape both the mapper's efforts and the user's queries, I will turn to a case study based on selected experiences from my 1970 to 1975 stint as cartographic editor of the *Atlas of Early American History*.

A Case Study: The *Atlas of Early American History*

The ostensible reason for creating the *Atlas of Early American History*,[6] as it is for virtually any atlas, was to fill particular needs for knowledge—that is, for cognitive consumption. The originator of the project, and ultimately editor in chief of the publication, Lester Cappon, had enjoyed a successful career as a teacher, author, editor, and archivist. As a historian, he had often felt personally the need for certain kinds of reference information that could best be obtained from maps, and so wanted to create an atlas. In order to do that, however, he first had to create the maps. Unlike some atlases, which are created utilizing a base of existing maps and data, this one had to be based on considerable original research.

The *Atlas* was conceived of as if it were the map equivalent of a history text, in essentially verbal terms, with verbal values. It was chiefly my responsibility to translate those terms and values into spatial representations, and into a coherent, high-quality exemplar of the category, historical atlas. In doing so, I learned what great differences in meaning are encompassed (and obscured) by the seemingly simple notion "map user needs"—an important phrase or theme in recent cartographic history, and an important concept in this assessment of the future. I also learned about the intrinsic shortcomings of printed maps in meeting such needs (however defined).[7] That experience can be used to demonstrate why I believe we need to conjecture about a future in which attempts to meet those needs no longer focus solely on the printed atlas.

Before proceeding to a specific example, we need to review briefly a few cartographic concepts that bear on the map-use problem. Working from a topical outline, as we were, and developing a set of virtually all-new maps (including primary-content research), there were few constraints on exactly what aspects of each abstract, verbal phenomenon or topic (e.g., Religion) we would map. This may sound ideal, but in fact choosing from many alternatives is never easy. In particular, I soon became painfully aware of how fundamental (and troublesome) were the notions of "application-specificity" and "application-neutrality" insofar as they must apply to maps, and of how ambiguous and nonrigorous is the common distinction between reference (or general) and thematic maps.[8] These two sets of notions commonly tend to be mingled in unexamined ways, and the situation becomes even less clear when the related but slightly different concepts of "inventory" and "message" maps developed by Bertin are introduced, as I believe it is useful to do.[9]

To make this vocabulary more comprehensible, we can look at a map that now exists in the *Atlas of Early American History*, "Religious Congregations in Massa-

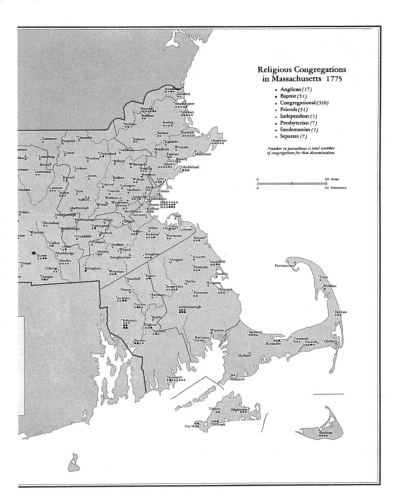

FIGURE 191 *"Religious Congregations in Massachusetts, 1775,"* Atlas of Early American History: The Revolutionary Era, *1760–1790 (Princeton: Princeton University Press, 1976). Library of Congress.*

chusetts, 1775."[10] (See Figure 191.) This full-page map is graphically straightfor-ward, showing every named location that had one or more religious congrega-tions. At each location there is a black dot pinpointing the named settlement, and then one or more colored geometric-point symbols identifying the denominations of each of the congregations that staff research showed existed there in 1775.

Once it was determined that there were enough historical data on congrega-tions to create this map, decisions had to be made on how to present it. Because this was an atlas, the form it took had to be a map—not necessarily the obvious alternative, when one realizes that all this place-attribute data (the topical com-ponent) could have been presented in a black-and-white table, or matrix, and place locations (the spatial component) could have been depicted on a consider-ably smaller, simpler, cheaper, black-and-white map.

Although the staff was not always explicitly aware of it, the general goal in cre-ating this map, as it was throughout the *Atlas*, was to map information as directly as possible, in the most application-neutral way. On the one hand, researchers wanted to avoid losing hard-won facts by classing observations or otherwise pro-cessing information, and on the other, they wanted each map to serve the great-est possible number of potential users.

Despite these goals, data loss and application-specificity were inevitable. In the process of doing research for this map, founding dates, congregation names, and other attributes were obtained but could not be put on the map. Similarly, by mak-ing the map design more or less application-neutral (that is, all denominations, congregations, and places were to be visually equal), no particular distribution took on visual form. In short, the data set from which the map was made contained much more potential for knowledge than could be obtained from the single pre-sentation form. Because of the considerable expense involved in creating a single, legible map in a printed atlas, that potential could not be fully realized.

It is difficult to classify such a map unambiguously. In conventional terms, it would tend to be called a thematic map, simply because we do not think of churches as base data. Yet there is no emphasis, conceptual or visual, on the struc-ture of a distribution, so in that sense it is not truly thematic. Using Bertin's ter-minology, it is an inventory map, useful for "look up" reference queries, not a message map conveying a striking concept or image. The same data could have been presented or designed differently; however, it is the nature of map *use* (and the potential for such use that the map provides) that is important in classifica-tion, not the map or the data per se.

The mapper, not the map user, is in control of the printed image, and there-fore, in control of the knowledge that can be gained from it. It is frustrating and futile to attempt to make decisions about map content and design for maps like this by asking what the user wants. It is likely that every user would approach the topic of religion in early Massachusetts history with different needs, and that a single map, even one that is intentionally application-neutral, would satisfy very few, if any, specific needs. The map does three things: it provides an inventory from which a user could conceivably structure a truly thematic or message map; it provides answers to some "look up" questions; and it presents a tidy image that might engender in a casual viewer a general sense of "knowing about Massachusetts churches in 1775." (See Figure 192.)

The issue to be addressed is not just cartographic, but involves value and values. This image was made at considerable expense, but it is probably safe to assume that the number of potential users is small, perhaps numbered only in the

FIGURE 192 *"A S.W. View of the Baptist Meeting House, Providence, R.I.," Massachusetts Magazine, 1 (August 1789). Library of Congress.*

hundreds. We have arrived at a point in the history of atlas making where enough general spatial information has accumulated so that newly printed products can only be increasingly specialized, application-specific, and limited in audience/ market potential. We must wonder whether it is wise to expend resources, skilled labor and money, in producing such documents that are relatively inflexible and user-limited. The *Atlas of Early American History* may represent the ultimate stage in the evolution of the atlas. The ecological niche of similar publications, a niche based on utility, may be disappearing. At the same time, technological developments are offering new alternatives for satisfying individual knowledge needs.

If we are indeed at the end of the atlas era, or even at the end of an era for selected kinds of atlases, the matter is of more than academic interest. Certainly at Donnelley we are concerned about our future in commercial, custom cartography (Donnelley produced the *Atlas of Early American History*), and what may be involved is the survival of cartography as we have known it.

ALTERNATIVES TO THE ATLAS: A UTILITY-BASED ANALYSIS OF AVAILABLE TECHNOLOGIES

Until now, the most efficient and useful forms in which spatial knowledge could be represented were maps and atlases. For the most part, these have been the only forms, regardless of users' needs and preferences. As we have shown with a few examples, however, these forms have limitations. Although not severe when information is scarce, they can become serious problems when information is abundant. Over the last several hundred years, spatial information has become abundant, and our society must find new ways of dealing with it. These ways do not simply include the creation and printing of ever greater quantities of ever more specialized maps and atlases. We are moving instead toward complementing or replacing these traditional tools with the products of a new tool—the digital computer. So far, cartographers have done little to try to characterize the virtues and limitations of computer technology insofar as the representation and use of spatial knowledge are concerned. Our interest in it originated primarily in a search for ways to facilitate traditional map production, but in the last few years we have realized how much more significant and pervasive its influence on our field might be.

The chief point to be made in this presentation is a limited one. It is probably a mistake to think that computer technology will have an equal impact on all map and atlas production and use. It is more suitable for meeting certain spatial knowledge needs than for others. For an analysis to be most functional, we need to distinguish more carefully than ever among different kinds of needs for spatial knowledge.

The most fundamental place and place-attribute mapping that occurs is usually conducted by governments, either for purposes of civil administration or for military reasons. The traditional product line, printed topographic and reference maps, also serves as primary data for various other derivative mapping efforts, such as commercial atlases, city maps, and the like.

In this domain, there was considerable impetus to make mapping more timely and map products more flexible, and only in this domain was funding available to support the very high cost of converting to an all-digital technology. As digital spatial data have accumulated, it is recognized that their utility goes well beyond serving as the grist for an improved mapmaking mill. Many questions formerly answered by using a topographic map can now be answered by querying a database directly, thereby eliminating the need for the intermediate image, the map. A series of questions about elevations, for example, does not need to involve imagery, and it will not, if answers can be obtained more efficiently from non-imaged data in a computer.

Furthermore, vehicles and weapons can be guided to destinations and targets directly from a database of earth surface elevations and features. The need for the intermediate map form is obviously eliminated from these applications. It is also easier to derive mental images of terrain from a series of pictures, generated directly from a database, than to obtain that same set of images by "reading" brown contour lines on topographic maps. In many military situations, maps as sources of spatial information will become entirely unnecessary.

The largest, most important commercial market for printed maps and atlases is that created by the needs of all kinds of motor vehicle drivers. As noted previously, the spatial knowledge needed to navigate successfully is twofold, and consists of driving instructions and images of street layout. The former are traditionally derived from maps, sometimes with considerable effort, but are not intrinsically or necessarily image-related. The latter are image-derived, but are not always essential nor preferred by many drivers. What is likely to happen is that the nonimaged on-demand itineraries will be derived eventually from digital databases. Map images will be reserved for "fallback" situations, where drivers depart from prepared itineraries (either intentionally or as when lost) or for the minority of the population which prefers to obtain and use comprehensive mental images of street arrangement as a basis for navigation.

Many of the "look up" needs the general public experiences and for which they now turn to printed reference atlases could as well be met by means of database queries, for example, "How far is it to Des Moines?" (and this is usually followed in everyday situations by "How do I get there?" which, as we have seen, can be answered satisfactorily without recourse to a map). Exactly how this nonmap reference market will develop depends partly on technological developments and partly on economics. Digital technology is not yet generally cost-effective, nor is it as widely available as printed maps and atlases are—but this can and very likely will change.

Small in quantitative terms but relatively important to the scholarly audience is the class of atlases described earlier, research/reference atlases like the *Atlas of*

Early American History. We must speculate about their future, and at the moment, I am most ambivalent about the future of printed products in this class. This ambivalence touches on some rather basic observations about the nature and history of mapping.

I have referred at several points to "look up" usage of maps and databases. The term is used to refer to specific questions about spatial information, either intrinsically nonimaged ("How far is it from Chicago to Los Angeles?"), or a combination of imaged/nonimaged ("Where is Berlin?"—the answer to this varying, depending on whether the user wants to know strictly in terms of distance from him, or where relative to an image of the European coastline), or completely imaged ("What does the world distribution of coniferous forests look like?"). For the most part it appears that such "look up" questions will be answered most efficiently (and probably most economically before long) by querying digital databases.

This situation will substantially erode, if not entirely eliminate, the need for printed maps and atlases. Electronic databases themselves are virtually application-neutral until a query is received, at which point the response is completely application-specific. They are updatable, flexible, and can search and custom-organize data in ways never before possible with printed information forms. Customers will pay only for data that are used, and storage space will no longer be a problem for users.

Currently, scholarly atlases (including maps in monographs, textbooks, and other research documents, as well as other special atlases such as national atlases) serve to meet "look up" needs, and often this is the only ostensible reason they are made—certainly this was true at the *Atlas of Early American History* project. However, there are other reasons atlases have been made, and it is difficult to envision ways that computer technology will improve upon or substitute for the printed documents that have been created for several hundred years.

Certain maps, and especially certain atlases, contribute more to human knowledge than just a set of specific spatial facts, however defined. Their very existence, for example, makes a statement about various values in a variety of situations. The success of county atlases in the nineteenth century, for example, was not just fact-based. Since they showed who lived where and who owned what acreage of land, their success was based on what they did for their purchasers' self-images. Those atlases served to confirm with concrete visible images the reality of ownership, possession, and control, even of being, itself—"I'm on the map, therefore I am."

Similarly, an atlas like the *Atlas of Early American History* provides a series of handsome, significant-looking images. They confirm the importance of early American history as a profession, the importance of our early national history, the reality of places and phenomena at a time which we cannot experience directly, and the permanence of a collective heritage. They can also stimulate and challenge.

State and national atlases are primarily important for similar reasons, not because many people use them to look up specific facts. All of the atlases described in this book originate not so much in the users' need to know as in the mappers' need to represent, display, and convey a point of view—artistic-emotional impulses, combined with certain cognitive goals.

Whereas the chief advantage of computer technology is its capability for providing unique, customized responses to individual demands, the chief advantage of the printed atlas is that it provides a fixed source of common images to be absorbed or even improved upon by the culture, with ultimate benefits such as shared values and a common intellectual vocabulary.

That printed atlases, by virtue of their inflexible form, impose unilaterally selected points of view and arbitrary depictions on users may even be seen as a powerful advantage, insofar as they focus attention on things. Certain kinds of information are still scarce and, consequently, valuable, but today—unlike 400 years ago—spatial knowledge is abundant, and excess rather than scarcity prevails in certain areas. As Simon points out, it is now attention, not information, that is the scarce resource: "In a world where attention is a major resource, information may be an expensive luxury, for it may turn our attention from what is important to what is unimportant. We cannot attend to information simply because it is there."[11]

This notion leads to the last situation to be considered: the use of maps and atlases in the process of children's formal education. Spatial meaning, like all other meaning, is fundamentally relational in nature. In order for children to become innovative adults, creating new relationships for themselves, they must be provided with certain conventions and fixed points of view that society has come to value and use. Just as they must learn conventional alphabets and grammar in order to synthesize novel utterances, they must learn to understand spatial facts in the form of traditional map images before they can utilize vast spatial databases effectively, to create images as well as other forms of spatial knowledge. They can hardly be expected to be able to spontaneously integrate the vast arrays of point data stored in a computer without knowing the ways such integration was accomplished by society in the past.

Furthermore, the more nebulous values associated with map images as described earlier are probably more important in the educational process than at any other time. There is a need for the widespread distribution of common images, not "on demand" but provided, even imposed, so that all children growing up in a society learn a common spatial vocabulary, and learn the value and utility of spatial knowledge in all its potential forms.[12]

CONCLUSION

As a society we are having entirely novel experiences with new technologies that will have a significant impact on the maps and atlases we have known. A new stage in an ongoing evolutionary process has begun; some products of the past may become extinct, others altered, and still others may flourish in surprising ways. There may be issues associated with these changes that we can actively address, where we can actively shape developments, while there will be others to which we can only respond passively. In either case, changes *will* occur in the future, and regardless of our vested intellectual or practical interests, we must prepare to function in that future.

NOTES

1   Denis Wood is the source for this general observation. It comes from a paper, "Now and Then: Comparisons of Ordinary Americans' Symbol Conventions with those of Past Cartographers," delivered at the Seventh International Conference on the History of Cartography, Washington, D.C., 1977.

2   This process is described and documented in Arthur H. Robinson, *Early Thematic Mapping in the History of Cartography* (Chicago: University of Chicago Press, 1982).

3   David Woodward, "The Techniques of Atlas Making," *The Map Collector*, no. 18 (March 1982), p. 5.

4   Wood, p. 36.

5   From approximately 1979 through 1981 cognitive psychologists, Perry W. Thorndyke and colleagues, at the Rand Corporation (Santa Monica, California) published a number of important studies describing how individuals acquire and process spatial information. See for example a Rand Corporation report, Perry W. Thorndyke and Cathleen Stasz, "Individual Differences in Knowledge Acquisition from Maps" (R-2375-ONR, January, 1979, a report prepared for Office of Naval Research), 43 pp.

6   *The Atlas of Early American History: The Revolutionary Era, 1760–1790* was created over a five-year project (1970–1975) based at the Newberry Library, Chicago, Illinois. Editor-in-chief was Lester J. Cappon, John Hamilton Long was assistant editor, and I was cartographic editor. The volume was published for the Newberry Library and The Institute of Early American History by Princeton University Press in 1976. Funding came from a great variety of sources; principal support was provided by the National Endowment for the Humanities.

7   My observations about this unusual experience with an unusual publication are recounted in, "Cartography and the Making of an Historical Atlas: A Memoir," *The American Cartographer* 4 (1977): 11–28.

8   Barbara Bartz Petchenik, "From Place to Space: The Psychological Achievement of Thematic Mapping," *The American Cartographer* 6 (1979): 5–12.

9   Jacques Bertin, *Semiology of Graphics*, trans. by William J. Berg (Madison: University of Wisconsin Press, 1983), p. 389ff.

10 *Atlas of Early American History*, p. 37.

11 H. A. Simon, "Rationality as Process and as Product of Thought," *American Economic Review* 68 (1978): 13, as quoted in Stephen Kaplan and Rachel Kaplan, *Cognition and Environment: Functioning in an Uncertain World* (New York: Praeger, 1982), p. 185.

12 Barbara Bartz Petchenik, "Facts or Values: Basic Methodological Issues in Research for Educational Mapping," *Technical Papers,* 7th General Assembly and 12th International Conference, International Cartographic Association. (Perth, Australia, 1984), pp. 788–803.

Contributors

HENRY W. CASTNER is Emeritus Professor of Geography, Queen's University, where he spent twenty-five years teaching and conducting research on map design and production, map perception, and most recently on the relationship between mapping and geographic education. This latter interest led to the publication in 1990 of *Seeking New Horizons: A Perceptual Approach to Geographic Education* by the McGill-Queen's University Press. He has also published two books on the history of Russian cartography, a children's study atlas of Ontario, and written on a variety of topics including tactual mapping, photomaps, tourist mapping, nautical charts, color charts, and maps in television news. Dr. Castner is a past president of the Canadian Cartographic Association and for 1994–1995 was president of the North American Cartographic Information Society. He is now living at 164 Fearrington Post, Pittsboro, NC 27312 where he continues his research and writing interests.

MICHAEL P. CONZEN is Professor of Geography at the University of Chicago. Educated at the Universities of Cambridge, Giessen, and Wisconsin, he has pursued broad interests in the historical geography of American settlement and urbanization, including the history of American commercial cartography. His books and edited works include *Frontier Farming in an Urban Shadow* (1971), *Chicago Mapmakers* (1984), *World Patterns of Modern Urban Change* (1986), *The Making of the American Landscape* (1990), and *A Scholar's Guide to Geographical Writing on the American and Canadian Past* (1993). He has published articles on American landownership mapping in *Imago Mundi*, *Agricultural History*, and *Chicago History*, and is currently completing a book-length study on the subject.

JOHANNES DÖRFLINGER was born on October 12, 1941, in Baden near Vienna (Lower Austria). He studied history and geography at the University of Vienna and taught history and geography in grammar school. In 1969 he received the Ph.D., and from 1970 was employed in the Department of History, University of Vienna. He achieved his Habilitation in 1980 for modern history.

Since 1989 he has been Professor of Modern History at the University of Vienna. He lectures on the history of cartography at the Universities of Vienna and Munich. His publications on the history of cartography include, with Robert Wagner and Franz Wawrik, *Descriptio Austriae: Österreich und seine Nachbarn im Kartenbild von der Spätantike bis ins 19. Jahrhundert* (Wien: Tusch, 1977); *Die österreichische Kartographie im 18. und zu Beginn des 19. Jahrhunderts unter besonderer Berücksichtigung der Privatkartographie zwischen 1780 und 1820*, 2 vols. (Wien: Österr. Akademie der Wissenschaften, 1984–1988); as editor with Ingrid Kretschmer and Franz Wawrik, *Lexikon zur Geschichte der Kartographie*, 2 vols. (Wien: Deuticke, 1986); and with Helga Hühnel, *Atlantes Austriaci*, part 1: *Österreichische Atlanten 1561–1918*, 2 vols. (Wien: Böhlau, 1995).

RONALD E. GRIM is currently Specialist in Cartographic History in the Geography and Map Division, Library of Congress. Prior to this appointment he served in a number of cartographic reference assignments including the head of the Reference and Bibliography Section in the Geography and Map Division and the assistant chief for Reference in the Center for Cartographic and Architectural Archives in the National Archives and Records Service.

He received a Ph.D. degree in historical geography from the University of Maryland, College Park, in 1977. His publications include *Historical Geography of the United States: A Guide to Information Sources* (Detroit: Gale, 1982), and co-editor, *World Directory of Map Collections*, 2d ed. (Munich: Saur, 1986), as well as numerous book reviews and articles in geographical, historical, and map librarianship serials and publications. He has curated three Library of Congress exhibitions: "ACSM Award Winners: Communication through Map Design" (1984); "World of Names: Celebrating the Centennial of the United States Board on Geographic Names" (1990); and "Deutsche in Amerika: Die Einwanderung im Kartenbild" (which opened in Dresden, Germany, September 1994).

J. BRIAN HARLEY (1932–1991) was Professor of Geography and Director of the Office for Map History of the American Geographical Society Collection in the Golda Meir Library, and a member of the faculty of the University of Wisconsin–Milwaukee since 1986. Prior to that he taught in the Universities of Exeter and Liverpool in the United Kingdom. He was a graduate of the University of Birmingham, receiving his Ph.D. in 1960 and the degree of Litt.D. in 1985 for his major published works.

Dr. Harley, a prolific author, was co-editor with David Woodward of the multivolume *History of Cartography* being published by the University of Chicago Press. His special research interest was in maps as ideological constructions. His most recent publication was *Maps and the Columbian Encounter*, an interpretive guide to an exhibition funded by the National Endowment for the Humanities.

He was a Fellow in the Center for Twentieth Century Studies, University of Wisconsin–Milwaukee.

MEI-LING HSU is Professor of Geography and Chair of the Department of Geography, University of Minnesota, Minneapolis, where she teaches courses and does research on cartographic design and communication, history of cartography, and population and urban development of China. She received her B.A. from National Taiwan Normal University, and her M.A. and Ph.D. from the University of Wisconsin, Madison. Her publications include: *Fidelity of Isopleth Maps;* and articles in the *Annals of Association of American Geographers, Cartography and Geographic Information Systems, Imago Mundi, International Yearbook of Cartography*, and *Urban Geography.*

CORNELIS KOEMAN was born August 19, 1918 in a village at the Zuiderzee in North Holland (province). He was a student in geodesy at the University of Technology at Delft during the years 1939 to 1946 and was also employed as a cartographic draftsman during the period 1938 to 1946. He served as assistant professor at the University of Technology at Delft until 1957. He founded and was the first incumbent of a chair of cartography at the University of Utrecht from 1958 to 1981 when he retired as Emeritus Professor of Cartography.

   He is the author of *Atlantes Neerlandici*, 5 vols. (1967–1971), a standard in the field of cartobibliography, and scores of books, articles, and reviews in the related fields of the history of cartography and surveying.

MARK MONMONIER is Professor of Geography at Syracuse University. He received a B.A. in mathematics from Johns Hopkins University in 1964 and a Ph.D. in geography from Pennsylvania State University in 1969. Before joining the geography faculty at Syracuse in 1973, Monmonier taught at the University of Rhode Island and the State University of New York at Albany. He has served as editor of *The American Cartographer* and as president of the American Cartographic Association. He received a Guggenheim Fellowship in 1984. He has published numerous papers on map design, automated map analysis, cartographic generalization, the history of cartography, statistical graphics, geographic demography, and mass communications, and is author of *Maps, Distortion and Meaning* (Association of American Geographers, 1977), *Computer-Assisted Cartography: Principles and Prospects* (Prentice-Hall, 1982), *The Study of Population: Elements, Patterns, Processes* (Charles E. Merrill, 1983; with George A. Schnell), *Map Appreciation* (Prentice-Hall, 1988; with George A. Schnell), *Maps with the News: The Development of American Journalistic Cartography* (Univ. of Chicago

Press, 1989), *How to Lie with Maps* (Univ. of Chicago Press, 1991), *Mapping It Out: Expository Cartography for the Humanities and Social Sciences* (Univ. of Chicago Press, 1993), and *Drawing the Line: Tales of Maps and Cartocontroversy* (Henry Holt, 1995). His current research projects include the development and refinement of computer-assisted methods to integrate maps and statistical graphics, and a book on the public-policy roles of hazard-zone maps.

MIREILLE PASTOUREAU served as Curator in the Département des Cartes et Plans in the Bibliothèque Nationale, Paris, from 1972 to 1994, where she was in charge of the early collections. In 1980, she completed her doctoral dissertation on the dynasty of French cartographers named Sanson d'Abbeville who flourished between 1630 and 1730. In addition to several articles and reviews on the history of cartography, she is the author of *Les Atlas français, XVIe–XVIIe siècles: répertoire bibliographique et étude*, published by the Bibliothèque Nationale in 1984. A subsequent volume on eighteenth-century French atlases is in preparation. She is also the author of *L'Atlas du monde de Nicolas Sanson d'Abbeville (1665)* (Paris: Editions Sand-Conti, 1988). She is currently Director of the Bibliothèque of the Institute de France, also in Paris.

BARBARA BARTZ PETCHENIK (1939–1992) integrated scholarly research interests in the nature of spatial knowledge and mapping with active participation in commercial cartography throughout her professional career. She was a Senior Sales Representative for R. R. Donnelley Cartographic Services, Mapping Services Division, and provided publishers in a wide variety of fields with high-quality custom-mapping capability and professional counsel since 1975.

From 1970 to 1975 she was Cartographic Editor, *Atlas of Early American History*, and from 1964 to 1970 was Cartographic Editor and Staff Consultant in Research and Design for *World Book Encyclopedia*. She held a B.S. degree in chemistry, and the M.S. and Ph.D. degrees from the University of Wisconsin in cartography and educational psychology.

Petchenik was co-author of *The Nature of Maps* (with Arthur H. Robinson) and contributed more than fifty articles, reviews, and essays to the professional literature, specializing in topics in map design, education, cognitive psychology and human factors, and computer-assisted vehicle navigation.

Petchenik was a member of the Mapping Science Committee, a National Academy of Sciences/National Research Council Committee advisory to all Federal mapping organizations; she was also the principal author of the Mapping Science Committee's 1990 report, "Spatial Data Needs: The Future of the National Mapping Program." Active in professional societies and organizations, she was also a vice president of the International Cartographic Association.

WALTER W. RISTOW was born in La Crosse, Wisconsin, in April 1908. He attended the University of Wisconsin–Madison from which he received a B.A. in Geography in 1931. He was awarded an M.A. in 1933 by Oberlin College and the Ph.D. in 1937 from the Graduate School of Geography, Clark University. From 1935 to 1937, he was instructor in Geography, Eastern Washington State College, Cheney, Washington. In September 1937, he was appointed head of Map Room and Chief of Map Division, New York Public Library, New York City. From 1942 to 1944, he also served as a civilian specialist in the U.S. Army Military Intelligence Service. He was appointed Assistant Chief in 1946, and was promoted successively Associate Chief and Chief of the Geography and Map Division, Library of Congress. He received the Library of Congress Distinguished Service Award upon retirement in 1978, after 32 years of service to the Library. Professional memberships include the American Congress on Surveying and Mapping (honorary and life memberships) and the Association of American Geographers, for which he served as national secretary, 1949 to 1950, and chairman, Middle Atlantic Division in 1951. He was active in other professional associations, and is the author of ten books and co-author and/or contributor to some twelve additional monographs. He is also author of some 125 articles in professional journals on the subjects of map librarianship, history of cartography, and the history of American cartography.

WOLFGANG SCHARFE was born in 1942, studied geography and mathematics, and was assistant at the Historical Commission, Berlin, 1967 to 1977. He has undertaken research on the history of cartography focusing on Brandenburg, Prussia, and Germany, as well as thematic and theoretical cartography. He has published extensively in the field. A lecturer since 1969, he was made professor in 1977, and since 1980 has been at the Cartographic Institute, Free University of Berlin. He has been chairman of the German working group "History of Cartography" since 1972, German member of the International Cartographic Association Standing Commission on the History of Cartography since 1973, and Vice President of the "Deutsche Gesellschaft für Kartographie," 1987 to 1989.

In 1979, he organized the 8th International Conference on the History of Cartography in Berlin (West), and since 1982 has been head of the biennial German-language colloquia on the History of Cartography (Bayreuth, 1982; Lüneburg, 1984; Vienna, 1986; Karlsruhe, 1988; Oldenburg, 1990; Berlin, 1992; Duisburg, 1994; Bern, 1996). His scientific research program on journalistic cartography, supported financially by the Deutsche Forschungsgemeinschaft, was terminated in 1993.

GÜNTER SCHILDER was born in Austria in 1942 and obtained his Ph.D. from the University of Vienna. At present he holds the Chair in the History of

Cartography at the University of Utrecht, The Netherlands. He is the author of numerous publications in the field of the history of cartography and discovery, among them *Australia Unveiled: The Share of the Dutch Navigators in the Discovery of Australia* (Amsterdam: Theatrum Orbis Terrarum Ltd., 1976); *Voyage to the Great South Land: Willem de Vlamingh, 1696–1697* (Sydney: Royal Australian Historical Society, 1985); *Wall Maps of the 16th and 17th Centuries: A Series of Full-size Facsimiles of Wall-maps Published in the Low Countries*, 4 vols. (Amsterdam: Nico Israel, 1977–1981); and *Monumenta Cartographica Neerlandica*, 4 volumes published so far (Alphen aan den Rijn: Canaletto, 1986–1993).

VLADIMIRO VALERIO, who was born in 1948, received his degree in architecture at the University of Naples in 1971. From 1972 to 1993, he was affiliated with the Istituto di Matematica della Facolta di Architettura di Napoli, attached to the chair of geometry as a research fellow. In 1993, he moved to the Dipartimento di Configurazione e Attuazione della Architettura.

Although his first studies were in the field of algebra and linear systems, his interest in the history of cartography dates from 1980, with particular emphasis on the scientific relevance of old maps and the study of the geometric structure of cartographic images. A work entitled "A Mathematical Contribution to the Study of Old Maps" was presented and published in the *Proceedings of the IX International Conference in the History of Cartography* (1985). He is also the author of several articles in the *Lexikon zur Geschichte der Kartographie* (Vienna, 1987). Other recent publications include *L'Italia nei manuscritti dell'Officina Topografica conservati nella Biblioteca Nazionale di Napoli* (Naples, 1985); *Catalogazione, studio e conservazione della cartografia storica* (Naples, 1987); and *Società, uomini e istituzioni cartografiche nel Mezzogiorno d'Italia* (Florence, 1993).

HELEN WALLIS (1924–1995) was the Map Librarian of the British Library from 1973 to November 1986. Previously, she was Deputy Keeper, 1967 to 1973, and Assistant Keeper in the Map Room, 1951 to 1967. Wallis was awarded an OBE in the Queen's Birthday Honours, 1986. Holder of the M.A., Ph.D. (Oxon), she was awarded Hon. Litt.D. from Davidson College, North Carolina, in March 1985. Elected Membre d'honneur of the Société de Géographie, Paris, in 1982, she was also awarded the gold medal of the British Cartographic Society in September 1988, the Distinguished Achievement Award of the Society of Woman Geographers in May 1990, and the Caird Medal of the National Maritime Museum, Greenwich, in June 1990. She served as president of the British Cartographic Society, 1972 to 74; chairman of the Standing Commission on the History of Cartography of the International Cartographic Association, 1976 to 1987; and President of the International Map Collectors' Society from 1986. She is a prolific author of articles, reviews, and monographs, which are listed in *The Map Collector*, no. 40 (Autumn 1987), pp. 30–38, and *Imago Mundi* 47 (1995):

188–192. Her books include *The Map Librarian in the Modern World: Essays in Honor of Walter W. Ristow*, ed. with Lothar Zögner (München, 1979); *Carteret's Voyage Round the World, 1766–1769* (2 vols., Cambridge: Hakluyt Society, 1965); *The Maps and Text of the Boke of Idrography presented by Jean Rotz to Henry VIII now in the British Library* (Oxford: The Roxburghe Club, 1981); and *Cartographical Innovations: An International Handbook of Mapping Terms to 1900*, with Arthur H. Robinson (Tring, Herts.: Map Collector Publications, in association with the International Cartographic Association, 1987); and *Historians' Guide to Early British Maps* (London: Royal Historical Society, 1994).

JOHN A. WOLTER served as Chief, Geography and Map Division, Library of Congress from 1978 to 1991, and as Assistant Chief from 1968 to 1978. On his retirement in August 1991, he was honored with the Library's Distinguished Service Award. A native of St. Paul, Minnesota, he is a graduate of the University of Minnesota from which he also received a master's degree in library science and Ph.D. in geography.

Active in professional societies and organizations, he served fourteen years as the Library's member of the U.S. Board on Geographic Names and as Board Chairman, 1981 to 1983. He also served three terms as a government representative to the U.S. National Committee for the International Geographical Union and is a past president of the Society for the History of Discoveries. The author of numerous articles and reviews in the fields of geography and cartography, he serves or has served on the editorial boards of several publications. His most recent publication is *Progress of Discovery, Johann Georg Kohl*, with Hans-Albrecht Koch and Margrit B. Krewson (Graz: Akademische Druck-u Verlagsanstalt, 1993).

DAVID WOODWARD came to the United States from England in 1964 to do his graduate work in geography and cartography at the University of Wisconsin under Arthur H. Robinson. From 1969 to 1980, he was at the Newberry Library, Chicago, in various curatorial and administrative capacities, including the directorship of the Hermon Dunlap Smith Center for the History of Cartography. He has been editor of the Kenneth Nebenzahl, Jr. Lecture Series and *Studies in the History of Discoveries*. He is now Arthur H. Robinson Professor of Geography at the University of Wisconsin–Madison, and a director of *Imago Mundi*. He is author of *The All-American Map*, numerous articles and book chapters, and editor of *Five Centuries of Map Printing*, *Art and Cartography*, and the *History of Cartography*, of which three volumes have appeared. Volume 2.1 received the Association of American Publishers' *Hawkins Award* for the best scholarly book published in 1992. He teaches introductory cartography, map design, and the history of cartography. The research for the topic addressed for this symposium was begun on a Guggenheim fellowship to Italy in 1977 to 1978.

Selected Bibliography

JOHN A. WOLTER AND RONALD E. GRIM

The hundreds of references cited in these essays constitute a relatively up-to-date bibliography for the time period and areas of concern for each author. However, it was felt that additional, and in some cases more general information was needed, particularly for those readers whose expertise is not in this field.

The Library of Congress Geography and Map Division has for several decades published cartobibliographies describing important parts of its collection. Of particular value in the study of atlases is the nine-volume *A List of Geographical Atlases in the Library of Congress, with Bibliographical Notes* (Washington, D.C., 1901–1992). The first four volumes were compiled under the direction of Philip Lee Phillips, first Chief of the Map Division. Four additional volumes were compiled by the Division's Bibliographer, Clara Egli LeGear. The ninth volume, a comprehensive author list for the 18,435 titles listed in volumes 1, 3, 4, 5, 6, and 7 was also compiled by Clara LeGear with the assistance of Ronald E. Grim and Kathryn L. Engstrom of the Division's Reference and Bibliography Section. Volume 9 is particularly interesting for its preface, which describes selected current atlas bibliographies. The introduction to volume 9 lays out in some detail the somewhat complicated history and structure of the entire set. It also includes a short biography of Clara LeGear and a chronological list of her publications. It must be noted that she finished compiling the last volume in her ninetieth year, an extraordinary achievement! Another atlas bibliography compiled by Clara LeGear that is still useful pertains to American atlases: *United States Atlases: A List of National, State, County, and Regional Atlases in the Library of Congress* (2 vols., Washington, D.C.: Library of Congress, 1950–1953).

Those readers who wish to pursue research on the history of the atlas should also examine the five volumes of the *Bibliography of Cartography* (Boston: G. K. Hall, 1973) and its two-volume *Supplement* (1980) for items of interest from the hundreds of references to articles, monographs, reviews, biographies, bibliographies, and other materials in several languages, to atlases and atlas making compiled for over a century by Division bibliographers. Though citations to current literature can be found in several publications, the most important and comprehensive is the *Bibliographia Cartographica,* published annually by the Staatsbibliothek zu Berlin under that title since 1974, but issued from 1957 to 1974 as the *Bibliotheca Cartographica.* A more select bibliography focusing just on historical citations is found in the bibliography section of *Imago Mundi, The Journal of the International Society for the History of Cartography,* which is also published annually.

Journals devoted to cartography, which currently number over sixty, also include many articles on various aspects of atlas history and publication. Lists of journals and bibliographies, and descriptions of their contents and areas of interest can be found in the articles by Wolter, Stevens, and Gilmartin. The following citations have been selected not only for their pertinence to the essays in this volume, but also to show the wide variety of materials (e.g., atlas catalogs, checklists, bibliographies, monographs, and articles) which are available for research into this fascinating area of cartography.

Akerman, James R. "On the Shoulders of a Titan: Viewing the World of the Past in Atlas Structure." Ph.D. dissertation, Pennsylvania State University, 1991.

Allen, Phillip. *The Atlas of Atlases: The Map Maker's Vision of the World: Atlases from the Cadbury Collection, Birmingham Central Library.* New York: Harry N. Abrams, 1992.

Atlases on Parade: Five Centuries of Map Books. Baltimore: Peabody Institute Library, 1964.

Badziag, Astrid and Petra Mohs. *Schulatlanten in Deutschland und benachbarten Ländern vom 18. Jahrhundert bis 1950: Ein bibliographisches Verzeichnis.* Munich: K. G. Saur, 1982.

Bagrow, Leo. *History of Cartography.* Revised and enlarged by Raleigh A. Skelton. 2d edition. Chicago: Precedent Publishing, 1985.

Blakemore, Michael J. and J. Brian Harley. "Concepts in the History of Cartography: A Review and Perspective." *Cartographica* 17, no. 4 (Winter 1980). Monograph 26.

Bosse, David. "A Canvasser's Tale." *The Map Collector,* no. 57 (Winter 1991), pp. 22–26.

Brown, Lloyd A. *The Story of Maps.* Boston: Little, Brown and Co., 1949.

Campbell, Eila M. J. "The Early Development of the Atlas," *Geography* 34 (1949): 187–195.

Chubb, Thomas. *The Printed Maps in the Atlases of Great Britain and Ireland: A Bibliography, 1579–1820.* London: Homeland Association, 1927.

Churkin, V. G. "Atlas Cartography in Pre-revolutionary Russia." In *Essays on the History of Russian Cartography, 16th to 19th Centuries.* Translated by James R. Gibson. Cartographica Monograph no. 13. Toronto: B.V. Gutsell, 1976.

Conzen, Michael P., Thomas A. Rumney, and Graeme Wynn, eds. *A Scholar's Guide to Geographical Writing on the American and Canadian Past.* University of Chicago Geography Research Paper no. 235. Chicago: University of Chicago Press, 1993. See especially "Historical Atlases and Map Series," pp. 183–195.

Dörflinger, Johannes. "The First Austrian World Atlases: Schrämbl and Reilly." *Imago Mundi* 33 (1981): 65–71.

——— and Ingrid Kretschmer, eds. *Atlantes Austriaci: kommentierter Katalog der österreichischen Atlanten von 1561 bis 1994.* Two volumes in three parts. Vienna: Böhlau, 1995.

Edney, Matthew H. "The *Atlas of India, 1823–1947:* The Natural History of a Topographic Map Series." *Cartographica* 28, no. 4 (Winter 1991), pp. 59–91.

Ehrenberg, Ralph E. *Scholar's Guide to Washington, D.C.: Cartography and Remote Sensing Imagery.* Washington, D.C.: Smithsonian Institution Press, 1987.

Engelmann, Gerhard. "Der Physikalische Atlas des Heinrich Berghaus: die kartographische Technik der ältesten thematischen Kartensammlung." *Internationales Jahrbuch für Kartographie* 4 (1964): 154–161.

———. "Der Physikalische Atlas des Heinrich Berghaus und Alexander Keith Johnstons Physical Atlas." *Petermanns Geographische Mitteilungen* 108 (1964): 133–149.

Espenhorst, Jürgen. *Andree, Stieler, Meyer & Co. Handatlanten des deutschen Sprachraums (1800–1945) nebst Vorläufern und Abkömmlingen im In- und Ausland. Bibliographisches Handbuch.* Schwerte: Pangaea Verlag, 1994.

Fullard, Harold. "The Problem of Communication between Editors and Users of Atlases." *Internationales Jahrbuch für Kartographie* 5 (1965): 187–193.

Gerlach, Arch C. "Problems in Atlas Making." *Internationales Jahrbuch für Kartographie* 5 (1965): 180–186.

Gilmartin, Patricia. "Twenty-five Years of Cartographic Research: A Content Analysis." *Cartography and Geographic Information Systems* 19 (1992): 37–47.

Gole, Susan. "An Early Atlas of Asia." *The Map Collector,* no. 45 (December 1988), pp. 20–26.

Grim, Ronald E. *Historical Geography of the United States: A Guide to Information Sources.* Detroit: Gale Research Co., 1982. See especially chapter 5, "Historical Atlases," pp. 53–67.

Harley, J. Brian and David Woodward, eds. *The History of Cartography.* Two volumes in three parts. Chicago: University of Chicago Press, 1987–1994.

Herbert, Francis. "The *London Atlas of Universal Geography* from J. Arrowsmith to E. Stanford, 1830s–1930s." *Imago Mundi* 41 (1989): 98–123.

Hinkel, Heinz. "Die Kartenbeschriftung als Gestaltungsmittel in Geschichtsatlanten." *Kartographische Nachrichten* 40 (December 1990): 221–226.

Hodson, Donald. *County Atlases of the British Isles Published after 1703: A Bibliography.* Vol. I: *Atlases Published 1704 to 1742 and Their Subsequent Editions* (Tewin, Welwyn, Hertfordshire: Tewin Press, 1984).

Horn, Werner. "Zur Geschicte der Atlanten." *Kartographische Nachrichten* 11 (1961): 1–8.

Joerg, Wolfgang L. G. "Post-War Atlases: A Review." *Geographical Journal* 13 (1923): 583–598.

Karrow, Robert. *Mapmakers of the Sixteenth Century and Their Maps.* Chicago: Speculum Orbis Press, 1993.

Koeman, Cornelis. *Atlantes Neerlandici: Bibliography of Terrestrial, Maritime and Celestial Atlases and Pilot Books Published in the Netherlands up to 1880.* 5 vols. Amsterdam: Theatrum Orbis Terrarum, 1967–1971.

———. *Atlantes Neerlandici.* Vol. 6: *Supplement to Volumes 1–5 and a Bibliography of the Geographical Atlases Published in the Netherlands between 1880 and 1940.* Alphen aan den Rijn: Canaletto, 1985.

———. *Collections of Maps and Atlases in the Netherlands: Their History and Present State.* Leiden: E. J. Brill, 1961.

———. *Joan Blaeu and his Grand Atlas: Introduction to the Facsimile Edition of La Grand Atlas, 1663.* Amsterdam: Theatrum Orbis Terrarum, 1970.

Kretschmer, Ingrid, Johannes Dörflinger, and Franz Wawrik, eds. *Lexikon zur Geschichte der Kartographie von den Anfängen bis zum ersten Weltkreig.* 2 vols. Vienna: Franz Deuticke, 1986.

Krogt, Peter van der. "Von 'Atlas' tot atlas." *Kartografisch Tijdschrift* 20 (1994), no. 3, pp. 11–18. Translated and summarized as "From 'Atlas' to Atlas." *Mercator's World* I (1996), no. 1, pp. 61–63, 93.

Lodynski, Marian. *Centralny katalog zbiorow kartograficznych w Polsce.* Vols. 1–4: *Katalog atlasow i dziei geograficznych.* Warsaw: Instytut Geografii, Polska Akademia Nauk and Biblioteka Narodowa, 1961–1968.

Loy, William G. "State Atlas Creation." *American Cartographer* 7 (1980): 105–121.

Meurer, Peter. *Atlantes Colonienses: Die kölner Schule der Atlaskartographie, 1570–1610.* Bad Neustadt a.d. Saale: Pfaehler, 1988.

———. *Fontes cartographici Orteliani: des Theatrum Orbis Terrarum von Abraham Ortelius und seine Kartenquellen.* Weinheim: VCH, Acta Humaniora, 1991.

Mickwitz, Ann-Mari and Leena Miekkavaaara. *The A. E. Nordenskiöld Collection in the Helsinki University Library: Annotated Catalogue of Maps Made up to 1800.* Vols. 1–2: *Atlases.* Helsinki: Helsinki University Press, 1979–1981.

Mood, Fulmer. "The Rise of Official Statistical Cartography in Austria, Prussia, and the United States, 1855–1872." *Agricultural History* 20 (1946): 209–225.

National Atlases: Their History, Analyses and Ways to Improvement and Standardization. Cartographica Monograph no. 4. Toronto: University of Toronto Press, 1972.

Pastoureau, Mireille. *Les atlas français, XVIe–XVIIe siècles. Répertoire bibliographique et étude.* Paris: Bibliothèque Nationale, 1984.

———. Les Atlas imprimés en France aux XVIe et XVIIe siècles." *Imago Mundi* 32 (1980): 45–72.

Pedley, Mary Sponberg. *Bel et Utile: The Work of the Robert DeVaugondy Family of Mapmakers.* Tring, Herts.: Map Collector Publications, 1993.

———. "The Subscription List of the 1757 *Atlas Universel:* A Study in Cartographic Dissemination." *Imago Mundi* 31 (1979): 66–77.

Ristow, Walter W., comp. *A la Carte: Selected Papers on Maps and Atlases.* Washington, D.C.: Library of Congress, 1972.

———. *American Maps and Mapmakers: Commercial Cartography in the Nineteenth Century.* Detroit: Wayne State University Press, 1985.

———. *Maps for an Emerging Nation: Commercial Cartography in Nineteenth-Century America.* Washington, D.C.: Library of Congress, 1977.

———. "Some Recent Regional Atlases: A Review" *Geographical Review* 41 (1951): 479–484.

Robinson, Arthur H. *Early Thematic Mapping in the History of Cartography.* Chicago: University of Chicago Press, 1982.

———— and Barbara Bartz Petchenik. *The Nature of Maps: Essays toward Understanding Maps and Mapping.* Chicago: University of Chicago Press, 1976.

Schwartz, Seymour I. and Ralph E. Ehrenberg. *The Mapping of America.* New York: Harry N. Abrams, 1980.

Schilder, Günter. *Monumenta Cartographica Neerlandica.* 4 vols. Alphen aan den Rijn: Canaletto, 1986–1993.

Seboek, Lou. *Atlases Published in the Netherlands in the Rare Atlas Collection.* Ottawa: Public Archives of Canada, National Map Collection, 1973.

————. *French Atlases in the Rare Atlas Collection.* Ottawa: Public Archives of Canada, National Map Collection, 1974.

Skelton, Raleigh A. *County Atlases of the British Isles, 1579–1850: A Bibliography.* Vol. I: *1579–1703.* London: Carta Press, 1970.

————. "Early Atlases." *Geographical Magazine* 32 (1960): 523–543.

————. *Maps: A Historical Survey of Their Study and Collecting.* Chicago: University of Chicago Press, 1972.

Stephens, John D. "Current Cartographic Serials: An Annotated International List." *American Cartographer* 7 (1980): 23–38.

Stephenson, Richard W. "Atlases of the Western Hemisphere: A Summary Survey." *Geographical Review* 62 (1972): 92–119.

———— and Mary Galneder. "Anglo-American State and Provincial Thematic Atlases: A Survey and Bibliography." *Canadian Cartographer* 6 (1969): 15–45.

Tessier, Yves. "Cartes et atlas: tendencies récentes dans la production des atlas." *Cahiers de Géographie du Quebec* 33, no. 88 (April 1989), pp. 73–88.

Thrower, Norman J. W. "The County Atlas of the United States." *Surveying and Mapping* 21 (1961): 365–372.

Tyner, Judith A. *Development of the American Atlas, 1790–1980.* Los Angeles: California Map Society, 1989.

Valerio, Vladimiro. *Atlanti napoletani del diciannovesimo secolo (1806–1860).* Naples: Luigi Regina, 1980.

————. "Italian Atlases and Their Makers, 1770–1830." *The Map Collector,* no. 45 (Winter 1988), pp. 10–18.

Wallis, Helen M. and Arthur H. Robinson, eds. *Cartographical Innovations: An International Handbook of Mapping Terms to 1900.* Tring, Herts.: Map Collector Publications in association with the International Cartographic Association, 1987.

U.S. Library of Congress. Geography and Map Division. *A List of Geographical Atlases in the Library of Congress, with Bibliographical Notes.* 9 vols. Washington, D.C.: Library of Congress, 1901–1992. See especially, "Preface," by John A. Wolter and "Introduction," by Ronald E. Grim, of volume 9 (1992).

————. *The Bibliography of Cartography.* 5 vols. Boston: G. K. Hall, 1973. *First Supplement.* 2 vols. 1980.

————. *United States Atlases: A List of National, State, County, and Regional Atlases in the Library of Congress.* 2 vols. Washington, D.C.: Library of Congress, 1950–1953.

Wawrik, Franz. *Berühmte Atlanten: Kartographische Kunst aus fünf Jahrhunderten.* Dortmund: Harenberg Kommunikation, 1982.

Winearls, Joan, ed. *Editing Early and Historical Atlases: Papers Given at the Twenty-ninth Annual Conference on Editorial Problems, University of Toronto, 5–6 November 1993.* Toronto: University of Toronto Press, 1995.

Wolf, Armin. "What Can the History of Historical Atlases Teach? Some Lessons from a Century of Putzger's 'Historischer Schul-Atlas'." *Cartographica* 28, no. 2 (Summer 1991), pp. 21–37.

Wolf, Eric W. *The History of Cartography: A Bibliography, 1981–1992.* Washington, D.C.: Washington Map Society in association with Fiat Lux, 1992.

Wolf, Hans, ed. *Vierhundert Jahre Mercator, Vierhundert Jahre Atlas: "Die ganze Welt zwischen zwei Buchdeckeln"; eine Geschichte der Atlanten.* Bayerische Staatsbibliothek Ausstellungskataloge 65. Weissenhorn: Anton H. Konrad, 1995.

Wolter, John A. "The Heights of Mountains and Lengths of Rivers." *Library of Congress Quarterly Journal* 29 (1972): 187–205.

———. "Saxton's Atlas of England and Wales." In *Visions of a Collector: The Lessing J. Rosenwald Collection in the Library of Congress*, pp. 372–375. Edited by Kathleen T. Mang. Washington, D.C.: Library of Congress, 1992.

———. "Source Materials for the History of American Cartography." In *American Studies: Topics and Sources*, pp. 81–95. Edited by Robert H. Waller. Westport, Conn.: Greenwood Press, 1976.

Woodward, David. *The All-American Map: Wax Engraving and Its Influence on Cartography.* Chicago: University of Chicago Press, 1977.

———. *Art and Cartography: Six Historical Essays.* Chicago: University of Chicago Press, 1987.

———. *Five Centuries of Map Printing.* Chicago: University of Chicago Press, 1975.

———. *The Maps and Prints of Paolo Forlani: A Descriptive Bibliography.* Chicago: The Newberry Library, 1990.

———. "The Techniques of Atlas Making." *The Map Collector*, no. 18 (March 1982), pp. 2–11.

Yonge, Ena L. "National Atlases: A Summary." *Geographical Review* 47 (1957): 570–578.

———. "Regional Atlases: A Summary Survey." *Geographical Review* 52 (1962): 407–432.

———. "World and Thematic Atlases: A Summary Survey." *Geographical Review* 52 (1962): 583–596.

Zeigler, Donald J. "Critical Atlas Reviews: Writing to Learn About Maps." *American Cartographer* 15 (1988): 357–362.

Index

Page numbers for illustrations are in italics

WITHDRAWN